MONEY

MONEY

Institutions, theory and policy

J. Struthers and H. Speight

Longman London and New York

Longman Group Limited
Longman House, Burnt Mill, Harlow
Essex CM20 2JE, England
Associated companies throughout the world

*Published in the United States of America
by Longman Inc., New York*

© Longman Group Limited 1986

First published 1986

British Library Cataloguing in Publication Data
  Struthers, J.
    Money: institutions, theory and policy.
    1. Money
    I. Title II. Speight, H.
    332.4 HG221
  ISBN 0-582-29667-6

Library of Congress Cataloging in Publication Data
  Struthers, J.J.
    Money: institutions, theory, and policy.
    Bibliography: p.
    Includes index.
    1. Money. 2. Financial institutions. 3. Monetary
  policy. I. Speight, H. II. Title.
  HG221.S886 1985   332.4   85-5162
  ISBN 0-582-29667-6

Printed and Bound in Great Britain by
Robert Hartnell (1985) Ltd., Bodmin, Cornwall

Contents

PART A: The institutional framework

vii

List of figures

List of tables

Preface

No branch of economics has absorbed so much attention, stimulated so much original research and thinking, and evoked so much controversy as the field of monetary economics. Terms such as 'monetarism', 'the money supply', 'the PSBR' etc. have become, in the UK at least, household names, often being used by individuals even though they understand very little about the subject-matter of monetary economics from whence they derive. This can probably be attributed to the fact that more and more governments in both the developed world and the less developed have in recent years adopted policies which may loosely, and in some cases, very loosely, be termed 'monetarist'. Also, the impact of 'monetarist' policies, or even just monetary policies of any description, can be so all-embracing and so rapid that few individuals can hope to remain immune from their overall effects, whether harmful or beneficial.

There is a vast literature on the subject now both in textbook form and in journal articles, but much of it deals either with theoretical issues or questions of policy with little attention being paid to the rapidly evolving institutional characteristics of a financial system. This text, because it attempts to provide a comprehensive coverage of the three aspects of monetary economics – institutional, theoretical and policy – should therefore be regarded not only as a useful teaching device, but also, hopefully, a text which deepens and broadens the reader's understanding of a rather complex subject.

For pedagogic reasons, the text is divided into three distinct parts, corresponding to the three themes mentioned above. Part A deals with the institutional dimension, along with an introductory chapter on the crucial question of what actually constitutes money in a developed economy. The emphasis is on the UK financial system, though occasional references are made to other systems, notably in Chapters 4 and 5 which deal with the secondary markets and other financial institutions (OFIs). The discussion continually relates to that which follows in the theoretical and policy sections. This is done in order to bring out the essential interdependence of the three elements. Part B covers some traditional ground in comparing the various theoretical approaches to the subject. By nature, theory evolves at a much slower pace than either policy or the institutional dimension. Nevertheless, the four chapters in this section have been written with the objective of presenting a crystallisation of long-established principles, alongside the more sophisticated refinements of modern theory. Where possible, mathematical exposition is kept to a minimum, though use is made of diagrams. Empirical tests of some of the more heated debates between the various protagonists occupies a significant place in this section, especially in Chapter 10 wherein issues such as the stability of the velocity of circulation; the exogeneity of the money supply; and the relative strengths of money versus 'real' expenditure multipliers receives extended discussion. The final Part of the book considers the broad area of monetary policy with both a theoretical discussion of monetary policy (Ch. 12) as well as a chapter which analyses and appraises monetary policy in practice, again in a UK setting and almost exclusively covering the post-1971 period (Ch. 13). The setting for Chapters 12 and 13 is provided by Chapter 11 which deals with the twin problems of inflation and unemployment. This chapter draws on theoretical explanations of these phenomena, but also presents some basic data for the UK economy. Once again, in this Part there is discussion of the empirical tests of the various theories and this draws on studies undertaken in the US as well as in the UK. Consideration is given also to the much discussed rational expectations hypothesis with the emphasis being on the theoretical and policy implications of this approach rather than the econometric testing of the various formulations that it can take.

After reading and absorbing this book it is anticipated that the reader will agree with the authors in their belief that the impact of something so apparently innocuous and harmless as money on an economy is invariably extremely complex and difficult to predict in advance. Indeed, it could be asked of readers, in advance as it were, whether they would endorse the sentiments expressed in the following two quotations, one from John Stuart Mill, the other from Milton Friedman; which, despite the long passage of time which separates them and the somewhat different terminology used, essentially seem to be saying the same thing.

> 'There cannot be intrinsically a more insignificant thing in the economy of society than money; except in the character of a contrivance for sparing time and labour. It is a machine for doing quickly and commodiously what would be done, though less quickly and commodiously, without it; and like many other kinds of machinery it only exerts a distinct and independent influence of its own when it gets out of order' (John Stuart Mill)

> 'because (money) is so pervasive when it gets out of order it throws a monkey wrench into the operation of all the other machines . . .' (Milton Friedman)

Acknowledgements

This book represents the product of a number of years' effort and reflection on the rapidly developing subject of monetary economics. The initial inspiration behind the book was my co-author Harold Speight who, in the final stages of the book's preparation, tragically died after a lengthy and painful illness which had previously enforced his early retirement from the School of Economic Studies at the University of Leeds, where he had lectured for 30 years. To him I owe much gratitude and I sincerely hope that the book will be viewed as a tribute to him by all its readers.

Others have contributed whether knowingly or not. Professor A. J. Brown, Harold Speight's former colleague at Leeds, provided support and encouragement to me after Harold's death. My own former professor, Professor Peter J. Sloane (now at Aberdeen University), should also be thanked for providing just enough pressure at the right time to complete the book. Dr Alistair Young, my Paisley colleague, was always ready to discuss particular aspects of theory despite the pressure of other commitments. There were others who provided indirect help in the form of suggestions and discussions, including: Dr Martin Myant, Dr Madhavi Majmudar, Dr Stewart Cochrane, Dr Terry Wanless, Mr Stuart Dunlop (all of Paisley College) and Dr David Cobham of St Andrews University whose own writings on monetary economics clarified my thoughts on the subject.

Finally, I would like to thank the typing and secretarial staff at Paisley College, in particular Jean Craft, Ella Kininmonth, Janette Johnstone and Margaret Jamieson for their cooperation and diligence over the typing of numerous drafts of the manuscripts especially at the beginning of one academic session when they were under severe pressure. Lucy Docherty, former technician in the Department of Economics and Management, and staff at the Educational Development Unit, both Paisley College, are also thanked for their help in producing some of the tables and diagrams in the text. Of course, any remaining errors or omissions remain the responsibility of the authors.

We are grateful to the following for permission to reproduce copyright material:

Philip Allan Publishers Ltd for equations 8.1, 8.2, 8.3, 8.4 p 23 *The Rational Expectations Revolution in Macroeconomics: Theories & Evidence* (1st edn 1982) by D K M Begg; George Allen & Unwin for equations 4.1, 4.2 pp 76, 86 *Post War International Money Crisis* (1st edn 1981) by V Argy; Bank of England for table 2.1 from pp 20, 21, 32 *Bank of England Report & Accounts 1984*, tables 3.1, 5.3, 11.3, fig 5.1, appendix from pp 53, 212, 465, 218, 79 *Bank of England Quarterly Bulletin* (Sep 1983, June 1984, Dec 1983, June 1983, March 1984); FT Business Information Ltd for tables

4.1, 4.2, 4.3 from pp 111, 107, 39 *The Banker* (Nov 1983, Nov 1981, Jan 1984); Barclays Bank Plc for table 13.4 from p 2 *Barclays Review* (Feb 1984) & *Barclays UK Financial Survey* (May 1984), fig 31.2 from 'Monetary Aggregates in the United Kingdom' by A E Davies p 3 *Barclays Review* (Feb 1984); Basil Blackwell for fig 12.1 from p 63 *The Theory of Monetary Policy* (2nd edn 1979) by Victoria Chick; Cambridge University Press for table 11.2 from 'The immediate contributions to inflation' by R C D Allen p 160 *Economic Journal* Vol 85 (1975); Free Press, a Division of Macmillan Inc for fig 9.3 from p 45 *An Introduction To The Theory of Finance* by B Moore Copyright © 1968 by The Free Press; The Controller of Her Majesty's Stationery Office for table 5.1 from table 9.4 p 95, table 5.2 from table 9.2 & supp tables pp 94, 141, tables 13.1 from data p 75, table 13.2 p 72, table 3.3 from table 8.2 p 87 *Financial Statistics* (July 1984, Dec 1977, April 1978, Jan 1977); Southern Economic Assn & the authors for equations 8.5–8.15 from pp 315–6 'Rational Expectations of Government Policy: an application of Newcomb's Problem' by Frydman et. al. *Southern Economic Journal* vol 49 (Oct 1982); John Wiley & Sons Inc for figs 12.2, 12.3, 12.4 from pp 201, 202 'Optional choice of Monetary policy instruments in a simple stochastic macromodel' by W Poole in *Quarterly Journal of Economics* Vol 84 (1970).

PART A

The institutional framework

CHAPTER ONE

Introduction

What is money?

One of the most important characteristics of the modern world is its interdependence. We live and work in communities which could not exist without the cooperation and the coordinated efforts of their members, and every day of our life we depend on the work of thousands of other men and women, most of whom we will never meet. This has been said so often that it has become platitudinous and is so obvious that we never give it a thought. We assume that we shall always be able to get as much water as we want simply by turning a tap, that the newspaper and the milk will arrive on our doorstep every morning, that there will be a train or a bus to carry us wherever we want to go, and that whatever we want to buy, somewhere in town there is a shop which sells it. It is only when supplies are interrupted by war, or natural disaster, or a major strike that we become consciously aware of our interdependence and, perhaps, realise that the complicated machinery of production and distribution is something to marvel at rather than take for granted.

Money is important, and monetary economics is a worthwhile study, primarily because without the institution of money this complex and convenient world simply would not be possible. Our world is an interdependent world because it is a world of specialisation. We are all specialists, producing – or more likely, helping to produce – some good or service not for ourselves but for other people who, in turn, produce other goods and services for us. Clearly, if we are to specialise we must be able to exchange our goods for other goods which we want but do not, and in most cases could not, produce for ourselves. Without some easy and convenient means of exchange, this elaborate network of specialisation would collapse overnight. The primary and – let us be clear about this from the outset – unique function of money is to act as a *medium of exchange*.[1]

The only alternative to the use of money is exchange by barter, the direct exchange of goods for goods. In any community producing more than a handful of different goods and services, barter is inconvenient, for two reasons:

1 Any exchange necessitates what is called 'the double coincidence of want'. If I can only make a direct exchange – say, of X for Y – I must find someone who both wants my X and is able and willing to supply Y in exchange. As Sir Dennis Robertson (1965) put it: '. . . the textbooks are full of the agonies of

two men, one with a spare fish, the other with a spare pair of boots, vainly seeking each other'. And what happens if I want a pair of boots but the only thing I have to offer in exchange is a fully grown horse? If I could sell my horse for money, three important consequences would follow. First, I can sell it to more people; I don't have to find a buyer who can offer boots in exchange. Second, I can spread the buying part of my exchange over as many different goods as I wish; I am not limited to the exchange of a horse for boots. Third, I do not have to spend the money immediately; by making possible the division of a single exchange into its two component parts, a sale and a purchase, the use of money also enables us to separate them chronologically and defer the buying operation if we wish.

The real importance of this possibility of separating the operations in time is that money becomes a very convenient asset to hold. It is a more efficient store of wealth than animals, which must be fed and eventually die, or goods, which take up storage space and deteriorate.

2 There is the problem of calculating the ratios of exchange between the different goods on offer. In the most primitive form of barter, where purchases are made by a single exchange, no system of prices is called for. If I go into the market offering eggs and want either a scythe or a feeding trough in exchange, I only need to know how many eggs I would have to pay for either. I can then compare the two offers just as easily as if I were told that eggs are 70 pence a dozen, a scythe would cost £15 and a feeding trough £20. It is when I must put through more than one transaction to get what I really want that the comparisons required to maximise my utility, or my returns, become complicated. Suppose, for example, that I cannot find anyone with the appropriate double coincidence of wants, so that the only way to buy a scythe is to exchange my eggs for apples, then exchange the apples for a scythe. Now suppose someone offers me 3 lb of apples per dozen eggs. Should I accept? The answer depends on how many apples I would have to pay for a scythe. Now let us move to a stage of development a little nearer to the market economy, in which eggs and apples and scythes are all being widely traded for each other and there is no longer any need for a double coincidence of wants. I have the choice of buying my scythe in a direct swap for eggs, or through an intermediate exchange for apples. If I want to be sure of making the best bargain, I must know the price of apples in terms of eggs, the price of a scythe in terms of eggs, and the price of a scythe in terms of apples. There are three goods and three price ratios. If I am also considering buying a feeding trough as an alternative to the scythe, I will also need to know how many eggs, and how many apples, I would have to give for a feeding trough. Note that there are now four goods, but five exchange ratios. If I were to consider the possibility of exchanging a scythe for a feeding trough, or vice versa, there would be six ratios to consider. The point at issue is that the number of exchange ratios increases faster than the number of goods being traded against each other. With A, B and C there are three ratios − A:B, A:C, and B:C. With four goods there are six ratios − A:B, A:C, A:D, B:C,

B:D, and C:D. In fact the number of exchange ratios increases according to the formula $n/(n-1)/2$ where n is the number of goods traded. A ten-commodity market would have 45 exchange ratios, a twenty-commodity market would have 190 ratios, and so on. The calculation of relative exchange-costs, or market values, is enormously simplified if all prices can be expressed in terms of one object. Suppose it were apples. Then the traders in eggs, and scythes and feeding troughs only need to know three market-prices – namely, the price of eggs, scythes, and feeding troughs in terms of apples. It is then a simple matter to work out their market values in terms of each other. There are now four goods but only three market prices, because one of the four has become the 'standard of value' for the rest: it is the unit of account or *numeraire*, in terms of which the values of all other goods are expressed. The price of the numeraire itself is, of course, always unity. The price of a pound of apples in terms of pounds of apples, = 1. Apples would then be performing the second basic function of money, which is to act as a *standard of value* a *unit of account*.

It is interesting to speculate which is likely to have come first, the adoption of a unit of account or the adoption of a means of payment. We shall never know the answer, and in any case the answer may be different for different communities. Money is not something which was invented in one place and then spread to the rest of the world. But a unit of account would, as we have seen, be very useful even in a market where there was no medium of exchange. It immediately reduces the number of market prices from $n(n-1)/2$ to $n-1$. If 100 goods are being exchanged against each other and one of them is adopted as the numeraire, all that is necessary for an easy calculation of the exchange ratio between any pair is that each of the other 99 shall have a price in terms of the numeraire.

Even in an economy with no markets, some unit of account would be needed for rational economic calculation and accounting. Unless everyone is to be given exactly the same real income – the same quantities of the same foods, the same clothes, identical houses, and so on – we need some way of calculating how big a slice of the community's total output each man shall receive, and we must then find some means whereby he can choose what goods and services he wants to make up that slice, and some way of ensuring that the total demands for each good or service do not add up to more than the total supply. We would need to compare the efficiencies of different forms of production, and we would be faced with problems which, put in the most simple possible form, are of this nature: if five units of capital and three units of labour can produce 100 gallons of petrol an hour, and six units of capital and two units of labour can produce 10 kilowatts of electricity per hour, ought we to build a new oil refinery or a new power station? Quite apart from the problem of deciding what we mean by a 'unit of capital' and a 'unit of labour', especially when there are different kinds of labour and capital in the two industries, we have to determine the comparative values of 100 gallons of petrol and 10 kilowatts of electricity. (And this example assumes that there are only two alternative uses for the capital and labour.)

Clearly, the first necessary step would be the adoption of some unit of account, some common yardstick in terms of which thousands of different goods and services, their costs and values, can be added and subtracted and compared.

We can have a unit of account even if we do not use a medium of exchange: but the wide use of a medium of exchange is inconceivable without the existence of a unit of account. To revert to our first example, if apples become the medium of exchange, it is almost inevitable that they will also become the numeraire if they are not so already; the values of goods being bought and sold for apples will be expressed in terms of apples. If the use of a medium of exchange came first, the adoption of a unit of account would surely, and quickly, follow.

Here we come to a rather important distinction between these two functions of money. The things which circulate as means of payment necessarily have some kind of physical existence. Notes and coins are tangible objects; they are pieces of paper or metal which we can touch and handle. Even that least material form of money, the bank deposit, can be seen: it exists as written or typed figures in the bank's ledgers and our bank statements. But a unit of account, like any other unit of measurement, is an abstraction. We can see and touch a yard of cloth, a ton of coal, a pint of milk, but no one has ever seen or touched 'a yard', or 'a ton', or 'a pint'. They are simply terms we use to identify or describe or define certain quantities of material objects and to indicate the relative sizes of different quantities. It is equally true to say that nobody has ever seen 'a pound' or 'a dollar': what we *can* see is 'a pound note' or 'a dollar piece', a bit of paper or metal which everyone will accept as having a purchasing power, a value, of 'one pound' or 'one dollar'. Nobody has ever spent a penny; we spend penny-pieces. The distinction is obscured by the fact that we commonly use the same terms to define our units of account and our media of exchange – the pound, the franc, the dollar, and so on. There are two reasons for this.

The first is that to do so is obviously more convenient than to separate them. It is a necessary characteristic of money-objects that they have a fixed value in terms of the numeraire: if different people set different values on a unit of money, exchange by the intermediary of money is impossible. We could have a unit of account different from the monetary unit. But why bother?

The second reason is historical. The original unit of account was often a commodity: values would be reckoned in terms of cattle, or skins, perhaps used as a common denominator in which to assess and compare personal wealth before it was used as a unit of account in trade. When, for reasons we will mention later, metals were adopted as the media of exchange, the unit of account became a certain weight of metal. When the media of exchange were given official approval by being minted into coins, the value assigned to each coin depended on the weight of metal it contained. This, after all, was one way of making the coins acceptable as media of exchange: if I am suspicious of the currency, it helps to know that a coin contains its face value of metal.

Money is, then, primarily a means of payment, the things we spend and which therefore circulate from hand to hand, or from bank account to bank account, in the conduct of trade. Money usually serves as the unit of account, but not always. In the course of man's history, hundreds of different objects or commodities have served one or other of these functions, but not necessarily both. Sometimes there exists a unit of account when trade is conducted by barter, and there are many instances of one object serving as a unit of account while something quite different circulates as the medium of exchange. If elephants are the standard in terms of which wealth is measured, as was once the case in Cambodia (or camels as is still the case among some nomadic tribes in the Sahara), the unit of account and the medium of exchange cannot be the same.

There have been examples of this separation of the two functions in advanced economies. During the German inflation of the early 1920s, wages and fees were often stated in terms of a commodity; the contract would be for the payment of that number of marks which, at the time of payment, would buy a specified quantity of wheat, or milk, or butter. In 1922 one German state issued rye bonds, and in 1923 a German company issued a loan of 200,000 kg of flax. In each case, the lender received in interest, and in repayment of the loan when it matured, the number of marks which would buy a certain amount of rye or flax (see Einzig 1966: 298); but this was an exceptional and disastrous period in German history. The identity of the unit of account and the unit of money is virtually universal. One minor exception is to be found in the British system; the guinea is one unit of account, but there is no longer a guinea coin.[2]

Inflation is the subject of a later chapter of this book, but we are all aware of some of its harmful consequences. An extreme inflation – a hyper-inflation – can disrupt an economy based on the use of money because it destroys the value of money. Because it is a unit of account, money is also used as a *standard of deferred payments*. Contracts which involve payment(s) at a future date are made in terms of money. Obvious examples are loans, purchases on credit, and hire purchase contracts. It is surely obvious that the value of money in terms of other goods must be reasonably stable if money is to perform this function efficiently. A lender who gives up a certain amount of purchasing power today expects to get back the same purchasing power when the loan is repaid. If a money is rapidly losing its value, people will refuse to make forward contracts in terms of that money. In the hyper-inflations in some European countries after the two world wars, contracts were often made in terms of a more stable foreign unit, e.g. the Swiss franc. The commodity bonds just described were a similar attempt to 'beat inflation'.

Money is also a *store of value*. Much of the money held in bank balances is held against prospective purchases of financial assets, bills and bonds and shares. The owners of those balances are interested in the prices of these securities rather than the prices of goods. But for those who hold money against emergencies or as capital to draw on when they retire, one would expect the price index of goods and services to be very important: they will measure the value of their savings not by the size of the nominal balances of money they hold, but by what those nominal balances will buy, i.e. their real balances. A depreciating asset is not a good store of value, and although savers seem to have a remarkable faith in the value of money, there is some rate of inflation which will destroy that faith and they will then forsake money for other forms of wealth-holding. Money must be a store of wealth to some extent if it is to act as a medium of exchange. It has to be held from one transaction to the next and, for our day-to-day payments, from one pay day to the next. In the most disastrous cases of hyper-inflation – for example in Germany in 1923 when prices doubled within hours – people refused to accept money in payment, and therefore it ceased to perform its primary function of acting as a medium of exchange.

Money and near-money

One of the major difficulties in identifying the objects which constitute money is that there are two purposes for which one requires a demarcation of money. First we would like to be able to list the assets which perform the function of money, and second we would like to be able to identify the group of assets which bear the closest quantitative relationship to income and economic activity and whose supply should therefore be controlled by the monetary authority. We leave consideration of this second question to later chapters and here confine our attention to the first problem. Conceptually, the answer is fairly easy: an object is money if it fulfils the functions of money. Money is a means of payment, a unit of account, and a store of value. The last two functions are, however, not relevant in the present context. A unit of account is an abstraction, and an object used as the standard unit for accounting purposes is not necessarily used as a means of payment. Money is only one of several stores of value; if this were the dominant criteria of moneyness, our houses would be money! The unique function then, and the only unique function, of money is that it is spendable; it gives 'immediate command over goods and services'; money is what we can hand over the counter in payment. It is perfectly 'liquid', and this quality of liquidity is both a necessary and a sufficient test of 'moneyness'. If we want to know whether or not a particular object is money, we need to ask only one question: can I spend it? If I can, it is money; if I can't, it isn't.

What objects constitute this means of payment? Notes and coins, obviously, and a current account on which I can draw cheques. The only difference, in this regard, between cash and cheques is that the acceptability of notes and coins in payment of debt is prescribed by law; they are legal tender, but cheques are not. The acceptability of a cheque depends on the payee's confidence that the payer has sufficient funds in the bank to meet the cheque and also on his presumption that the bank will put no restriction on the transfer of the proceeds to him in any form he chooses, be it currency, or his own account at the same bank, or his account at another bank. This legal tender aspect apart, a current account has the same monetary properties as notes and coins. Unused overdraft facilities are also money.[3] The formal conditions attached to a deposit account state that it is withdrawable at seven days' notice. Formally, therefore, it is not 'chequable' and is not money, but in practice it is: if I have a deposit account the bank will honour my cheques even if my current account is empty.

Perfect liquidity is thus a simple criterion by which we can distinguish money from everything else. The answer to the question 'What assets constitute the means of payment?' is not, however, as definite and clear-cut as we might suppose. Some non-deposit banks – some merchant banks and overseas and foreign banks – run a few current accounts and issue cheques. Since 1968, for example, we have had the National Giro, deposits which are used solely as a means of payment, while the National Savings Bank and the Trustee Savings Banks will make payments out of ordinary accounts by standing order. In short, one cannot compile a comprehensive list of the assets constituting the money supply which is valid in all places and at all times; the composition of the list changes and all we can do is to treat the question ad hoc and ask of each asset suggested for inclusion: can it be spent?

If we dropped the perfect liquidity or 'spendability' criterion, we would not know where to draw the line between money and other assets. We can in practice draw money against a building society account, whether it be a deposit account or a share account, as easily and as quickly as against a deposit account at a bank, and the same goes for National Savings Bank deposits up to a hundred pounds, and Trustee Savings Bank deposits.

How many occasions then are there when it is really impossible, or very inconvenient, to wait a couple of days for the money? Probably not many. In that case, there are several other assets which, for most purposes, are as close to money as makes no difference. Firms holding bills of exchange or Treasury bills (defined and described in Chapter 2) can turn them into money in a matter of hours. Savings certificates and savings bonds can be cashed within two or three days. All these 'non-money financial assets' have a high degree of liquidity, i.e. they can be turned into 'universal command over goods and services' (a) quickly, (b) at a very low cost in time and inconvenience, and (c) with a zero or negligible loss of value. They are so close to money that they are usually put into a separate category of assets, along with time and savings deposits, and labelled *near money* or *quasi-money*. Their only significant difference from currency and chequeable deposits is that one cannot actually spend them; they are not accepted in payment of debt.

Many other assets possess one or two of these elements of liquidity, but not all three. Bonds – which are certificates representing long-term loans, as contrasted with the bills mentioned above, which represent short-term loans – and shares in companies can be sold within the day on the Stock Exchange, and payment will be received some two to three weeks later. In addition, stamp duty and brokers' commissions will cost about 1.5% to 2% of the selling price, depending on the amount of the transaction and the type of security.[4] More important, however, is the fact that the market value is not fixed. The prices of these securities are determined by supply and demand on the Stock Exchanges, and if there are more sellers than buyers their prices fall. An insurance company will buy back an insurance policy before the end of its life, but only at its 'surrender value', which will always be less than the total of premiums paid to date.

Some 'real' – as opposed to 'financial' – assets can also be quickly turned into money, e.g. a car, furniture, and other consumer durable goods: but if I do want a quick sale I must be willing to accept whatever price I can get at the time. What particularly distinguishes these assets from near-money assets then, is that their money values can be less than what we paid for them if and when we sell them. It is mainly for this reason that they are less liquid. 'Liquidity', then, is not an absolute term; we cannot separate assets into two tight compartments labelled 'liquid' and 'non-liquid'.

On the contrary, the most we can say is that there are degrees of liquidity, with assets being arranged in descending order of liquidity, on the basis of two criteria: 'transferability' and 'reversibility'.

1   *Transferability.* An asset is liquid in so far as it is easily, quickly and cheaply transferable to another holder. It may be transferred by sale, in which case 'transferability' is synonymous with 'marketability'; or in the case of some securities – e.g. bonds, bills, savings certificates, insurance policies – through redemption by the borrower of the loan which the security represents. (Insurance premiums are, in a sense, lent to the insurance company for the term of the policy.) When we transfer an asset, we of course receive money in exchange. 'Transfer' and 'encashment' are synonymous.

2   *Reversibility.* An asset is liquid in so far as it is transferable without loss, i.e. in so far as the seller can recover the sum he paid for it. It is perfectly reversible, however, only if its money value is fixed and certain *and* if it is transferable at zero cost.

Which assets meet these requirements? We may suggest the following categories:

- *Money*: Notes and coins plus accounts at the deposit banks. Their liquidity is absolute. There is no question of their transferability or reversibility: these terms specify the difficulty or cost of converting other assets into cash or a bank account.

- *Near money*: Assets which are not actually money, but can be turned into money very quickly at a zero or negligible cost and/or loss of value. They comprise: (a) Deposits with building societies, Trustee Savings Banks, the National Savings Bank and similar institutions. (b) Loans at short notice to discount houses, finance houses and local authorities. (So long as the borrower is solvent, categories (a) and (b) have a fixed money value.) (c) Fixed-term securities very close to their maturity dates. (The maturity date of a security is the date on which the issuer will redeem it, i.e. take it back in exchange for a sum of money equal to its face value. It is therefore also known as the redemption date. Equity shares do not have a redemption date; only in the most exceptional circumstances will a company buy back its ordinary shares. The Government's Consolidated Loan Stock – 'Consols' – are the one category of Government bonds without a redemption date.) (d) Some long-term assets of fixed value, e.g. savings certificates, the cash value of insurance policies.

- *Other financial assets*: Government bonds and industrial debentures not included in (c) above, equity shares in companies, insurance policies and mortgage loans, and fixed-term deposits at banks. In each case the owner holds a certificate or other document which entitles him to repayment of a principal sum at a particular date or specified alternative dates, and/or the receipt of interest or a share in profits.

- *Real assets*: Consumer goods and industrial plant, land, buildings, stocks etc. Least liquid of all are assets with a very specialised use such as the fixed equipment of a mine perhaps.

Many of these non-money assets – the near-monies, in particular – can perform the asset function of money almost as well as money itself, their only disadvantage being a lower degree of liquidity which, in many cases, is slight. In a time of inflation, some of them – namely, real assets and those financial assets whose values are linked with the values of their underlying real assets, such as equity shares,[5] and to some extent with profit insurance policies – are better stores of value than money. Conversely, of course, when prices are falling they are inferior to money as a store of value or wealth; their prices – i.e. their money-values – will most probably fall along with other prices. Moreover, possession of them may have much the same effect on economic behaviour, in particular on decisions to spend or to save, as the possession of money itself. But if we were to accept this asset function as giving them monetary status, it would be impossible to fix a clear dividing line between money and other assets. We could not fix it at some arbitrarily chosen degree of liquidity because liquidity is not a quantifiable concept. Indeed, although we have listed assets in categories of descending order of liquidity, the boundaries between the categories can be quite blurred. If the transferability of A is higher, but its reversibility lower, than that of B, can we say that one is more liquid than the other, and if so which?

There is therefore a degree of arbitrariness in our, or any, choice of the assets which constitute near money, and the delimitation of near money is even more difficult than the delimitation of money. The range of degrees of liquidity is very wide, and unless we make an arbitrary decision that 'near moneyness' is to be defined as 'withdrawable on demand', the question 'What is near money?' devolves into the unanswerable question 'How near is near?'.[6] Despite these nuances, however, near money assets are particularly important in monetary theory. For one thing the existence of a large and varied supply of good quality 'near monies' reduces the demand for money as an asset (see Ch. 9).

Our definition of money as anything which constitutes 'immediate and universal command over goods and services', with emphasis on the word 'immediate', has led us into hair-splitting argument. We differentiate the various assets by the time, cost, inconvenience and possible capital loss incurred in converting them into the spendable asset, and so rarely is it important that this time, or the cost and inconvenience should be reduced to absolute zero, that the distinction – which between many assets is a very fine one anyway – in many cases seems to have little practical significance. It is also probably true that spending depends on the possession of non-money assets as well as on the possession of actual money, and it is via its effect on spending that money affects the economy. But only money can be spent; people cannot spend money they haven't got, and one technique of monetary policy is to alter the terms on which non-money assets can be converted into money. Our search for a precise definition of money may therefore have some practical importance after all.

Newlyn's definition

Professor Newlyn (1971) has suggested a different way of identifying money, one which permits the inclusion of time deposits at least in the UK and the clear exclusion of all other assets. His distinction rests not on the 'status' of assets from the owner's point of view – i.e. on whether or not he regards an asset as money, or 'as good as money' – but on the consequences of a transfer of the asset from one owner to another, what he calls 'operational effects on the economy'.

Suppose I pay a debt with notes or coin. The only consequence is a physical transfer of money from me to my creditor. The total amount of money in existence does not alter, and there is no further repercussion on the economy unless or until my creditor spends the money, which is something quite separate from the transaction between him and me. The same is true of payments by cheque drawn on current accounts at the banks. The total of bank deposits does not change; there is a change of ownership of deposits, and that is that. It is also true, in the British context, of a transfer of money from a current account to a deposit account or vice versa. Now suppose I draw on an account with a building society to make a payment. The building society has to draw on its money reserves (cash in the till plus its account at a bank) and no other society gains a like reserve. Since building societies maintain a minimum ratio of money to other assets, a loss of cash necessitates a reduction of other assets by some multiple of that loss. It will cut back its mortgage loans or sell securities, since these are its major assets. This does have further repercussions, in the housing market and/or in the markets for securities. One small withdrawal from a building society account would not, of course, have any repercussion, but large withdrawals would. Either fewer houses would be built because there were fewer mortgages available; or the building societies would have to raise the rates they pay on deposits and share accounts to attract more funds to lend, in which case mortgage rates would also be raised and the demand for houses would fall; or the building societies would have to unload securities on to the market, which would depress the prices of securities, i.e. raise interest rates.[7] Something very similar happens if payments are made by withdrawing funds from other institutions who thereby lose cash or bank deposits and who keep a minimum ratio between such liquid reserves and other assets consisting of securities and debts owed to them by borrowers, e.g. hire purchase finance houses, merchant banks, insurance companies, the National Savings Bank and Trustee Savings Banks (whose non-money assets are loans to national and local government).[8]

The banks also keep a minimum ratio of cash to deposits. If this differed from one type of account to another, then a payment out of a bank account could have repercussions. Suppose, for example, they were instructed to maintain a higher cash reserve against current accounts than against deposit accounts (as is the case, for instance, in the USA), then payments out of debtors' current accounts into deposit accounts of their creditors would raise the overall ratio of deposit accounts to current accounts; the banks could then increase their total assets by making more loans and/or buying more securities on the basis of a given reserve of cash. There would be repercussions in the securities markets and/or the market for bank loans. An American economist would, on this analysis, be justified in excluding time deposits from the money supply. Using this criterion, unused overdraft facilities are not money. Given that the banks maintain certain ratios between their reserves of cash and other liquid assets on the one hand and their deposit liabilities and total assets on the other, then an increase in actual overdrafts would, in the absence of any simultaneous increase in their reserves, compel them to unload some other assets – bonds or bills or call-money – leading to inevitable repercussions in the bond market or in the market for bill-finance.

It has been argued that there is one implicit assumption in the Newlyn analysis. It is that the payment out of a bank account must be held in the same form by the creditor as it was by the debtor. If the debtor draws a cheque on his bank account which the creditor pays into his own bank account, the analysis presented above holds good. Similarly, if the debtor pays notes out of his wallet, which the creditor then puts into *his* wallet. But if the debtor pays by cheque and the creditor cashes the cheque into currency, the banking system loses that much cash and must reduce its other assets by some multiple of that loss. Conversely, if the debtor pays notes which the creditor then pays into his bank, being credited with a bank deposit in exchange. Newlyn's reply is that the criterion applies only to 'the set of transactions which is necessary to make the payment'. What happens after the payment has been made is irrelevant to his definition.

Clearly, the task of defining what is and what is not money is not a simple one. Yet, no debate on the usefulness of monetary policy can be undertaken unless some attempt is made to do so. All too often those economists embroiled in heated debates as to whether 'money matters' in macro-economic policy-making have failed to recognise this (see Chs 8, 9 and 10). Charles Goodhart (1970: 160), in a seminal article, stated the problem very clearly: 'the distinction between that theoretical approach to monetary analysis which may, perhaps unfairly, be termed "Keynesian" and that approach which, equally unfairly, may be described as "neo-quantity" or "monetarist" turns mainly on divergent *a priori* expectations about the degree of substitution between money and other financial assets and between financial assets and real assets'. The fact that the distinguishing feature of assets described as 'money' is that they perform the function of a medium of exchange does not, on its own, allow us to draw a line of demarcation between those assets regarded as money, and those not. The issue as we have discussed above is more complex than that.

Notes

1 This is the term traditionally used to identify the unique function of money. Goodhart (1978) and others have made a distinction between the medium of exchange function which is not unique to money and the 'means of final

payment' function, which is. A transaction can be completed by the exchange of goods or services for evidence of debt, e.g. trade credit, a bill of exchange, or a charge account. But the buyer cannot be said to have *paid* for his purchase until he has surrendered money, nor will the seller consider that payment has been made until he has received money.

2 In recent times, also, barter trade has undergone something of a re-birth, with barter associations being established in the US (see Fieleke 1984); in the area of north–south trade, barter and reciprocal trade with developing countries has been intensified (see S. Jones 1984); while barter trade in east–west commercial relations is also fairly commonplace (see Miller 1981).

3 There is some justification for treating unused credit card facilities as money. They are used as a means of payment. Alternatively, they could be treated as a substitute for money to those who use them; their need to hold money is reduced.

4 There may also be a stamp duty, paid by the purchaser.

5 There is, however, some doubt about this, at least in the short or medium term. For example, the index of ordinary share prices was lower in the spring of 1977 than in the spring of 1972.

6 A reasonably clear-cut definition of near money would be 'perfectly reversible and quickly transferable non-money financial assets'. This would exclude bills and other securities 'very close to their maturity dates'. But once we allow for any loss of value on conversion we have to ask what is the maximum potential percentage loss of value which qualifies an asset as near money, a similar problem to that which arises if we include in money assets which are not perfectly liquid. The word 'quickly' is similarly ambiguous, but it is suggested in the text that this is less important.

7 The rate of interest on a security is synonymous with its 'yield'. A £100 bond with a 'coupon rate' of 4% pays £4 per annum interest. If I pay £100 for the bond, the yield on my investment is 4% per annum. If the market prices of the bond were £80, a purchase would yield 5%. To say that the prices of securities have fallen, or that rates of interest have risen, are simply different ways of describing the same event.

8 Payment out of a bank account, or with cash, is not different in this respect from payment out of, say, a building society account. If the creditor put the money received back into a building society, there would be no repercussions in the mortgage or securities markets.

CHAPTER TWO

Financial institutions and the traditional money markets

Financial markets

A market can be generally defined as a place in which, and/or a set of institutions by which, buyers and sellers can be brought together. It is not necessarily a particular geographical location. Although a large proportion of the financial transactions conducted in Britain do in fact take place in the City of London, the famous 'square mile', the buyers and sellers are spread throughout the world.[1] Further, London is not the only market centre; the market for funds is world wide. In some contexts, the term 'market' is used to refer not to a place or places where business is conducted, nor even to the institutions and arrangements for bringing primary and/or secondary buyers and sellers together, but simply to indicate the fact that there is a well-recognised and continuous demand for, and supply of, the type of asset in question; thus we see references to 'the markets' for building society deposits, for insurance and for mortgages.

One often sees references to 'the primary market' and 'the secondary market' for a particular negotiable instrument, but since many markets, on our opening definition, are both primary and secondary, we will instead consider here the 'primary' and 'secondary' activities of a market. The primary activity is to conduct the sale/purchase of a newly issued security. Its function is to bring surplus spenders and deficit spenders together and arrange transactions between them. It is by this activity that markets enable those with entrepreneurial ability to acquire funds from those who have neither the time, inclination, nor ability to use their funds in productive enterprise. Secondary market activity is the exchange of money for existing securities. It is in the secondary market that a primary lender/investor can 'monetise' his loan or investment by selling it. The existence of an active and efficient secondary market gives a high degree of liquidity to securities bought in the primary market; the lender/ investor can easily and cheaply change his mind, so to speak, reverse his decision to lend or invest. Clearly, both primary and secondary activities of markets are essential for a smooth and adequate flow of credit, and London retains its position at the centre of the most efficient set of financial markets in the world.

Just as we classify credit into long-term and short-term, so we can classify financial markets into long-term (usually termed 'the capital market') and short-term (usually referred to as 'the money market').

The capital market

The titles dealt in fall into two groups. First, bonds and shares and, second, other evidences of long-term lending, such as mortgages.

The primary market in bonds and shares consists of the institutions and methods by which new bonds and shares are sold to the primary holders. If an existing public company is raising new capital by an issue of shares, it must offer them first to existing shareholders (by a 'rights' issue) and it does so direct. The first issue by a new public company is invariably put into the hands of an issuing house, stockbroker or bank, which 'brings the firm to the market' either by inviting the public to buy the shares or by 'placing' them in bulk with financial institutions or Stock Exchange jobbers, who sell them piecemeal to the public. Mortgage loans may be negotiated directly with a building society or insurance company, or through an intermediary, usually an estate agent or a solicitor.

There is no secondary market in mortgages. The secondary market in bonds and shares is the Stock Exchange. There the shares are held by the jobbers; they do not deal direct with the public, only with stockbrokers who buy from and sell to the jobbers on behalf of their clients. Most of the stockbrokers' business comes from institutions which are, in reality, themselves acting as agents. The insurance companies, for example, are agents for their policyholders who supply their funds, the pension funds are agents for their subscribing members, and the investment trusts and unit trusts are the agents for their own shareholders and unit holders. One group of institutions – building societies, most banks, and the discount houses – is interested only in government and local authority bonds, i.e. gilt-edged stock.

The short-term market

If we identify it with 'the money market' it does not deal exclusively in short-term debt. Traditionally, the main market activity is the buying, selling and financing of bills of exchange, both those issued in the private sector (which are from hereon lumped together under the title 'commercial bills') and Treasury bills; but all the institutions operating in this market also buy, hold and sell gilt-edged bonds. However, probably at least 75% of the bonds they deal in are 'short bonds'; that is, they have a life to maturity of not more than five years. The market also deals in deposits, with banks, building societies, local authorities and finance houses, some of which are also now at fairly long-term, certificates of deposit, and short-term book account loans; e.g. call money lent to the discount houses. The money market is not a formally organised market in a particular place, like the Stock Exchange or the commodity exchanges. Most of its business is conducted by letter or telephone, or by personal visits to each other's place of business; but most of the major institutions who participate directly in the market, on their own behalf or as agents, have their head office or a branch in the City.

The money market is not, in fact, a fully unified market, but has two sections.

The 'traditional' market

This is often referred to as 'the discount market'. The participants are the discount houses and the deposit banks. The traditional money market is closely and directly linked with the central monetary authorities: behind or above these institutions stands the Bank of England, both regulating the market and supporting it as 'lender of last resort', prepared to supply money in exchange for, or on the security of, certain categories of bills or bonds to the discount houses on request. The Treasury does not participate, but is an important influence as the issuer of two of the main securities traded, the Treasury bill and the government bond. What distinguishes this market most sharply from the other money markets is that it is through the traditional market that notes and coins are issued, and it is in this market that the other, and larger, part of the traditional money supply, bank deposits, is determined and created.

The parallel markets

These are of more recent origin, and only came into prominence in the 1960s. They are parallel in the sense that they offer to lenders alternative facilities to those obtainable in the traditional markets. Both borrowers and lenders have a wider choice than in the traditional market and the terms allowed in the parallel markets are more flexible and more adaptable to changing requirements (see Einzig 1966:2). There are at the time of writing at least six parallel markets, differentiated from each other by the credit instrument traded. They are the markets in inter-bank, inter-company, local authority, finance house, and Eurocurrency deposits, and the market in certificates of deposit. The clearing banks and discount houses play a major role in some of the parallel markets, little or no part in others. Most of the markets' activities are conducted by the 'secondary banks', i.e. the merchant, overseas, and foreign banks, and by non-bank financial institutions such as insurance companies and finance houses. Industrial and commercial companies also take part; they constitute the inter-company market and participate in others as, for example, when they buy certificates of deposit or make loans to the finance houses or local authorities. Most of the business in these markets is conducted through deposit brokers. Some of them are descended from foreign exchange brokers, some began as local authority loan brokers in the 1950s. Some have up to a hundred branches in various parts of the world, others are one-man firms. Some are departments of stockbroking firms, while others are wholly or partly owned by discount houses. One distinguishing feature of the parallel markets is that they cannot use the Bank of England as lender of last resort (see Ch. 6).

The work of all these money markets consists essentially of the exchange of immediate purchasing power, money now, for titles to receipt of money in the future. The stock in trade of the markets is money and securities or other titles to future payment, e.g. local authority deposits, which they buy and sell to each other and to the general public or arrange the purchase and sale. Some of the institutions which organise a market and conduct most of its operations provide specialised services, e.g. building societies and insurance companies. They all, by their existence, help to create markets for funds and provide a wide variety of assets for savers and lenders enabling borrowers to tap a wide variety of sources of finance. They are all, in one way or another, financial intermediaries.

The functions of a central bank

No discussion of the traditional money market would be valid without some analysis of the role of the central bank. In the UK, of course, this is known as the Bank of England. But first of all how do we define a central bank?

The Bank for International Settlements (BIS) defines a central bank as 'the bank in any country to which has been entrusted the duty of regulating the volume of currency and credit in that country'. Sir Richard Sayers' (1967: 66) definition is much wider: 'the central bank is the organ of government that undertakes the financial operations of the Government and by its conduct of those operations and by other means, influences the behaviour of financial institutions so as to support the economic policy of the Government'.

Whichever of these, or other, definitions we choose, one thing is clear: a central bank has responsibilities which set it apart from all other banks. If it conducts commercial banking operations as well, they must in every way be secondary to its central banking operations. The central bank may show a profit but it must always treat profits as a coincidental by-product of its activities, not an objective. Its first concern must be for the national interest. This is the prime and obvious basis of sound central banking, the first difference between the central bank and all other operators in the money markets.

The constitutions and precise duties and powers of the central bank vary from one country to another, but there are certain functions which all must discharge; they are inherent in the definitions just quoted.

1. It must control the issue of notes and coin. The easiest way is to give it a monopoly of the issue, but that is not essential so long as the central bank has power to set a limit on private issues.
2. It must control the volume of credit-money created by banks.
3. In a sophisticated financial system, where the banks are no longer the only suppliers of credit, the central bank should have control, direct or indirect, over other credit-giving institutions. If spending is a function not simply of the quantity of money but of 'the liquidity of the economy', the central bank should, ideally, be able to control this 'liquidity'.
4. It must be able to support as well as control the financial system in order to prevent crises of confidence and violent, disruptive changes in the supply and cost of credit. It must be able to relieve shortages as well as prevent excesses.

5. As the Government's financial agent the central bank will, inevitably, be the Government's banker. It will hold the Government bank account and in all probability will on occasion lend to the government. In this capacity it will also manage and administer the country's National Debt, a task which goes as far back as 1715. This is, of course, always a temptation to an improvident government, and the Act establishing the Bank of England had a clause prohibiting it from making loans to the government without Parliament's permission; but it was rescinded in 1793.

6. It is also natural that the central bank will act as the official agent in its external financial relations. It will hold the Government's reserves of gold and foreign exchange; it will undertake such operations in the foreign exchange market and administer such controls on the purchase and sale of gold and foreign exchange as may be necessary to stabilise the exchange value of the domestic currency or to cause changes in it, as the Government desires. It will maintain contact with other central banks and international financial institutions and will conduct, or at least play a part in or advise on, negotiations with them.

The history of the origins of the Bank of England (in 1694) and its subsequent development and growth is well documented elsewhere (see Sayers 1977). For our purposes perhaps the most important date is 1947 when the Bank was nationalised. One of the most important clauses in the Act concerned was Clause Four, which gave certain statutory powers to the Treasury over the Bank and to the Bank over other banks. These powers are set out in sub-clauses (1) and (3) of Clause Four:

> The Treasury may from time to time give such directions to the Bank as, after consultation with the Governor of the Bank, they think necessary in the public interest . . .
>
> The Bank, if they think it necessary in the public interest, may request information from and make recommendations to bankers, and may, if so authorised by the Treasury, issue directions to any banker for the purpose of securing that effect is given to any such request or recommendation . . .

The Treasury must, however, give the banker concerned an opportunity to make representations with respect to the directive.

Important though Clause Four is constitutionally, it has so far made no difference to the relations between the three parties. Control by the Treasury and the Bank continues to be exercised, as hitherto, by consultation, persuasion and, for the most part, informal discussion between responsible people who are in almost daily contact with each other and whose experience is that cooperation and compromise are better than compulsion. No directive has yet been issued by either the Treasury or the Bank, although the Bank has issued requests on such matters as liquidity ratios, the amount of credit to be extended by overdrafts and bill finance, and the priority sectors for credit. When one such request in 1969 − to keep lending within certain prescribed limits − was not met, the Bank halved the interest on the banks' compulsory special deposits with it. The Bank has other sanctions: it could discipline a clearing bank by closing its account at the Bank; a recalcitrant discount house could be denied lender of last resort facilities; an accepting house could lose most of its business if its acceptances were made ineligible for rediscount at the Bank.

The Bank's control over the monetary system and its exercise of that control derive from its two main functions: it is banker to the Government and to the traditional money market.

Banker to the Government

The Bank has been the Government's banker since its foundation. Small accounts are kept at branches of the clearing banks by outlying offices of some government departments – e.g. the Department of Employment, Customs and Excise, and the Inland Revenue – but all payments and receipts eventually pass through accounts at the Bank. The Bank holds subsidiary accounts, the accounts of various statutory bodies and government organisations, e.g. of departments such as the Inland Revenue, the National Insurance Fund, the Exchange Equalisation Account (EEA), the Commissioners of the National Debt. There are two main government accounts:

1. The Exchequer Account, for receipt of revenue and payment of the expenses of government and internal transfers between the Exchequer and other departments.
2. The National Loans Fund (1968), through which pass all government borrowings and most of its lending.

As government banker, the Bank also acts as agent and adviser in all the Government's financial activities, both internal and external. It prints and issues the 1,800 million new notes put into circulation each year and withdraws and destroys old ones; the Note Issue Department is the biggest department of the Bank in terms of numbers employed. It is the Government's agent in its relations with the institutions which comprise 'the City', and the executor of monetary policy. It announces and administers new issues of government loan stock through the Government's stockbroker, conversions (the exchange of old loan stock for new issues), and the issue of Treasury bills both 'on tap' and by tender. It acts as registrar of the loan stock, collecting payment for new stock and making repayment at maturity, paying interest to stockholders, maintaining the register of stockholders and making repayment at maturity, paying interest to stockholders, maintaining the register of stockholders and recording transfers between holders by sale and purchase. It administers the Exchange Equalisation Account which holds reserves of gold and foreign exchange, and operates the control of purchases and sales of foreign exchange by residents through about 300 authorised banks with permission to deal in foreign exchange. In managing the EEA, it frequently intervenes in the foreign exchange market itself, buying or selling sterling/foreign currencies to reverse deviations of the exchange rate from its desired level. This intervention may be in the spot market – i.e. buying/selling for immediate delivery – or in the forward market, e.g. it may buy sterling for delivery one to six months hence to restore confidence in the short-term future value of sterling. It negotiates loans from or to official monetary institutions overseas and conducts or participates in any other discussions with them. In 1964, for example, the then Governor of the Bank, Lord Cromer, raised $3,000 million from other central banks in a few hours, to be used to relieve pressure on the pound in the foreign exchange markets which might otherwise have forced the new Labour Government to devalue. It is therefore in frequent contact with other central banks and with institutions such as the International Monetary Fund, the World Bank (International Bank for Reconstruction and Development) and the Organization for Economic Cooperation and Development.

Government and local authority borrowing

The Government and the local authorities also borrow at both short and long term. The Government borrows from the public in two ways:

1. By the sale of non-negotiable securities, that is, securities the title to which cannot be transferred from one holder to another and repayable only to the registered original holder. The main items in this category are (a) National Savings securities: National Savings Certificates, Savings Bonds, and Premium Bonds; and (b) a special category of security, Terminable Annuities, issued through the National Savings Bank and Trustee Savings Banks.
2. By the sale of negotiable securities: Treasury bills and Government bonds which together constitute the major supply of gilt-edged securities.

Treasury bills
The Treasury bill is classed as a bill of exchange; in fact, it is not an order to pay, but a promissory note. They were first issued in 1877.[2] Until 1914 there were severe statutory restraints on the uses of Treasury bill finance, and it was only during the First World War that the practice began of issuing new bills to repay maturing bills, the consequence of which was, of course, that outstanding bills have become a permanent part of the National Debt. With short-term loans to the Exchequer from government bodies and the Bank of England (ways and means advances), they constitute the 'floating debt'. They are issued in denominations of £5,000, £10,000, £25,000, £50,000, £100,000, £250,000 and £1 million and are all 91-day bills.
    Treasury bills are issued in two ways.

The tap issue Bills are created and issued, as required, to meet residual day-to-day requirements of the Treasury and to provide an investment for certain holders of temporarily surplus funds. Most tap bills are bought by other government departments and by various statutory funds such as the EEA, the National Debt Commissioners, the National Insurance Fund and the Public Trustee. Since all these are part of the Government sector, the lending and repayment of these funds is really only a piece of internal book-keeping designed to use as fully as possible the total funds available to the Government. Tap bills are also made available to overseas monetary authorities with deposits in London banks, and to the Issue Department of the Bank of England, which may later sell them to the public or the discount houses or the clearing banks in the conduct of an open market operation.

The Treasury bill tender Most bills are sold by tender. Each Friday the Bank of England announces the quantity of bills which will be on offer next week and invites bids (tenders) from a selected group of institutions: the London bankers (including the London offices of overseas banks), the discount houses, and the bill brokers. The Bank of England itself also puts in tenders on behalf of overseas central banks and for its own Banking Department. Anyone else wishing to tender will do so through a London bank, acting as his agent. Since the minimum tender is for £50,000 face value of bills, these private tenderers will be mostly financial institutions – building societies, savings banks, insurance companies, HP finance companies, etc. – or large commercial and industrial firms. From 1935 to September 1971, the clearing banks had an agreement with the discount houses not to tender on their own behalf, only as agents. The formal agreement was abandoned in September 1971, but the practice continues. They are large holders of Treasury bills, but they buy them from the discount houses not less than one week after the day of issue. Since 1971 they also buy them 'hot', i.e. on the day of issue or shortly afterwards.

The tender rate is, of course, the inverse of the percentage price offered. From 1924 to 1971 the discount houses tendered at a common price – 'the syndicated bid' – and since 1939 they have 'covered the tender', i.e. have collectively bid for the whole issue, the proportion of the total for which each house bids being determined by the size of its capital and reserves.[3] The discount house and Bank of England bids make up 'the inside tender' and the rest 'the outside tender'. The syndicate price would depend on the size of the issue as compared with the current state of demand for bills from the banks and others, the probable size of the outside bids, and the current and prospective cost of funds, which would depend very much on the antici-pated course of bank rate during the life of the bills. Since the discount houses cover the tender, an outside bidder must offer a higher price than theirs to get an allotment of bills. The discount houses get the remainder, the proportion depending on how many bills the outside tenderers have bid for at prices higher than theirs. Outside bidders must therefore try to guess the discount houses' bid prices, but their bids are also strongly influenced by expectations about government penal rates. If the tenderer expects this and market rates in general to fall, he bids heavily since he is expecting security prices to rise and if he is correct he will be able to sell his bills later at a profit or, alternatively, will be earning a return higher than the (later) current rate; if he expects rates to rise, he abstains. The proportions of the total issue obtained by the discount houses and the outside tenderers respectively can therefore change markedly from week to week. It is unusual for the discount houses to fail to get some bills; on the other hand, there are always some bids higher than theirs.

The security and liquidity of Treasury bills makes them a very suitable invest-ment for foreign central banks and other foreign institutions holding sterling balances. Until the 1960s this was how they used these balances, but then much of the overseas money – and company money – which used to go into the Treasury bill tender began to move into the more profitable parallel markets (see Ch. 6) although the foreign central banks continue to keep their sterling assets mainly in Treasury bills.

Government bonds

Government bond issues are the major source of long-term finance. They are issued at irregular intervals, the timing depending mainly on the need for finance but also on the 'state of the market' and the Government's strategy on interest rates. They carry a fixed return, expressed as a percentage of the par value (invariably £100) of a unit of the security, and this percentage is the coupon rate. This rate is not synonymous with, and can differ widely from, the market rate of interest, or yield, on the bond. Coupon rates vary and depend on the current yield on existing gilt-edged stocks of similar maturity; the Government cannot expect to raise 15-year money at 8% if an outstanding issue with fifteen years to go to maturity is currently available on the market at a yield of 10%.

More often than not, government stock is issued at a discount on the par value, giving the primary holder a capital appreciation if he holds the bond to maturity. All issues are negotiable and are traded on the stock exchanges, where their prices may, of course, be less than their par – i.e. redemption – values. In that circumstance also the (secondary) buyer makes a capital gain if he holds the bond to maturity. If at any time the market rate on a particular class of bond is lower than the coupon rate, its price on the market will be higher than its redemption value. There are, therefore, almost always two yields on any bond, its 'running yield' and its 'yield to redemption'.

Local authority borrowing

Local authorities also borrow in various ways, for various periods. They borrow, for example, from the banks on overdraft. In addition, they accept deposits, usually at seven days' notice and in large sums, £50,000 being a typical minimum figure. They tap small savings with mortgage loans for two to seven years secured on their rates revenue, available more or less continuously in multiples of £50 or £100 starting from a minimum of, usually, £500; they also issue transferable securities. Some large authorities issue 'revenue bills', analogous to Treasury bills in their original purpose, i.e. to finance day-to-day expenditure between receipts of rates. The larger authorities also make issues of bonds of various kinds (see Ch. 6).

Banker to the money market

About 100 financial institutions – including domestic banks, discount houses, and overseas banks – keep an account at the Bank. The most important accounts are those of the London clearing banks and the discount houses, because it is mainly by operations which affect these accounts that the Bank maintains its day-to-day control of the monetary system. A clearing bank's balance with the Bank is counted as cash in its balance sheet. It draws notes on demand against this account to replenish its tills and pays surplus or worn notes into it. Net debts to other banks at the daily clearing are settled by transfer out of this account. The banks thus use these bankers' deposits in much the same ways as a customer of a bank uses his current account, with one important difference: a bank's account at the Bank of England cannot be overdrawn and the Bank gives advances to only one category of its banking customers, the discount houses.

The Bank also holds a small number of private accounts. Its own staff, for example, are allowed to keep accounts with it. Most other private accounts date back to the era when the Bank was an active commercial bank, but in the last few years it has been prepared to open new accounts, mostly for firms in the City, probably because this small private business has the merit of giving the Bank direct experience of some of the banking problems that other banks face.

The Bank thus stands, perhaps at times uneasily, between the public sector of which it is part and the private sector in which it operates; it has to wear different hats. In close daily contact with the City, it represents the City to the Treasury; but it is also the instrument by which the Treasury makes its wishes known to, and its policies impinge upon, the City. It is the ultimate support and guardian of the institutions which comprise the City; in the liquidity crises of 1973–74, for example, it was the Bank of England which organised the 'lifeboat' committee (see p. 66). But it is also in the end their master. It is not a department of state, and it is not even subject to the same degree of control by the state as the other nationalised industries. Everyone assumes that it should be the agent of the Treasury but that it should also be its financial adviser, 'making an important contribution to the formation of policy in this field'.[4] An efficient central bank may be the creation of government, but must not be its creature. It must be prepared to speak out against policies which, in its considered opinion, are improvident, impracticable or irresponsible; a competent governor of the central bank must be prepared to offend his masters. On the other hand, the Government must be the final arbiter of policy and the Bank must be prepared to operate conscientiously a policy with which it does not agree. Its various roles can clash; the twin duties of support and control sometimes conflict, as we shall see. As the Government's banker, one of its duties is to raise finance for the Government; in so doing it may, necessarily, weaken the monetary policy which it is currently pursuing.

The balance sheet of the Bank of England

The operations of the Bank with which we shall be concerned are reflected in the weekly bank return and annual balance sheet. These are still presented in two parts, distinguishing the note-issuing function of the Bank from its banking business as prescribed by the 1844 Bank Charter Act, although the separation no longer has its original, or indeed any, significance (see Table 2.1).

Table 2.1 Balance sheet: 29 February 1984

Issue Department

1983 £000		1984 £000	1983 £000		1984 £000
	Notes issued:		11,015	Government debt	11,015
11,007,915	In circulation	11,457,345		Other securities of,	
17,085	In banking department	12,655	3,285,996	or guaranteed by, the British Government	2,001,111
			7,727,989	'Other securities'	9,457,874
£11,025,000		£11,470,000	£11,025,000		£11,470,000

Banking Department

1983 £000		1984 £000	1983 £000		1984 £000
				Liquid assets	
14,553	Capital	14,553	17,227	Notes and coin	12,828
383,970	Reserves	395,744	229,634	Cheques in course of collection	222,898
£398,523		£410,297	1,339,883	Treasury and other bills	1,113,860
			£1,586,744		£1,349,586
	Current Liabilities				
644,774	Public deposits	233,487	338,328	Investments	341,629
694,898	Bankers' deposits	766,960	1,372,718	Advances and other accounts, *less* provisions	540,349
1,781,231	Other accounts	1,046,537	25,309	Subsidiary companies	25,342
23,000	Payable to Treasury	21,750	219,327	Premises and equipment	222,125
£3,143,903		£2,068,734			
£3,542,426		£2,479,031	£3,542,426		£2,479,031

Source: *Bank of England Report and Accounts*, 1984: 20, 21, 32

The sole liability of the Issue Department is the note issue. Most notes have passed into circulation and are held by the public; the rest are held in the Banking Department as a reserve against calls for them from the banks with accounts at the Bank. The assets held against the note issue are almost all government securities, bonds and Treasury bills, which the Issue Department takes up as it prints and issues more notes. It is these bonds which the Bank uses when it operates in the gilt-edged market in managing the National Debt (see p. 20). The 'other securities' are bonds issued by authorities other than the British Government, e.g. Commonwealth governments. The Issue Department used to hold the reserves of gold coin and bullion, but most of this was transferred to the EEA in 1939, and the remainder in 1970. The Bank therefore no longer holds any gold 'backing' against the note issue, which is thus entirely fiduciary.

The important liabilities of the Banking Department are the deposits held with it by the Government and official agencies – public deposits – and by the banks and discount houses – bankers' deposits and special deposits. The latter are compulsory deposits called from time to time from the banks (until September 1971, from the clearing banks only). The 'other accounts' are deposits by private customers of the Bank and by overseas central banks and other financial bodies. Against these liabilities the Department holds a small reserve of notes and coin against calls on the bankers' deposits, and mass of bills and bonds (but note that most of its securities are held in the Issue Department) with which it conducts open-market operations. The item 'other securities' is a mixture of several kinds of non-British Government securities. It includes bonds issued by Commonwealth governments, some shares and debentures which the Bank acquired in the 1930s when it helped with industrial reconstruction and development, commercial bills which the Bank frequently buys from the discount houses to check the quality of bills circulating in the City, and bills discounted for its own customers. Advances also includes loans to its customers, but the significant part of this item for our purpose is lender-of-last-resort loans to, and discounts for, the discount houses.

The discount houses

The discount market includes eleven discount-house members of the London Discount Market Association, plus two discount brokers, and the money trading departments of five banks which carry on the same kind of business as the discount houses. There are also six firms of stockbrokers, called money brokers, who help to make the market in gilts using money borrowed from the banks (see Revell 1973: 221–3).

The traditional function of a discount house is to buy bills of exchange and hold them, i.e. to finance bills. The practice of discounting is probably nearly as old as the bill itself, but until about the second quarter of the nineteenth century the bill-brokers were pure brokers, intermediaries between borrowers and lenders who arranged bill finance and arranged the discounting of bills both by wealthy individuals and by the banks, of which there were about a thousand by the early nineteenth century (see Scammell 1968).

Nowadays the main function of the discount house is to discount and hold bills with funds borrowed at call from the banks, and rediscount them with the banks or the central bank. But the development of the London Discount Market to its present form and size did not really begin until the second half of the century and was not based on the internal bills but on bills used to finance foreign trade. During the two world wars, commercial bills were largely replaced by Treasury bills in their portfolios, but are now again a major asset.

They were able to expand slowly by diversifying into the parallel markets. In 1964, they took up the first issues of short-term local authority bonds made under the

1963 Act and have continued to make a market for local authority bonds and bills. Soon they began to deal in dollar certificates of deposit (CDs) not long after they were introduced into the London market and have made a market in sterling certificates since they first appeared. In addition, they operate in the Eurocurrency market as dealers in bills and CDs. Indeed, more than one-third of their reserves are now deployed in parallel market assets, and a majority of the members of the Discount Market Association have a stake in firms of brokers in the parallel markets. The new arrangements for monetary control introduced in 1971 helped the discount market; money lent to the market could, without limit, be included in banks' reserve assets.[5]

Clearly, the great strength of the discount houses has been their ability to adjust to change, and find new activities to replace or supplement the old. Beginning as discounters of and dealers in commercial bills, they have successively turned to Treasury bills, to bonds, and to the new credit instruments and the new money markets. Throughout their history, and in all their many activities, two features of their operations persist. First, they operate almost entirely on borrowed money and, second, they lend at longer terms than they borrow.

As for *sources of funds*, they accept deposits at seven days' notice at the same rate as the clearing banks and also take some money at longer than seven days at higher rates, as well as overnight money from lenders outside the money markets: but most of their funds come from the market, predominantly as money at call and short notice from the banks – the deposit banks, overseas and foreign banks, the TSBs and the acceptance houses – and a wide range of other financial institutions, including Giro – over 250 in all. The London clearing banks are, however, the major source (see McRae and Cairncross 1974).

All loans are made against 'eligible collateral' – securities of a quality defined by the lender – good bills and CDs, government bonds of up to five years' life, and (usually, but not always) local authority bonds. The collateral must have a value slightly higher than the loan, and this margin on the collateral must be maintained by the deposit of further securities if the market value of the collateral already pledged declines. The houses keep a stock of unpledged securities, financed of course from their own resources, for this purpose. Only the discount houses have the privilege of borrowing from the Bank of England, and the Bank's standard of eligibility is particularly high; it usually only takes government bonds of up to five years' maturity, Treasury and local authority bills and, if necessary when the houses are short of these, bills accepted by a substantial British bank; but since the mid 1940s it has occasionally taken good trade bills. A minimum proportion of the collateral against last resort loans must be Treasury bills.

As we shall see, the rate at which the Bank discounts bills or lends on the security of bills depends on its interest-rate policy at the time. It may charge the same rate as the Bank of England charges (previously the bank rate, then minimum lending rate). These were penal rates; they were kept higher than the rates at which the discount houses discounted bills, so they lost money on these loans or rediscounts. Or it may charge only the current market discount rate.

From the mid 1930s until September 1971 the discount houses had an agree-

27

ment with the clearing banks under which the latter lent them 'regular' or 'good' money, normally renewable every day, at a low rate of interest ($1\frac{5}{8}$% below bank rate) and the discount houses did not compete with them for funds by offering more than the clearing banks for deposits.[6] In addition, they lent money at rates which varied from day to day, and even within the day, depending on the going rate on Treasury bills and general market conditions: 'the clearing banks keep a lively eye on the market's profit margins on bills, and are quick to squeeze the discount market by altering the terms on which they lend money to the market' (Radcliffe Report, para. 168). Finally there was 'privilege money', taken late in the day and lent overnight only, to enable a house to balance its books. It was borrowed only if the discount house could not find money elsewhere, and in comparatively small amounts (usually not more than £5 million in total); the rate charged was about $1\frac{1}{8}$% below bank rate.

All this changed after September 1971. The clearing banks' cartel rate for regular money, and the concept of 'regular money' itself, was abandoned.[7] The rates the banks charged, and the rates the discount market would pay, became competitive with other rates, especially rates in the inter-bank market. The 'privilege facilities' would be withdrawn.[8] But in their place the Bank of England gave the market limited overnight borrowing facilities at a non-penal rate. With the growth of new markets offering better rates than this, the discount houses' proportion of funds from the non-clearing banks had fallen in the 1960s. This decline in call money from the secondary banks was quickly reversed, helped by the fact that such money counted as part of the new compulsory minimum ratio of reserve assets to eligible liabilities (see Ch. 13).

Uses of funds

The funds that discount houses borrow are used to buy (discount) commercial bills and local authority ('corporation') bills; to pay for Treasury bills allotted to them at the tender; to buy bonds issued by the Government, local authorities, public corporations and some Commonwealth and Dominion governments, and dollar and sterling CDs; to lend to the finance houses; and to operate in the inter-bank market, where they both borrow from and lend to (accept deposits from and place deposits with) a wide range of banks. A discount house's holding of any security is likely to be temporary; it is bought, held for a while, then sold again. Their main customers are the banks, who regularly buy from them parcels of bills which they then usually hold to maturity. They also sell parcels of bills to other institutions and to industrial and commercial firms, who like the banks hold them as a short-term investment. They also act as jobbers in the other securities they hold, adjusting their prices and the proportions between their assets in search of maximum profits. The potential capital losses and gains on holdings of bonds are substantial. For this reason they like to keep their bonds 'short' and they increase or reduce their holdings according to their interest rates expectations (and other considerations).[9] In short, both their activities – intermediation and jobbing – are risky, and their profit margins tend to be unstable.

28

The functions of the discount market

The discount houses and brokers are useful in three ways.

Supply of credit

They supply credit to industry and commerce by discounting bills; to the Government and local authorities by buying their bills and bonds; to the finance houses by deposits; and to the banks by taking up certificates of deposit. Since nearly all the funds they lend are borrowed funds, they are only channels for credit, but by providing a market for credit documents they increase the flow of credit.

Services to the financial system

1 By making a market in bills, certificates of deposit, bonds, and day-to-day deposits of sterling (call money), they provide a convenient and flexible means of employing money, and so help to attract foreign funds to London; they made an important contribution to the development of London as a financial centre.

2 They economise on the total stock of money in two ways:

(a) The existence of an organised market for Treasury bills and short bonds means that some money which might otherwise be idle flows into these securities.

(b) When one bank has a surplus of funds, another may be short. The surplus/shortage is adjusted through the market by the extension/calling-in of call money. They thus drain off spare credit. And in a time of general shortage they ensure that what credit is available is put to use.

3 They provide valuable services to the banks:

(a) Call money is an excellent liquid asset for the banks. Because of the discount houses' privilege of recourse to the Bank of England as lender of last resort, the liquidity of call money is absolutely secure, and the banks therefore have an assured means of adjusting their cash position very quickly. Call money therefore reduces the banks' minimum safe reserve of cash and provides earnings for spare funds. Bills are also a liquid income-earning asset and it is the discount houses who make the market in bills.

(b) They make up convenient portfolios of bills for the banks, i.e. portfolios with a run of maturity dates. They also buy bills from the banks.

(c) By making a market for bonds, they help the banks to switch between bonds (investments) and advances, or between bonds and liquid assets. Bonds are a reserve of liquidity.

4 Most important, they act as a shock absorber between the operations of the Bank of England and the clearing banks. Because the discount houses can always borrow from the Bank to repay call money, the banks can transfer to

them the impact of any sudden reduction in their own cash reserves by calling in loans.

Services to the authorities

1 It is readily accepted that their obligation to cover the tender of Treasury bills is useful to the authorities in two ways:
   (a)   The Exchequer is assured that its need for short-term finance will be met. The discount houses, in effect, underwrite each weekly issue of Treasury bills. (They can only do this, of course, if the Bank of England acts as lender of last resort and does not impose a penal rate too often. Ultimately, it is the Bank which underwrites the Treasury bill issue.)
   (b)   Knowing this, the authorities can deliberately create a shortage of cash in the money market by issuing more Treasury bills than are necessary to meet prospective net disbursements, so that in the following week the Treasury is taking in more money than it is paying out. They can then influence interest rates by the terms on which the Bank relieves this shortage.
2 Because they tap surplus funds to relieve any shortage, any general scarcity of money in the market is revealed in the discount market or can be created by operating there. The authorities do not need to deal with each individual bank but have one central point at which to inject/withdraw funds for the whole system. This simplifies the administration of monetary policy. It is through the discount houses that the authorities exercise day-to-day control over the monetary system; it is through them that it acts as lender of last resort to the money market and so effects the Bank's interest rate policy.

No doubt all these functions can be performed by the Bank of England and/or the clearing banks, by direct dealings between the banks and the Bank of England. But some of them are specialised functions which would mean the setting up of new departments and – as the Bank said in evidence both to the Radcliffe Committee and to the Select Committee on the Nationalised Industries in 1967 – they probably perform them as cheaply as any one could. Certainly, the evidence is that both the Bank of England and the rest of the market want them to survive and continue to bear the peculiar risks to which they are subject.

After the publication of 'Competition and Credit Control' (CCC) in September 1971, the activities of the discount houses changed significantly. The most important changes were:

1 Operations within the discount market; the discount houses, discount brokers, money brokers, and the money trading departments of the six banks were not to be subject to the new combined reserve ratio. It was agreed to keep not less than 50% of these borrowed funds in certain categories of public debt; Treasury and other public sector bills, tax reserve certificates, and government nationalised industry and local authority bonds with not more than five years to final

maturity. In fact, this was rather less than the proportion of such assets they held in September 1971. This rule was changed in July 1973.

2 The discount houses were to abandon the syndicated bid for tender Treasury bills. Though permitted to agree the price at which they will underwrite the tender, i.e. take up any surplus, each house was to be free to bid its own price for any quantity of bills it wishes. The discount houses agreed, however, to continue to cover the tender; in return the Bank continued to 'confine to the market their extension of last resort facilities' (which was necessary if the high liquidity of call money was to be preserved) (*Bank of England Quarterly Bulletin* (hereafter BEQB) September 1971: 314). Occasional 'indirect help' by the purchase of bills from the banks would continue. The Bank, however, would require the discount houses to provide part of the collateral against last resort loans in the form of Treasury bills, up to a minimum proportion to be agreed. The agreement by which the clearing banks did not bid on their own account was also cancelled; but the banks in fact do still refrain from tendering on their own behalf.

3 The existing structure of rates on call money was abandoned. There would no longer be a common basic rate for 'regular' money; there would be no 'regular' money or 'overnight' money in the old sense. All rates on call money would be negotiated ad hoc.

On the whole the discount houses enjoyed an enhanced position in the market under the new system:

1 They retained their privilege of last resort borrowing at the Bank, a privilege denied to all other institutions, although several other banks – the clearing banks, merchant banks, and overseas and foreign banks – keep accounts there.

2 Loans to the discount houses continued to count as reserve assets, but the only advantage attaching to loans to other banks is that they reduce eligible liabilities. The importance of call money was increased by the fact that the secondary banks were now required to hold a minimum reserve ratio, and call money counted as a reserve asset without limits. In the first year of operation of CCC, loans to the discount houses by accepting houses, overseas banks and other banks in the UK rose from £450 million to £859 million, so the discount houses remained and still remain major operators in the markets for all the traditional reserve assets.

3 They held assets which are not reserve assets for the banks; 1–5 year bonds, non-eligible commercial bills, local authority bonds and certificates of deposits; and those classed as public sector debt counted as reserve assets for the discount houses. Since they are held against call money, they effectively became reserve assets for the banks; the banks could increase their reserves by lending call money to the discount houses for the purchase of such assets. Hence the authorities' request that they should not engage in 'window dressing' operations, buying non-reserve assets with call money.

4 The discount houses did not incur reserve ratio obligations when they borrow; their only obligation was to hold 50% of their assets in public sector liabilities.

This '50% rule' could, however, be an embarrassment. The new policy on gilt-edged made larger fluctuations in gilt-edged prices probable, with bigger risks of capital losses. After heavy losses in 1972 and the ending of the 50% rule in 1973, they reduced their holdings of gilt-edged rapidly. They also need a good stock of assets such as Treasury and local authority bills which can be turned into money when there is a dearth of funds in the call money market. It follows that the houses depend on a continuous flow of new Treasury bills, and a shortage can be embarrassing for them. It was estimated that in the summer of 1973 they lost some £25–£30 million, and their profit in 1972 was £7 million. It was in these circumstances that the 50% rule was abandoned in July 1973, in favour of a regulation that holdings of 'undefined assets' (briefly, private sector paper) must not exceed twenty times their capital and reserves. 'Defined assets' included balances at the Bank of England and public sector bills and bonds with not more than five years to final maturity.

The deposit banks

There are three groups of deposit banks, which are also called joint stock banks, primary banks, and *retail banks*. They are:

1 The six London clearing banks (LCBs), who settle cheques drawn on each other daily through the Bankers' Clearing House. They include the 'Big Four' – Barclays, National Westminster, Midland and Lloyds – and two smaller banks, Williams and Glyn's Bank and Coutts and Co. Williams and Glyn's is owned by the National and Commercial Banking Group in which Lloyds has a 16% interest, and Coutts is a subsidiary of National Westminster. The Big Four hold about half the total sterling deposits in UK banks, and more than 12,000 out of some 15,000 branch offices in the UK.
2 Three Scottish clearing banks and four Northern Ireland banks. The Scottish banks are the Bank of Scotland, part-owned by Barclays, the Clydesdale Bank, owned by Midland, and the Royal Bank of Scotland, which in 1985 became fully merged with Williams and Glyn.[10] Those in Northern Ireland are the Northern Bank, owned by Midland, the Ulster Bank, owned by National Westminster, the Bank of Ireland and Allied Irish Banks Ltd., both owned by Eireann banks.
3 Seven 'other deposit banks': the Cooperative Bank (now a member of the Bankers' Clearing House), C. Hoave and Co., the Isle of Man Bank (owned by National Westminster), Lewis's Bank (owned by Lloyds), the Yorkshire (jointly owned by Barclays, Lloyds and National Westminster), and the offices in Great Britain of two Eireann banks.

The Big Four not only own other deposit banks; they own, or have a share in, merchant banks, finance houses and (except Lloyds) banking consortia. They have also spread their activities abroad through subsidiaries, besides their membership of consortia. Barclays Bank International conducts deposit banking in every part of the world through more than 1,700 branches, Lloyds Bank International has over 180 offices, most of them in South America, and Grindlays, in which Lloyds has an interest, has over 200 branches in Asia and Africa. National Westminster and International Westminster have 26 branches in major financial centres, including 13 in Europe, five in the USA and one in Tokyo; it also has a minority interest in three European banks. The Midland Bank is widely represented abroad through associated and correspondent banks, has close links with a group of European banks (EBIC) and also has shares in three overseas banks.[11]

The activities of the deposit banks

Traditionally, the particular activities of the deposit banks which distinguished them from the secondary banks were:

1 They engaged in retail banking, the acceptance of small deposits and the handling of small transfers between accounts.
2 They accepted only two kinds of deposit: (a) deposits at 7 days' notice,[12] in which all the London clearing banks paid the same rate of interest, minus 2%.[13] Since September 1971 the rate has been set at a variable interval, under the bank's 'base rate'. The banks adjust their base rates according to the supply and demand for funds, roughly following inter-bank rates. They also fix them independently, but their rates have not so far differed from each other for more than a few weeks; (b) deposits on current account, which with some exceptions earn no interest and are withdrawable on demand. About half the adult population have an account of some kind with a clearing bank. A deposit constitutes a liability of the bank to pay cash to the owner, or his payee, or to another bank through the clearing.
3 Because notes and coin reach the public through them as their deposits are universally accepted as money, and because they have branches throughout the country, they have become the main operators of the payments mechanisms.[14] Other institutions offer the same or similar facilities for the transfer of money – e.g. National Giro, other banks, the TSB – but the deposit banks still dominate the field.
4 They lend by creating deposits: loans create deposits. In so doing they create money. The greater part of our money supply is bank-created money.
5 Their lending to the private sector is predominantly by overdrafts, 80% of them to industry and commerce. Traditionally, the banks make 'self-liquidating' loans to provide working capital, not to finance long-term projects, but since overdrafts are more often than not a renewable or continuing facility they are, in practice, often used for longer-term purposes.

In the mid 1960s they all bought or acquired a share in finance houses and more recently have set up or bought secondary bank subsidiaries to take fixed-term deposits and use them to make term loans and to operate in the parallel markets.

They have also taken on themselves activities which they used to leave to the merchant banks, accepting bills and granting acceptance credits, administration of share issues and registrar services, the management of unit trusts and private investment portfolios, and insurance broking. There have also been *innovations* on the liabilities side. They accepted deposits, saving deposits on terms similar to those of the TSB, and long before 1971 they had been offering higher rates for large deposits. All this *diversification* was speeded up after 1971, with the new freedom to compete.

The major innovation of recent years has of course been in the mortgage market. It was estimated in 1984 that 30% of their loans (exclusive of those mentioned on page 57, which accounted for another 15%) were at medium or long term. Some of them have brought in new schemes to attract medium-term deposits. One explanation for these changing functions is that the banks have been responding to fierce competition from non-bank financial intermediaries, particularly the building societies. This is an issue to be taken up in Chapters 4 and 5.

Notes

1   For an absorbing account of day-to-day operations within the City see Clarke (1979).

2   There is a brief history of the Treasury bill in Midland Bank Review (hereafter *MBR*) (February 1961).

3   From 1956 each house has been able to increase its allotment by putting in a small independent bid at a slightly higher price than the syndicated bid.

4   'Report of the Committee on the working of the Monetary System', *The Radcliffe Report* (Cmnd 827, HMSO 1959, para. 333).

5   With the shortage of Treasury bills during the 1960s discount houses became increasingly involved in the holding of commercial bills (amounting to 30% of their total assets by 1970).

6   This agreement was with the discount houses only, not with the brokers and money-trading banks.

7   But the clearing banks soon afterwards began to lend them for fixed periods ('fixtures') up to three months. According to Wilson *et al* (1976: 28) about 55% of call money was 'fixtures' in 1975.

8   In fact they were not, but the facility is used less frequently and is more expensive.

9   In fact, although they are still heavy traders (jobbers) in bonds, they no longer hold them as investments.

10   During 1981 the Royal Bank of Scotland was subject to take-over bids by the Hong Kong and Shanghai Banking Group and Standard Chartered. These were the first bids for a British clearing bank for over a decade, and the £500

million bids came up before the Monopolies and Mergers Commission.

11   Also at the end of 1980 the Midland launched a successful take-over of an American bank, the Crocker National Bank (see *The Banker* (hereafter *TB*) March 1981: 27).

12   In evidence to the Wilson Committee in 1977, the London clearing banks stated that 75% of their sterling deposits were still at eight days' notice or less. See 'The London Clearing Banks, Evidence by the Committee of London Clearing Bankers to the Committee to Review the Functioning of Financial Institutions', the *Wilson Report* (Cmnd 7937, HMSO, 1980).

13   The Scottish clearing banks used to offer rather less than this. There are a number of differences between them and the LCBs: for example, they held, and still hold, only very small balances at the Bank of England, but a much higher total ratio of cash to deposits than the London clearing banks. The first-line reserves of the 'other deposit banks' before 1971 consisted almost entirely of deposits with other banks, and their holdings of notes and coin and balances at the Bank of England are still negligible in relation to their deposit liabilities (see Revell 1973: 157–61).

14   They offer other ways of making payments, credit cards, standing orders to the bank to make specified payments at specified dates, and credit transfers. Of course, in recent years with the speeding up of technological progress in the banking world, money transmission services have been revolutionised. Cash dispensers or automated teller machines (ATM) are now commonplace, not only at bank branches but also, for example, at places of work. A more ambitious future development could be the introduction of electronic funds transfer at point of sale (EFTPOS), with debits communicated via electronic link to the banks.

CHAPTER THREE

Banks and the creation of money

The creation of deposits

Bank deposits are money; they are generally accepted in settlement of debt. How do they come into existence?

1 Those of us who have a personal account at a bank probably acquired our deposit by paying in cash or cheques. That is how our deposit was created. We exchanged one form of money (cash) for another (a bank deposit) or we exercised the claim to money which possession of a cheque gives us. But neither transaction necessarily, nor even probably, increases the aggregate of bank deposits. The cheque will have been drawn on another account and merely transfers a deposit from one owner to another and probably from one bank to another,[1] leaving bank deposits as a whole unchanged. The notes and coin may also have been withdrawn from another bank account. The only payments of cash into a bank which increase aggregate deposits are those which constitute a net inflow of cash; they occur only when someone decides to hold less currency and more bank deposits. Significant changes in the aggregate preferred ratio of currency to bank deposits do not occur suddenly.

From this brief discussion we draw the conclusion that saving does not, in the UK at least, increase bank deposits. A firm draws, say, £1,000 of currency against its bank account and pays it out in wages. This currency will sooner or later find its way back into the banks, unless the public (which, of course, includes retailers, wholesalers and producers) decide to hold more currency. If a wage-earner decides to save £5 and put it into the bank, the only difference is that this £5 goes back into the bank rather more quickly than it otherwise would. It circulates, or remains 'active' for a shorter period. If people retain their savings as cash, then an increase in saving is an increase in the public's demand for cash, additional to what they require for making payments. This extra cash is drained from the banks and, as we shall see later, other things being equal, it induces a reduction in bank deposits. Most salary-earners are paid by cheque or by direct credit to their bank account. If a salary-earner saves, all that happens is that part of his bank deposit stays idle; it is not transferred to other (successive) depositors in payment for goods and services. Of course, his bank deposit will be bigger than if he had not saved, but the gain to his deposit is balanced by the loss to the deposits of those who would have received payments if he had not saved. Saving does not change the total quantity of money, either currency or deposits; it merely reduces the *velocity of circulation* of money.

There is, however, one exception to this statement. Savings held in a bank are probably transferred from some current account to the saver's deposit account where they will earn interest.[2] In some countries – e.g. USA – the ratio between deposits and the cash which banks must hold as a reserve is higher for deposit accounts than for current accounts; they can build up a bigger total of deposit accounts than for current accounts on a given cash base. A transfer of deposits from current to deposit account thus 'frees' some cash; it allows the banks to create more deposits, more money, without receiving more cash. Saving therefore probably causes an increase in aggregate bank deposits.

2   The payment into a bank account of a cheque drawn on an account held abroad and in a foreign currency is a net addition to bank deposits. If, for example, I pay into my account a cheque, denominated in dollars, drawn against an account in a New York bank, the sum will be credited to my account and probably now be expressed in sterling. This is not a transfer of ownership of a UK bank deposit. I have, in effect, sold foreign exchange to my bank for a bank deposit and there is no reduction in any other deposit in the UK; in return for a deposit obligation to me my bank holds a claim to a dollar deposit in New York. It may sell it to the exchange equalisation account, receiving in exchange a credit to its account (banker's deposit) at the Bank of England. Such credits are equivalent to cash in the till, since they are an immediate source of cash.

3   One or other of the deposit banks similarly receives cash and acquires an equal deposit liability whenever the government, or other public authority which banks with the Bank of England, or the Bank of England itself, makes a payment to the private sector (which includes the banks). In a particular week, the government may pay out more for goods and services, or in loans and subsidies, or in repayment of debt, than it receives in payment for goods and services, in taxes, in repayment of loans and in new borrowing. Or the Bank of England may buy more securities from the private sector than it sells. The recipients of these net payments out of the public sector will receive cheques drawn on the Bank of England. These cheques will eventually be deposited with a bank. New bank deposits are created and no existing deposit is reduced. In return for the deposit liability the bank receives a claim on the Bank of England which it adds to its account there.

There are two points to note about these three origins of new bank deposits. First, they all increase one bank's holdings of cash, or its equivalent, a balance at the Bank of England. Such deposits are often referred to as *primary deposits*. Second, the banks play a passive role in the action. The deposits are created on the initiative of the public, a government body, or the Bank of England. The bank concerned must, of course, be willing to play its part but there is no compulsion to sell securities to the central bank nor to accept cash or cheques from any member of the public.

Most bank deposits, however, are *derivative*; that is, they derive from operations undertaken by a bank on its own initiative. This could take the form of a purchase of securities by a bank. Not only may the bank buy (discount) some bills from their original owner, they may also buy many more (previously discounted) bills from the discount houses. Treasury bills or gilt-edged bonds may also be bought either in the primary market (i.e. by subscription to new issues) or in the secondary market (the Stock Exchange). Government securities bought in the primary market will be paid for by transfer from the bank's account at the Bank of England to public deposits. Securities bought on the Stock Exchange and bills discounted will be paid for by crediting the seller's bank account; that is, by an increase in bank deposits. This deposit thus derives from, and is created by, the purchase of the security.

4 Banks also create deposits when they lend. Most bank lending is of two kinds. First, they lend for very short periods, from one day to one month, to discount houses, to brokers in bills and gold bullion, and to jobbers on the Stock Exchanges. Second, they lend by straight loan or overdraft. When a bank makes a loan, it does so by creating a current account deposit in the borrower's favour, against which he can draw cheques. The deposit appears, of course, as a *liability* in the bank's monthly published accounts, and the advance is an asset. When a bank lends by overdraft it does not credit the borrower with a deposit, but gives him permission to draw cheques against a non-existent deposit, so to speak. A deposit is created when the recipient of the cheque pays it into his account — which may be held at another bank — and it is, of course, a deposit in favour of the payee, not the borrower. All lending creates deposits, but overdraft facilities create deposits not only when they are granted but when they are used. If the borrower's cheque is paid into an account held at his bank, that bank acquires an overdraft asset, the borrower's liability to repay, and a deposit liability to the payee. If it is paid into another bank the lending bank acquires an asset, the borrower's liability to repay, and a liability to pay cash to the payee's bank through the clearing.

Certain conclusions can be drawn from the discussion so far:

1 Bank deposits are money, and everyone who acquires a bank account gives an asset in exchange, currency or cheque, foreign exchange, a security, or a promise of repayment. The first two are an exchange of one form of money for another; the second two can be described as 'monetisation of a non-money asset'.
2 A bank's accounts follow the practice of double entry, every debit entry has a corresponding credit entry and vice versa.
3 Primary deposits supply the bank with cash or its equivalent in exchange, for deposit liabilities; derivative deposits do not.

4 All derivative deposits are a net addition to the supply of domestic money held by the public. This is not true of all primary deposits; a deposit acquired by paying into one's account domestic currency or a cheque on a domestic bank is not a net addition to the money supply.

5 Derivative deposits are, quite literally, created by the bank. The deposit of currency or cheques with a bank creates nothing; it exchanges one form of money for another, or transfers money (a bank deposit) from one owner to another. The deposits and cash assets arising from payments by the public sector to the private sector, or from the purchase of foreign exchange by the EEA, are created by the Government or its agent, not by the bank. But when the banks buy securities or lend they create money on their own initiative, and that money is not a 'real', manufactured money substance. It is created out of thin air, so to speak, and exists materially only as strokes of ink in the bank's books. Banks are the only institutions in the private sector with the power to create money, and they have that power because their deposit liabilities are generally accepted as money and cheques are universally accepted in payment of debt.

Many bankers would deny this. They do not accept that 'loans create deposits' and argue that they can only lend out money which has been deposited with them. This is true for any single bank, but it is not true for banks in the aggregate.

The multiple creation of deposits

Let us say a bank is founded and gradually builds up deposit liabilities of 100 'units' (we can take a unit to be a pound, or a million pound, or any sum we wish). The counterpart of the deposits is cash deposited for safekeeping, and the banker makes a charge for the service. His balance sheet would be:

Liabilities	Assets
Deposits 100	Cash 100

The banker gradually realises that his customers are leaving most of this money with him continuously; deposits and cash never falling below, say, 80. His customers are making payments not by withdrawing cash for the purpose, but by handing to their creditors a banker's receipt for money deposited with him or written instructions to the banker to pay money to them, and the creditors in turn are not withdrawing the money but asking the bank to transfer ownership of it to themselves on the authority of this written instruction.

The banker therefore begins to lend out this surplus cash, at interest, until all the 80 units are in circulation outside the bank. His balance sheet is then:

Liabilities	Assets
Deposits 100	Cash 20
	Loans 80

The next stage comes when borrowers have also formed the habit of not withdrawing the cash lent to them but are instead making payments with written instructions to the banker to transfer ownership of the cash to a named person. The banker now finds that little of the cash ever leaves his vaults. Every depositor and every borrower has the right to withdraw cash, but few of them exercise that right. Receipts are circulating between debtors and creditors without being presented at the bank.[3] Meanwhile, the legal tender stays in the bank and the banker can make loans by giving borrowers not temporary ownership of the cash in his vaults, but the right to withdraw cash if required. Since few exercise that right, either as depositors or as borrowers, the sum of rights to withdrawn cash can safely exceed the amount of cash available for withdrawal. The 'right to withdraw cash on demand' is one definition of a demand deposit, and the banker is now at the final stage of development; when he is lending by creating deposits in favour of the borrower and these deposits are circulating as an alternative money to coins.

At the final stage, the bank's accounts would take some such form as:

Liabilities		Assets	
Deposits		Cash	100
by cash	100	Loans	900
by loan	900		1,000
	1,000		

Assuming that this balance sheet shows the bank in its 'full loaned up'[4] position, we presume that the banker has decided that 10% is a safe minimum ratio of cash to deposits (which was, in fact, the ratio adopted by the UK deposit banks until 1946, when it was reduced to 8%). Note that this cash reserve and the accepted minimum ratio of cash to deposits are the only constraint on the creation of bank money. If there were only one bank, and if the only money in use were bank deposits, there would be no intrinsic limit to the money-creating power of the bank. It is the liability to repay deposit holders with a money, which the bank itself cannot create, that constrains its deposit-creation. For every extra £10 this *monopoly* bank received in deposits of cash, it could extend further loans to the tune of £90, in so doing creating deposits of £90 in addition to the deposit of £10 which reflected its receipt of cash. Its *deposit multiplier* (see pp. 42–3 for a fuller discussion) would be:

$$\Delta D = \frac{\Delta R}{r} \qquad\qquad [3.1]$$

where R = cash reserve
         r = cash ratio

Or, if we assume that, as D increases, deposit-holders withdraw cash to maintain some desired ratio, a, of cash-holdings to deposits, this becomes:

$$\Delta D = \frac{\Delta R}{r + a} \qquad\qquad [3.2]$$

Deposit creation in a competitive banking system

With more than one bank in operation, there is another and more restrictive constraint on the ability of any one bank to create deposits. It then becomes true to say that a bank can only lend out what depositors have lent to it; or, to be more precise, it can only lend more if, and to the extent that, it acquires cash in excess of the minimum required to support its level of deposits. It is, however, also correct to say that the banks as a whole can lend (create deposits) to some multiple of any cash they hold.

Suppose again that our first bank, now a member of a multiple banking system, receives cash on deposit to the value of 100. Suppose it proceeds to increase the value of its balance sheet in line with its cash reserves by creating loans and deposits to the sum of 900, to reach the 'final stage' of the example on page 40. The new borrowers now draw cheques on their accounts and, to assume the worst situation from the point of view of the lending bank, all these cheques are deposited by the payees in accounts held at other banks. These other banks could, of course, use the cheques to acquire deposits at the lending bank, but are unlikely to do so. They will rather claim cash from the first bank and cash the asset on which they can build up their own interest-earning loans. Bank A is therefore faced with a demand to transfer something like 900 units of cash to other banks, and it only has 100 units.

Clearly the only safe course for bank A is to lend a sum equal to, not a multiple of, its excess reserves. Its safe balance sheet is then:

Liabilities		Assets	
Deposits: by cash	100	Cash	100
by loans	90	Loans	90
	190		190

Then, as the borrowers spend their deposits of 90, leading to claims from the other banks on the lending bank for 90 cash, the balance sheet changes again to:

Liabilities		Assets	
Deposits: by cash	100	Cash	10
by loans	0	Loans	90
	100		100

The two 'loans' items are different, because the borrowers have spent their deposits (90) with deposits at other banks, but they still owe their own bank 90.

To simplify, let us now suppose that all the cheques drawn on the new deposits (90) at bank A are paid into one other bank, B, or that there are only two banks in the system.[5] This bank's deposits and cash reserve now rise by 90. It has learned caution, and expands deposits only to the extent of its excess reserves. It requires an extra cash reserve of 9 against the new deposits 90 so, assuming that it was fully loaned up before it received the new cash and new deposit liability, it can safely expand its deposits by 91, which it does by lending this sum. As in the first stage, we assume that these loans are spent, and we further assume that all the cheques are paid into bank A. A thus acquires new deposits, and cash, from B to the value 81. The changes in B's balance sheet are as follows:

Liabilities		*Assets*	
(I) After receipt of deposits and cash from A:			
Deposits by cash	+ 90	Cash	+ 90
(II) After making further loans of 81:			
Deposits by cash	+ 90	Cash	+ 90
by loans	+ 81	Loans	+ 81
	+ 171		+ 171
(III) After A has claimed cash, 81:			
Deposits by cash	+ 90	Cash	+ 9
by loans	+ 0	Loans	+ 81
	+ 90		+ 90

Bank A now has extra cash, and deposits, to the value of 81, and excess cash reserves of $81 - 81/10 = 72.9$. It raises its loans and deposits by 72.9, loses cash to bank B to the sum of 72.9; bank B then increases its loans and deposits by $72.9 - 72.9/10$, loses cash to bank A, and so on . . .

The sum of the additional deposits created when the whole chain of receipts of cash and increases in lending has worked through will be:

$$100 + 90 + 81 + 72.9 + 65.61 + \ldots$$

This can, alternatively, be expressed as:

$$100 + (100 \times 0.9) + (100 \times 0.9^2) + (100 \times 0.9^3) + (100 \times 0.9^4) + \ldots$$

It is a convergent geometric series whose sum is: $100/(1 - 0.9) = 1,000$.
Similarly, the total extra lending is:

$$90 + 81 + 72.9 + 65.61 + \ldots$$

This can, alternatively, be expressed as:

$$90 + (90 \times 0.9) + (90 \times 0.9^2) + (90 \times 0.9^3) + (90 \times 0.9^4) + \ldots$$

This is also a convergent geometric series whose sum is:

$$90 \times \frac{1}{1 - 0.9} = 900$$

The banking system as a whole, therefore, like the single monopoly bank, can expand its deposits by $10 \times$ any increase in cash reserves C, and its loans by $9 \times C$. The deposit multiplier is still $\Delta D = \Delta C/r$, or $\Delta C/r + a$, as the case might be. As deposits increase, so does the public's desired holding of cash, and their only source of cash in the banks. At each stage of the series of deposit expansions an expanding bank loses cash, therefore, not only to other banks but also to its customers; cash drains out of the banking system as a whole. Note again, however, that the banks can engage in multiple deposit creation only because deposits are accepted as money. If borrowers withdrew money in cash, which was not returned to the banks, the banking system *as a whole* could only expand loans up to the amount of their excess cash reserve; if there were occasions on which all holders of deposits withdrew them all in cash, the banks could not lend, or could not intermediate between depositors and borrowers, at all.

The destruction of deposits

Deposits are destroyed by an action which is the reverse of one of those which create a deposit:

1 The withdrawal of cash by a depositor.
2 The purchase of foreign exchange from the bank by a depositor.
3 A net excess of payments from the private to the public sector over payments in the reverse direction.

(In each of these cases, the bank's cash reserve and deposit liabilities fall by the same sum. If the bank concerned previously held only the minimum ratio of cash to deposits, its cash ratio will now be deficient (e.g. 9/99 is a smaller fraction than 10/100), and a further secondary contraction of deposits will be necessary.)

4 A sale of bonds by the bank to the non-bank private sector. The buyer will pay for them with a cheque drawn on a bank deposit. If this deposit is held at the bank selling the securities, its 'investments' asset (see the next section) and its deposit liabilities fall equally; if held at another bank, the selling bank's deposits are unchanged, but there is a transfer from the other bank's account at the Bank of England to that of the selling bank, which thus loses one asset (investment) and gains another (cash), while the other bank's deposit liabilities and cash reserves fall equally.

5 The redemption at maturity of a bill of exchange held by a bank. The drawee of the bill will redeem his debt out of a deposit. If the deposit is held with the bank which holds the bill, its asset item 'bills discounted' (see the next section) and deposit liabilities both decline by the value of the bill. If the deposit is held at another bank, the bank holding the bill will gain cash from the other bank. One could trace a complicated series of inter-debts between banks resulting from the discounting and redemption of a bill, but the simple fact remains that the drawee must hold a deposit somewhere with which to redeem the bill, and when he does redeem it the deposit vanishes. If the bill were redeemed with cash the bank's deposit liabilities will not change, and the cancellation of the 'bills discounted' asset would be balanced by an increase in the bank's cash reserves. But such payments must be rare.

6 Repayment of a loan or overdraft. Again, the bank loses an asset ('loans and advances'), and either loses an equal deposit liability or gains cash from another bank. Suppose a borrower uses a cheque to repay his overdraft. If the cheque was drawn by a customer of the creditor bank, the bank loses an asset (loans and advances) and an equal liability (deposits); if it was drawn on another bank, the creditor bank loses a loan asset and gains an equal credit to its account at the Bank of England, while the other bank's cash and deposits fall.

Retail banks' balance sheet

Banks, like other firms, publish their accounts – their profit and loss accounts and balance sheets – annually. They also, unlike other firms, publish interim statements, in balance sheet form, once a month (see Table 3.1).

These monthly accounts are a mixture of 'monetary' and 'business' items; they give in one statement a picture of the bank both as a monetary institution and as a trading firm. They therefore include items which are of no relevance to the study of money. The liabilities include not only deposits but capital subscribed by (and

Table 3.1 Retail banks' balance sheet, 16 May 1984 (£ million)

Liabilities		Assets	
Sterling deposits	91,804	Sterling assets	
Other currency deposits	31,596	Notes and coin	1,780
Other liabilities	20,104	Balance with the Bank	
		of England:	
(Eligible liabilities: 74,156)		Cash ratio deposits	324
		Other	139
		Market loans	17,735
		Bills	
		Treasury bills and	
		others	272
		Eligible bills	2,561
		Advances	66,139
		Investments (UK	
		Government stocks	
		and others)	8,447
		Other currency assets	33,678
		Miscellaneous assets	12,429
Total	143,504	Total	143,504

Source: *BEQB*, June 1984, Table 3.2.

therefore owed to) the shareholders, and accumulated profits set aside as general reserves against ill-fortune or for expansion of the business (e.g. building new branches) or as special provisions against future liabilities (e.g. to pay taxes). Assets include some major non-monetary items such as premises and furnishings, and investments in other banks and financial institutions.

Liabilities

The monetary item on the liabilities side is deposits. Until April 1975 these were classified into current accounts, bearing no interest and withdrawable on demand by cheque, and deposit accounts, earning interest and formally subject to seven days' notice of withdrawal but in practice withdrawable on demand subject to a small loss of interest. In the new classification – sight deposits and time deposits – sight deposits comprise balances, 'whether interest-bearing or not, which are transferable or withdrawable on demand without interest penalty (or interest indemnity). It includes money immediately at call and money placed overnight' (*BEQB* Notes to Tables).

Assets

Notes and coin

The banks keep a float of cash in the tills against withdrawals of cash by depositors. This float can be replenished by drawing cash against their accounts at the Bank of England. The non-clearing banks and other institutions accepting deposits which can be withdrawn in cash keep accounts at the clearing banks against which they can withdraw cash. A bank's account at the Bank of England is also used to meet cheques drawn against it and paid into other banks and passing through the clearings, or to the Government, and 'honoured' by a transfer of deposits at the Bank of England.

It is the unpredictability of cash withdrawals by customers and through the clearing which makes 'cash in hand and at the Bank of England' an essential asset. If withdrawals were perfectly predictable, a bank need only hold assets which mature − i.e. are 'monetised' − in time to meet withdrawals. The withdrawals in question are, of course, *net* withdrawals, gross withdrawals minus concurrent payments into the bank. The larger the number of accounts and the more diversified their owner-ship − e.g. geographically, industrially − the more likely is it that withdrawals will be matched by payments into accounts and the smaller will fluctuations in deposits be. A bank with several scattered branches and thousands of small accounts does not need such a high cash ratio as a bank operating in only one centre and with a small number of large accounts. Personal accounts are fairly stable; business accounts are bigger and more actively used and show wider fluctuations, the most erratic being accounts held by financial institutions. But nearly all accounts are subject to seasonal drains, e.g. personal accounts during the holiday season and at Christmas, industrial and financial accounts (and personal accounts) during the tax-gathering season in the first quarter of the year. From 1951 to 1971 the LCBs were obliged to maintain a ratio of cash to deposits not less than 8%. After September 1971, the only cash obligation was a $1\frac{1}{2}$% ratio of balances at the Bank of England to 'eligible liabilities', and this applied only to the LCBs; the actual ratio of cash, including till money, to deposits varied; for the LCBs it was some $4\frac{1}{2}$–$5\frac{1}{2}$%.

In March 1981, alterations to the cash reserve requirement were proposed, as foreshadowed in the Green Paper 'Monetary Control' of November 1980 (Cmnd 7858). Henceforth, the only requirement was one 'whereby recognised banks and licensed deposit-taking institutions in each case above a minimum size will be required to hold cash balances on special non-operational non-interest-bearing accounts with the Bank ...' (*BEQB* March 1981: 38). Though initially some confusion prevailed as to the precise basis of calculation, the new requirement was to apply uniformly. Under the existing arrangements it amounted in total to the equiva-lent of not more than $\frac{1}{2}$% of 'eligible liabilities', though the LCBs were permitted to maintain, on their ordinary accounts with the Bank of England, those balances necessary for clearing purposes. In addition, recognised banks, and licensed deposit-taking institutions, as customers of the Bank, were allowed to maintain balances on their ordinary accounts at the Bank, providing these were consistent with business conducted through such accounts.

Reserve assets

This category of assets was in operation between 1971 and 1981 and all banks agreed to maintain them in a minimum ratio of $12\frac{1}{2}$% to a sub-category of deposits, termed 'eligible liabilities' (see Ch. 13).

Money at call. This is secured and immediately callable money lent to discount houses, brokers and jobbers.

Other bills are commercial bills eligible for rediscount, or as collateral for loan, at the Bank of England, up to a maximum of 2% of eligible liabilities.

Special deposits are compulsory deposits with the Bank of England which cannot be included in reserve assets or, before 1971, in liquid assets.

Market loans other than reserve assets include a variety of short-term loans to, or deposits with, other banks and discount houses, and money lent through brokers to the parallel markets, e.g. the local authority and finance house markets (see *BEQB* Notes to Tables).

Bills other than reserve assets are all commercial bills. Cash in hand and balances with the Bank of England, all money at call, and all bills discounted used to constitute 'the liquid assets' of the banks. Call money and bills were generally regarded as the secondary reserve, after cash, against deposit liabilities. Prior to 1971 the ratio of these assets to deposits was termed 'the liquidity ratio' of the banks, which the LCBs maintained at or above a certain minimum, 30% up to 1963, 28% thereafter.

Investments. These are bonds, not equities. Most of them are UK Government loan stocks, but the item also includes some bonds issued by Commonwealth governments and by local authorities. The banks prefer securities with a comparatively short life to maturity (not more than 10 years) because the nearer the maturity date the smaller are the fluctuations in their market prices. The present value of a bond has two parts:

1 The series of future income receipts all discounted back to the present.
2 The redemption value of the bond, discounted back to the present. The nearer the maturity date of the bond, the greater is this second element in its value compared with the (fewer) annuity payments receivable. And the nearer the maturity date, the less is the effect of a change in interest rates on the present value of the redemption price. The relevant formula is:

$$P = \sum_{i=1}^{n} \frac{R_i}{(1 + r)^n} \qquad [3.3]$$

where P = the present value of R, the redemption value
r = the rate of discount
n = life of the bond

Given R, P depends inversely on r and on the number of times (n) $1 + r$ is multiplied by itself. The influence of a change in r on P thus depends on the value of n.

Investments have long been regarded as a kind of residual asset, one which could be expanded or contracted to offset changes in the level of advances demanded or permitted. In 35 out of the 52 quarters 1959/11 to 1972/11, advances and investments changed inversely (see Wadsworth 1971: 462–3). Indeed, it is arguable that investments rather than cash, call money and bills are the true, active liquidity reserve. Thus liquidity pressures upon the clearing banks are evidenced not by variations in their cash ratios . . .

> but by signs of unwillingnes among the banks to reduce further their holdings of gilt-edged in order to restore their holdings of (conventionally) more liquid central government debt to that proportion of assets necessary to satisfy the prescribed ratio (*BEQB*, June 1969: 177).

Advances. The biggest single item in the balance sheet and generally the most profitable. Until 1971 the rate charged on loans and overdrafts by all the clearing banks was 2% above bank rate with a minimum of 5% to most borrowers, shading down to 1% above bank rate and a 4½% minimum for large loans to exceptionally creditworthy customers, e.g. the nationalised industries, who could turn to the Government for support in a crisis.

The liquidity of bank assets

Cash is perfectly liquid but earns nothing. The liquidity of any other asset is a function of its convertibility into money, which has three aspects. First, the speed with which it can be converted. Second, the ease of conversion: the smaller the effort and/or inconvenience involved, the more liquid is the asset. Finally there is the cost of conversion, which takes two forms: (a) the fees and taxes (usually a stamp duty) incurred, if any, and (b) the loss on the buying price, if any. This last item in liquidity, unlike the others, is quite unknown until the asset is converted into money. The possibility of loss is different for different assets, and this aspect of liquidity is a function of the potential loss and of the risk that such loss will occur, neither of which is calculable with any precision. For many assets – e.g. bills and investments – there is a link between the time aspect and the risk-of-loss aspect of liquidity. If I hold a government bond maturing two years hence, there is no risk of loss if I am prepared to wait two years for conversion. Alternatively, I can sell the bond on the Stock Exchange today and receive the money in 11 to 25 days' time, but I would then have to pay the broker's fee and stamp duty, and I may not get the price I paid for the bond.

Loans at call and short notice are convertible in a matter of hours at no expense, minimal effort, and no loss of value. Most of them are to discount houses who can always borrow from the Bank of England to repay call money: these loans can, in effect, be shifted onto the central bank. Bills discounted have differing degrees of liquidity; most of them are bought from the discount houses and mature in *echelon*, some tomorrow, some the next day, and so on over a period of two months or more. In specifying the maturity distribution of the bills they take up from the discount houses the banks have regard to their probable liquidity requirements over the next few weeks, and in normal circumstances, therefore, their holdings of bills are, overall, as liquid as they need to be. Only in a time of exceptional monetary stringency would the banks need to unload bills, and in such circumstances the Bank of England would take them up. Bonds are also held in echelon but, of course, with much longer spread of, and intervals between, maturity dates. They are less liquid than bills both because of their longer maturity and because, for that reason, their prices can change more sharply. It is because of this relationship between maturity and risk of loss on sale that the banks prefer comparatively short bonds. Since they are held in echelon, it will often be the case that some of their bonds are very short indeed, as liquid as some of their bills.

Advances are usually the most profitable asset and are also usually considered to be the least liquid monetary asset. From the time aspect alone they are more liquid than most investments, but they are the one asset on which there is a risk of default, small though it may be. The banks only lend to creditworthy borrowers, but no borrower can count himself immune from insolvency. Further, they are the one asset which is not immediately shiftable onto the market or onto the central bank. If a borrower, denied renewal of a loan by one bank, can borrow from another bank or a non-bank lender, the original lending bank can be said to have shifted the loan onto another lender, but the market for loans is not like the markets for bills and bonds, where one can always find a buyer (including the Bank of England) if one is prepared to accept the market price. A borrower unable to repay may not find an alternative lender and the bank may only have the choice of renewing the loan or bankrupting the customer. Overdraft limits are notoriously difficult to reduce. Apart from the risk of default, advances have capital-certainty, but not shiftability, while investments are shiftable but their capital values are not certain. Some part of advances is always in process of repayment. The real difference between advances and investments then is not so much that one is more liquid than the other, but rather that they have different liquidity attributes.

From 1946 to 1971 the monthly published cash ratios of the London clearing banks varied only by a few decimal points from the 8% minimum. Assuming that this was also true from day to day, it is clear that only very minor calls on bank liquidity were met out of cash reserves. Once the actual holdings of cash, or of any other asset, fell to a required minimum, it ceased to be a true reserve. The crucial reserves, those which can be drawn on to meet a serious drain of cash out of the banks, individually or collectively, are those which are shiftable and/or saleable and are held in excess of a minimum or are not subject to a minimum. In most years the liquidity ratio was above the minimum as the banks built up a cushion of reserves against the heavy transfers of cash to the Government as taxes on income are paid in the early part of the year. Clearly, then, it is call money which can be withdrawn quickly from the discount houses, and the bills which can be unloaded onto the discount houses or directly onto the Bank of England, which are the liquidity reserves to meet any sudden increase in the public's demand for cash. As we have seen, investments are also a source of liquidity. It is misleading therefore to regard the cash ratio, or even the liquidity or reserve ratio (after 1971), as the sole and adequate indicator of a bank's liquidity. As we saw earlier the liquidity of call money and bills rests ultimately on the Bank of England's willingness to act as lender of last resort to the discount houses and, since in that capacity the Bank will usually accept only first-class bills, the quality of the bills held by banks and discount houses becomes an important part of liquidity. And since the degree of capital certainty of an asset is one component of its liquidity, the maturity structure of a bank's investments is part of its liquidity. The liquidity of a bank is therefore not a measurable quantity, indicated by the ratio of one asset or a few assets to liabilities, although that is an important part of it; it is rather a characteristic of the whole balance sheet. Hence the care which the banks take, the constraints they impose on themselves, in terms of the quality and maturity of their assets.

The management of bank assets

Portfolio management

Wealth can be held in various forms, usually grouped into money, non-money financial assets, and real assets, each of the last two covering a wide spectrum. Thus non-money financial assets include bills, bonds and ordinary shares; bills and bonds may be issued by governmental or private organisations, and shares are issued by firms of widely varying size and quality, engaged in many different kinds of industrial or commercial activity. Real capital may be land, domestic or industrial or commercial property, precious stones or metals, works of art, houses and consumer durable goods, and so on. Every owner of wealth therefore has a problem of choice: he has to decide in what forms he shall hold it. His object will be to achieve the highest possible income consistent with a degree of security. Security is identified as stability of the income from the asset (including capital appreciation), and the assets which offer the highest prospective return are likely to be also those on which the return is subject to wide fluctuations. One can, however, reduce the risk associated with a given prospective return if one 'diversifies the portfolio', distributing one's wealth over a variety of assets on which the returns may be expected to fluctuate in a compensatory way. One chooses assets whose returns are negatively correlated. How far one diversifies depends on the value one sets on security. The utility of a portfolio is maximised (for a 'risk-averter') by equalising the marginal returns, each discounted for risk, from all the assets held.

Banks are profit-maximising enterprises, and we would therefore expect them to follow similar equi-marginal rules. As multi-product firms, selling credit of various kinds and facilities for the transfer of money, banks would supply each service up to the point at which the marginal cost of supplying the service is equal to the marginal revenue derived from it; or, if they cannot distinguish the marginal costs of the various services, up to the point at which the marginal revenue from all the services are identical and equal to the marginal cost of the bank's total operations. With free competition, each bank would compete actively for deposits, paying interest on current as well as on deposit accounts and making a charge, related to the cost, for entries on each kind of account. On the assets side of the balance sheet, one would expect them to equalise marginal returns net of risk. As each bank expanded its activities we would suppose that sooner or later they would have to bid up rates on deposits with the result that the marginal cost of attracting them would rise. At the same time, in order to lend more and as their demand for securities increased, they would have to reduce the rate on loans, perhaps take on riskier ones, and pay more for securities; the marginal returns on their activities, net of risk, would fall. Consequently the volume of each bank's deposits and lending would be determined by the profit-maximisation formula, marginal revenue equals marginal cost. For the banks as a whole, of course, expansion would depend on their ability to attract cash deposits from the public, i.e. to persuade the public to make more use of cheques and less use of cash; this persuasion one may presume, would only succeed at a rising cost (Baltensberger 1980).

Constraints on the banks' portfolio management

In fact, the clearing banks' profit-maximising behaviour, and their portfolio management, have long been constrained by various conventions and by the nature of their functions and status in the economy. They buy their non-cash assets – their call loans, bills, bonds, and loans and overdrafts – with deposits created in favour of the seller or borrower. These deposits are assets to the holder and liabilities of the bank; liabilities to pay cash on demand or at short notice either to the depositor or to other banks through the clearing. They are also money. But they are not legal tender; the acceptability of cheques depends on confidence that the drawer's deposit or overdraft facility is sufficient to meet the cheque and confidence that the bank can meet the cheque with cash across the counter or through the clearing. It only needs a whisper of doubt about the drawer of a cheque or about his bank to destroy this acceptability. Neither the clearing banks nor anyone else can guarantee the integrity and solvency of every drawer of every cheque; that is why bank deposits cannot be declared legal tender and their acceptability, their 'moneyness', guaranteed and enforced. But they can, and today the major banks do, make sure that confidence in themselves remains unimpaired. They do this by giving solvency and liquidity priority over profitability: solvency, maintaining assets at least equal to liabilities, and liquidity, maintaining these assets in forms which ensure their ability to meet punctually all demands for cash. The fact that our payments system would break down if confidence in the primary banks were shaken, and the consequent crucial importance of solvency and liquidity, inhibit the banks' search for profits. Their portfolio behaviour therefore differs in a number of ways from that of most other investors:

1　They do not diversify their portfolios as widely. They do not, as bankers, hold equities or real property, but only gilt-edged or equally safe securities. This is, no doubt, part of the tradition of 'sticking to one's last', concentrating on banking and taking no direct share in industry and commerce, but it is also due to the belief that the quality of a bank's assets should be beyond question.

2 They do not diversify by choosing securities with negatively correlated yields and values; the returns on all their assets tend to rise and fall together. They do spread their loans between industries and regions and between the industrial, financial and personal sectors of the economy. This is partly for security, partly so as not to be accused of discrimination.

3 The risk element in their assets is not variability of running return, which is known in advance and is constant over the period of the investment. (The rate on loans and overdrafts is not fixed for the life of the loan, but any changes are decided by the banks themselves.) The risk is twofold: first, in the case of bonds, the variability of market value and a consequent possible capital loss on sale; and second, in the case of advances, the risk that the asset may not be quickly convertible into cash. Advances are also, as noted previously, subject to a risk of default, but this is minimised by care in the choice of borrowers, by the deposit of collateral security in some cases, and by industrial and geographical diversification. The risk of having to sell bonds at a loss is reduced by holding them in echelon. They balance the rate of return, which usually increases with the length of life to maturity of the security against capital certainty which diminishes with length of life.

4 A major constraint is the overriding priority given to liquidity. There are circumstances – e.g. inflation, or a confidently expected fall in interest rates (rise in capital values) – when a rational investor would 'go illiquid', i.e. would hold no money at all. This can never be the case with the banks; they must always keep an adequate reserve of cash. The importance of maintaining an overall liquidity-structure of assets adequate to meet all likely demands for cash, plus a margin to spare for any emergency, is the key to the deposit banks' portfolio behaviour. It explains the practice of holding, in addition to their non-earning primary reserve of cash, a significant proportion of their assets in a secondary reserve of low-yielding assets – call money and bills – which are convertible into cash very quickly and at their face value, or, in the case of not-yet-mature bills, very close to it. It explains the practice of holding bonds in echelon and their preference for comparatively short bonds; and their relative concentration on short-term, self-liquidating loans. The banks could earn bigger profits if they held only cash and long bonds and/or medium-term or long-term loans. They would be perfectly liquid if they held only cash and balances at the Bank of England, and loaded all their costs onto their charges for administering accounts; but then they would, of course, cease to perform one of their main functions, which is to provide credit. They would be only a repository of funds. It has often been said that the structure of the clearing banks' assets is a compromise between liquidity and profitability, or between their obligations to their depositors and their obligations to their shareholders.

If, however, their obligation to depositors were the only explanation of their liquidity-structure, one would expect that structure, in particular the proportions of cash and other liquid assets, to be much less rigid and uniform than it is. One would, for example, expect a small bank operating in one or a few places to maintain a higher cash ratio than a large, national, multi-branch bank. This has not been the case (see Turner 1972). If they can borrow from the central bank or from other banks to meet a sudden heavy demand for cash, to do so might be cheaper than selling off high-yielding assets, probably at low prices (which are concomitant with high yields), to obtain cash; liquidity will be less important, banks can safely hold less cash and more earning assets. Their cash ratios would be a function of the interest rate on such loans relative to the yields on assets, varying directly with the former and inversely with the latter. The cash ratio, and hence the deposit multiplier, would be a function of the relation between these two rates so long as the desired cash ratio was not less than what they considered to be the minimum safe ratio. Banks can operate with lower cash ratios if the financial system contains assets which can be turned into cash very quickly without loss, such as, for example, call money lent to the London discount market. If the banks can lengthen the term of their liabilities — say by offering higher rates on deposits at longer notice of withdrawal or by issuing certificates of deposit of varying terms — then again, reserves of cash and very liquid assets become less important; the clearing banks can move in the direction of matching the maturity of their assets to the maturity of their liabilities, as has been the regular practice of some other banks (see page 80). This the clearing banks have done in the last few years. Portfolio management then includes the management of liabilities as well as assets; they can adjust their liquidity by changes on either side of the balance sheet.

A rise in interest rates on bonds and advances might be expected to induce the banks to economise on cash and liquid assets, especially if they expected those rates to fall again in the near future. A rise in the expected rate of interest, on the other hand, would be a reason for selling investments since the rise, when it comes, will reduce their market value. It follows that the effect on holdings of investments of an actual rise in the rate of interest would depend on whether it produced expectations of a further rise or of a reversal. If the return on investments rose relative to that on loans, a profit-maximising bank would tighten up on advances and buy more bonds, subject again to expectations regarding bond prices. Similarly, a rise in bill rates as compared with bond rates would induce them to hold more bills and fewer bonds, and vice versa.

In fact, the clearing banks do not operate even this modified profit-maximising portfolio policy. Not only do they never 'go illiquid'; the cash ratio varied little from 10% up to 1946, and even less from 8% between 1946 and 1971, and has been mostly within the range of $4\frac{1}{2}$–$5\frac{1}{2}$% since 1971. On their response to changes in relative interest rates, the evidence is not unanimous. Parkin, Gray and Barrett (1970), looking at portfolio changes by the LCBs, 1953 to 1967, found that a rise in the Treasury bill rate induced the banks to substitute short-term liquid assets for bonds, except that the biggest effect was a fall in one liquid asset, call money. A rise in the rate on short bonds had the opposite effect, a switch out of short-term assets into bonds, but again the effect on call loans was perverse. They did not include advances in the study, regarding them as outside the control of the banks. Brechling and Clayton (1965), on the other hand, writing on the portfolio behaviour of the LCBs and the Scottish and Irish banks in the period 1951 to 1963, concluded that a rise in the Treasury bill rate had no effect on the liquidity ratio, and while it induced a fall in the ratio of advances to deposits, the investments/deposits ratio rose. The explanation they suggest is that a rise in the bill rate was associated with a restrictive credit policy, in response to which the banks moved out of advances into investments. They found an inverse relationship between the yield on short bonds (bonds of 5 years' life) and the investments/deposits ratio and suggest two probable reasons for this: (a) a rise in bond rates generates expectations of further increases, so the banks sell before prices fall further; (b) the rise in bond rates is associated with difficulty and high cost of alternative finance, so the public are 'driven into the banks'. Similarly, Sheppard (1971) found a fall in the investments/deposits ratio and a rise in the advances ratio as long-term rates rise. This evidence seems consistent with the assertion earlier that investments are a residual, and a reserve, to accommodate changes in advances.[6]

5 Not only have the authorities regulated in some degree the composition of the banks' portfolios by cash and liquidity ratios; in the 1950s and 1960s they exercised two forms of control over advances. First, there were ceilings on advances, requests to the clearing banks to curtail advances or not to increase them by more than a certain percentage. Second, there were requests to concentrate their lending in particular sectors – e.g. agriculture, the exporting industries – and/or to restrict their lending to other sectors, e.g. to importers, to persons, to property developers. In 1958, the Bank of England announced that it would take powers to call for special deposits from the LCBs and the Scottish banks. The first call was made in 1960 and there have been several calls and repayments since. What happens is that part of the bank's deposit at the Bank is transferred to a special account and neutralised, i.e. it can no longer be counted as part of the bank's cash reserve, nor even as a liquid asset (reserve asset) (see Ch. 13).

In so far as these constraints compelled banks to hold a bigger proportion of non-earning or low-earning assets than they would choose to hold, they imposed an implicit tax on the banks and on their depositors.

6 A final constraint on the banks' portfolio choice is the fact that, quite apart from ceilings imposed by the monetary authorities, they cannot alone determine the volume of their advances, and so cannot freely determine what proportion of their total assets shall be held in this form. To see why this is so, let us regard advances as being sold by the banks to their customers. The quantity sold will

be determined by demand and supply and will therefore depend on the public's willingness to borrow (buy advances) as well as on the banks' willingness to lend (sell advances). The banks could determine the size of their aggregate advances, within a wide range of possible values indicated by the slope and height of the demand curve for them, by varying the price they charged. In fact, they have not tried to do so; until 1971, for many loans they followed a convention of charging a rate fixed at a certain interval above bank rate, which in turn was fixed by the monetary authorities. Since the 1860s they followed a similar convention on deposits, paying no interest on current accounts and bank rate minus 2% on deposit accounts. They did not compete on price, but engaged increasingly in various forms of non-price competition: advertising, increasing the number of outlets (branches), and the provision of ancillary services to depositors. This section of banking was thus in much of its activity an *oligopolistic* industry selling at a fixed price, externally determined, and frequently subject to an upper limit on the volume of sales.

Another look at self-liquidation

Clearly the banks' management of their assets is constrained by the need to maintain an adequate degree of liquidity. Since all the non-cash assets are loans − to discount houses and brokers (call money), to governments (Treasury bills and investments) − there are two ways of converting them into money. First, by repayment at due date; if this were the sole means of conversion, liquidity would be a function solely of the maturity of the asset and the integrity and solvency of the borrower. The second way is to shift the burden of lending onto another lender. In pursuit of their twin goals of liquidity and profit, therefore, the banks choose assets which are shiftable and as far as possible without risk of capital loss, and/or mature within a short time.

This *shiftability* or 'self-liquidating' quality of most bank assets is, however, largely illusory. Call loans can be guaranteed to remain shiftable in a crisis because the Bank of England acts as lender of last resort to the discount market. If the banks call in these loans and the discount houses cannot repay out of their own resources and maturing bills and bonds, they can always borrow from, or rediscount bills with, the Bank of England. What may not be generally realised is that the other assets' liquidity also depends, ultimately, on the existence of a lender of last resort. Bills are rediscountable on the market, investments can be sold on the Stock Exchange, but in a liquidity crisis, when there is widespread pressure to liquidate assets, rediscount and sales would be at best expensive in terms of capital loss, and at worst impossible. Advances are not, of course, shiftable by sale or rediscount; there is no negotiable instrument transferable to a third party. Loans can only be liquidated by non-renewal when they mature; most loans are, in fact, renewed. Having repaid one loan from the proceeds of one set of transactions, firms usually require a further loan to finance the next set; having repaid his overdraft after the harvest, the farmer will want another next spring. Working capital is a *revolving fund*, and both those who use overdrafts and those who use bills or any other form of short-term finance tend to do so fairly continuously. If one bank refuses to renew a loan, therefore, the disappointed borrower is likely to turn to another source of finance: the loan is then not in fact self-liquidating, but rather is shifted onto another lender. The asset which appears to be liquid because it is self-liquidating is, in practice, liquid in so far as it is shiftable, and just as the so-called shiftable assets are liquid only if there are buyers for them, so also the so-called self-liquidating assets are liquid only if there are alternative sources of loans. Again, any widespread attempt to liquidate loans would precipitate a financial crisis. Industry and commerce depend on the banks as a whole maintaining credit; and assets are self-liquidating only if most of them are not being liquidated. Therefore most of the assets of the banking system are ultimately neither self-liquidating nor shiftable unless there is some external supporting institution which will step in to uphold the system in a crisis. If it were not for the existence of a central bank which we know would take any exceptional measures necessary to support the banks in a liquidity crisis, the supposed liquidity of the banking system, which seems secure if we look at each bank separately, is illusory.

The banks and corporate finance

Bank lending to the private sector was an issue of central concern to the Wilson Committee. Indeed, a main objective of the committee was to assess whether financial institutions in general were making adequate funds available to industry in the UK. For a number of years the view had prevailed that, compared to rivals Germany, France and Japan, lending policies in this country were highly cautious. In the area of long-term funding, for example, whereas in the UK the average formal term was 2½ years, in Japan the period was 15 to 20 years and in Germany 7 years. Not surprisingly, British industry was forced to rely on *internal funds* for its investment capital (between 1974 and 1979 as much as 70%). In Germany, industry was able to borrow almost three times as much money as industry in the UK.

UK banks traditionally adopted a highly conservative attitude towards a firm's *debt-equity ratio*, the ratio which indicates the extent to which it raises loan capital as opposed to capital from the owners. Analysis had shown that the average ratio was 22, which compared badly with the USA's 31, France's 39, Germany's 57 and Japan's 85. Moreover, the apparent weak position of British firms was compounded by the banks' policy of refusing to offer credit when a firm's *gearing ratio* (the ratio of long-term and short-term debt to shareholder's interest) was in excess of one-third of asset value. Certainly UK banks are usually prepared to allow loans to *roll-over* by lending additional funds, but even when the initial loan is approved the asset valuation is invariably in terms of what the assets would earn in the event of bankruptcy, and not the asset value of a going concern.

In response to these criticisms the clearing banks, in their own evidence to the Wilson Committee, rejected the charge that they were reluctant to finance British industry. In their view, the problem was quite the reverse: the reluctance of industry to seek funds. To support their case they pointed out that in 1979 the manufacturing sector utilised only 45% of the available resources, and the service sector only 60%, and that they were currently providing almost 50% of their loans to industry in the form of fixed-term agreements; many of them with maturities of ten years and more, with the possibility also of capital repayments holidays.

Ironically perhaps, the final report of the committee appeared to come down on the side of the banks: 'It is the demand for credit, not the supply of credit that is and has been the limiting factor' (Wilson Report). 'Low productivity, low profitability, low demand and problems caused by government policies are regarded as far more important factors (than "the way the financial institutions operate") behind our poor industrial performance' (Progress Report).

To the committee then, the true cause of the low take-up of funds by British industry, and the manufacturing sector in particular, was the combined effects of economic recession and inflation plus the governments' reaction to these problems; stringent monetary policies and concomitant high interest rates. The question of who really is to blame is one that is still being discussed in banking circles. If it is the banks, what can the Government do about the problem? Since the present administration is unlikely to contemplate nationalisation of the banks (unlike the French who recently did just that) – this being an alternative discussed but rejected by the Wilson Committee – some, notably the TUC in 1982, have argued for the setting up of a National Investment Bank to channel funds into Britain. If such an institution was to be established, the pension funds and long-term insurance funds would be expected to deposit a minimum of 10% of their new funds annually.

However it is more realistic to believe that the present government will prefer to rely on market forces in the financial sector to stimulate increased lending to the corporate sector. This is happening on a significant scale anyway, as we shall discuss more fully in Chapter 4. The role of the Government will probably continue to be one of *supervisor* and regulator of the financial system, and in an era of rapid *innovation* this is a role which takes on added significance (*BEQB*, September 1983: 358–77).

Evidence on bank lending is presented in Tables 3.2 and 3.3 below. In 1979 it accounted for 23% of total Industrial and Commercial Companies (ICC) sources of funds. Atkin (1981: 53) attributed the growth of bank lending to industry to the collapse of the debentures market during the seventies, plus increased competition in sterling lending from foreign banks. Capital markets in general have been extremely volatile in recent years because of rapid inflation and historically high nominal interest rates, which rendered the prices of both ordinary shares and fixed-interest securities unstable.

The banks increased their share of ICC *external* finance in the 1970s. Whereas in the 1960s they provided substantially less than 50% of the total, by the late 1970s and early 1980s they were contributing 60% and upwards. In addition, many banks have established (or taken over) *leasing* subsidiaries. As we shall see in Chapter 4, this has been a rapidly expanding market in recent years. In 1970 leasing accounted for only a small proportion of new fixed investment by manufacturing industries; by 1975 it amounted to only 6% of the total; in 1984 it was as high as 17%. Though

Table 3.2 Sources of funds of industrial and commercial companies (ICCs) (1958–79) (per cent of total sources)

	1958–62	1963–67	1968–72	1973–77	1973	1974	1975	1976	1977	1978	1979
Undistributed income	72	67	52	49	44	32	53	51	62	67	59
of which depreciation	28	30	28	34	19	30	47	38	38	39	42
Capital transfers (net)	—	2	8	3	3	3	5	3	2	2	2
Bank borrowing	10	12	19	24	34	41	6	18	18	15	23
Other loans and mortgages	4	3	4	3	6	1	5	4	1	2	3
Import and other credit received	—	—	3	5	4	7	3	7	4	3	7
UK capital issues: Ordinary shares	11	3	3	5	1	1	12	6	4	4	4
Debentures and preference shares	—	9	4	—	—	—	2	—	1	—	—
Overseas	3	4	6	11	7	15	14	11	10	7	2
Total	100	100	100	100	100	100	100	100	100	100	100

Source: *Wilson Committee Report*, Table 34: 133

Table 3.3 Sources of capital funds of industrial and commercial companies (ICCS) (£ billion)

	1979	1980	1981	1982	1983	1984*
Internal funds	24.3	18.3	20.1	18.1	26.5	34.8
Capital transfers	0.4	0.5	0.7	0.6	0.6	0.6
Import and others credit received	1.6	0.01	1.3	0.3	0.5	1.5
Bank borrowing	*3.9*	*6.3*	*5.8*	*6.5*	*1.9*	*12.0*
Other loans and mortgages	0.7	0.1	0.4	0.7	0.6	0.4
UK capital issues: Ordinary shares	0.8	0.8	1.6	0.9	1.7	0.4
Debentures and preference shares	−0.02	0.4	0.08	0.06	0.4	0.1
Capital issues Overseas	−0.05	−0.03	−0.03	−0.04	−0.04	−0.02
Overseas direct investment in securities	0.07	0.7	0.7	0.1	0.4	−0.5
Other overseas investment	0.4	1.2	0.5	1.3	2.1	−1.4

*The figures for 1984 are estimates based on actual figures for first quarter.
Source: *Financial Statistics*, July 1984, Table 8.2

usually arranged at fixed rates of interest, a growing proportion is now written at floating rates.

Whereas prior to 1970 the bulk of bank lending was in the form of overdrafts, after Competition and Credit Control (CCC) in 1971, UK banks began to offer more *term loans* (up to 10 years). These are loans which are normally priced at a mark-up on three-months' or six-months' money in the sterling inter-bank market (see Ch. 6). Rates are reviewed every three or six months but fixed at the outset of each period at an agreed margin over the London inter-bank offer rate in the money market. Since the early 1970s, term lending has grown rapidly and currently accounts for 40% of total bank advances. Its attraction is that it is invariably offered at flexible interest rates which theoretically enhances companies' liquidity positions. The banks also benefit because they are able to monitor more accurately the growth of their overall lending.

Conclusion

There is, of course, an interrelationship between the banks' contribution to corporate finance and the Government's monetary policy (Moore and Threadgold 1980). With bank lending increased even at the height of the recession, this meant a boost to the banks' deposit bases and inevitable consequences for the money supply. To this extent, given the Government's commitment to end the recession via market forces, higher interest rates were counter-productive. So, while the Government wished to encourage greater reliance on external sources of funds on the part of British industry, it also had to concern itself with the possible inflationary repercussions of excess liquidity in the economy. Much corporate borrowing in the late 1970s and early 1980s was involuntary. This was because the raising of interest rates had the perverse effect of increasing the amount of borrowing undertaken by firms rather than reducing it. In the next chapter the emphasis will be on the growing competition between the mainstream banks and the whole range of *Other Financial Institutions* (OFIs) who go to make up the British financial system.

Notes

1   In the latter case there will also, *ceterus paribus*, be a transfer of cash between the banks, through the clearing.
2   There have been moves recently to offer interest on current accounts also. During 1981 the Co-op Bank announced its intention to resume paying a rate of interest (up to 10%) on current accounts (see *Financial Times*, 10 Dec. 1981). A number of other banks now offer rates on current accounts, or *Free Banking Services* to current account holders in credit (for example, the Bank of Scotland).
3   They, in fact, were the forerunners of our modern banknote. The written instructions to the banker were akin to our cheques.

4   By the expression 'full loaned up' is meant that banks fully extend their credit up to the maximum permitted in terms of internal prudential ratios, and government controls; for example cash–deposit ratio and reserve assets ratio. In general terms, American banks are 'loaned up' to a greater degree than their British counterparts.

5   If there are only two, or a few banks, we would expect a proportion of the cheques to be paid into accounts at the lending bank. If so, it would still have some excess reserves when all the cheques had been cleared and could lend again. The other bank(s) would, of course, receive less cash from the first bank and their loans would increase by less than is indicated in the text. But the aggregate increase in loans and deposits would, clearly, be the same.

6   See Bewley (1981). There appears to be a similar diversity of evidence in the case of American banks (see Besen (1965) and Fraser and Rose (1973)).

CHAPTER FOUR

Financial intermediation: The secondary banks

A classification of financial institutions

There are many ways of classifying the financial intermediaries who operate 'the financial system'. The one which follows is based on that set out in Revell (1973).

The banking sector

1 *The Banking Department of the Bank of England.*
2 *The deposit banks*: (a) the London clearing banks; (b) the Scottish clearing banks; (c) the Northern Ireland banks; (d) other deposit banks.
3 *The secondary banks*: merchant, overseas, foreign and consortium banks. Their deposits are now counted as part of the money supply, as officially defined.
4 *The discount houses and brokers.* They take loans from the banks and others, some of which, because they are repayable at a few hours' notice, are almost as liquid as money, and use them to lend both to the private sector and the public sector by the purchase of bills, certificates of deposit and bonds. They have been called 'bankers to the banks'.
5 *The National Giro.* Takes deposits, provides a payment mechanism, and makes personal loans. Revell includes it in the deposit banking system.

Other financial intermediaries

1 *Other deposit institutions.* Their work is the acceptance of deposits which, in general, are repayable on demand, or within a few days, and the lending of them in specialised ways. They do not offer a cheque service and their deposits are not counted as part of the money supply; but because they are so liquid they are termed 'near-money' or 'quasi-money' and the institutions themselves are sometimes classified as 'near-banks': (a) the building societies; (b) the hire purchase finance houses; (c) the National Savings Bank and the Trustee Savings Banks.
2 *Insurance and provident institutions*: (a) the insurance companies; (b) the pension funds.
3 *Portfolio institutions*: (a) unit trusts; (b) investment trusts. They raise money from the public by issuing debentures and shares or 'units' and use it to buy securities, mostly shares and debentures in industrial and commercial public companies.

4 *Special investment agencies*. Their funds come from the Government, the banks, and other large financial institutions, or from the capital market, and they lend to, or buy an equity in, trading firms. Some specialise in helping particular industries. Examples are Finance for Industry, the Agricultural Mortgage Corporation.

In essence, this financial system has three essential functions:

(a) To provide an efficient means of making payments.
(b) To facilitate the flow of credit by providing efficient intermediation between lender and borrower and by making a market in negotiable instruments of credit.
(c) To perform these tasks honestly and responsibly; only if the public trust their financial institutions will the flow of credit and of money payments be maintained.

Financial intermediation basically arises from the actions of the owners of surplus funds. The owner of surplus funds who does not wish to keep his money idle may invest it himself. A large proportion of industrial investment (70% in 1984) is financed internally, out of profits put to reserve; people use their savings for the deposit on a new house. An individual may lend directly to a borrower, or make a direct investment, as when he buys new company shares. Or he may hand his money to an institution which will lend or invest it on his behalf, as when he puts money into a building society or finance house, pays insurance premiums or buys shares in an investment trust or a unit trust; these institutions are the financial intermediaries. An intermediary buys 'primary securities' – e.g. shares, mortgages, promises to repay loans – from the 'ultimate borrowers' with funds obtained from 'ultimate lenders' to whom it issues claims on itself, e.g. insurance policies, deposit accounts, unit trust units, investment trust shares. These claims, its own liabilities, are 'secondary' or 'indirect' securities. Financial intermediation can thus be defined as the purchase of primary securities from ultimate borrowers and users of funds and the issue of indirect claims to ultimate lenders and investors. Essentially, then, financial intermediaries come between lenders and borrowers not as agents for one or the other but as independent operators, seeking profits themselves (although some like the building societies claim to be non-profit making) and making separate contracts between themselves and the lenders and themselves and the borrowers. Thus their ostensible function is to organise a vast flow of credit.

The advantages of intermediation arise almost entirely from the centralised administration of numerous small blocks of funds, i.e. from economies of scale. They are:

1 Professional management. Without intermediation, lenders would have to seek creditworthy borrowers, and borrowers seek lenders, willing to borrow (lend) on mutually acceptable terms for mutually convenient periods of time.

The flow of credit would, clearly, be seriously hampered by the time, inconvenience and cost involved. Intermediaries acquire, and use on behalf of the ultimate lenders, expert knowledge of the creditworthiness and – with varying degrees of success – the prospective returns on different investments.

2 They can combine diversification with large unit investment because they collect several small loans or investments into a large block. The small lender/investor can thus get a much wider diversification of his funds, and get a given degree of diversification much more cheaply, than if he lent directly to the ultimate borrower. The dealing costs (e.g. broker's commission and contract stamp) and administrative costs of a large investment are lower, per pound invested, for large investments than for small. A deposit of £100 in a large building society will be spread over thousands of mortgages; £100 in a unit trust or investment trust will be spread over anything from, say, 50 to upwards of 400 different shares and/or bonds. The ultimate lender thus gets security at low cost.

3 Because they can diversify, they can undertake more risky investments than the small investor could without reducing significantly the security of the whole portfolio. They can thus support innovation and thereby speed up economic progress.

4 They can take advantage of the law of large numbers or 'massed reserves'. The greater the number of individual lenders/investors, the greater the probability that withdrawals will be matched by new injections of funds. Intermediaries can therefore, up to a point, safely *borrow at short-term to lend at long-term*. They can provide a variety of terms of repayment of loans and a variety of liquidities of claims on themselves without a perfect matching of the terms of loans and claims. Fewer portfolio changes are needed; an individual investor must sell an investment whenever he needs money, but an intermediary need only sell primary securities when *net* withdrawals exceed surplus liquid reserves. This reduces the cost of administering the portfolio of assets.

5 They can transform illiquid primary securities into claims on themselves which are almost as liquid as money itself. Building society funds, for example, are employed in mortgage loans with a life of twenty to thirty years but the depositor can withdraw his deposit on demand. Insurance policies can be surrendered (but only at a considerable loss of premiums already paid), unit trusts will buy back units at any time, investment trust shares can be sold on the Stock Exchange. They thus increase the liquidity of the economy. By offering assets which are almost 'as good as' money yet earn a return, they reduce the demand for money as an asset, and increase the velocity of a given stock of money.

6 By offering a variety of assets to lenders, with different combinations of risk, rate of return, convenience and liquidity, and a variety of terms and conditions to borrowers, they can reconcile the different requirements of borrowers and lenders.

7 They enable borrowers to tap wider sources of finance and borrow small

savings more cheaply. It is cheaper to issue large batches of primary securities to a few financial intermediaries than hundreds or thousands of small batches to the primary lenders. The interposition of the strength and reputation of the intermediary between borrower and lender enables the borrower to tap funds from lenders who, because of ignorance or fear of loss, would not buy the primary securities themselves or would only do so for a very high return. Savers will accept a lower return on the safer and more liquid liabilities of the intermediaries than they would accept on the primary securities: even after taking into account the cost of intermediation, the cost of finance is probably reduced.

8 By providing a safe return on savings, plus liquidity, and a wide variety of assets, they encourage both saving itself and the direction of savings into productive investment. In so far as investment is determined by the cost of capital, the existence of an efficient intermediated capital market stimulates investment.

The economic significance of financial intermediation

By taking relatively illiquid primary securities (e.g. mortgages and hire purchase loans) and turning them into liquid assets for the primary lenders, they increase the stock of liquid assets available to owners of wealth. They can exchange their bank deposits for income-earning assets which are good substitutes for money in its store-of-value function, which can satisfy the speculative motive, and some part of the precautionary motive for holding money (see Ch. 8) as well, or almost as well, as money itself. The main consequence of intermediaries then is that they increase aggregate expenditure, which they do in two ways. First, in so far as expenditure is a function of the liquidity of wealth, the ultimate lender is unlikely to spend significantly less because he holds intermediary liabilities rather than money, as he might if he held primary securities; and the ultimate borrower can spend more. Second, much of their acquired funds probably comes out of idle balances; by lending it to spenders, they activate that idle money, thereby increasing the velocity of circulation. Some of them, especially the secondary banks, attract funds to London and since so many of these funds now go into the parallel markets rather than Treasury bills, the Treasury bill rate can be lower, providing it is consistent with the maintenance of a given level of reserves, than it could otherwise be[1] (see Revell 1973: 287). Indeed, financial intermediaries have been largely responsible for the growth of the parallel markets.

There are times, of course, when it is expedient to restrain the activities of the intermediaries. Their ability to expand credit and increase the velocity of circulation of money weakens anti-inflation policies (see Ch. 11).

What is a bank?: The need for supervision

The question may seem a strange one to ask at this stage, but in fact there is no useful statutory definition of a bank in the UK. The Bills of Exchange Act of 1882, for example, defined a bank as 'a body of persons, whether incorporated or not, carrying on the business of banking' but did not say what 'the business of banking' is. Palmer's *Company Law* says: 'it is generally accepted that the usual characteristics of banking business are (1) the collection of cheques from customers; (2) the payment of cheques drawn on the bank by customers; and (3) the keeping of current accounts'. This definition makes no mention of one major activity which one associates with the term 'banking', namely lending. In a famous legal action in 1966 the plaintiff, United Dominion Trust, rested its case on a claim that it was a bank. The Court of Appeal accepted the claim, not because it met Palmer's three requirements – it did not – but because it was generally regarded in the City as a bank.

There is a strong case for confining the term 'bank' to the eighteen institutions recognised as deposit banks by *the* Bank, the Bank of England. They are the only institutions who provide current accounts and cheque facilities for, and lend on overdraft to, the general public. It is through them that notes and coins are issued and withdrawn. They are the only institutions for whom the operation of current accounts and the provision of a money transfer mechanism is a major activity and they have a dominating position in this aspect of banking; and, correspondingly, they are the only institutions whose deposits are universally used and accepted as money. But one must then recognise that the secondary banks perform precisely the same services but in a more limited or specialised field, and that some banking operations are performed by institutions which are not recognised as, and would not claim to be, banks. The building societies and finance houses, for example, take deposits and make loans. The building societies will make payments on behalf of their depositors, and depositors are said to be using their deposits more and more like bank accounts, making more frequent withdrawals. Deposits with both are, in practice, withdrawable without notice up to quite large sums, and the finance houses offer personal loans not tied to a purchase of goods. The Trustee Savings Bank operates a personal current account and cheque service, and offers loans, as does Giro. There is no reason therefore why the big deposit banks should continue to dominate the operation of the payments mechanism or retain their near-monopoly of the creation of money. They have achieved their position simply because their deposits have come to be universally accepted and used as a means of payment.

The institutions generally recognised as banks (designated as secondary banks) differ from the deposit banks (designated as primary banks) in the following ways:

1 Although they have some current accounts, and some at least issue their own cheques, their deposits do not circulate widely; they play only a small part in providing the economy's payments mechanism. Most of them, for example, do not lend on overdraft.

2 They keep only small working reserve balances at the Bank of England and before September 1971 were not subject to day-to-day control by the Bank.
3 They are not members of the Bankers' Clearing House.
4 They carry on a different kind of business. Their deposits are overwhelmingly in large units, as are their loans; they are 'wholesale bankers', whereas the deposit bankers, who will accept any sum, however small, are also 'retail bankers'. Most of their deposits and loans are for a fixed term, which is often counted in years, and a large part of their deposits and loans is from/to clients overseas.
5 Their management of their balance sheet is very different from that of the deposit banks.

The need for a legal definition of the term 'bank' was shown in 1974, when several institutions calling themselves banks were caught in a liquidity crisis. They had been taking deposits and using them to invest in property and shares and to lend to property developers, and in 1973–74 share prices and property values fell heavily. The crisis was sparked off by the failure of London and County Securities early in 1974. This shook confidence in the other smaller banks, who quickly lost deposits obtained from the public and on the money markets. Many of them had insufficient liquid assets to meet these withdrawals; too much of their resources being tied up in rapidly depreciating, and in many cases practically unsaleable, assets. At least six banks failed, and about thirty had to be rescued by a 'lifeboat committee' of the London and Scottish clearing banks and the Bank of England, and as a result the clearing banks alone lost an estimated £50 million in bad debts. The word 'bank' is linked in the public's mind with the clearing banks, with a branch in every town and an unassailable reputation. Thousands of depositors and shareholders, however, learned to their cost that the inclusion of 'bank' in a title does not necessarily imply that the company concerned is a safe repository for their money. The consequence was that the Bank of England decided to set up a new supervisory department in July 1974, to collect from a wide circle of smaller banks and finance houses quarterly information on the maturities and quality of assets and deposits, provisions for bad debts, standby credits available from other banks, and so on. But what is really needed is a clear dividing line between banks and other institutions, with the banks both subject to official supervision of the quality of their business and, at the same time, assured of some form of last resort assistance either from other banks or from the Bank of England.

In October 1975, the Government announced its plan to bring in legislation applying to credit institutions who wished to call themselves banks or to accept deposits. The nature of this proposed legislation was outlined in a White Paper, 'The Licensing and Supervision of Deposit-Taking Institutions' (Cmnd 6584), published on 3 August 1976. Deposit-taking institutions would be classified into two groups:

First, those institutions entitled to call themselves banks. Though the term 'bank' was still not defined, there was to be 'exacting' criteria for recognition, not specified in detail but including:

(a) A minimum amount of capital and reserves.
(b) They had to conduct 'a wide range of activities judged to be characteristic of banking'.
(c) Reputation and status in the financial markets.

It was anticipated that upwards of 300 institutions would qualify for recognition as banks.

Second, those institutions not recognised as banks, but licensed to accept deposits from the public. The criteria for the grant of a licence was:

(a) Minimum capital and reserves. Again, the minimum was not specified, but was to be a level adequate to provide security but 'not so high that it constitutes an undue deterrent to otherwise suitably qualified persons'.
(b) Adequate liquidity and solvency. The balance sheet would be satisfactory in terms of such matters as the matching of assets and liabilities, the degree of risk attached to assets, the sectoral distribution of assets, provision against bad debts, loans to associated companies, and so on.
(c) The quality of management, which must show itself to be 'honest, trustworthy, and suitably qualified'.

No other institutions were to be permitted to accept deposits from the public for on-lending. Building societies, the NSB, the TSBs, National Giro and Friendly Societies, excluded from the legislation, were already controlled by existing laws.

Both groups of institutions were to be subject to continuous supervision by the Bank, except that it was to be left to the authorities in the countries of origin to supervise the UK branches of foreign institutions. The Bank was then authorised to withdraw a recognition or a licence if an institution ceased to fulfil the required conditions, and it was required to make an annual report on its supervision to Parliament and to the Select Committee on Nationalised Industries.

In July 1978 a draft Banking Bill, the Banking and Credit Unions Bill (Cmnd 7303), was published. Part 1 dealt with the procedures for recognising deposit-taking institutions as banks, and for the granting of licences to take deposits. According to Hindle (1978: 23), it would effectively 'create a first and second division in banking' with the Bank of England empowered to 'promote and demote institutions from one division to another'. The most controversial section of the Bill was *Part 2* which proposed the setting up of a *deposit protection fund*. All recognised banks and licensed institutions were to contribute with initial contributions adding up to a total fund of between £5 million and £6 million. Raised by *compulsory* contributions from all institutions covered by the new arrangements, the objective was to insure depositors against loss, up to the sum of £10,000. In calculating initial contributions, a minimum of £5,000 for the smaller institutions and a maximum of £300,000 for the larger ones was recommended. These were based on the size of each institution's 'deposit base'; defined broadly as sterling deposits taken by the institution in the UK *excluding* inter-bank deposits, secured deposits, deposits with an original term to maturity of more than five years, and deposits in respect of which a Certificate of Deposit has been issued. At an early stage bankers raised serious objections to the proposal.

The clearing banks argued that because they take a smaller proportion of their total deposits from inter-bank sources compared to other institutions, their expected share was unduly high. The merchant banks and the London offices of overseas banks believed that because a large proportion of their deposits come in wholesale quantities, the fund would not provide adequate protection. The discount houses, whose deposits are mostly inter-bank, secured and in wholesale quantities, saw no justification in the requirement that they should pay the minimum contribution of £5,000.

It was also difficult for such institutions to accept that the public sector bodies such as the National Girobank and the National Savings Bank as well as the building societies were to be exempt from the scheme. The building societies indicated their intention to set up their own arrangement, and the Trustee Savings Bank were to be incorporated into the *fund* at a later date. Nevertheless, despite assurances from the Treasury that public sector profit targets would be weighted in order to take account of their preferential treatment, the clearing banks questioned the rationale of making special cases of such institutions when it was they, the clearing banks, who were least likely to go bankrupt.

Moreover, the banks pointed out that the 0.3% contribution ceiling (which could in fact be raised to 0.6% if the Treasury deemed it necessary) would amount to £140–£150 million. Not only was this in excess of the £300,000 envisaged as the maximum *initial* contribution, it was also the approximate cost of the 'lifeboat'. In that sense, to the banks, the fund would confuse the insurance objective with a rescue facility; if the Bank of England performed its new supervisory role effectively such a scheme should not be required. Even if a similar arrangement had existed at the time of the 'lifeboat', in the banks' opinion little use would have been made of it.

However, to introduce the 'lifeboat' into the debate probably obscured more fundamental issues. The ostensible purpose of the lifeboat was to neutralise or, at minimum, re-cycle deposits out of dubious institutions into safe ones such as the clearers; it was originally seen as an ad hoc facility for deposit insurance. In any case, in terms of its objectives, the lifeboat enjoyed a high measure of success. It served to stabilise the deposit markets, thereby enabling those institutions who had experienced sudden withdrawals of deposits to regain confidence in the markets. The acid test was whether they would be able to repay their debts to the lifeboat or not. In the event, most of them did. Those who did not cannot be regarded as innocent victims of panic withdrawals, but rather as basically unsound financial institutions.

The issue of bank supervision was highlighted by the collapse of Johnson Matthey Bankers in 1985 which lost £248 million despite being lent £134 million by the Bank of England. At the time of writing, Johnson Matthey was simultaneously attempting to sue Arthur Young, its auditors, and also under investigation by the fraud squad. The Bank of England was also criticised for failing to carry out its supervisory role effectively. A series of reform proposals and a new Banking Bill have been suggested. The reforms include: the replacement of the two tier system of recognised banks and licensed deposit-takers (LDTs) with a single authorisation to take deposits; regular dialogue between the Bank and bank's auditors; a 25% exposure limit on single and related borrowers as a percentage of capital; and an increase in the Bank's supervisory staff (see Financial Times 21 June 1985).

Financial intermediaries: The secondary banks

The merchant banks

The term 'merchant bank' is applied to such a wide variety of institutions that it is impossible to define it precisely. Of the 300-odd institutions in London classified as banks, probably about 100 would class themselves as merchant banks. Seventeen of them make up the exclusive Accepting Houses Committee, all of whom are also members of the fifty-eight strong Issuing Houses Association; the title implies that they are both merchants and banks. Most of the older institutions bearing the title began life as merchants and developed their banking activities later, and some still are merchants, for example in timber, rubber, sisal, coffee, ferrous metals, gold and silver; but not all have kept their merchanting business, and for those who have, trading in goods is now only a small part of their operations. As banks, they engage in (for the most part) *wholesale intermediation*, taking large deposits (£25,000 or more), more than half of them in foreign currencies and many of them from overseas residents, and investing them in call money, bills and bonds, certificates of deposit, and loans and advances; the latter are also mostly on a large scale (£50,000 or more), usually more than half in foreign currencies and a large proportion to overseas residents. In their other activities they act as advisers and intermediaries (in the everyday sense of that term), providing services rather than funds.

The traditional function of the merchant banker is to accept bills of exchange on behalf of the drawee. The use of the 'bill on London' which in the late nineteenth century financed most of the world's international trade was developed by family firms, most of them merchants and a few of them already bankers, most of them of European or American origin, who in the first half of the century had either transferred their business to, or opened branches in, London, which was then the world's centre of trade and finance. The merchants were importers and exporters and had acquired an expert knowledge of the day-to-day operation of foreign trade and of the integrity and creditworthiness of their counterparts in the countries with which they traded. Their own reputations were sound, and bills drawn on and accepted by them were freely negotiated. The London Accepting House's signature on a bill guaranteed payment at maturity. Most of the houses who survived the financial crises of the nineteenth century and are still in existence today (some of them, meanwhile, having amalgamated) are members of the Accepting Houses Committee, the leading acceptors whose acceptances are 'eligible paper' for rediscount at the Bank of England.

Their reputations and connections also made them the natural agents for foreign governments wishing to raise money in London, and so began their other traditional function, the arrangement of bond issues in London for foreign governments and municipalities and, later, debenture and share issues for large foreign companies. It has been estimated, for example, that 40% of the £3,600 million of overseas loans between 1870 and 1914 were arranged by merchant banks. They naturally also became the agents for the payment of interest and dividends on these loans and investments.

All their present multifarious activities seem to follow logically from these beginnings. (a) The old bills of exchange have, for large sums, evolved into revolving credits covering a series of transactions, some of them running into several millions of pounds, often financed by a syndicate of accepting houses and banks. Some of these are of a new kind developed in the 1960s, the 'clean credits' unsupported by documentary titles to goods. They have also been active in arranging long-term credits for the export of capital goods, again syndicated. From the arranging of short-term credit by accepting bills for clients and presenting them for discount, they have developed services to deal with almost any financial problem facing the firm. In so doing they have, of course, provided themselves with alternative sources of income to replace those which declined with the decline of the international bill of exchange and the bill on London. (b) Their concern with importing and exporting has enabled them to provide a complete service to handle the shipping as well as the finance of the exports of small firms. This involves the insurance of cargoes, and some merchant banks now have general insurance broking departments. (c) Their commissions were often received in foreign currencies; this led them into the exchange of currencies, and several of them have used the experience so acquired to become important dealers in foreign exchange. They pioneered the Eurocurrency and Eurobond markets, and they arrange syndicated loans – e.g. by the issue of bonds – from foreign lenders to foreign borrowers denominated in currencies other than sterling.[2] In the 1940s and 1950s their international business was severely curtailed by exchange controls and they turned their attention more to domestic business. With the general liberalisation of trade from the late 1950s onwards, culminating in the adoption of flexible exchange rates and ultimately the abolition of exchange controls in 1979, they have turned their eyes abroad again. (d) Members of the Issuing Houses Association administer issues of shares and debentures for domestic companies and of bonds for local authorities. An issuing house advises on the timing and method of raising long-term capital, will draft the prospectus and have it published in the newspapers, handle the applications for shares and allot them if the issue is over-subscribed, underwrite the issue or arrange for it to be underwritten by one or more large institutions (the insurance companies are frequent underwriters), or place the shares with the institutions. This business of arranging domestic issues developed in the 1920s and 1930s. Perhaps the best recent example of a share issue was the £3.5 billion flotation of British Telecom in 1984 which was administered by Kleinwort Benson. They also act as registrars to smaller companies and foreign governments, keeping the register of stockholders and administering the payment of interest and dividends. They will advise on dividend policy, the timing of rights issues to share-holders, the preparation of the annual accounts and even on the organisation and management of the firm. Indeed, they are also prepared to engage in takeover bids or mergers and are equally willing to plan and conduct a campaign of opposition to a bid. (e) They arrange medium- and long-term finance for large capital projects at home and abroad, and 'bridging' loans for property companies to cover the purchase and development of land and property for resale. So though in terms of the sums involved, they mainly act as intermediaries between the borrowers and the large banks and institutions who supply the finance, they are also, as we have seen, bankers themselves. (f) Some merchant banks provide 'venture capital' to develop inventions or to nurture a small business to the point where it is ready to make a public issue of shares. McRae and Cairncross (1974) say their experience with venture capital has not been very happy: they have not usually improved the performance of their clients nor made much money for themselves. (g) Some of them have taken a stake in factoring and leasing and in hire purchase finance. (h) They operate as agents or principals in all the parallel markets. (i) Their knowledge of business and finance which they acquired as acceptors and issuing houses is the basis of their considerable business as investment advisers. For example, they manage portfolios of shares for wealthy individuals, and for institutional investors such as pension funds, unit trusts and investment banks; they rarely accept a portfolio less than £50,000 or £100,000. (j) A few have their own trusts through which small investors can tap their skill in this field. (k) Individual merchant banks like Brown Shipley & Co. have developed a market in foreign banknotes, supplying them to banks and travel agencies.

'Merchant banking', then, appears to cover virtually every financial activity and service except retail banking (though some are now accepting small deposits). Not all merchant banks engage in all these activities. Some – e.g. Hill Samuel – aim to provide as wide a range of services as possible; others specialise in a few; e.g. Robert Fleming announced in 1968 that they would concentrate on investment management and corporate finance.

Can they survive?

Since the early years of this century the merchant banks have come up against increasing competition in every area of business and there is now not one which is peculiar to them. The Midland Bank opened its first foreign branch in 1905, offering both current and deposit accounts and loan facilities, and all the London clearing banks now have branches and/or associates in the major trading countries, offering much the same services as the merchant banks. They and the foreign banks in London and overseas banks based in London offer acceptance credits and other means of financing trade; but the members of the AHC are responsible for nearly half of all London acceptances.[3] Both the clearing banks and some stockbrokers handle issues of shares, manage investment portfolios and have their own unit trusts. The larger London banks, both British and foreign, participate in international consortia to provide large-scale finance without the intermediation of the merchant banks. First the foreign and overseas banks and now the clearing banks are bidding for large deposits at medium-term by the offer of special rates and the issue of certificates of deposit. In the mid-1960s the clearing banks set up subsidiaries to operate in the parallel markets. Even some insurance companies are moving into wholesale banking, e.g. Guardian Royal Exchange in 1971 and Norwich Union in 1972. Some of these institutions, e.g. the large American banks, can offer a full range of financial services in every part of the world, backed up by much larger resources than any of the older merchant banks can command. Some have set up their own merchant banking subsidiaries in London, as have three of the London clearing banks (Barclays,

Midland and Natwest).[4] In one field after another, the older merchant banks are meeting more competition. With more than half their liabilities in the form of foreign currencies, fluctuations in sterling since 1971 have strained their resources and continuing inflation has necessitated high retained profits to maintain the 10% ratio of free assets to liabilities which the Bank of England has adopted as a guideline.

Legislative changes may have their effect too. For example, the extension of the privilege of eligibility of bills for discount at the Bank of England could threaten the position of the accepting houses particularly. They, together with the UK clearing banks and overseas banks, are the group which traditionally enjoyed the advantage of their bills being automatically acceptable at the Bank for rediscount and therefore commanding the best rates in the market. With the establishment of the new system of monetary controls and the Bank's more market-oriented approach to the determination of interest rates, this privilege has been extended to other banks.

Yet the accepting houses do not on the whole seem too worried about this change. Indeed, some merchant banks, such as Brandts and Gibbs, which have recently left the AHC, have reported that they have experienced no appreciable difference in their operations as a result of the changes. So the change, while likely to broaden the range of top quality bills available on the market, is unlikely to make any real difference to the senior merchant banking houses.

The other main legislative change stems from recent banking legislation. The question of status under the Banking Act is likely to affect significantly a number of financial institutions who have in the past been able to describe themselves as carrying out merchant banking activities. Now licensed deposit-taking institutions that are UK based can no longer use the name bank, and some of the smaller more specialised institutions may feel that their client relationships will suffer as a result.

This is not to suggest that the merchant banks do not retain their unique role in the City of London. Throughout their history they have been remarkably flexible and successful in finding new activities, new sources of livelihood, but if they are to retain their prosperity and independence, they must again seek new pastures. They are, traditionally, independent and small. Their great problem now is whether they can stay both small and independent. Must they amalgamate to fight back? Even then they would still be small compared with their rivals. Or should they go under the umbrella of the big banks? In 1972, the Bank of England announced that the clearing banks would in future be allowed to take more than a 25% stake in acceptance houses and EEC banks more than 15%. Midland already had a 33% stake in Montagu Trust and National and Grindlays owned William Brandt. Now Midland took complete ownership of Samuel Montagu via the Montagu Trust, Guinness Mahon amalgamated with the commodity trader, Lewis and Peat, and S G Warburg was linked, by cross-holdings of shares, with the Banque de Paris at Pays-Bas. The Hongkong Shanghai Bank has completely bought out Anthony Gibbs, causing it to leave the exclusive AHC, and other banks have accepted injections of capital from abroad.[5] Consequently by mid-1984 only six of the major accepting houses remained independent. More recently, some merchant banks have begun to further diversify their activities by becoming linked to insurance companies, and in some cases have

taken them over. During 1984, for example, one of the 'giants', Charterhouse 5
Rothschild, announced a £1 billion merger with Hambros Life Assurance (see *The
Times*, 12 April 1984). (See also Clay and Wheble 1978; Parker in *The Banker*
(hereafter *TB*), July 1977.)

The British overseas and foreign banks

By September 1984 there were 460 banks with offices in London whose business is
mainly with clients overseas. Table 4.1 shows the rapid expansion in the number of
these banks. Even during the difficult 1980–81 period, the numbers rose considerably. Some of these – the small group of *British overseas banks* – are British owned,
have their head offices in London, and were established, most of them in the nineteenth century, to finance trade between Britain and her overseas trading partners
and colonies, and to provide a banking service to traders and producers (most of
whom would originally be branches or subsidiaries of British firms) in those countries.
Some are owned by London clearing banks, e.g. Barclays Bank International, International Westminster Banks, and Lloyds Bank International, formed by a merger of
the Bank of London and South America (BOLSA) and Lloyds Bank Europe.

Table 4.1 How London's foreign banking community has grown, 1967–84

Year	Directly represented*	Indirectly represented**	Total
1967	114	—	114
1968	135	—	135
1969	138	—	138
1970	163	—	163
1971	176	25	201
1972	215	28	243
1973	232	35	267
1974	264	72	336
1975	263	72	335
1976	265	78	343
1977	300	55	355
1978	313	69	382
1979	330	59	389
1980	353	50	403
1981	355	65	420
1982	377	70	447
1983	391	69	460

*Directly represented through a representative office, branch, or subsidiary.
**Other banks indirectly represented through a stake in a joint venture or consortium bank.

Source: *TB*, Nov. 1983: 111

There is some degree of geographical specialisation. Barclays being heavily
represented in Africa and the Caribbean area, Lloyds in South America, Grindlays in
India, Pakistan and Africa, Standard Chartered in Africa and the Middle and Far

East. As their operations overseas have been subjected to more restrictions, and to nationalisation, the overseas banks have turned to the parallel markets to generate earnings and are trying to develop merchant banking operations in Europe and America as well as their traditional areas of operation. The overseas banks usually invested some of their surplus overseas deposits in London. As the countries in which they operated needed overseas loans – e.g. to finance crops – the banks were at times net borrowers in London. They also acted as London agents for firms and wealthy individuals. As the emerging countries came to require funds for development, the overseas banks sought them in London. This financing was originally in sterling, but in the 1960s it also helped to develop the Eurodollar market.

Several of the original overseas banks have disappeared. Some have seen their operations overseas nationalised by new governments in the Commonwealth. Some have merged with other banks in London. They have established other links and activities, e.g. Grindlays is half owned by an American bank and owns William Brandt, a merchant bank; Standard Chartered owns a merchant bank, Tozer Standard Chartered, established in 1973, and renamed Standard Chartered Merchant Bank, has a controlling interest in the bullion broker Mocatta and Goldsmid; Hongkong and Shanghai Bank has completely bought out Anthony Gibbs (renamed Wardley in 1983).

The *Commonwealth banks* have their head offices, and operate as domestic banks, in one or other of the countries of the Commonwealth, e.g. the Royal Bank of Canada, the National Bank of Nigeria Ltd. etc. They maintain branches in London. The second group are the *foreign banks*, with head offices abroad, who have branches or subsidiaries in London and/or have bought a share in a British bank. Many of the wholly or partly-owned offshoots of American banks were newly established merchant banks; some of these were established simply to develop the parent bank's syndicated lending, and underwriting and dealing in Eurobonds; some engaged in medium-term lending to industrialists and property developers. London has more foreign banks than any other financial centre. Currently (1984) their total sterling deposits are equal to about one-third of those of the London clearing banks, and the American banks alone control more funds than the London clearing banks. Total assets of the foreign banks are about 60% of the total of the UK banking sector.

Many of the London subsidiaries or branches of foreign banks have been in existence for several years, starting with the Bankers' Trust (America) in 1860. But the real growth came after 1958: there were 53 foreign banks with offices in London in 1950, 77 in 1960, 159 in 1970, and 248 in 1974; a further 91 had stakes in London-based consortia. Many of these foreign banks also have offices in Britain, outside London. *The Banker* (Nov. 1983: 123) reported that as many as 40 foreign banks had 196 offices outside London. The total deposits of the overseas and foreign banks in London multiplied twenty times between 1958 and 1971, and they trebled between 1970 and 1974. The most important group is the American banks, with three-quarters of the total deposits of foreign banks in London. Today the number of the world's largest 100 banks not directly represented in the City with their own branch or representative office is just four.

There are several reasons for this remarkable growth. In 1958 exchange control was relaxed for non-residents; sterling became more freely exchangeable by them into foreign currencies, and vice versa. Resources could therefore be employed in London without being locked into sterling. In addition, London was developing the parallel money markets, so that London was the most flexible market in the world, i.e. it offered the widest variety of uses of money, and it had an extremely efficient foreign exchange market for the speedy, cheap and convenient transfer of funds from one currency to another. A further reason was that Britain did not try to keep foreign banks out or put any restrictions on competition with British banks. The American banks also came to provide a banking service here for their customers back home who were setting up branches or subsidiaries in Britain. They came because their own domestic exchange controls restricted their customers' ability to buy foreign currency for foreign investment, and because their domestic growth was hampered by Regulation Q (see p. 123), which limited the rates they could pay on deposits. They came especially in the late 1960s seeking funds, particularly Eurodollar balances, to transfer back to their head offices because of the credit squeezes in the USA. Some set up branches, some bought into British banks, e.g. First National City bought a 48% stake in Grindlays. According to *TB* (May 1973), there were then nine wholly-owned or majority-owned merchant banking subsidiaries of US banks in London. Likewise most of Japan's foreign trade is financed in dollars, and the Japanese banks came to London partly in search of dollars when their supply from banks in the USA itself was restricted by credit squeezes there. Rapid growth in the number of Arab banks has also occurred, especially in the wake of the oil price explosion of 1973 and the subsequent need for re-cycling. By December 1983, thirty Arab banks were directly represented in London, twenty arriving in the previous eight years and twelve of these in the previous six years (see *TB*, Dec. 1983 for a review of Arab banking). Some foreign banks, such as the Ghana Commercial Bank, are mainly concerned with the finance of trade in their own country's exports and imports. But perhaps the biggest attraction to foreign banks in general was the fact that London had become the main centre for trading in Eurocurrencies, in which these banks play a much bigger part than UK banks (see Ch. 6).

Market share

Recent banking legislation has obviously affected the status of many of these banks. Immediately after the Banking Act of 1979 there was a sudden rush of applications from foreign banks. By November 1981, of the 220 foreign banks granted authorisation under the Act (excluding the 133 rep. offices), 180 had been granted recognised bank status and 40 the status of a licensed deposit-taking institution, and a number of the latter have been 'promoted' to banks.

New areas of business have opened up to foreign banks operating in the UK. A number of them have now been added to the list of institutions whose bills are eligible for discount at the Bank of England, for example, and foreign banks are now able to participate in areas of ECGD, backed export finance business, an activity previously closed to them. Table 4.2 shows the inroads foreign banks have been making into the

UK bankers' market share, with their share of sterling advances by all banks increasing to 19 per cent by the middle of 1981 (compared to 17 per cent at the same time in 1980). Similarly, their share of foreign currency advances increased to 72 per cent (71 per cent in 1980).

Table 4.2 Foreign banks' UK market shares, 1975–81

(£ million; figures in parentheses show percentages of totals)

| | All banks in the UK | | | Foreign banks in the UK | | |
	Total assets	Sterling advances	Currency advances	Total assets (%)	Sterling advances (%)	Currency advances (%)
May 1975	124,488	24,589	19,478	64,760(52)	3,314(13)	13,585(70)
Dec 1975	139,793	24,101	23,089	77,529(55)	3,429(14)	16,167(70)
Dec 1976	175,123	27,314	30,239	104,358(60)	4,399(16)	21,580(71)
Dec 1977	190,802	30,295	32,379	110,981(58)	4,937(16)	23,167(72)
Dec 1978	218,929	35,203	37,692	127,638(58)	5,581(16)	27,690(73)
Dec 1979	263,843	42,743	39,677	152,370(58)	7,271(17)	28,700(72)
Dec 1980	303,234	52,933	45,751	174,344(58)	10,069(19)	32,464(71)
July 1981	391,698	58,764	61,137	237,887(61)	11,428(19)	43,885(72)

Source: *TB*, Nov. 1981: 107

With the abolition of exchange controls in October 1979, many of the foreign banks have increased their capacities for customer-related foreign exchange operations. In particular, there has been a significant growth in (forward) deals as more companies take advantage of their new-found freedom, and the banks have reacted to this speedily. Though the relaxation has made life more difficult for the monetary authorities in their attempt to control the growth of the money supply, it has at the same time added to the flexibility and attraction of London as a centre for international financial activities.

Consortium banks

A recent development is the consortium bank and the banking 'club'. A group of banks jointly establish a separate institution of which they are collectively the only shareholders. Through them the shareholding banks can, as one director puts it, 'focus their considerable resources and far-reaching geographical coverage by working together'. In January 1984, *TB* listed twenty-four consortia based in London. The Midland Bank has shares in banks based in New York, Paris and Brussels as well as in Midland and International Bank (MAIBL), and Barclays participates in some Paris-based banks and a number of London-based consortia. All but one (Lloyds) of the London clearing banks are members of one or more consortia.

Initially, their own capital resources were small; but they can call on the specialised knowledge and expertise of their shareholders and, to some extent, on their resources. Some are owned within one country; two are owned by Japanese banks, for example, and there are seven American consortia. The majority, however, are owned by shareholders in different countries. MAIBL is owned by two London, one Australian and one Canadian bank; while one of the biggest, Orion Bank Ltd, in 1984 had shareholders in America, Italy, Japan, Britain, Canada and Germany. Sometimes the term 'consortium' is reserved for banks wholly owned in one country and the remainder are termed 'multinational banks', but the Bank of England defines consortium banks as 'banks which are owned by other banks but in which no one bank has a direct shareholding of more than 50% and in which at least one shareholder is an overseas bank'. Some specialise geographically, e.g. the Iran Overseas Investment Bank, the Anglo-Romanian Bank (which specialises in trade with Eastern Europe); some specialise industrially, e.g. the International Energy Bank; but this does not mean that they confine their activities entirely to one area or one branch of industry. With much of their capital in sterling and more than 80% of their assets in foreign currencies, their capital ratios are susceptible to fluctuations in the value of sterling as was clear in the immediate post-1971 period (Bee 1984).

Probably no two of these consortia undertake exactly the same range of business, but between them they supply most of the services provided by all other kinds of bank, except that they do not usually provide a cheque service and everything they do is done on a large scale. They accept large deposits and provide large medium-term loans (up to ten years) to, and organise and underwrite bond issues for, firms and governments in any part of the world and in any major currency.[6] Some of them have been active also in financing oil exploration in the North Sea. The consortia MAIBL have been active in arranging, with up to fifty other banks, medium-term loans for as much as one billion dollars, one of them to the UK Electricity Council. They have been particularly active in the Eurodollar market. Indeed, most of them were established to conduct Eurocurrency operations of one kind or another, and McRae and Cairncross call them 'Eurobanks' because they rely on the Eurocurrency markets for their funds.[7] Yassukovich (1976) divides them into four groups. First, there are those 'devoted primarily to medium-term lending in the Eurocurrency market', a group which includes the oldest and biggest consortia. Second, there are those who take on a wider range of activities which we associate with merchant banking: arranging international mergers and acquisitions of companies, financial advice and other specialist financial services, and project finance.[8] Their advantage over domestic merchant banks and investment banks is, of course, their large collective resources, expertise and wide geographic coverage. Third, there are the consortia formed to penetrate a particular market, or to finance economic expansion of a particular area, e.g. the Libra Bank and the Euro-Latin American Bank in South America. Fourth, there are the consortia established on the initiative of governments to secure their own finance for the development of their national resources and 'to educate their own institutions in international banking methods, in order to better negotiate with the international market'. Brazil, Mexico, Iran, Saudi Arabia and others have formed such consortia, bringing in European and North American banks to provide extra funds and/or expertise and training of their own personnel.[9]

The main advantage of the consortium bank is the large funds to which it has access. Any one member can initiate business in the knowledge that he probably has a ready-made syndicate to finance it, or to arrange the financing. The danger, however, is the possibility of conflict of interest between the shareholders and the consortium. The shareholders themselves almost invariably have a wide geographical spread of activities, and any one might come into competition with its own consortium. This happened in the 1970s as several of the shareholding banks expanded and developed their overseas representation sufficiently to participate directly in large-scale operations. This applies particularly to the American banks; a dozen or so of them have pulled out of consortia, and others have bought out their partners, e.g. American Express bought up Rothschild International in 1975, the Chemical Bank took over London Multinational in 1977, the Royal Bank of Canada acquired Orion in 1982, Standard Chartered took over MAIBL and, most recently, Den norske Creditbank took over Nordic in 1983. Since 1976 there have been a total of seven buy-outs. Some London merchant banks – e.g. Hambros, Rothschild, Kleinwort Benson – have also withdrawn from consortia as the latter developed their specialised merchant banking and advisory services.

Overseas and foreign banks

Banking clubs are somewhat different from consortia. They are associations of banks from different countries to cooperate in particular ventures or activities requiring large-scale finance, and to provide such facilities as the withdrawal of money by customers travelling abroad. They are all European, and originated partly as a response to the invasion of Europe by the American banks, partly as a means of exploiting the opportunities for large-scale finance which the EEC was expected to create. The biggest are: Associated Banks of Europe (ABECOR); Europartners; European Banks International Company (EBIC); and Inter-Alpha. Barclays Bank is a member of ABECOR, the Midland Bank of EBIC, and Williams and Glyn's of Inter-Alpha. EBIC has consortia in America, Europe, Australia and the Far East associated with it, and one can contact EBIC or its associates through any one of more than 9,800 branches of the member banks (see *TB*, Aug. 1977: 83–7).

Operations

All three kinds of bank described in this section offer a variety of services, sometimes in association with partners and subsidiaries among the British banks. Not every bank engages in all these activities, but one or other of them will manage an investment portfolio, administer a share issue, finance an investment or trading project by short or medium-term loan or with equity participations, arrange insurance, offer leasing and factoring facilities, provide or arrange acceptance credits, issue and deal in certificates of deposit, and operate in one or more of the parallel markets. The one service most of them do not offer is retail banking; they do not accept deposits of less than £10,000 and for many the minimum is £50,000, more if it is a foreign currency deposit.

Some of their deposits are at very short notice; they will accept overnight deposits, withdrawable next day. But the majority of their deposits are at longer term than this, ranging up to one year. They have also been issuing increasing quantities of certificates of deposit. Lacking a network of branches, they do not have the same access as the domestic banks to sterling deposits from the general public. Their domestic deposits come mainly from large firms, other banks and financial institutions. They used to pay the same rates as the London clearing banks on seven-day deposits, but that convention was abandoned in the late 1950s. Rates are now negotiated, and depend on rates in the parallel markets. Most of their deposits are from overseas: from their own branches or head offices, from other banks, from international agencies such as the Bank for International Settlements in Switzerland, from large companies, from trusts and from wealthy people, and most of them are denominated in a foreign currency.[10] However, in addition to their large deposits in the Eurocurrency market, the inter-bank market is now also a major source of funds.

The banks use these deposits for a variety of purposes. In the early days of the influx of American banks, many dollar balances were on-lent to their head offices. The probable result would be that the head office acquired a claim against another bank inside the USA, since it was a balance in an American bank which was being on-lent. The major advantage of this was that while the parent bank also acquired an equal deposit liability to its London branch, it did not have to maintain a minimum ratio of cash to such a liability, as it would have if the liability were to a resident in the USA. This on-lending declined after 1969, when American domestic banks were required to hold reserves against borrowings from foreign banks, and a much higher reserve against an increase in their borrowings from their foreign branches.

Their major asset is loans for overseas trade and investment, mostly in foreign currencies. Just as they accept deposits in specific currencies and for a specified time, so are their loans usually made in fixed sums for fixed terms rather than by overdraft, and in particular currencies. And their loans, like their deposits, are in large units: a 'typical' loan is probably in excess of £500,000 and some run to several millions of pounds or their equivalent. Although balances deposited with them are not necessarily on-lent in the same currency but exchange for a balance in a third country which is then on-lent, they must have the first currency available when the deposit matures. These banks must therefore try to match the two sides of their balance sheets in two dimensions, the currency dimension and the maturity or term dimension, and they are therefore important operators in the foreign exchange markets. When they sell a balance in one currency spot (for immediate delivery), they will usually buy a similar amount of the same currency forward (for delivery at a named future date but at a price fixed today) to guarantee their future liabilities to depositors. In seeking the most profitable outlets for funds they will sometimes exchange sterling for balances abroad, sometimes change foreign currencies into sterling; but, their holdings of sterling are a small part of the total. They are put to a number of uses: advances, loans at call and short notice to the discount houses and others, the purchase of Treasury bills and government stocks, loans to local authorities and finance houses, and certificates of deposits, and involvement in the inter-bank market.

The overseas and foreign banks were not until 1971 subject to any minimum liquidity ratio, although they actually held a fairly high proportion of their assets in liquid form (as do the merchant banks), since a few large deposits are subject to greater risk of withdrawal than a multitude of small accounts. If the key word in deposit banking is *liquidity*, the key word for these banks is *matching*. They must, as far as possible, match the currency and maturity of their assets to those of their liabilities. Their ideal balance sheet has been compared to a Christmas tree on which opposite branches are of the same length.[11]

Competition with UK banks

UK banks also accept deposits and lend in foreign currencies, both from/to UK residents and overseas residents. Why, then, were the overseas and foreign banks so successful in the 1950s and 1960s? Why did their deposits increase much faster than those of the clearing banks? There are two answers. *First*, they had some advantages over the domestic deposit banks in the expanding field of international trade and investment. The overseas banks' long experience abroad gave them a detailed knowledge of firms (and their trading practices and customs) in the countries in which they operate. The majority of international transactions were conducted in US dollars; the most important foreign banks, the American, had a dollar capital base and had access to dollar loans at last resort from their central bank. Sterling, on the other hand, was a weak currency. *Second*, and more important, they were not bound by the customs, traditions and constraints which for so long inhibited the UK banks. The latter traditionally accepted only two kinds of deposit, current account deposits and deposits withdrawable at seven days' notice. They paid no interest on current accounts and they all paid the same rate on seven-day deposits. Their minimum lending rate was also uniform, set at a fixed interval above the deposit rate, and the whole structure rigidly geared to bank rate. Their loans and overdrafts were subject to review at intervals; and prior to 1971 they were obliged to maintain minimum cash and liquidity ratios. The secondary banks' deposits were not subject to any price cartel or tradition or 'seven days only' rule, but adjusted to the market. Similarly in their lending, they tailored the service to the customer's needs as to the term of the loan and the method of repayment: and the rate is negotiable. In so doing they must have captured some business from the clearing banks, but a large part of it is of a kind which clearing banks would have been unable or unwilling to handle, except through a subsidiary or associated firm.

The American banks, in particular, have brought new techniques and new attitudes into banking in Britain. They are accustomed to competing actively for deposits and have brought their aggressive competitive attitudes with them. 'In the US, there is little in the way of a logical distinction between money and any other commodity. Both can be *sold* with all the ingenuity at the disposal of a powerful marketing organisation'. They are skilled at keeping their clients' money active, 'masters at not letting money stagnate' (Spiegelberg 1973: 98). This is most clearly seen in their approach to lending which differs from that of the clearing banks. They look for security to the borrower's ability to generate future cash flow rather than to his assets. This approach requires closer involvement with the borrower's affairs and monitoring of his financial ratios. In recent years there has been evidence of severe strain and differences of opinion between consortium bank management and shareholders, in some cases resulting in joint ventures being taken over by one of the participants, or leading shareholders withdrawing. This happened with both Orion Bank and Scandinavian Bank in 1980. In May 1981 it was announced that Orion Bank was to be bought out by one of its shareholders, Royal Bank of Canada. The problem, it seemed, was that Orion, as a general Eurocurrency and international banking operation, had come increasingly into competition with its owners, especially National Westminster and Chase Manhattan.[12]

Undoubtedly, the banks have been experiencing pressures. The climate of the Eurocurrency and Eurobank markets has been far from healthy. One reason for this is, of course, the renewal of the huge OPEC surpluses as a result of the last oil price rise, which though it generated a buoyant flow of funds in the markets, did not nullify the excessive risk exposure and concern about the shortage of good quality borrowers that previously pervaded the markets. Likewise, in the Eurobond markets the extreme volatility of interest rates and exchange rates has adversely affected bond dealing activities. Margins on syndicated loans, in particular, have fluctuated, with the rise in sterling at the end of 1980 reducing the sterling value of earnings, but subsequent reductions in sterling causing it to increase.

Some banks have argued that in many cases the shareholding banks have outgrown the need to expand in numbers. Considering that many consortium banks were set up at a time when Euromarket banking was new and many commercial banks were relatively inexperienced in that area, now that the main commercial banks are able to conduct the Eurobusiness themselves, many of the consortia may find their services no longer required. In an era of intense competition, the commercial banks may no longer find it necessary to share in the profits of a consortium which is competing with them for business. Some of the big banks in particular are taking this view. The Bank of America, for example, has over recent years been running down its commitments to joint ventures.

Despite these pressures, however, the consortium banks have been able to weather the storm. As is usual in banking, when some banks are under threat, paradoxically, new ventures are set up. This has been particularly true of joint ventures and consortia (see Blanden in *TB*, Mar. 1981) which suggests that the unique features of consortium banking remain as valid as ever. Perhaps their real merit is their diversity: not only do they bring together leading banks from different countries or from one country, they also provide a platform for smaller banks to engage in international markets. As Blanden (1981: 99) says, 'they enable international experience to be associated with local knowledge; they bring together different types of banks with special expertise, such as commercial and merchant banks'.

Table 4.3 shows that the consortium banks have continued to perform rather well. For the group as a whole there was a 23% growth of profits in the last year for which data is available (1982). Their average pre-tax return on assets for the last year was 1.18%, which compared favourably with an average of 0.62% for the twenty largest banks in the world, 0.81% for the five largest US banks, and 0.84% for the four

Table 4.3 Consortium banks' profits (1982)

	Latest year	Previous year	Change (%)
Total assets (£m)	14,250	11,330	+26
Pre-tax profits (£m)	150.9	122.8	+23
Post-tax profits (£m)	82.0	66.8	+23
Return on average assets:			
Pre-tax 1.18%			
Post-tax 0.64%			

Source: Bee R N 'London Consortium Banks and the debt crisis', *TB*, Jan 1984: 37–39.

major UK clearing banks. Bee (1984: 39) argues that the banks have successfully weathered the continuing world debt crisis, in marked contrast to their condition during the 1974–75 crisis. One reason given by the banks themselves is that though still mainly dependent on Eurolending business, they have been trying to extend the scope of their activities. Fee income, from managing international issues as well as other types of merchant banking and advisory services, has become very important. So also has dealing in foreign currencies and on the money markets, as well as project finance and *leasing*.

Clearly, the consortium banks, like the merchant banks discussed earlier, have survived ostensibly as a result of their ability to adapt to the rapidly changing institutional environment.

Notes

1   On the other hand, the dependence of some borrowers – e.g. the local authorities – on foreign funds reduces the authorities' freedom of manoeuvre on interest rates for fear of an embarrassing withdrawal of funds. Further, foreign currency exchanged into sterling at the Exchange Equalisation Account increases the quantity of money. The effect can be offset by sales of government bills and bonds, but a heavy inflow can 'swamp the defences' and weaken monetary control.

2   In the more competitive climate of recent years the merchant banks have been affected greatly, as can be seen in the trend of accepting a low spread for short-term loans. And it has been in the Eurocurrency loan markets that the banks have been most severely stretched, for it is here that the foreign banks present a real challenge to them. In contrast to the late 1960s when they had a virtual monopoly of this market, by the end of the 1970s it was the American banks who began to dominate. They have, however, retained a strong influence in the Eurobond market, especially when big issues are involved.

3   Indeed, members of the AHC account for about 40% of the acceptances held by all banks in Britain and for about 62% of the acceptance business done by purely British banks.

4   In addition, two other 'big banks', Lloyds and the Bank of Scotland, have extended their involvement in merchant banking. Lloyds, in October 1979, created a new merchant banking unit with the title Merchant Banking Division (Corporate Financial Advice), although to date it does not lend money or take equity stakes but acts in a purely advisory capacity. Likewise, in 1977, the Bank of Scotland revived its non-trading subsidiary, British Linen Bank, and launched it as its merchant banking arm. By contrast, Williams & Glyn's Bank has moved in the opposite direction and run down its merchant banking team, mainly because it found that many of its bigger customers were unwilling to move their business away from their traditional merchant bank.

5   Some of them have quite significant foreign owners. Since the Phillip Hill Investment Trust sold off its 16% stake in Hill Samuel in 1980, the two biggest shareholdings in the bank are the 5% of the Banque Arabe et Internationale d'Investissement and the 3% of the First City Bancorporation of Texas. The US insurance giant, the Prudential, owns 9.5% of equity (though only 2.3% of the votes) in the Hambros Trust. Cook Industries of Memphis owns 13.8%, the Securities Group of New York 9.8% and the Munich Reinsurance Group 5.2% of Arbuthnot Latham (*TB*, Aug. 1981: 46).

6   One consortium arranged an 80 million dollar loan for the Government of Iran.

7   They also participate in the bond market, arranging issues of Eurobonds and using some of their deposits to subscribe to them.

8   This is the provision of large medium-term loans for specific projects, e.g. sinking an oil well, the purchase of a new ship. The security for the loan is not the borrower's existing assets, but the oil, copper, gas, ship etc. which the project will produce.

9   One of the most impressive examples of recent years was the Arab Banking Corporation (ABC) set up in 1980 with a paid-up capital of $375 million subscribed by the governments of Kuwait, Libya and the United Arab Emirates. Based in Bahrain, its birth is an indication of the determination of Arab oil exporters to become more involved in investment in banking, as well as to participate more fully in the re-cycling of their surplus funds.

10   For example, the owner of a balance with a German bank will transfer it to a bank in London, receiving in exchange a deposit at the London bank. Although it is with a London bank, the deposit will be entered in that bank's books as a certain number of deutschmarks and when the deposit is withdrawn the depositor will receive a credit at whatever German bank happens to be the correspondent of the London bank (a large London bank might well have more than one correspondent bank in Germany).

11   Providing nobody defaults, it is a self-liquidating balance sheet. There is no need for liquidity as such (Revell 1973: 244). Of course, perfect matching will rarely, if ever, be achieved. In any case, against the security it offers must be set its low profitability; profits are made by *successfully* 'taking a view of the market', shortening assets and lengthening liabilities when interest rates are

CHAPTER FIVE

Financial intermediation: The non-bank financial intermediaries

Despite the fact that rapid institutional change in the financial system has blurred many of the distinctions between financial institutions, it nevertheless remains necessary to classify the non-bank financial intermediaries separately from the mainstream banks discussed in Chapters 3 and 4.

The finance houses

These are institutions whose main function is to finance hire purchase, credit sales and other forms of instalment credit. Hence they are often termed hire purchase finance companies. Some describe themselves as industrial bankers. There are about 1,900 companies operating in this field, but the forty-two members of the Finance Houses Association (FHA) (September 1984) do about 90% of the total finance house business. In 1971 it was estimated that the fourteen houses brought under the umbrella of Competition and Credit Control accounted for 80–85% of all instalment credit written by finance houses. Most of the big companies are owned by firms outside the instalment credit industry. Barclays Bank owns Mercantile Credit, National Westminster owns Lombard North Central, Midland owns Forward Trust and Lloyds and Scottish is largely owned by Lloyds and National and Commercial. The Hodge Group has been taken over by Standard Chartered Bank, and Bowmaker is owned by the C T Bowring group. In 1981 the TSB Group, the old Trustee Savings Banks, was forced into an outright bid for the only large house still independent, United Dominions Trust. Other banks, and some of the insurance companies, partly own several houses. Some manufacturers and large retailers finance their own instalment credit, and some of them have established separate subsidiary companies for one purpose, e.g. Ford Motor Credit (Drury 1982).

Finance houses have operated in one form or another since the early nineteenth century. According to the FHA, total credit outstanding by the end of 1981 (exclusive of that supplied by the clearing banks) was £10.11 billion. Rapid growth in the 1950s and 1960s was probably a consequence of rising incomes, which increased demand for consumer goods, especially cars, and full employment, which reduced families' reluctance to commit themselves to extended regular repayments. In the 1970s, inflation, which encouraged people to acquire durable goods quickly, was probably a significant factor. Hire purchase finance has grown rapidly in spite of restraints frequently imposed. These restraints curtailed their traditional activities, especially in the 1960s, and the finance houses reacted by diversifying.

The activities of the finance house

Today the finance houses use their loanable funds in several ways:

1 More than 60% of funds are still employed in instalment credit. The proportion fell from 80% in 1963 to 66% in 1971 as a result of the controls on consumer credit.[1] A hire purchase agreement may be made direct with the finance house, the retailer acting as agent, drawing a commission from the finance company and receiving from it, immediately on sale, the cash price of the goods. Some agreements are made with the retailer, who then sells the hire purchase debt to the finance house: this is known as 'block discounting'.

2 They lend to industry and commerce in several other ways. They are active in *leasing* and contract-hire, they pioneered *factoring*, they offer bill-finance for the purchase of stocks and, to their dealer–agents, longer loans for the improvement of premises. They lend large sums to car dealers to finance stocks of cars. They give bridging loans on mortgage to property development companies to finance the purchase and redevelopment, or building, of property for resale, though this business has declined in recent years. They also lend to householders and firms on second mortgage, a loan secured on the difference between the outstanding mortgage and the value of the property. They provide trade credit for importers and exporters. A recent development is *chattel mortgage*, loans secured by a charge on moveable assets. According to the Wilson Report, around half of new instalment credit extended by FHA members is to corporate bodies.

3 Some finance houses have joined international consortia – the 'credit clubs' – to provide medium-term finance in large amounts to industry and commerce. Each member of a consortium represents it in his own country and collects payments from borrowers in his country – e.g. for imports financed by a foreign member of the consortium – as if it were a domestic agreement.

4 They have been coming closer to the banks, e.g. by new forms of lending such as personal loans; by the offer of current account facilities to personal customers; by activities which we associate with merchant banking; and in the 'money shops' which two of them (Western Credit and United Dominion Trust) set up.[2] Six of the largest houses have been classified as banks, and some of the biggest houses have merchant banking subsidiaries at home and abroad, although the recent banking legislation may threaten this status. Provident Clothing, a check-trading company, tried to develop a full banking service for its customers in The People's Bank acquired for this purpose, but was prohibited by the 1979 Banking Act from utilising the title 'bank'.

Sources of funds

In 1984 about one-sixth of their funds came from their own capital and reserves. The remainder, their borrowed funds, came from two sources:

1 *Loans from the money markets:* about 38% of the total. They borrow from the banks on overdraft and by term loans and from the discount houses by the discounting of bills. These bills are created in two ways: (a) a finance house arranges an acceptance credit with an accepting house or other bank offering acceptances and draws bills against it as required; (b) a bank draws a bill against the finance house in exchange for a deposit. Bills of either kind are 'finance bills' or 'accommodation bills'.[3] The houses recognised as banks can issue certificates of deposit, and their acceptances are classified as 'bank bills'. Bank lending to finance houses, however, has never been one of the priority classes to be protected in times of restraint; therefore, they cannot rely on its continuance. But they are better placed than some borrowers when cash loans are scarce, the money borrowed is not locked into investments with no immediate cash flow; they have a regular, continuous flow of repayments.
2 *Deposits.* They accept deposits, at various terms of notice of withdrawal, from two sources. First there are deposits by the general public, usually in comparatively small sums; the minimum initial deposit accepted is often as low as £25 or £50. A few houses advertise in the newspapers for deposits. The terms of notice of withdrawal offered range from eight to six months, and in some cases up to a year. They offer higher interest rates, of course, the longer the term. On average, they borrow at a much shorter term than they lend, and this can cause losses when interest rates rise.

Much more important in total are the bigger deposits, running up to hundreds of thousands of pounds, placed with them by companies, by secondary banks both on their own account and on behalf of clients, by other financial institutions and by wealthy individuals. In 1984 more than half of their borrowed funds came from the banks and discount houses in one form or another, about 20% from deposits by the public, some of these from companies and other non-bank institutions, and 2–3% from overseas. They take deposits from foreign residents, but only in sterling. They also accept sums up to £100,000 'in the normal course of business' and deposits bigger than this 'by negotiation' with the rate and terms negotiated direct or through a bank or money-broker.

In seeking deposits the finance houses must, of course, compete with other borrowers such as the building societies, local authorities and banks operating in the parallel markets, hence they must offer competitive rates. In fact, their rates are slightly higher, the differential varying with the size and reputation of the house concerned, the amount deposited, and the term of withdrawal of the deposit. For example, the rate on a deposit at three months' notice has usually been $\frac{1}{4}$ to $\frac{3}{4}$% above the corresponding local authority rate. Their rates tended to change with minimum lending rate (MLR), but not at a fixed interval, and some houses' rates have been stickier than others. Since 1970 the FHA have had their own published base rate to which the rates they pay/charge are related. It is determined on the last day of the month, by a formula which gears it rigidly to the inter-bank three-month rate over the preceding eight weeks which is widely used as the representative market rate. Deposits may be for a fixed term, or at agreed periods of notice of withdrawal, which again may be as long as a year. Some companies also borrow in the parallel markets at call or at seven days' notice.

Just as they have taken on some of the activities of the banks, so the deposit banks, freed by Competition and Credit Control, moved more and more into some of their activities. The liquidity crisis of 1973–75 brought several houses into trouble, with funds locked up in businesses with inadequate cash flows, especially property companies. In mid-1976, for example, UDT still owed £400 million, at a high rate of interest, to the 'lifeboat committee' of the Bank and the clearing banks. This experience made them realise, if they did not realise it before, that borrowing short to lend long (most of their lending is from two to five years) can carry a high liquidity risk as well as the interest-rate risk mentioned earlier, and they are now trying to devise a medium- or long-term borrowing instrument.

Those finance houses which are listed bankers have been subject to credit control by the Bank of England. They were required to observe the $12\frac{1}{2}\%$ minimum reserve ratio (before its phasing out in November 1980) and have been subject to other controls when they applied to banks, such as the supplementary special deposits scheme. Additionally, some other non-bank finance houses agreed to maintain reserve ratios of 10% and were also subject to the supplementary special deposits scheme, and have from time to time been requested by the Bank of England to control their level of advances and to give priority to certain sectors (see Ch 13).

Recent performance

Like most of the financial institutions discussed in this chapter, the finance houses have performed surprisingly well, despite the recession. After the misfortunes which beset some of them after the property bubble burst in 1973, performance in recent years has been quite buoyant.

A major proportion of the houses' business remains the granting of instalment credit on motor cars, and this market has been affected greatly by the inflation of recent years. So much so that the FHA pressed for some relaxation of the controls on instalment credit, which they argued had remained unchanged since December 1973 (a change from one-third deposit and twenty-four months to repay to a longer repayment period). The Government's response to this was that it would simply result in more imported – particularly Japanese – cars being sold in the UK market. But some of the larger houses, Mercantile Credit, for example, have been able to implement longer term repayments.

During the high interest rate period of 1979–81, trading margins were certainly squeezed, competition was very keen and bad debts rising, yet the industry's key profits indicator, the FHA base rate, managed to fall from its excessively high level. Although there has been a trend to upgrade the amount of business written on variable rates, most of the houses' trading is dominated by fixed-rate medium-term lending, so that the trend of interest rates is crucial to profitability. In 1980 the FHA base rate was 17% on average; by September 1984 it had fallen back to 11¼%.

The pattern of new business in recent years, however, has been inconsistent. There has been a slump in industrial lending, and consumer business has made slow progress. But leasing operations have continued to grow and by September 1984 accounted for almost two-fifths of total business outstanding. The growth rate of 44% in leasing for the first quarter of 1984 over the same period for 1983 stood in marked contrast to a gain of only 8% for consumer credit, while industrial lending – which accounted for 30% of new business in the quarter (approximately the same as leasing) – dropped by 33%.

Two other factors have seriously affected the behaviour of finance houses, increasingly fierce competition and bad debts. Many industrial companies severely affected by the recession have had increasing difficulty in meeting their financial obligations and bad debts have risen markedly over recent years. Fierce competition has also forced many houses to adopt more 'cut-throat' margins on industrial lending, and some new leasing business, notably vehicle leasing, has become increasingly competitive.

Despite these pressures, profits have continued to improve as borrowing costs decline, but the existence of these pressures has forced the houses to write a greater proportion of variable rate business. By September 1984, as much as 30% of the industry's business was indexed, which should reduce the cyclical variation in future profits. Finally the relaxation of hire purchase terms announced in 1983 is likely to have a beneficial effect on their future performance.

Building societies

No other sector within the financial system has experienced more rapid and spectacular growth than the building societies. With a tradition going back as far as 1775, when the first building society on record was founded in Birmingham, they have expanded rapidly in this century, especially since 1960. Between 1921 and 1965 their shares and deposits grew 9.7% p.a.; between 1921 and 1939 the rate of growth was 12.3% p.a. More than two million new houses were bought with building society loans between 1919 and 1939. The next major expansion came in the 1960s: shares and deposits, and mortgages outstanding, multiplied more than five times during the period 1960 to 1973. They lent more than £5,000 million in 1975, £6,000 million in 1976 and more than £20,000 million in 1984.

Another noteworthy development has been the growth in the average size of the societies. There is a large size range, and with the 160 or so members of the Building Societies Association currently holding 99% of the total assets of the movement, there must be several too small for efficient operation. In 1984, out of the 217 building societies operating, the five biggest (with assets exceeding £2,000 million each) held 56% of total assets; the biggest thirty-six held 90%. There were 109 societies with assets of less than £2,000,000, and whose total assets were only 0.1% of the total. At the end of 1984 the combined assets of the two largest societies, the Halifax and the Abbey National, were between a quarter and a third greater than the entire assets of the National Savings movement (excluding Trustee Savings Banks). Economies of scale are, however, limited. Ghosh (1974) writes that there are few economies in management expenses once assets rise above £1,000,000, and the lowest total costs per £100 of assets are found in the £1 million to £10 million asset range. But there were wide differences between individual societies in the same size group. It seems, therefore, that efficiency is not to any important degree a function of size.

Liabilities

The major liability (around 93% in 1984) of the building societies is to their depositors and shareholders. A deposit is a loan to the society, and in the event of liquidation depositors rank as creditors, with priority over shareholders for repayment. Shareholders enjoy limited liability; they hold the equity of the society and therefore have no guarantee of repayment of their investment if the society becomes insolvent. These are the only resemblances to shares in a company. A building society does not have fixed share capital, does not make public issues or placings of specific numbers of shares, and its shares are not transferable. It is not a profit-making institution, but does acquire surpluses in which it puts to reserve. One becomes a shareholder by opening a share account, in exactly the same way as one would open a deposit account. There will usually be a small minimum initial shareholding, and the maximum for any one person is currently £20,000.

In practice, a shareholding is merely another kind of deposit, carrying a slightly higher (usually $\frac{1}{4}$% or $\frac{1}{2}$%) rate of interest but a lower priority for repayment in the event of liquidation. Share accounts also have a longer minimum notice of withdrawal than deposit accounts, but in practice withdrawals are allowed on demand or at very short notice. About 97% of lenders to building societies take shareholdings. Currently share funds dominate deposit funds in the ratio of about 29:1. Interest on both types of account is paid net of tax; the society pays tax on the gross interest but at less than the standard rate. There are two hidden subsidies here: first a subsidy from those depositors who do not pay tax at the standard rate to those who do. Second, a subsidy to borrowers; without the tax concession the societies would have to pay higher rates to attract funds and hence charge higher rates to borrowers.[4] There is also tax relief on the interest element in repayments of mortgage loans if the loan does not exceed £30,000, though this only applies to one mortgage, not more than one.

Many accounts are short term, but many people use their building society account for long-term saving and these accounts are second only to insurance as a vehicle for personal saving. Most building societies offer fixed-term shares and contractual saving schemes at higher rates of interest, and participate in the Save As

You Earn scheme. More than a hundred societies have joined with insurance companies to offer life insurance linked with 'building society bonds' or monthly investments in the society over the life of the policy.

Assets

Around 80% of the building societies' assets are mortgage loans, and currently they undertake about 80% of all lending for house purchase. Most mortgages are secured on owner-occupied houses, but they also lend on shops, blocks of flats, rented property, farms and industrial premises. The period of the loan is usually between twenty and thirty years, but since at any time total debt will consist mainly of 'old' loans at various stages of repayment and most mortgages are repaid before their full term (usually because the mortgagee has sold his house), the average life of outstanding mortgages is usually less than ten years. Most societies advance up to 80% of their own (usually conservative) valuation of the property, or up to 95% if the borrower can provide additional collateral. However, more recently 100% loans have become common as the societies try to live with competition from the banks in the mortgage market. The building societies also lend to the privately organised, non-profit-making mutual housing societies up to 50% of the cost of their projects. A small proportion of their loans is to property developers to finance house-building.

All assets other than mortgages and their own fixed assets – land and buildings and equipment, constituting about 1% of total assets – are classed as liquid assets. These include cash in hand, bank deposits, and public sector securities. Building societies have been subject to supervision since 1836, but their legal requirements were not affected by Competition and Credit Control. The form and maturity structure of their assets is regulated, under the Building Societies Act of 1962, by the Chief Registrar of Friendly Societies.

He specifies the kinds of security to be held as liquid assets and their maturity structure, i.e. the proportion in which different maturities shall be held. Societies must also observe a minimum ratio, $7\frac{1}{2}$%, of net liquid assets, as defined, to total assets. In fact, their liquidity ratio has for some years ranged between 16% and 20%; and in July 1984 it was 18.1%. They must also maintain a further minimum ratio, the reserve ratio, defined as the ratio of general reserves, plus balances carried forward, to total assets; this varies according to the size of assets and ranges from $2\frac{1}{2}$% on the first £100 million down to $1\frac{1}{4}$% on assets in excess of £1,000 million.

These liquid and other reserves are held against possible losses on mortgages or investments, and to maintain lenders' confidence. In fact, such losses have so far been negligible, and it is doubtful if many depositors and shareholders know what their society's ratios are. In any case, the minimum ratio is not big enough to meet a panic rush to withdraw shares and deposits. Cash in hand and bank deposits vary widely as a percentage of total assets: in 1972 it ranged from 8.3% for societies with less than £1 million assets to 1.6% for those with more than £250 million assets. At the end of 1984 the overall average was about 5.4%. A reduction in the reserve and liquidity ratios would enable the societies to lend more, probably with a smaller

91

difference between their borrowing and lending rates since fewer assets would be in a non-earning or low-yield form. This is an argument in favour of amalgamation, in view of the lower cash ratios of the big societies.

The interest-rate problem

The primary function of the building society movement is to provide finance for the purchase of property, especially houses for owner-occupation. The advantages of the modern society are that on the one hand the borrower can obtain funds to buy a house immediately and repay over several years and, on the other hand, it offers a safe interest-bearing asset to savers whatever the purpose of their saving. The depositors and shareholders who supply the funds are, by and large, not the borrowers who use them. They are the most important lenders in this area, holding 80% of the outstanding debt for house purchase in 1984.

They are also important financial intermediaries, administering in 1984 funds of more than £80,000 million, collecting the savings of millions of surplus spenders and putting them to productive use, and converting an illiquid primary security (the mortgage) into a liquid asset for depositors and shareholders which offers all the benefits of security, convenience and expert management. They dominate their market as lenders, but as borrowers they have several competitors: savings bank accounts and other forms of National Savings, deposit accounts at the banks, unit trusts, gilt-edged securities and industrial debentures and shares. We may assume that of these the strongest competitors are the closest substitutes, namely safe fixed-return assets. Their deposits and shares do have certain characteristics likely to attract the small saver: virtually complete security, a high degree of liquidity, ease and convenience of deposit and withdrawal, and the fact that regular payments into an account are a convenient way to accumulate funds for the down-payment on a house and probably give the depositor some priority for a mortgage loan when funds are scarce. Nevertheless, the societies' ability to attract funds seems to depend significantly on keeping their rates in line with those offered by competing assets. Their net receipts (new deposits minus withdrawals) have fluctuated not only with changes in total personal saving but also with changes in their rates relative to those offered by other channels for savings. They also seem to change with the fortunes of the Stock Exchange; building society managers say that people withdraw funds when share prices are rising and put them back when they are bearish about shares.[5] Their relative rates fluctuate because they are slow to change their absolute rates. This is because their lending rates change infrequently, and the main reason for this is their reluctance to alter the rates charged to existing borrowers; a change either way is expensive to administer and a rise in the rate is obviously likely to be embarrassing and worrying to borrowers. Further, most mortgage contracts oblige the lender to give three months' notice of change in the rate.[6]

Although they are non-profit-making enterprises, they must, like any other firm, also avoid losses if they are to stay in business. As a result, the rates they pay as borrowers are closely geared to the rates they earn as lenders. The rates they offer are, therefore, also sticky; changes in them lag behind changes in other rates. Professor Revell (1973: 385) notes that from January 1955 to April 1971, bank rate changed thirty-seven times; and seven of these affected either deposits only or mortgages only. The consequence is that they tend to lose funds in periods of rising interest rates, and vice versa. There is a further lag – about six months on average – between changes in their net receipts and changes in their net lending; in the interval they appear to offset the resultant dearth or glut of new funds by drawing on or accumulating liquid assets. But these reserves have in recent years been inadequate to offset large inflows and outflows, and this has led to alternating gluts and shortages of mortgage loans. Indeed, at times, they have been accused of exacerbating the rise in house prices by lending too freely; this was so in 1972–73. Yet in February/March 1974, they suffered a net outflow of funds, and in April the Government made them a short-term loan of £500 million.

Competition with the banks

In recent years, commentators have tried to assess the extent to which expansion in the activities of building societies has been at the expense of the clearing banks. Some have argued that in terms of tax advantages, prudential regulation and the impact of monetary policy, the building societies have enjoyed preferential treatment by the Government. There is no doubt that during the 1960s and 1970s at least, the building societies went from strength to strength, and Table 5.1 presents some indicators of this. Total funds lodged with the societies stood at £5 billion at the end of 1965; by the end of 1984 the figure was over £86 billion. In 1950 the building societies had less than 10% of funds in the personal sector, while the National Savings movement, the savings banks and the clearing banks shared the other 90%. By 1984 the National Savings share of the market had declined to less than 20% while the societies' share was almost half. The clearing banks' share also dropped, especially after 1971, but not to the same extent as that of the National Savings sector.

In their evidence to the Wilson Committee, the clearing banks claimed that the building societies were able to grow during these years mainly because of special privileges they enjoyed within the financial system (Benson 1978). Clearly the societies enjoy certain 'natural' advantages over the banks; they lend into a favoured market, i.e. most recent governments have placed a high premium on owner-occupancy in allowing mortgage interest alone to qualify for tax relief; their business does not involve complicated services and on the whole is cheaper to operate than conventional banking business; they are open for business on Saturday mornings. However, the banks' complaints go much wider than this. What tax advantages, then, do the building societies enjoy? There are three main ones:

The *first*, and probably the most important one, is the *composite rate of tax* arrangement. This allows the building societies to discharge the basic rate tax liability of their investors without having to pay the basic rate of tax, but a reduced rate to reflect the fact that a high proportion of building society investors are not liable to pay tax. The composite rate is designed to secure for the Inland Revenue the same amount of tax as would be collected if all building society investors were separately assessed. In 1983–84 the composite rate was 25.5% compared to a basic rate of 30%. The *second* is the lower rate of *corporation tax* paid by the societies on their surpluses (40% as opposed to the standard rate of 52%). This concession only cost the Government about £35 million in 1984–85. The *third* main advantage is, of course, the tax relief on interest paid on mortgages on a principal residence (up to a maximum of £30,000) which is received whether or not the money has been borrowed from a building society. The cost of this relief in 1984–85 was estimated at around £1,750 million. There are some other advantages enjoyed; notably the absence of stamp duty on properties valued below £25,000, and the zero capital gains tax on the sale of a main residence.

The Wilson Committee, in fact, made the recommendation that the societies' preferential composite tax arrangement should be abolished, and that they should be required to pay corporation tax at the standard rate. This was in line with their view that the tax arrangements for all licensed deposit-taking institutions (LDTs) should be put on a common footing; namely, that all interest should be paid gross, with an exemption from tax at the basic rate on deposit interest received below a certain minimum level.

Table 5.1 Personal sector liquid assets, 1973–84

Period	Increase in balances during period						
	National savings	Local authority temporary debt	Deposits with monetary sector	Deposits with savings banks	Deposits with building societies	Other	Total
	(£m)	(£m)	(£m)	(£m)	(£m)	(£m)	(£m)
1973	107	80	3,407	162	2,188	−102	5,842
1974	−11	−24	2,973	62	1,969	−77	4,892
1975	423	−31	86	211	4,161	−18	4,832
1976	440	−76	1,357	475	3,301	40	5,537
1977	1,290	−40	534	633	5,932	−22	8,327
1978	1,525	30	3,222	549	4,899	35	10,261
1979	−508	74	6,353	2,433	5,833	102	14,287
1980	1,376	14	6,565	756	7,175	50	15,936
1981	6,052	19	4,165	−1,560	7,082	−24	15,732
1982	3,466	−44	4,056	—	10,294	18	17,555
1983	2,942	0	3,566	—	10,489	24	17,021
1982 Q.1	1,315	−15	586	—	1,772	−2	3,599
Q.2	393	14	2,242	—	2,520	—	5,170
Q.3	697	−29	560	—	2,693	13	3,933
Q.4	1,115	−14	605	—	3,309	7	5,022
1983 Q.1	712	14	2,329	—	1,840	−2	4,943
Q.2	617	11	1,720	—	2,050	1	4,349
Q.3	676	−20	227	—	2,587	10	3,026
Q.4	872	−5	−727	—	4,021	15	4,176
1984 Q.1	923	1	117	—	3,406		

Period Balances outstanding end-period

	National savings (£m)	Local authority temporary debt (£m)	Deposits with monetary sector (£m)	Deposits with savings banks (£m)	Deposits with building societies (£m)	Other (£m)	Total (£m)
1973	7,565	374	16,317	2,533	16,347	162	43,298
1974	7,554	350	19,290	2,595	18,316	85	48,190
1975	7,977	319	19,376	2,806	22,477	67	53,022
1976	8,417	243	20,733	3,281	25,778	107	58,559
1977	9,707	203	21,267	3,914	31,710	85	66,886
1978	11,233	233	24,489	4,463	36,609	120	77,147
1979	10,725	307	30,842	6,896	42,442	222	91,434
1980	12,101	321	37,407	7,652	49,617	272	107,370
1981	18,153	340	41,570	6,092	56,699	248	123,104
1982	21,673	296	51,685	—	66,993	92	140,668
1983	24,615	296	54,887	—	77,482	116	157,396
1982 Q.1	19,468	325	48,215	—	58,471	72	126,551
Q.2	19,861	339	50,457	—	60,991	72	131,721
Q.3	20,558	310	51,017	—	63,684	85	135,654
Q.4	21,673	296	51,622	—	66,993	92	140,676
1983 Q.1	22,385	310	53,951	—	68,833	90	145,619
Q.2	23,002	321	55,757	—	70,883	91	150,054
Q.3	23,678	301	55,530	—	73,470	101	153,080
Q.4	24,550	296	54,803	—	77,491	116	157,256
1984 Q.1	25,473	297	54,920	—	80,897		

Notes: 1. From the fourth quarter of 1979 deposits with the Trustee Savings Banks' ordinary department are included in deposits with savings banks. They were formerly included in National Savings.

2. From the first quarter of 1981 deposits with the National Savings Bank Investment account are included in National Savings. They were formerly included in deposits with savings banks.

3. Other includes deposits with other financial institutions and tax instruments. From the first quarter of 1982 tax instruments only are included.

4. The monetary sector includes, from the first quarter of 1982, the former banking sector, the trustee savings banks and some small previously non-reporting institutions. There is a slight break in the series as a result of the introduction of the new sector, and another slight break in the first quarter of 1983.

Source: *Financial Statistics*, Table 9.4.

During 1984, a number of changes in the societies' tax arrangements were announced. In February, the facility whereby the societies enjoyed relief from capital gains tax on gilt-edged securities held for more than one year was scrapped. In future, they will pay corporation tax at a rate of 40% on their gilts' profits. This move came as something of a surprise to the societies since many of the gilts they had been buying were specially created by the Bank of England to suit their needs – low-yielding stocks on which a maximum tax-free capital gain could be earned – and by March 1983 the societies owned as much as 9.4% of all tradeable gilts, most of them with a short date to maturity and a low coupon. Since 1975, the societies' share of short-dated gilts had risen from 10.6 to 23.9% in 1983 (see *The Economist*, 3 Mar. 1984: 76). Jones (1984: 42) has argued that this amendment is the first step on the way to complete equality with the banks on the amount of corporation tax paid by the societies.

Other changes announced during 1984 included the new arrangement, from April 1985 onwards, whereby bank interest will be taxed in the same way as building society interest, i.e. basic rate tax will be withheld from the interest before it is paid, and banks will hand over a large lump sum to the Inland Revenue in lieu. In addition, the Chancellor in the March 1984 Budget intimated his intention to progressively reduce corporation tax, from the present rate of 52 to 35% by 1986–87, beginning with an immediate cut to 50% in the current financial year, followed by a reduction to 45% in 1984–85 and to 40% in 1985–86.

The question remains, however, whether these proposed changes will eliminate the apparent advantages enjoyed by the building societies. The debate has gone on for some years. Leigh-Pemberton (1979), on the side of the banks, argued in favour of complete fiscal neutrality for all types of savings, with incentives offered to all institutions, or none at all. Though admitting that the disadvantages faced by the banks were to some extent alleviated by Competition and Credit Control – for example, the banks can supplement their deposits by borrowing from the wholesale markets – they can gain also from the issue of certificates of deposits; to Leigh-Pemberton these improvements have failed to materialise. This is so, because of the approximate breakdown of sterling deposits – current accounts 40%, 7-day accounts 30%, and wholesale deposits 30% – and the fact that as much as 75% of the sterling deposits are, in reality, repayable on demand or within seven days. The effect of this is that the banks' liquidity and capital requirements are much higher than those of the societies.

Another factor is that because the societies are, in essence, just mutual organisations with narrowly defined objectives, they are owned by their members. As a result, their capital is their reserves which they are concerned to maintain at a minimum level sufficient to retain trustee status. Though this varies from one society to another, the minimum reserve ratio of 3% is about half that of the banks. The banks' *free capital ratio*, which is a measure of their protection against lending risks, and is defined as capital resources minus book value of their infrastructure, has, according to Leigh-Pemberton, declined considerably since 1972, thereby leaving the banks exposed (see Fig. 5.1).

Not surprisingly, there has been some reaction to these views. Boleat (1979, 1980) and Congdon (1979) argued that additional controls on the societies would not be the solution. While agreeing with the evidence of the clearing banks to the Wilson Committee that the societies enjoyed a favoured position in the financial system, the solution was more freedom for the banks and not less freedom for the societies. As for the tax arrangements under which building societies operate, the benefits are not always assured. The composite tax facility, for example, benefits them only if those who are liable to pay tax at the basic rate are more interest-sensitive than those not

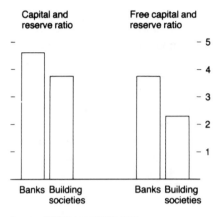

Source: *BEQB* June 1983: 218

Fig 5.1 Capitalisation of banks and building societies: 1981

liable to pay such tax. Indeed, on this question the Building Societies Association (BSA) disagreed with that part of the clearers' evidence which tried to argue that tax-paying investors are more interest-sensitive than non-tax-paying investors. In the view of the BSA, it was impossible to argue on this issue on one side or the other. Similarly, according to Boleat, the differential corporation tax had to be seen in its proper historical context. The differential came into operation in 1973 in order to prevent tax discrimination against building societies. Without it, the higher rate of tax would have been passed on to equity shareholders. Given that the societies are mutual associations, this would have meant a low level of deposits, which would have been contrary to the perceived need to increase the level of owner-occupancy in the UK.

Boleat, in a subsequent article (1983; see also Boleat 1982), reinforced these views. In a discussion of tax arrangements, he made two distinct points in defence of the building societies. The first concerned the fact that the banks pay interest on current accounts in the form of the notional interest which is used to offset bank charges. If complete equality is the objective, Boleat argued that such interest should be taxed. Of course, as Boleat himself admitted, this tax would become explicit if the banks as a whole paid out interest on current accounts. This implicit advantage which the banks enjoy was, according to the author, similar in principle to the composite tax arrangement enjoyed by the societies. The second and more substantive point concerns the arrangement on corporation tax. To Boleat, the belief that the banks pay the 52% rate was erroneous. He argued that they pay much less than this because they are able to take advantage of *leasing* arrangements. He pointed to the fact that during 1981 the average corporation tax paid by the banks was a mere 19.3%.

Boleat received some support for his views from the 1984 chairman of the BSA, Herbert Walden (see Walden 1984). He endorsed the view that the banks benefit substantially from their leasing business. This was so because the societies are not

97

only liable to pay 40%, but they actually do so, given that they have no leasing arrangements with which they could mitigate some of their tax liability. Certainly a major part of the benefits from leasing are passed to the lessees. Indeed, one study mentioned by Walden, and commissioned by the Midland Bank, calculated that as much as 80% goes to the lessees. Yet, this still represents a substantial gain to the banks, and in Walden's view probably negates any advantage enjoyed by the societies. In any case, according to Walden 'Building societies have nothing to fear from equal treatment in respect of taxation on the interest which they and the banks pay to investors . . . equality of treatment does not necessarily mean the same treatment . . .' (p. 36). Evidently, debate on these issues will continue for some time to come. However, such debate should also incorporate the wider questions of monetary policy. Once again, there are contrasting views.

Building societies and monetary policy

Bankers also criticised the Government's monetary policies for highlighting *sterling M3* as the target variable to control. This is defined as notes and coin plus sterling deposits, including CDs held by UK residents in the public and private sectors, and therefore excludes building society deposits. The societies are a significant force in the national debt market as evidenced by the fact that at the end of 1984 they held 8% of total outstanding government stock and 27% of stock with maturities of less than five years. Certainly, the societies' deposits are included in *PSL2*, which is another of the money supply variables monitored by the Bank of England (see Ch. 13), but during the 1970s, at least, sterling M3 was the important variable.

However, criticisms of monetary policy go deeper than this. For one thing, the societies were never subject to the various monetary restrictions imposed on the banks, such as the reserve assets ratio, which until its phasing out in November 1980 stood at $12\frac{1}{2}$%. Neither did they come under the Special Deposits or Supplementary Special Deposits (the 'Corset') Schemes. These, of course, have also been abolished, but their non-application to the societies when they were operated must have reduced the effectiveness of monetary policy. At least this was the view of some bankers. Indeed, one commentator (Johnson 1979) suggested that the Government adopt a new target variable, labelled *M4*, which would include building society deposits, as well as those of the savings banks, the trustee savings banks etc. Currently, as we shall see in Chapter 13, monetary policy is much more than the control of a single target variable, whether M3, M4 or PSL2, but rather involves a complex plethora of indicators as well as targets.

Nevertheless, the banks also pointed out that because building societies were traditionally subject to different prudential controls from those faced by banks, they have been able to grow at the expense of other financial institutions. The societies, for example, were never obliged to contribute to the controversial deposit protection fund which was discussed in Chapter 4.

Leigh-Pemberton, in particular, argued against the notion that the building societies' deposits required to be subsidised in these ways simply because their lending is nominally long-term. The fact is that the average period of a building society loan is not twenty years, but only about eight years, and the societies, unlike the banks, lend on the best possible security, that is property. To this extent, the bankers' case is probably a strong one. The problem has been that the perfectly valid aim of encouraging greater competition between financial institutions has invariably been confused with the objectives of overall monetary policy. Perhaps, as Leigh-Pemberton says, if the authorities had retained the spirit of Competition and Credit Control instead of becoming pre-occupied with the problem of financing a massive public sector borrowing requirement (PSBR) by the sales of government debt to the non-bank sector, some of the distortions manifest in the UK financial system would not have developed: 'there is little advantage in Britain having the best housed unemployed in Europe . . .' (1979: 10).

Another crucial issue in this debate is whether the banks lose deposits as a consequence of the intermediation services offered by building societies. There are two views on this. The 'old view' is that because building society reserves are held within the banking system, a receipt of funds by them will change the ownership of bank deposits, but not their total value. If there is a movement of funds from the banks to the societies, the extent to which the latter invest a proportion of their liquid assets in public sector debt may, however, cause the banks to lose deposits. By contrast, the 'new view' is that the banks have to recognise that the demand for bank deposits is not infinite, and therefore need to make their liabilities more attractive in order to survive. The problem, at least for the banks, is that as a financial system becomes more sophisticated, the share of bank deposits in total liquid assets tends to decline anyway. This has been true of the UK financial system. Between 1946 and 1977, for example, the ratio of London clearing bank (sterling) deposits to national income fell from 53 to 23%, while the ratio for building society deposits increased from below 10 to almost 30%.[7]

However, though the societies can (to a limited extent) create credit in the mortgage market in so far as the money they lend to housebuyers returns to them via vendors' deposits, their credit activity, by definition, has a smaller impact on the economy than that of the banks. This is so because of the vital distinction between bank deposits and building society deposits. For while the former is money (i.e. a means of payment) the latter is not, but is at best only a store of value. Boleat (1980), for example, has shown that almost 80% of the loans given by the societies are on existing dwellings, so that the bulk of their loans simply involve an exchange of assets and liabilities between individuals. How long this remains so will depend ultimately on the speed at which the societies extend their range of services within the financial system. There are already clear indications that they intend to develop a whole range of services traditionally reserved for the banks, including cheque facilities, overdraft facilities and payment by standing orders. A number of them have also installed automated teller machines (ATMs), which indicates that they have no intention of being left behind as the pace of technological progress in the financial system quickens (*BEQB*, June 1983: 216–20).

In July 1984 a Green Paper entitled 'Building societies: A new framework'

(Cmnd 9316) was published with the objective of addressing many of the above-mentioned questions. This pointed out that there was a great need to review existing legislation governing building societies. The Building Societies Act of 1962, which still regulates the activities of the societies, was considered grossly out of touch with modern developments in the UK financial system, and it was the stated intention of the Chancellor to introduce new legislation governing building societies during the duration of the present parliament. However, while envisaging a loosening of the legal restraints under which the societies had operated for more than a century, the Green Paper proposed an even more active role for them, not only in the provision of housing finance but also in the full range of money transmission services.

Of course, in the early 1980s, the details of this debate changed somewhat as it was the turn of the societies to feel the pressure of competition from the banks in the mortgage market. Bank lending for house purchase has more than doubled since 1978, and as a result the building societies' share fell from around 95% in 1977 to about 75% in 1984. One probable reason for this was the abolition of the 'Corset' in 1981 which allowed the banks to enter the mortgage market with renewed vigour (see Ch. 13). Indeed, the bank's share of the market actually went as high as 41% of formal net advances for house purchase during 1982, with the societies' share going

Table 5.2 Loans for house purchase, 1973–84

Period Net advances during period

Period	Building societies	Local authorities	Insurance companies and pension funds	Monetary sector	TSBs	Other public sector	Total
	(£m)	(£m)	(£m)	(£m)	(£m)	(£m)	(£m)
1973	1,999	355	183	310		46	2,893
1974	1,490	557	189	90		113	2,439
1975	2,768	619	150	60		133	3,730
1976	3,618	67	103	80		60	3,928
1977	4,100	4	119	120	1	18	4,362
1978	5,115	−43	73	270	5	17	5,437
1979	5,271	293	234	590	7	74	6,469
1980	5,722	461	357	500	93	251	7,384
1981	6,331	268	270	2,265	182	346	9,662
1982	8,147	554	6	5,078	−	329	14,113
1983	11,041	−306	153	3,597	−	103	14,588
1982 Q.1	1,298	223	7	1,078	−	74	2,680
Q.2	2,019	151	2	1,289	−	85	3,546
Q.3	2,139	116	−2	1,508	−	85	3,846
Q.4	2,691	64	−1	1,203	−	85	4,042
1983 Q.1	2,821	−78	−9	848	−	85	3,667
Q.2	2,828	−93	32	997	−	6	3,770
Q.3	2,607	−98	79	1,049	−	6	3,643
Q.4	2,785	−37	51	703	−	6	3,508
1984 Q.1	2,932	−19		417	−	5	
Q.2	3,977						

Period   Balances outstanding end period

	Building societies	Local authorities	Insurance companies and pension funds	Monetary sector	TSBs	Other public sector	Total
	(£m)	(£m)	(£m)	(£m)	(£m)	(£m)	(£m)
1973	14,624	1,696	1,317	1,160		159	18,956
1974	16,114	2,253	1,484	1,250		272	21,373
1975	18,882	2,872	1,533	1,310		405	25,002
1976	22,500	2,939	1,572	1,380		465	28,856
1977	26,600	2,943	1,580	1,510	10	483	33,126
1978	31,715	2,900	1,623	1,790	15	500	38,533
1979	36,986	3,193	1,854	2,380	23	574	45,010
1980	42,708	3,654	2,117	2,880	116	825	52,297
1981	49,039	3,922	2,205	5,145	298	1,171	61,780
1982	57,186	4,476	2,211	10,751	—	1,500	76,124
1983	68,227	4,170	2,364	14,238	—	1,603	90,712
1982 Q.1	50,337	4,145	2,211	6,751	—	1,245	64,446
Q.2	52,356	4,296	2,212	8,040	—	1,330	67,992
Q.3	54,495	4,412	2,210	9,548	—	1,415	71,838
Q.4	57,186	4,476	2,208	10,751	—	1,500	76,124
1983 Q.1	60,007	4,398	2,199	11,559	—	1,585	79,791
Q.2	62,835	4,305	2,231	12,596	—	1,591	83,561
Q.3	65,442	4,207	2,310	13,645	—	1,597	87,204
Q.4	68,227	4,170	2,364	14,238	—	1,603	90,712
1984 Q.1	71,159	4,151		14,655	—	1,608	
Q.2	75,136						

Notes: 1. The figures for insurance companies and pension funds are less reliable than those for other institutions.
2. The monetary sector incudes, from the first quarter of 1982, the former banking sector, the trustee savings banks, and some small previously non-reporting institutions.

Source: *Financial Statistics*, Supplementary Tables, and Table 9.2.

as low as 47%. Since 1982, there has been something of a retreat by the banks with their overall loans reduced by half (see Table 5.2).

Activity in the index-linked national savings market has also presented the societies with fresh challenges in recent years. During 1981, for example, the Treasury, struggling with an unbalanced equation of an increasing PSBR, a gilt-edged market which was approaching saturation level and rising world interest rates, decided to eat into £1 billion of personal savings by offering an index-linked national savings contract for the over-sixties, the so-called 'granny bonds'. Later the age limit was scrapped altogether as the Government attempted to raise another £3½ billion. These initiatives proved threatening to the societies, and further issues of National Savings Certificates in 1983 and 1984 seriously affected the societies' receipts. A recent example of this was in September 1984 when the Post Office decided to withdraw its 28th issue of certificates, to the great relief of the societies. Though this had proved successful in the Government's objective of taking in a large portion of the £3,000 million required to help finance the 1984–85 PSBR (indeed, in the first five

101

weeks of its existence £800 million was received), to the societies it was extremely threatening, as indicated by the fact that during August 1984 they took in just £133 million, as opposed to the £800 a month required every month to satisfy mortgage demand. The alternative would have been another rise in mortgage interest rates which, following on the heels of the major 2½–3% rise announced during the summer, would have been a body blow to borrowers, not to mention the Government in its continued fight against inflation (see Table 5.3).

Table 5.3 Financing of the PSBR from the OFI and personal sectors £ billions: 1983 prices

	1973–77*	1978–82*	1982	1983
Contributions to the PSBR				
Central government	+12.2	+12.5	+8.3	+14.4
Local authorities	+ 3.5	+ 1.0	−2.2	− 2.4
Public corporations	+ 1.9	− 0.5	−0.9	− 0.4
PSBR	+17.6	+13.0	+5.2	+11.6
Financing the PSBR				
Purchases of BGS by:				
OFIs	+ 5.7	+ 7.4	+4.9	+ 6.7
Personal sector	+ 2.0	+ 1.8	+1.3	+ 1.3
National savings (personal sector)	+ 1.0	+ 2.9	+3.7	+ 2.9
All other financing	+ 8.9	+ 0.9	−4.7	+ 0.7
of which, purchases of commercial bills by the Issue Department	− 0.1	− 1.7	−5.0	+ 0.7

* Annual averages

Source: *BEQB*, June 1984: 212

Yet, like many of the financial institutions discussed in this chapter, the building societies are likely to survive these threats to their dominance by adapting to the changed environment. Already some of the larger ones have taken the lead. Abbey National, itself hardly under threat, declared its intention of trying to 'raise the cheapest housing finance through retail selling' and the organisation of a sales team to look into new channels of advertising. Other innovations by Abbey National include the High Option Bond Scheme, offering a one-year term guaranteeing a 1% differential over the share rate on a minimum investment of £25,000, and the 40 + bonds which with a minimum investment of £500 on a ten-year term loan will guarantee 2% over the share rate. Abbey also launched its own 'Granny Bonds' in October 1980 to compete directly with the Government's, offering people over the age of 60 an extra 3% interest. In the first three tranches issued, an inflow of more than £450 million was secured[8] (McLachan 1981).

The societies have also departed from convention by making approaches to the money markets in the City. Alliance started this by issuing a 'yearling bond' in September 1980, and was followed by four of the smaller societies who raised £100 million through the money market. By far the most innovative measure however, was the application by Nationwide in July 1981 to the Bank of England for permission to issue six-monthly certificates of deposit for about £25 million. In addition, Nationwide's negotiable bond was given trustee status by the Inland Revenue, and by December 1981 was the only one of its kind on the secondary market carrying a full stock exchange quotation. By then the society had raised £30 million. Coupons of those already on the market ranged from 14 to 16%, and an issue of October 1981 offered a particularly attractive rate at 16%. The bonds are issued at par with a one-year life, and can be bought through a stockbroker for as little as £1,000. The big question, of course, is who will actually make secondary markets for such instruments?

During 1983–84 the societies engaged in a series of initiatives which commentators believe will make them look more and more like the clearing banks, against whom they have been competing so aggressively. In September 1983, for example, the five leading societies hoped to regain some lost ground by issuing two-year term shares. These paid a guaranteed $1\frac{3}{4}$% above the ordinary share rate, but were available only for a limited period sufficient to attract an additional £1 billion to help reduce the existing mortgage queues. Other moves included the introduction by the Nationwide of depositors' Access cards; the Abbey National cheque facility with the Co-op bank, and a similar arrangement between the Alliance and the Bank of Scotland; and possibly the most adventurous move to date in the offer by the Nottingham Building Society of home banking services with the cooperation of the Bank of Scotland. The Halifax meanwhile, has launched its own ATM with the installation of Cardcash machines in early 1985. Finally, there have been fresh moves into the wholesale money markets with the objective of tapping large corporate as well as private deposits. The Finance Bill of 1983 made it possible for the societies to issue Certificates of Deposits, so making it possible for them to obtain funds at rates comparable to those which the banks can borrow. The 1985 Budget also gave the societies permission to pay interest gross to non-residents who are not able to reclaim composite-rate tax and to pay interest on Eurobonds to non-residents without withholding tax. The Halifax was the first to take advantage of this concession with a £150 million Eurobond issue in September 1985.

Whether these moves provide more stability in the societies' monthly receipts is the crucial issue. During 1983, average monthly receipts were £700m which left them with substantial shortfalls for most of the year. The same probably applies to 1984, though the previously mentioned interest rate increases reversed this to some extent.

Despite these developments the societies have not been immune from criticism. Some of the larger ones particularly have been attacked for encouraging a proliferation of new schemes. If the smaller societies attract too much high-cost money, they may find themselves in difficulty if there is a change in market conditions. Also under attack has been the *recommended rate cartel*. The Wilson Committee said that this arrangement protected inefficient societies and encouraged them to engage in wasteful *non-price competition* in areas like the number of branches. Because the recommended rate responds slowly to changes in prevailing interest rates, the consequence is invariably a recurrent feast and famine in mortgage lending, and so the committee recommended that it should be abolished. Real competition between the societies and other financial institutions, it argued, would only be achieved if the automatic link between the rates paid to depositors and those charged to borrowers was broken. The cartel, in fact, collapsed in 1983 after a revolt led by Abbey National, and this probably implies even fiercer competition with banks in the years ahead.

Where then can the societies go from here? Have they, in a sense, been too successful for their own good? With upwards of 25 million people holding deposits at building societies, three times as many as in 1970, possibly the only avenue of growth is if they continue to become more and more like banks and other financial institutions, competing aggressively for all types of savings, large and small. In the end the personal saver can only benefit from more competition.

Probably the real solution is for greater diversity in the arrangements for providing housing finance. Britain, in fact, is unusual in the extent to which building societies dominate housing finance, with upwards of 80% of all outstanding housing loans. By contrast, in Canada six different types of institutions each have between 10 and 20% of outstanding loans. Also in some European countries, a variety of arrangements exist for house purchase, ranging from the 'saving for building' scheme in West Germany, France and Austria, where banks and other institutions agree to provide a housing loan once the saver has built up a previously agreed sum, usually over a period of two to four years; to the mortgage bond which with a specified maturity and interest rate operates in West Germany and in the Scandinavian countries. Variation also exists as far as the length of the loan is concerned. In Britain loans are offered up to twenty-five years (and in some cases up to thirty years as the societies try to offset the effects of high interest rates in the economy generally). In France, the maximum is fifteen years, and in West Germany ten to twelve years. In addition, in some countries mortgage rates, which are traditionally sticky here anyway, are fixed for the duration of the loan (e.g. America's S and L scheme). Of course, with inflation, fixed-rate mortgages are not really acceptable, but compromise arrangements are possible. In the USA new mortgages are sometimes reviewed after two years, and to benefit first-time buyers there is a scheme to 'index' the capital value of the loan to some measure of inflation which would allow lenders to charge a lower nominal interest rate. The initial payments would be lower and though they would rise over time would stay constant in real terms.[9] A similar arrangement, a 'low-start' mortgage, was set up in Canada in 1978 with annual payments rising during the first ten years. Ultimately, of course, the lenders may not be too enthusiastic about such schemes, as they will inevitably involve the acceptance of lower interest rates at the beginning in return for higher rates later on, but this is probably where government subsidisation of the housing market can be truly non-discriminatory, and yet still encourage owner-occupancy.

Insurance companies

Insurance is essentially a collective protection against the risk of financial embarrassment or loss. An insurance company collects premiums from thousands of policy-holders to provide a fund out of which it compensates those policy-holders who suffer the loss against which all have insured. To ensure that the fund will be adequate to meet all the losses, the ratio of premiums to benefits is determined by calculating, on the basis of past experience, the degree of risk involved, i.e. the probability of loss. The policy-holder can thus 'substitute certainty for uncertainty'; for a fixed premium payment he is protected against an uncertain, but potentially much greater, loss.

Insurance business is classified into life, and non-life or general, insurance. We can take insurance against almost any conceivable kind of calculable risk, but the main categories of general insurance are property; marine, aviation and transport; motor vehicle; personal accident and sickness; and third-party liability including employer's liability. Life insurance is of three kinds: (1) *Term assurance*, under which benefit is paid only if the insured person dies within the term of the policy; (2) *Whole-life*, in which the benefit is payable on death only; and (3) *Endowment*, in which the benefit is payable at the end of a fixed number of years (the term of the policy) or at earlier death. Endowment policies may be 'without profits', which pay a fixed guaranteed benefit, or 'with profits' which offer a smaller guaranteed benefit plus bonuses which depend on the success of the insurance company's investment policy. In the 1960s, a new type of policy appeared, the 'unit-linked' policy, under which premiums were invested in a named unit trust or property bond, or a separate investment fund managed by the company itself. The Industrial Life Offices write life insurance policies sold through various channels, and substantial amounts of general insurance. They account for about half the total regular premium life insurance not covered by group schemes. The Prudential is easily the biggest industrial office and the biggest life office.

Life assurance enjoyed a major tax concession in the personal relief given for qualifying premiums up to a limit of the greater of £1,500 or one-sixth of an individual's total income. The 1984 Budget abolished this. Previously relief was given directly, with premiums paid by the policy-holder net of a deduction of 15% (from April 1981). (The benefit was also given to those below the tax threshold.) The insurance companies then reclaimed the appropriate amount from the Inland Revenue, which during 1979–80 was estimated as £430 million. In general, the Wilson Committee was against the special encouragements given to long-term contractual savings and life assurance (and pension funds) in particular, and suggested that the tax relief given to life assurance premiums should be extended to cover any other form of contractual medium- or long-term savings.

There are a large number of insurance companies authorised to carry on business in the UK, many of them incorporated overseas and many of them authorised to carry on more than one type of business. In 1984, there were 330 companies authorised to carry out ordinary long-term insurance business (and twelve authorised to carry out industrial life insurance together with fifty-five collecting friendly societies). All of this number were authorised to carry out each of the seventeen types of general business distinguished by the Department of Trade (though many of the individual companies that received permission formed part of larger groups). In addition, many trade unions provide life and/or sickness insurance for their members. Some of the companies are 'mutual offices', whose profits go to the policy-holders and who should, in theory, be able to offer lower premiums or higher benefits if they invest their funds as successfully as the commercial companies. They conduct more than 25% of the life business and 10% of general assurance. Finally, there is Lloyds, the 300-years-old insurance market responsible for most marine insurance, where one can insure almost any thing against almost any kind of disaster with any of the 17,000 underwriting agents of one of the 360 or so 'syndicates' of wealthy men who put up the money to cover the risks.

The investment requirements of the general funds differ from those of the life funds. Most of their liabilities are short-term since most policies can be cancelled or renewed annually, and most premiums are held for only a short time before being paid out in claims, expenses, taxes and profits. The main characteristic of their investment must be quick and easy marketability. Most holders of whole-life endowment policies, on the other hand, enjoy a normal life-span and their premiums accumulate over several years. The accumulating funds are invested to produce an income out of which to pay bonuses (one of the companies' main instruments of competition) on with-profit policies and offer guaranteed returns on without-profit policies. For most of their customers, the policy is an investment as well as an insurance. In 1984 the Life Funds' income from assets was equal to more than 50% of their premium receipts, and more than two-fifths of their total income was added to their assets. At the end of 1984, total long-term funds had a market value of almost £84 billion. The general insurance companies, whose total annual premiums exceed those of the life offices, had funds of over £17 billion.

There is a sizeable degree of concentration in the British insurance industry. The Wilson Committee reported that in terms of assets the nine largest companies (on a group basis), each with total assets of more than £1¼ billion, accounted for 45% of the total assets held at the end of 1978. In addition, there were a further fifty-two companies with assets larger than £100 million (as well as fifty-eight pension funds of at least this size). The Wilson Committee suggested that increasing institutionalisation of savings was a cause for concern, especially because the larger companies often have several quite separate funds controlled by separate managers and pursuing different objectives, though based on common assessments of the prospects for individual companies etc. However, excessive concentration was not a feature highlighted by the committee as a source of concern. Similarly for the same year the ten largest insurance groups accounted for 61% of UK premiums for general business and 52% of those for long-term business. The committee noted that for big companies, with 1973 as the first year for which comparable figures are easily available, this represented a decrease in concentration in the former and an increase in the latter. Indeed, it was believed that over the long run, in both general and long-term business, small- and medium-sized companies have been increasing their market shares at the expense of the larger groups. At the same time the larger groups who used to concentrate either on long-term business or on general business have more recently been dividing their attention more equally between the two.

The insurance industry in the UK has been extremely versatile, and has been at the forefront in designing cover for new types of risks: re-insurance is a good example of this. Unit-linked policies have also assumed increasing importance in recent years. Essentially these are unit trusts with an element of insurance thrown in. Each premium buys a unit in either a unit trust or a special fund; and a small proportion of each premium also buys a modest amount of life assurance cover. Obviously, investments in unit trusts are riskier than an endowment policy, but the premiums can be split between a number of funds, and usually are. Units can be bought in trusts linked to commodities, from the stock exchange, property and the overseas markets. Since the abolition of exchange controls, unit trusts have exploited the new freedom to the full by offering units in many more overseas markets.[10]

Perhaps the most innovative development in recent years has been the 'loan-back option'. This allows planholders to borrow from their own pension fund, and money borrowed can then be used for any purpose. If it is for an approved purpose such as buying a house or a partnership in a business, tax relief is allowed on the loan interest payment. Interest charged on loanbacks is usually around 3% over variable bank base rates, though the amount actually credited to your fund will be $1\frac{1}{2}$ to 2% less because of deductions by the insurance companies to cover expenses and management charges. The consequence is that the fund grows at less than the short-term interest rate and, historically, returns of long-term investments are 3 to 4% higher than short-term rates. This, ultimately, will adversely affect the value of a policy.

Insurance companies as investors

The insurance companies and pension funds, especially the life offices, thus have enormous funds at their disposal, to which billions of pounds are added every year. In 1982 the insurance companies incorporated in the UK received £11,053 million in premiums derived from all territories, and this represented a more than 14.5% increase over 1981. Prudential is said to be Britain's largest single investor. Many of the premiums, especially at Lloyds, are paid by non-residents and in 1984 insurance services made the biggest single contribution to net invisible exports (around 50%). Each company must, in the interests of policy-holders and shareholders, and to meet competition from other insurers, put its premiums to profitable use. They lend on mortgage, buy public and private sector fixed-interest stocks, ordinary shares and property. They are, collectively, the biggest investors in the capital market, the most important of the 'institutional investors'. Their influence has been growing fast during recent years; for example, whereas in 1973 the Diamond Commission estimated that insurance companies and pensions funds together accounted for 28.4% of UK listed equities, by 1984 this figure was around 40%.

Traditionally, the insurance companies look for stability of income and security of capital in their investments, rather than a high return. The post-war inflation, and intense competition in the market for the increasingly popular with-profits policies whose bonuses offer some hedge against inflation, have led them to invest more heavily in assets which are likely to maintain their real value, especially equities and property. The distribution of assets varies widely from one company to another, but the average proportion invested in ordinary shares was 3% in 1927, 10% in 1947, 22.5% in 1976 and 28.3% in 1984. The proportion invested in real property was 17% in 1976 and 23.5% in 1984. Since 1959, equities have in fact been the biggest single item in the insurance companies' portfolios. But ordinary shares and property still make up on average around two-fifths of their total assets and one-third of their annual investment. One might have expected them to seek more protection against inflation. The main reason they have not done so is that many of their liabilities to policy-holders are expressed in fixed money terms and fall due regularly and, for the most part, predictably. This is, to a large extent, true of the with-profits endowment policies as well as policies with no bonus element. When a company declares a bonus for the year of 4%, for example, on a £1,000 policy, it promises to pay the policy-holder £40 some years hence, in addition to the guaranteed £1,000, whatever happens to the company's income and assets in the interval. It is still important, therefore, to try to secure an assured income and match the maturities of assets to the maturities of liabilities. Another reason is that they are such large investors that their investment policy must depend partly on the relative supplies of different assets; to buy heavily in the equity market at a time when ordinary shares are in comparative short supply, perhaps because there is a dearth of new issues or because the market in general is bullish, is likely to drive up prices and reduce their prospective yields. Their investment policies do, in fact, show much flexibility both within the year and from year to year; they switch quite heavily between investments according to changes in relative supply and relative prospective returns as they see them.

Investment income is obviously heavily influenced by variations in the level of interest rates as well as by fluctuations in sterling. Thus in 1976 the portfolio invest-ment income of the companies and Lloyd's rose by almost 35% at a time when interest rates in many industrialised countries were rising and sterling was very weak. In contrast, during 1977, when interest rates in several countries were lower at least for part of the time, and sterling improved, especially against the dollar, the combined portfolio investment income dropped by 14%. Since 1979 as sterling has fluctuated in value considerably the companies have been subject to the inevitable repercussions. However, the abolition of exchange controls has come to their aid. In the short term a fall in the pound increases the sterling value of overseas earnings, providing they are not offset by higher sterling costs. While this benefits those who have claims payable in foreign currency, over the longer run there can be adverse effects on those who have to make foreign payments out of sterling resources. When exchange controls were operated this caused problems, as insurers were unable to convert assets from sterling into foreign currencies in order to match fully their overseas liabilities, and were thereby exposed to an exchange risk.

Most parts of the insurance business have, however, been facing increasing competition, and as the 'Committee on Invisible Exports' in their evidence to Sir Harold Wilson argued, the companies have had to put up with restrictive policies in many overseas countries, including nationalisation and requirements that insurance should be placed with local companies. Fortunately for the insurance companies, this has not affected total earnings too much, as the capacity of local markets in developing countries is limited and much of the direct business written there has been re-insured on the international market.

Pension funds

These are similar to life assurance funds to the extent that they are primarily concerned with long-term liabilities, and therefore require to accumulate a substantial fund to cope with these liabilities as they mature. Pensions enjoy special tax status, more so indeed than any other form of savings. All contributions to pension schemes are relieved of tax and pension funds pay no tax either on income or capital gains. Pensions are, however, taxed when they are paid out, though they are not classed as unearned income but earned income. The reason for this is that pensions are considered a type of deferred income. Every employed person in the UK will retire on some sort of pension though often it will not live up to expectations. The state pension scheme provides for a maximum pension of $1\frac{1}{2}$ times average earnings which for many high-rate tax payers will be substantially below final salary levels.[11]

Company pension schemes usually offer a pension equivalent to two-thirds of final salary, but the problem is that to enjoy the maximum pension employees have to be in the same scheme for forty years. Some employees try to supplement their schemes. One tax-efficient method is through additional voluntary contributions (AVCs). Under this scheme an employee can pay up to 15% of his gross salary (less any contribution to his employer's main scheme), with all contributions being tax-free. For the self-employed it is a different story, and on the whole they have to make their own arrangements to top up their state pensions. Since the 1980 Finance Act the self-employed have been able to contribute up to $17\frac{1}{2}$% of so-called relevant earnings (that is gross taxable earnings) to a pension scheme and receive full tax relief on their contribution. Prior to this the upper limit was £3,000 a year.

As far as the use to which pension funds are put the objective, clearly, must be to use contributions to acquire assets with a high degree of security and a return compatible with the rate of wage inflation. The other problem, of course, is for pensions currently in payment to be increased to compensate for cost of living increases. The Wilson Committee reported the results of a recent (1979) analysis of 440 pension schemes, which showed that a high proportion (68% of the 395 private sector schemes) made some provision for discretionary pension increases, to compensate, albeit partially, for cost of living increases. On average, discretionary provisions amounted to almost 60% of the increase in retail prices over the previous five years. There was, however, significant variation between different schemes. The remaining forty-five schemes in the public sector gave increases which matched increases in the cost of living.

During the 1950s and 1960s the bulk of pension funds were invested in equities which at first proved lucrative as the return on equities was consistently higher than both the return on gilt-edged stocks and the increase in retail activity (Pratten 1979). More recently, with the poor performance in the company sector and severe inflation, the return from equities, allowing for capital values, has failed to keep ahead of the rise in prices. Short-term movements in the value of equities do not, however, have any direct impact on the variability of pension funds, since the funds, at least until they reach maturity, have a steady inflow of revenue and are therefore not constrained by the need to sell their assets at any particular date. The variability of pension funds, then, will depend upon the income from their assets keeping pace with inflation, that is the real rate of return on their assets over the long run, and not merely upon a composite return which takes capital values into account at the end of a particular fixed period. It is when inflation is unpredictable that the financing of pension funds is made difficult because providing accurately for liabilities that lie far into the future is inevitably more problematic.

Currently over half of the pension funds assets are in the form of company securities (around 90% of which are equities), with most of the rest in government stocks and in property. Funds have been increasing their holdings in gilts and other fixed-interest stocks in recent years because of the very high yields obtainable, and as long as interest rates remain high and the yield differential between gilts and equities also stays high, this trend is likely to continue.

However, in the same way as the building societies' own success seems to have been too much for them to cope with, so also with the pension funds. Indeed, at the end of the 1970s there was a fear that a money mountain would appear with too much money chasing too few investments, and few equities available. Leaders in the field, however, have argued that this need not happen as long as the market is allowed to operate freely with yields adjusting to ensure equilibrium. The pension funds, of course, have been under attack from industry for withholding equity funds from UK manufacturing industry, and this indeed was one of the issues that the Wilson Committee was set up to examine. In its deliberations the committee exonerated the institutions, but for a time there was talk of 'force-feeding' capital into industry through direction of industry via a central fund (Bain 1983).

The insurance companies and pensions funds are quantitatively the most important financial intermediary. They finance about one-fifth of total net fixed investment, and they collect, pool and invest or on-lend a bigger proportion of personal savings than any other category of financial institutions. Additionally, among all the financial institutions, insurance companies are the largest holders of UK government securities (around 30% of total non-official holdings at the end of 1984) with the pension funds coming next (at around 16%). In ordinary shares the pension funds are the largest holders with approximately 40% of listed UK ordinary shares at the end of 1984, with the insurance companies next at around 18%. Inevitably, this accumulation of securities has brought the institutions to the dominant position they hold today within the financial markets. They have, indeed, enjoyed phenomenal growth over the last twenty years, with their assets in aggregate rising from £7 billion at the end of 1957 to around £190 billion at the end of 1984, and even allowing for increases in inflation this involves a vast increase. And though this growth was less than the expansion in the inflow of savings into the building societies and banks over the same period, unlike the latter the major part of the life and pension funds are invested in long-term securities markets, so much so that the Wilson Report said that their increasing dominance of both the gilt-edged and equity markets was one of the most important developments in the financial system since the time of the Radcliffe Report.

Investment trusts

An investment trust, the first of which was established in the 1870s, is not a trust in the legal sense; its assets are not held by a trustee to whom the administrators of the trust are responsible for their management. It is rather a public company which raises capital by the issue of debentures and shares to the public, and the only way one can participate in an investment trust is by subscribing to such an issue or by purchasing shares on the secondary market, the Stock Exchange. An investment trust is thus a 'closed-end' trust, whereas a unit trust is 'open-ended'. An investment trust is forbidden by law to buy back its own shares. Some trusts are managed by specialist investment trust management companies, some of whom also manage unit trusts; several are off-shoots of firms of stockbrokers and merchant banks.

The funds acquired are used to buy holdings of a wide variety of securities. At the end of 1984, there were 200 investment trusts making returns to the Bank of England and about thirty smaller trusts which did not make returns. At the end of 1957, total assets held by investment trust companies were valued at £1.1 billion, and these assets grew rapidly during the 1960s, though they have shown little growth in the 1970s. In fact, the Wilson Committee reported that over the period 1973–77 the investment trusts made net disposals of assets. About 83% of the £14.2 billion of assets held at the end of 1984 by companies making returns were ordinary shares, about 3% were loan stock and preference shares, and most of the remainder was short-term fixed interest assets.[12] These portfolios are highly diversified: not more than 15% of their assets can be invested in any one company and a large trust may have up to 400, or even more, blocks of shares and loan stocks. The Wilson Committee reported that a much wider proportion than the permitted maximum of 15% was held in unlisted company securities. At the end of 1984 the nine largest management groups together managed sixty-eight investment trust companies, accounting for around 47% of the total funds under management.

They acquire shares on the Stock Exchange by subscribing to new issues and taking up 'placings' of shares, and some of them underwrite new issues and acquire some of their shareholdings in that way. They do not engage in short-term speculation, but neither do they hold shares in perpetuity. Like most investors, they switch between investments according to their changing views of the prospects for particular securities and for the market in general.

The revenue of an investment trust is the interest and dividends on these assets. From this revenue the managers of the trust deduct their management fee and expenses, which together range from about 0.1 to 0.5% p.a. of the value of the assets. A small proportion – not more than 15% – is usually put to reserve and the

111

remainder distributed to shareholders. Because the companies issue fixed interest debentures and preference shares, the ordinary shareholders gain from the gearing effect when income is rising, lose when it is falling. A company with a £1 million issue of 8% debentures outstanding has a fixed call of £80,000 p.a. on its revenues. Any earnings on this £1 million in excess of 8% accrue entirely to the holders of the equity of the trust. More important, probably, is the similar effect on the net asset values of the equity from changes in the capital value of its investments.

Unit trusts

A unit trust performs the same economic function as an investment trust: it pools funds subscribed by a large number of investors and uses them to buy securities. There are, however, certain important differences between them.

First, a unit trust is a trust in law, as well as in name. Like an investment trust, it is established and administered by professional managers who make a fixed percentage charge for their services, but they are required to appoint an independent trustee, usually a bank or insurance company, in whose name the assets are held and to whom the managers are responsible for the prudent and honest management of the funds. The trust is established under a trust deed, which must be approved by both the trustee and the Department of Industry. The deed stipulates among other things that the managers must retain sufficient money to cover management expenses, must publish to unit-holders regular audited accounts, must operate a satisfactory method of calculating the prices of units and their yields. Advertisements inviting the public to buy units must be approved by the trustee, who can also change the management of the trust, or veto a proposed change, if it appears to be in the best interests of the unit-holders to do so. Investment trust companies may not advertise their shares, apart from the usual announcement of new issues.

Second, the operation of a unit trust is subject to other stringent controls. The trust (as opposed to the company which manages the trust) cannot raise 'prior charge' capital, e.g. by the issue of debentures and preference shares. There are strict formulae for the calculation of management fees and the differences between the 'bid' price at which the managers will buy units and the higher 'offer' price at which they will sell them, on any day.

Third, a unit trust is not a company, raising capital by the issue of shares.

Unit trust management

They are established and administered by unit trust management companies, some of which are subsidiaries of financial institutions such as banks, insurance companies and stockbrokers.

Funds are obtained by the sale of units of the trust to the public, on request. The buyer of units acquires 'the right to participate on equal terms with other "units" in the beneficial ownership of the portfolio of securities . . . held by the trust' (Radcliffe Report, para. 278). Any member of the public can buy units at any time, either through an 'authorised agent' – a banker, stockbroker, accountant or solicitor, to whom most managements pay a commission on the sale – or direct from the trust. Units can only be bought from/sold to the managers; they are not transferable. Some trusts occasionally make 'block issues' of units; they advertise in the national press that they are offering a certain number of units, or any number of units, within a limited period, at a named price or at the price ruling on the day of purchase, whichever is the lower. A unit-holder can also require the trust managers to repurchase from him, at any time, all or any part of his holding of units. The managers thus make the market in units.

The funds invested can vary from day-to-day and without limit except insofar as the managers may have set an upper limit to the size of the trust, which is very rare. That is to say, a unit trust is 'open-ended'. The daily price of units is based on the current value of the portfolio of securities held by the trust. Thus in a trust with ten million units in issue and assets valued at £2 million, the basic price of a unit would be 20 pence. If a week later the Stock Exchange prices of the underlying assets rises by 10%, the basic price of units would be 22 pence. The bid price would be less than this; the offer price would be higher. The difference between the two prices covers the cost of buying or selling the underlying assets on the Stock Exchange (brokerage and stamp duty) and a contribution to management expenses known as the 'initial services charge', which is chargeable on all new units sold. In practice, the managers can often 'marry' purchases and sales of units without disturbing the underlying assets. It is only when there are significant net sales or net purchases that they have to buy or sell securities. In addition to the initial service charge, the managers also receive a half-yearly fee for managing the portfolio and administering the trust. Both *were* subject to strict maxima. The initial service charge was not to exceed 5% of the sum invested by the buyer of units, and this plus the half-yearly management fee, usually $\frac{1}{2}$ or $\frac{3}{16}$ of the value of the trust, up till December 1979 was not to exceed $13\frac{1}{4}\%$ of the value of the trust over a period of twenty years. From December 1979, however, unit trust managers have been free to fix charges at any level.

The managers are responsible for the choice of investments, sometimes with outside expert advice. Every unit trust invests its unit-holders' funds in a diversified portfolio of securities, but the degree of diversification and the investment policy vary widely between the 350 or so trusts operating and making returns at the end of 1984. There are *general trusts*, and there are *specialised trusts* which invest in specified groups of industries, particular areas of the world or particular kinds of market 'special situation'. Some specialise in domestic securities, some in overseas; a few are invested entirely in fixed interest securities. There are trusts aiming at high yields and trusts whose main or sole object is capital appreciation. There are staid funds which make only infrequent changes in their portfolios and there are so-called 'go-go' funds whose managers inform subscribers that they intend to switch investments as often as necessary to achieve quick capital growth. There appears to be little difference, on average, between the performance records of the two kinds of trust. Most are suitable for the small saver, allowing a minimum initial purchase of £100 or less and thereafter in multiples of five or ten units; and most units are priced at less than £1.00. A few have a larger minimum initial purchase, usually from £1,500 to £2,500, offering in return a low initial service charge. Most trusts operate savings schemes for the investment of a fixed monthly sum, and many offer unit-linked insurance policies. Another difference between investment trusts and unit trusts is that the latter are not allowed to accumulate assets by putting profits to reserve. All their income from the underlying assets is, after deduction of expenses, paid out as income to unit-holders.

Unit trusts are of more recent origin than investment trusts. The first unit trust (an M and G trust) was set up in 1931. At the end of 1984, there were over 340 unit trusts making returns to the Bank of England with total assets over £11 billion; this compares with 176 trusts in 1968 with assets of £1.3 billion. There has been substantial growth in the size of unit trusts' funds over the last twenty years (in 1957, total assets amounted to £60 million) though in recent years the number of unit-holders' accounts has declined. At the end of 1984 the four largest management groups administered seventy-nine trusts with assets above £5,000 million and 51% of the total. Investment policy has changed somewhat in recent years with the proportion of assets invested in UK company securities declining and an increase in holdings of overseas company securities and short-term assets. In contrast to investment trust companies, unit trusts normally have an inflow to be invested, though there is a tendency for this to be cyclical and related to the strength of the stock market. At the end of 1984 the proportion of total assets made up by ordinary shares was almost 60% while other company securities (loan capital etc.) accounted for around 2%. The proportion taken up by cash and other short-term assets (net) was 6% (compared to 2% for the investment trusts).[13]

The unit trusts also hold gilt-edged stock and in early 1984 the Inland Revenue threatened to come down heavily on their growing numbers of 'gilt unit trusts'. Though still exempt from capital gains tax on these, the tax authorities now believe that the trusts have been 'over-trading', that is turning over their gilts portfolio at a rate faster than six times a year, and the possibility of unit trusts (just like the building societies discussed earlier) being asked to pay the full rate of corporation tax on their gilts profits is a very real one.

Investment trusts and unit trusts are in fact the typical financial intermediary. They pool thousands of comparatively small sums and use them to finance industry and government. They offer the saver a cheap and convenient means of investing in primary securities, and a non-money asset which is both income-earning and easily cashable. They offer the security of diversification, professional management and economies of scale; they increase the demand for primary securities which is also the supply of finance, and so on; all the advantages of intermediation listed on pages 62–4.

Savings banks

The final category of secondary banks is the savings banks. The major savings banks are the National Savings Bank (before 1969 known as the Post Office Savings Banks) and the Trustee Savings Banks. The POSB was founded in 1861 and the NSB is now reported to be the largest institution of its kind in the world, with deposits exceeding £6,500 million. One can deposit in, or withdraw from, one's account at any of 21,000 post offices. The first Trustee Savings Banks also appeared in the nineteenth century, and by 1984 they had 1,600 branches and held over 11 million accounts and total deposits of more than £7,000 million. Each Trustee Savings Bank is an independent institution, managed by a board of honorary trustees and salaried officials, but subject to government regulation and supervision by the National Debt Office. Both the NSB and the TSBs offer two kinds of deposit account. First there is the *ordinary account*, for which the current (1984) interest rate is 3%, paid without deduction of tax, but from April 1985 interest will become taxable. Interest rates will probably increase as a result. Rates are notoriously sticky. The rate on an ordinary account at the POSB was $2\frac{1}{2}$% from 1861 to 1970. Maximum withdrawals of £100 can be made from the NSB, but there is no longer any limit to withdrawals from TSBs. The other is the *investment account*, bearing a higher rate of interest than the ordinary account ($12\frac{1}{4}$% in February 1985). Investment accounts are subject to a minimum notice of withdrawal of seven days. The TSBs now accept deposits at three months' and six months' notice (and recently up to five years) at higher rates of interest. Tax is not deducted from interest on investment accounts at source but all interest is subject to tax. In 1983–84 the TSB introduced an interest-bearing cheque account.

Deposits in the ordinary accounts of both banks are lodged with the National Debt Commissioners, who invest them in government securities. The interest on these securities is, of course, the income out of which depositors' interest is paid. The funds of the investment accounts of the NSB are also invested in government securities by the Commissioners, and the investment policies of the trustees of the TSBs for their investment account funds are closely circumscribed by instructions issued by them. Until 1978, a minimum of 20% of the funds had to be held in assets which the regulations class as liquid. Of these, at least half were to consist of cash, temporary loans to local authorities, and marketable government and local authority stocks with not more than five years to final maturity; and the remainder to be held in local authority stocks with a life of less than one year. The other 80% had to be invested in gilt-edged stocks, local authority mortgage loans, and debentures of the Agricultural Mortgage Corporation and the Scottish AMC. Since 1978 all of these funds have become available for investment elsewhere as restrictions were eased. This should provide a challenge to them to find suitable homes for these funds. The TSBs now have a unit trust, quite separate from their banking business, which does hold private sector assets, including equities. The funds of the NSB are held in the same forms, but not necessarily in the same proportions. With far more accounts than any one TSB, it can operate with a lower degree of liquidity.

The TSBs offer a current account and cheque service. Both the NSB and the TSBs make regular payments out of an ordinary account 'by standing order'. In 1976, the TSBs began a personal loan and overdraft service. In 1975, the Central TSB joined the London Clearing House. The Trustee Savings Bank has now also become quite heavily involved in the mortgage market, although at the lower end of the market. Indeed one, the Birmingham Trustee Savings Bank, has a long history of doing this. For statistical purposes, the NSB and TSBs ordinary accounts are considered in the national financial accounts as part of central government, and deposits with these accounts are treated as directly financing the central government borrowing requirement. The NSB investment accounts and the TSB (Special Investment Department until 1976) 'new department' account are classified within the 'other financial institutions' sector, and their transactions in central government and other public sector securities are treated as part of market financing of the public sector borrowing requirement.

The *PO Giro* is quite separate from the NSB and is a means of making payments. All Giro account records are held at a central office, and one makes payment by completing the appropriate form and sending it to this office.[14] The sum named on the form is then transferred from the payer's Giro account to that of the payee, the whole process taking about three days. If the payer does not have a Giro account, he pays cash, plus a transfer fee, at any post office, for the credit of the payee. If the payee does not have a Giro account, he receives a cheque cashable at a post office. One can draw on one's Giro account on demand. No interest is paid on current accounts though it is on deposit accounts. Giro's growth has been slow; it had only about a million accounts in 1984 and the Government itself makes little use of its payments facility.[15] It was given permission to allow overdrafts in 1975.

Following the Report of the Committee to Review National Savings (the Page Committee) in 1973, legislation was introduced in 1975 under which the TSBs were, over a period of ten years from November 1976, to be gradually freed from all government control and develop a full range of banking services, including overdrafts. Partly to this end, the seventy-three TSBs amalgamated into sixteen regional banks, and in 1983 the four regional banks in Scotland merged to form TSB Scotland. In 1984, legislative plans to sell off the TSBs were fairly advanced. By then the TSB empire, which included United Dominion Trust, TSB Trustcard (Credit Card Operations) and TSB Trust Company (insurance services and unit trusts), held assets in excess of £9.5 billion.

Clearly, the money services offered by the TSBs and Giro represent a growing threat to the clearing banks. The Wilson Committee Report, as a consequence of the Page Report and the Trustee Savings Bank Act, predicted that they would evolve into a 'third force' in UK banking, providing the full range of banking services, and would ultimately be treated the same as other banks for monetary and prudential purposes. This has not quite happened so far but there is no doubt that these banks will continue to diversify their activities. For example, in addition to their consumer and house-purchase loans, they have recently become involved in the refinancing of export credits and from July 1981 have been permitted to engage in medium-term commercial lending.

Recently, their share of the market has been adversely affected by the loss of tax-free status on their savings accounts, as well as the increasing competitiveness of the High Street banks. And, though the TSBs, unlike the private sector banks, are not required to pay dividends to shareholders, the £1 billion of their funds which is tied up with the National Debt Commission earning a lowly $7\frac{1}{2}\%$ p.a. remains a great burden on them. They have also been severely constrained in their activities by a shortage of capital. Just to maintain their market share over recent years would have required their asset base to have risen by a third to £10 billion and this would have necessitated an injection of capital to the sum of £200 million.[16]

Notes

1   The Crowther Committee estimated that in 1969 the percentages of total expenditure financed by credit were: motor cars 45%, furniture 41%, radios and electrical goods 42%, clothing and footwear 20%. They also finance the hire purchase of machinery and vehicles by firms.
2   UDT closed down all its shops in 1974–75.
3   They also borrow Eurodollars switched into sterling by the banks.
4   The tax concession does not apply to tax at more than the standard rate, nor to corporate depositors and shareholders.
5   Some studies have shown that the real rate of return to building society deposits increased throughout the 1960s and most of the 1970s. Pratten (1979), in a comparison of the real rates of return for building societies deposits and equities over the period 1961 to 1978, discovered that there was a substantial negative real rate of return on building society deposits, whereas equity values kept up with inflation. Deposits, of course, can be withdrawn at their monetary value, but the fact that building society deposits grew rapidly despite high inflation clearly indicates the extent to which investing in a building society has become very popular amongst the general public, and the tax advantages enjoyed both by the societies and by individual investors must be a major explanatory factor.
6   With the continual fluctuations in interest rates during recent years, some building societies have decided to change their rates on an annual basis only.
7   Llewellyn (1979) points out that banks may actually gain deposits as well as lose them; e.g. building societies may attract deposits as an alternative to personal sector investment in some form of public sector debt (gilts, National Savings securities, TSB deposits) thereby adding to bank deposits and reserve assets. This would, of course, be constrained by the extent to which the societies themselves purchase public sector debt. Also some building society deposits are, for people without bank accounts, an alternative to holding notes

and coin, and as the loans of the societies are fed back to the banking system, bank deposits will be increased. In the end, competition from the building societies will produce a *trend effect* on bank deposits (as a result of their general competitiveness) as well as a *cyclical effect*, associated with the short-term flows of funds through the societies.

8   Abbey has also engaged in cooperation with some local authorities by offering to top-up funds promised by them, and has broken new ground with the formation of its own housing association in Tower Hamlets, thus becoming the first building society to build property for sale *or* rent. The housing association route was chosen to get around the law forbidding building societies from owning land.

9   In July 1984, the Nationwide announced its intention to arrange index-linked mortgages.

10 Indeed, by December 1983 some of the larger insurance companies were attempting to obtain a foothold in the highly lucrative but volatile US insurance market. Commercial Union was one such company despite failing with a similar venture in 1975; a failure that cost it £100 million.

11 See Arthur (1978) for an interesting account of the development of state pensions in the UK.

12 A substantial proportion of total assets is held in overseas shares (around 30% in 1984).

13 There has been criticism of late of the tendency of unit trusts to maintain excessive levels of liquidity, sometimes as high as 15%. The normal level is about 5% but on occasions, when the risks are regarded as excessive, the liquidity ratio may rise. An example was Britannia's Japan Fund which at the end of 1981 stood at 30%. Also before the stock market collapse of 1974, unit trusts were not permitted to hold cash. However, they are now allowed to hold cash on deposit (see *Sunday Times*, 15 Nov. 1981, 'Is your unit trust playing it too safe?').

14 In mid-1981 the National Girobank made a successful application for membership of the London Clearing Bankers House.

15 In Holland, one in four people have a Giro account compared to one in twenty in the UK.

16 This group of banks is often referred to as 'public sector banks' but, strictly speaking, the Co-op Bank is the purest type of 'public bank'. Currently owned by some 10 million small co-operators spread throughout the country, though with a mere seventy full branches, under 1 million customers and assets of around £700 million, its influence is limited. The Co-op Bank actually pioneered the paying of interest on current accounts, though stopped doing so for a time. The bank was seriously affected by the Government's windfall profits tax on the banks announced in the 1981 Budget which took almost two-thirds of its 1980 profits.

CHAPTER SIX

The parallel markets

Introduction

Having discussed the role of secondary banks in Chapter 4, it is now time to turn to another strata of financial institutions or markets. These are known as the *parallel markets* (Einzig 1971). The term parallel is used because these markets, while not in the mainstream of the financial system, tend to run alongside the traditional and secondary banking sectors, offering as they do their own particular brands of financial instruments. We have already mentioned the extent of product differentiation in the financial system, and these markets should be viewed as further evidence of that phenomenon. Like the secondary banks and other financial institutions (OFIs), these markets, especially the now colossal Eurocurrency and Eurobond markets, have enjoyed substantial expansion in recent years. Therefore, the same questions which were asked of the former will be asked of these institutions. What is their economic significance? How far do they compete with institutions in the non-parallel markets? And what influence do they have on the Government's monetary and financial policies?

The following markets will be considered: (a) the local authority market, (b) the Eurocurrency market, (c) the inter-bank market, (d) the certificate of deposit market, and (e) the inter-company market.

The local authority market

The local authority market engages in two methods of borrowing, long-term and short-term:

Long term

Local authorities raise longer-term finance by the issue of stocks and bonds.

Stocks are long-term fixed interest securities. As in the case of government bond issues, the issue is announced in the press and subscriptions invited. The timing of issues is controlled by the Bank of England; the minimum issue is £3 million, and most are much bigger than this; only the large authorities issue stocks. They used to be mainly of 10–20 years maturity, but in recent years of high interest rates they have tended to concentrate in the 5–8 years bracket. Local authority stocks are traded on the stock exchanges.

Bonds are medium-term securities, of three kinds:

1 Mortgages secured on the authority's revenue, sold on tap mainly to smaller lenders, the minimum being usually £500 or £1,000. They have a life of two to five years, but frequently there is a right to repayment at a few days' notice.

2 Bonds sold on tap, again in small sums. The difference from mortgages is that there are fewer legal formalities and less documentation attached to them. For this reason they have largely replaced mortgage loans since their introduction in 1964.

   Mortgages and bonds are sold in larger amounts, the usual minimum being £20,000 for smaller authorities and £50,000 for big authorities, through brokers. The terms range from one to ten years or more and yields are $\frac{1}{4}$ to 1% (according to the standing of the authority) above that on gilt-edged stocks of similar maturity, mainly because there is no formal secondary market in them.

3 When temporary borrowing was restricted in 1964, local authorities were allowed to issue bonds with a minimum life of one year. They are negotiable securities, and they are still referred to as 'yearlings' although they are issued for terms up to five years. The total which any authority may issue is subject to control by the Bank. Some are issued through the Stock Exchange, some are sold direct to discount houses and other financial institutions, in amounts ranging from £200,000 to £1 million. Their attraction for the discount houses is that a one-year bond fills a gap in the maturity distribution of their assets between bills and short gilt-edged. Under the 1971 'Competition and Credit Control' regulations, they were also regarded as eligible public sector assets. The 1981 'Monetary Control' Paper (Cmnd 7858) initiated some changes in the definitions of assets regarded as eligible, but these had only a negligible effect on local authority issues (see Ch. 13). These bonds cannot, however, be used as collateral for loans from the Bank.

Short term

Loans of less than one-year duration comprise:

1 Bank overdrafts – local authorities borrow comparatively little by overdraft, using funds so obtained mainly to maintain their day-to-day cash position and as a stop-gap against withdrawals of other temporary loans.

2 Bill finance – until 1974, this method was severely restricted but is now available, subject to Treasury consent, to any authority with a gross rate income in excess of £3 million per annum. They are issued in maturities of three to six months. They are popular in the money market: bills with an original maturity of less than six months are eligible paper (collateral) at the Bank, and since the 1971 arrangements were regarded as eligible reserve assets

for the banks and public sector assets ('defined assets') for the discount houses. The yield is higher than the Treasury bill rate but, because they are eligible securities, lower than the sterling certificate of deposit rate – usually about $\frac{1}{16}\%$ lower.

3 The bulk of their short-term finance comes by way of deposits, in large sums, at terms ranging from overnight at call, to seven days' notice, to fixed terms up to 364 days and, occasionally, for longer periods. Loans are arranged, usually through brokers, in multiples of £50,000 (though they can go down to £5,000). Deposits of £1 million or more are quite common. The authority issues a deposit receipt, but this is not transferable; there is no secondary market in deposits. Rates vary from day to day and within the day according to the treasurer's need for funds on any particular day and the amounts available from the major suppliers, that is large firms and financial institutions, in particular the merchant and overseas and foreign banks. Deposits are renewable, but most are repaid at the original maturity date, being matched against the liabilities of the depositors.

A significant part of local authority finance, especially deposits, comes from overseas. Some has come direct from foreign lenders and depositors, some is on-lent by the banks, but since the Government offered them and the nationalised industries forward exchange cover – that is repurchase of foreign currencies at a given rate of exchange – a few larger authorities have raised large medium- and long-term loans on the Eurocurrency market, switching into sterling.

The market in local authority loans was the first parallel market to develop in the later 1950s. Originally, the main outlet for funds was local authority deposits; this was the main growth area after 1955. Its importance declined after 1971, when all banks were obliged to maintain a $12\frac{1}{2}\%$ ratio, because local authority deposits were not classed as reserve assets. There are, of course, active secondary markets in local authority stocks, negotiable bonds and bills, and a specialised market in larger mortgages.

The Eurocurrency market

The origins of Eurocurrencies

A Eurocurrency deposit is a bank deposit denominated in a currency other than that of the country in which the bank is situated. The main Eurocurrency is the Eurodollar, but there are also Eurofrancs, Euromarks, Euroyen, Eurosterling, and so on.

A Eurodollar begins as an ordinary deposit with a US bank, probably acquired by a non-resident holder in any one of several ways: as earnings from exports to the USA; by selling another currency for dollars; by selling for dollars an asset located in the USA, either real assets or securities. These are all typical ways in which foreigners can acquire a bank balance in the USA. This deposit becomes Eurodollars when the original owner transfers it to a bank outside the USA, in exchange for a deposit denominated in dollars or in the currency of the receiving country. The bank concerned might be, for example, a London bank or the Paris branch of an American bank. There are several reasons why American residents might wish to hold dollar-dominated balances abroad (see the next section); the originator of Eurodollars is not necessarily a non-resident (Glendinning 1970; Einzig 1973; Bell 1973; Quinn 1975; Hewson and Sakakibara 1974; Hogan and Pearce 1982; Kane 1983).

The first bank A may then lend the dollar deposit to bank B. (Either bank may, of course, sell the dollar balance with an American bank to someone with a debt to pay in America. It then becomes a deposit owned in the USA and disappears from the Eurodollar scene.) The Eurodollar market is the network of institutions who borrow and lend these balances. Note that Eurobalances are borrowed and lent, not bought and sold. It is called 'Euro' because it originated with participating banks situated in Europe, but there are markets in Japan, Canada, Singapore, the Middle East and the Caribbean; the latter area, with its tax advantages for the banks, is now the biggest market after London. About 40% of total world Eurocurrency deposits are held in London, and the reasons for this relative importance are clear. London has the largest number of foreign banks, the largest foreign exchange market, and the largest concentration of experience and expertise in international finance; and foreign banks were allowed to establish themselves in the UK without hindrance. All Eurocurrencies are often brought under the single title 'Eurodollars', because these are the main Eurocurrency, constituting 70% of the Eurodeposits in the eight major European centres (Benelux, France, Germany, Italy, the Netherlands, Sweden, Switzerland and the UK).

The origins of the market

The acceptance and on-lending of deposits denominated in foreign currencies is not new; some UK banks practised it in the 1920s. But it virtually ended with the international financial crisis of 1931. The revival dates back to the 1950s, and there were a number of reasons for it:

1 One of the measures taken in the sterling crisis of 1957 was a ban on the use of sterling acceptances to finance trade between non-sterling countries, because London acceptances were usually discounted in London, creating a supply of sterling which the foreign holder probably wished to convert into another currency. London banks looked for deposits in dollars, the strongest currency, to use instead of sterling for the finance of trade.

2 During 1958 the major European currencies were made more freely convertible, at least for current, that is trading, transactions. The dollar, the strongest currency at the time, was the most popular currency to hold as a working balance; to pay and receive payment in dollars saved the cost and exchange risks of converting one's own currency into some other foreign currency.

3 In the late 1950s and early 1960s there also came a series of events which

increased the supply of dollars to banks in Europe. In 1959, the US balance of payments moved into a long series of deficits. Foreigners were earning more dollars than they spent, and there were two discouragements to the employment of their dollars in the USA. The first was *Regulation Q*, which until 1975 set maximum rates that American banks could pay on time deposits. Banks were also forbidden to pay interest on deposits with a term of less than thirty days. Regulation Q applied only to domestic deposits; there was no maximum rate for dollar deposits held abroad, and competition for such deposits was a major reason for the establishment of branches of American banks in London in the 1960s. American firms transferred spare funds to London to earn the higher rates, some were then lent back to banks in the USA. Second, from 1964 to 1974 the US Government imposed an interest-equalisation tax on foreign borrowing in the USA. This increased the cost of raising dollar loans in America (which increased demand for the alternative Eurodollars) and/or reduced the net return on lending (thus inducing holders of dollar deposits to transfer them to the more profitable Eurodollar market).

4   A further supply of Eurodollars came from holders who, for reasons other than the interest differential, did not wish to invest in the USA. One of the main participants in the Eurodollar market from the earliest days was the London-based Moscow Norodnay Bank. Several writers say that this bank, collecting dollars from East European State banks and placing them on the London market, initiated the Eurodollar market.

The market grew phenomenally in the 1960s and early 1970s. Eurodeposits, which totalled about $1 billion in 1960, were $19 billion net for the European centres in 1967, $57 billion in 1970, $215 billion in 1975 and $1,050 billion at the end of September 1983.[1] During the years 1965–78 the market, as measured by the Bank for International Settlements, grew at an annual rate of 30%, three times the growth rate of world money supply.

Eurobonds

The interest equalisation tax also stimulated the growth of long-term loans for Eurodollars: Eurobonds; and the use of Eurodollars was given a further impetus in 1968–73 when American borrowers were forbidden to use domestic funds for overseas investment (Park 1974). Eurobond issues over the period 1963–73 came to $33 billion. In 1981, the total issue of Eurobonds amounted to $27.4 billion; in 1982, the figure was $45–46 billion, while in the period May 1983 to May 1984 the figure rose to $58 billion. They are always large, usually syndicated and underwritten (the fee for each service having a maximum of ⅜%) and are long-term, usually ten to fifteen years.[2] The associated instruments are negotiable, and Eurobonds are traded on the major stock exchanges throughout the world. It was estimated in 1977 that about 60% of the $55 billion of Eurobonds outstanding were held by persons, 15% by banks and 25% by 'institutions', for example pension funds, insurance companies, Arab monetary authorities. A recent development is the syndicated Eurocredit, a loan made originally for three, six or twelve months but renewable at the end of each term at the going market rate. This renewal facility converts a short-term loan into a medium- or long-term loan if required. Starting in 1971, Eurocredit lending grew quickly, and $23 billion were issued in 1973, including two for $1,000 million, to the British Electricity Council and to the Italian equivalent, ENEC, and $28 billion in 1976.

Sources and uses of Eurocurrencies

The primary lenders are persons and institutions seeking a temporary profitable use for spare balances held in US banks, and one feature of the market is the wide range of maturities it offers, from overnight to five years or more. They include commercial banks, central banks and governments, international monetary organisations such as the International Monetary Fund and the Bank for International Settlements (BIS), large companies, especially multi-national companies, and, presumably, some wealthy people. In the early days, the main suppliers were central banks who put dollars, often bought from their residents (for example, through exchange stabilisation funds such as the Exchange Equalisation Account (EEA)), into the market either directly or via the BIS, or through 'swap' arrangements (see below) with their commercial banks. In 1971, the Group of Ten major industrialised countries agreed not to place further funds in the market, but other governments not party to the agreement have been earning dollar surpluses and converting them to Eurodollars. Up to 1973, the main net source was really the US deficit. In 1972–74 the exporters of primary products were the main contributors. The OPEC countries became the biggest net lender in 1974; their contribution then tailed off quickly, but revived in 1976. The eight European countries running the main Eurodollar market have collectively been the biggest suppliers and users of funds, and usually net suppliers. However, more recently the non-oil less-developed countries have been the major borrowers. In 1980, Mexico was the largest user, with China also significantly involved; in 1984, it was the turn of Brazil with a massive borrowing of $6 billion.

There are, likewise, many uses and users of Eurodollars: governments and central banks have used the market to offset surpluses and deficits in the current balance of payments. In a country with a chronic surplus – for example, Germany – the central bank, having paid out domestic currency to the banks in exchange for an inflow of foreign currencies, would claw it back by a 'swap' arrangement under which the commercial banks bought dollars from the central bank, with the right of reconversion into marks at a fixed rate of exchange. The banks then on-lent the dollars. Meanwhile, the effect of the inflow of dollars on the domestic money supply was neutralised by the swap. Conversely, countries with a deficit have bought from domestic banks dollar and other balances on the market. Some of these dollars were often redeposited on the market temporarily. Governments – notably those of Belgium, France, Italy and the UK – and local authorities, nationalised industries, the Electricity Council and the Post Office have raised large loans. The British Government, for example, arranged a credit for $2,500 million through the London

Clearing Banks in 1974. A further loan of $1.5 billion for seven years was raised through a syndicate of thirteen American, German and UK banks in January 1977. A number of UK local authorities have raised large Eurodollar loans. The arrangement will be that one or more banks take up a Eurodollar deposit, exchange it for sterling 'spot' either on the foreign exchange market or with the EEA, then lend the sterling to the local authority. The private sector uses Eurodollars for many purposes. Probably the main outlet is the finance of international trade, but large sums are borrowed at medium-term, usually for five to seven years, to finance investment both at home and abroad. Loans are used to buy new issues of bonds or shares in the currency concerned. Some Eurodollars are on-lent to US firms at lower rates than they could get from their domestic banks. Many Eurodollars are switched into the domestic currency, some by banks (subject to some restriction in the UK; spot foreign currency assets must exceed spot liabilities), who sell them to the central bank or to other banks in exchange for domestic currency assets.

During the credit squeezes of the 1960s, especially in 1966 and 1969, American banks drew heavily on the Eurodollar market. Their foreign branches accepted dollar deposits which they immediately on-lent to their parent offices in the USA receiving, of course, a credit balance at the head office. They could bid freely for these deposits since Regulation Q did not apply to them, and until October 1969 the parent bank was not obliged to hold any liquid reserve against these 'repatriated' dollars. Whether or not the US banking system as a whole can increase its deposits by this repatriation depends on how the foreign branch acquired the Eurodollars. If they came from an owner in the private sector, then all that happens is that a dollar balance in, say, New York is transferred from owner 'X' to the London branch of American bank 'Y', which transfers it to the head office. If the dollar balance was previously held with another bank, 'Z', then 'Y' can expand its deposit liabilities but 'Z' must reduce its deposits equally, unless 'Z' happens to have excess reserves or a higher ratio of time deposits to current account deposits than 'Y'. The effect is the same as if 'X' had transferred his deposit to a domestic branch of bank 'Y'.

Suppose, however, that the Eurodollar balance came from a central bank's reserves. This could happen if, for example, a Germany company bought a dollar balance from the Bundesbank and placed it with a Eurobank, which then lent it to the London branch of a US bank. Let us further suppose that this dollar balance was part of a Bundesbank working balance held with the Federal Reserve, or perhaps borrowed from the Federal Reserve, or obtained by selling gold to the US government. The US bank then receives from its branch a claim which is, ultimately, on the Federal Reserve Bank (FRB), the central bank of the USA. It can then expand its deposits and liabilities without contraction by another bank. Apart from the above-mentioned temporary concession on branch credits, it is only if the overseas branches acquired US notes and coin, or gold, or balances with the Federal Reserve, for transmission to head office, that total deposits in the USA can be increased by repatriation.

Again, the effect of repatriation is the same as that of a similar domestic transaction; any claim, domestic or foreign, on the Government or the FRB which is credited to a commercial bank permits an increase in total bank deposits. The converse of this is that when, say, a foreign central bank uses dollar balances in US commercial banks to buy US government securities, the US money supply falls. If these are dollar balances created by loans to US residents and used to pay for excess imports, there can be excessive lending by the banks which is not reflected in the money supply. If policy is guided solely by the level or rate of growth of the money supply, the excess lending may be supported by reserves supplied to the banks by the FRB.

The market mechanism

All participants in the market are banks, including the consortia. Particularly active are the overseas and foreign banks, who were mainly responsible for developing the market in the first place. The largest operators are the London branches of American banks.

All business is conducted, by telephone or telex, by the foreign exchange departments of the banks concerned, some of it direct and some through foreign exchange brokers, some of whom are subsidiaries of discount houses. Loans are unsecured, i.e. without collateral, but every bank sets a limit on the amount it will lend to (that is deposit with) any other bank. The normal unit for an inter-bank transaction is $1 million, and transactions of up to $100 million have been recorded. Banks will, of course, pass on Eurocurrencies to their own customers in much smaller sums, the minimum probably being $50,000. Because there is wide flexibility in the terms of deposits and loans, banks can match the terms of their assets (loans, or deposits made at other banks) with their liabilities (deposits received) closely, or can speculate on changes in the rates, borrowing short to lend long if they expect rates to fall, and vice versa. There is some forward-forward business, for example a two-month loan to be taken up one month hence. They also switch between Eurocurrencies according to their expectations regarding exchange rates, and make similar switches for customers, for example the multi-national companies. All deposits and loans are at fixed term and bear interest, but the range is very wide, from overnight to seven years in the case of loans, overnight to one year or more in the case of deposits. It appears, however, that most loans and deposits are for months rather than years. Most loans (deposits) are now of the 'floating rate' type; the term is fixed but the rate of interest is adjustable periodically within the term. As money market rates change, the rate is set at a variable interval above the corresponding London inter-bank offer rate (LIBOR). This has also been tried for Eurobonds. Banks take a large volume of certificated deposits (CDs) in Eurodollars and there is an active secondary market in these certificates. CDs also are now available at floating rates. Since 1970 some large companies have issued 'Eurocommercial paper' – bills of exchange expressed in Eurocurrencies – direct to lenders, with a bank acting as intermediary broker.

Some Eurodeposits are on-lent directly to a user of dollars, who then spends the dollar balance in the USA. The dollars then go into the internal circulation in the USA and are lost to the market. But a large proportion pass from one bank to another before they reach their ultimate destination, the dollar-spender.

Each time a Eurodeposit changes hands the lending bank requires from the borrower a margin over the rate it is paying its own depositor, but this inter-bank margin, at $\frac{1}{16}-\frac{1}{8}\%$, is lower than the margin which the ultimate lending bank will charge the ultimate non-bank borrower. Since with each transaction someone undertakes a liability to make a future payment of dollars, and often converts the dollars presently received into another currency, there will clearly be much forward covering of Eurodollar transactions. A bank switching dollars into sterling, for example, will buy dollars forward on the foreign exchange market if it wants to be sure of the price it will have to pay for dollars when its own obligation to pay dollars matures.

Each time a Eurodollar deposit is on-lent to another bank, it creates a new Eurodollar deposit and asset. For example, bank A received a dollar balance in New York from a customer; he acquires a Eurodollar asset and bank A a dollar asset and a Eurodollar deposit liability. Bank A then lends the New York balance to bank B; A acquires an asset (the deposit at B) to match its loss of dollars, but B acquires an asset (the dollar balance) and a Eurodollar deposit liability (to bank A). But there is still only the one dollar deposit in New York. Further, these deposit liabilities/assets remain in existence for their full term, even if the dollar balance in New York has been on-lent to an ultimate borrower and passed out of the Eurodollar system. The total quantity of Eurodollars is thus a multiple of the dollar deposits in the USA on which they are based.

The Eurodollar multiplier

Any balance, or part of a balance, which has passed out of the market into the international circulation may, of course, sooner or later come back into the market. There is, in other words, a Eurodollar multiplier analogous to the bank deposit multiplier (see pages 40 and 41) (Dufey and Giddy 1978; Argy 1981; Levi 1983). Eurodollar deposits are not like internal bank deposits which, being the usual means of payment, automatically remain in large part within the banking system. The most likely redepositor is a central bank which takes in, say, dollars in exchange for its domestic currency; but it may equally well convert the dollars into gold or add them to its reserve at the US Federal Reserve Bank. We do not know what the multiplier is. Argy (1981) presents a useful summary of empirical work on the Eurodollar multiplier. He compares the so-called 'fixed' multiplier models with 'flexible' versions. If, for example, there is a shift of a deposit (say 100 units) out of a US bank and into a Eurobank, what are the likely repercussions on the traditional bank multiplier? This 'fixed' version of the multiplier contains three assumptions:

1 The central bank will sterilise the liquidity effects on the balance of payments.
2 The central bank declines from depositing any component of their dollar deposits in the Euromarket.

3 The monetary effects in the USA of differential reserve requirements on demand and time deposits as well as different preferences by both the central bank and the public for financial assets generally, are ignored.

The 'fixed' multiplier defines the dollar components of the world money supply to include private sector holdings of Eurodeposits but excludes Eurobanks' holdings of cash in the US banking system. Thus, there is merely a change in the ownership of the deposit. The possibility of a multiplier effect arises out of the likelihood, indeed certainty, that the Eurobank will lend some proportion of the cash deposited. Though initially the amount on-lent will appear as a private deposit in a US bank, if this, in turn, is redeposited in the Eurobank, the whole process will start again.

If r is the cash/deposit ratio, and d is that part of the loan proceeds actually redeposited, the multiplier is as follows:

$$\frac{\Delta M}{A} = \frac{1 - r}{1 - d(1 - r)} \qquad [6.1]$$

where this is derived from the series:

$$\Delta M = (1 - r)A + d(1 - r)^2 A + d^2(1 - r)^3 A + \ldots d^{n-1}(1 - r)^N A \qquad [6.2]$$

with M = the money supply
A = initial Eurodeposit.

The final outcome depends on the size of d: if $d = 0$, the multiplier would be $(1 - r) < 1$; while, if $d = 1$ (that is there is 100% redepositing), the multiplier would be: $1 - r/r$.

If we take an arbitrary value for $r = 0.09$, the multiplier is 10.11. If r is lower than 0.09, the multiplier increases above 10.11. Much of the debate on the Eurodollar market centres on the extent of the redepositing which actually takes place.

As to the size of the multiplier in the 'fixed' model, estimates vary. One estimate (Klopstock 1968) has it in the range 0.5 to 0.9. By contrast, Makin (1972) puts it at the extremely high figure of 18.4 for 1963–66. A major study by Lee (1973) estimates that the multiplier was 1.26 in 1963 and rose steadily to 1.92 because large firms found it profitable to hold more of their working balance in Eurodollars and central banks were redepositing more of their dollars in the market. McKinnon (1977), using a slightly amended version of the multiplier equation, obtained a multiplier value of 1.15. There are, however, two essential differences between the Lee and the McKinnon versions.

The first concerns the source of the additional deposit in the Eurobank. Whereas Lee assumes that it derives from an increase in the base of the system, McKinnon contends that there is an exogenous shift in the propensity to hold Eurodollars. On balance, McKinnon's version is more useful in explaining the effects of preference changes for Eurodollars as, for example, those which occurred in the early 1970s with the growth of OPEC oil revenues and the like.

The second difference relates to the definition of the base in the system. McKinnon's base, all US deposits including those held by US residents, is much broader than Lee's which is restricted to foreigners' deposits in the US banking system. The broader the base of the system, the larger the assumed 'leakage' and the smaller the multiplier. The fact that, since January 1974, US residents have been able to deposit in the Euromarket implies that Lee's base may be too narrow. But, by the same token, because McKinnon's base includes a sizeable proportion which probably do not transact in the market, given the large minimum transactions involved, his base is probably too broad.

Other commentators (Hewson 1975; Niehans and Hewson 1976; Hewson and Sakakibara 1974) argue that the 'fixed' multiplier approach is useless. Their contention is that the theory of non-bank intermediaries is of more relevance than simple banking theory. There are two differences between their approach and those previously discussed.

First, they attempt to derive, from a *general equilibrium* framework, a gross deposit multiplier which allows for portfolio adjustments. Second, irrespective of the size of this gross deposit multiplier, the significance of the Euromarkets is in their effects on private sector liquidity, which in turn depend on the degree of *maturity transformation* of the market. Put simply, these 'flexible' versions of the multiplier model allow for the effects of inflows into the Euromarket on *both* the demand and supply of funds. If maturity transformation is near to zero, the Eurobanks' addition to net liquidity in the private sector is also close to zero. Niehans and Hewson (1976) show that in the early 1970s there was indeed close matching of the maturity structures of their liabilities and assets, suggesting that their net liquidity effect was small. Hewson and Sakakibara (1974) suggest that the multiplier was only a little higher than 1 in the years 1968–72. However, as evidence from *BEQBs* tends to show, in more recent years there seems to have been considerable maturity transformation, with the result that the Eurobanks have probably made a significant contribution to net liquidity after all (Little 1979).

Whatever the size of the multiplier, there seems to be some justification for believing that these Euromarkets have added considerably to the world supply of funds and liquidity. As was argued in Chapter 5 in connection with the growth of the non-bank financial intermediaries such as the building societies, the entry of another intermediary in the form of the Euromarkets is likely to have a considerable expansionary effect. The domestic monetary repercussions of this will be discussed below.

The significance of the market

The market has provided a new outlet for lenders and a new source of funds for borrowers. Eurodollars are not wholly a net addition to the international flow of funds, but they have probably increased the flow. So long as its convertibility is maintained, a Eurocurrency constitutes a new, non-government reservoir of international liquidity which can be titled towards one country or another as relative demands and interest rates change. International mobility of funds through the banks also brings banks in different countries into closer competition with each other. Both the mobility of funds and the competition between banks will tend to reduce differences in interest rates. In all these ways, Eurocurrencies have created a new, efficient international market which has been of undoubted benefit to lenders and borrowers alike. It has helped countries to adjust to balance of payments deficits and surpluses; it was to bolster up the £ without using our reserves to buy sterling that the Chancellor in his Budget Speech in March 1973, by offering cover against exchange risks, encouraged local authorities and nationalised industries to borrow in the Eurodollar market (which they did, to the tune of £1,000 million in 1973). In the case of the USA, the new means of employment of dollars held by non-residents meant that fewer of them were presented for conversion into gold; the strain on US reserves has been less than it would otherwise have been, given the deficit. On the other hand, some of the dollars coming on to the market would be offered on the foreign exchange markets against other currencies. Their effect on the dollar is similar to that of an export of capital; it is exchange-value reducing. If the exchange is affected by or results in a sale of dollars to the US stabilisation fund, it will reduce the official reserves of gold or foreign exchange.

There are dangers and problems. There were ten defaults on Eurobonds in the years 1963–77. More efficient financial intermediation, by reducing interest rates and by facilitating the flow of funds from countries where money is easy to countries where it is tight, has some inflationary effect on the world economy. The fact that interest rate discrepancies induce flows of funds which tend to iron out these discrepancies means that it is difficult to conduct an interest rate policy geared to the internal situation and independent of what happens to interest rates elsewhere. On the other hand, of course, it does make more effective the deliberate use of interest rates as a means of attracting or repelling funds. Any relief to the balance of payments arising from an inflow of Eurodollars for conversion into the domestic currency can only be temporary; Eurodollar deposits have to be repaid in dollars eventually, and the foreign exchange situation thus gains 'spot' but loses 'forward'. Eurodollars can become a new form of 'hot money', moving out of one currency into another not only in response to interest rate differentials but also because of expectations of currency revaluations; they then increase the downward pressure on a weak currency and the upward pressure on a strong currency (Kern 1979). However, none of this is peculiar to Eurodollars; 'hot money' was a well-known problem in the 1930s, and would still be a problem if there were no Eurodollar system.

They can be a danger to the banking system, dealing in unsecured loans in a market with no lender of last resort. Banks often borrow short to lend long; for example, in February 1976 the London banks' Eurodollar liabilities of up to 7 days' maturity exceeded their lending at similar maturities by $7.3 billion and, conversely, their loans of more than one year exceeded their deposit liabilities of similar terms by $30.4 billion. There are two inherent dangers in this. The first is that it can lead to discrimination in favour of banks with ready access to the hard currencies. For example, in 1983 and 1984, US banks in London were taking in deposits above the corresponding inter-bank and CD rates while German banks were paying almost 1% above the inter-bank rates. Second, and much more important, is that in a chain of on-lendings there can be a weak link. If one borrower defaults, the next one back in the chain would have to buy dollars on the foreign exchange market to meet his obligations to the next bank. If a number of chains were broken, there would be an unholy scramble for dollars which could seriously weaken one or more other currencies. In the worst case, national reserves could not meet the demand. The banks can, and do, guard against this by holding assets – for example, dollar certificates of deposit and other dollar securities – which can be sold to meet their liabilities, and by arranging stand-by lines of credit with banks abroad; but in a severe crisis these may not be adequate. However, virtually all the banks operating in the market are strong institutions.

One solution would be to impose controls on foreign currency borrowing by resident banks and others. Another would be to impose reserve ratios and interest rate ceilings on Eurobanks. An objection is that they impose direct, administrative controls on the flow of international finance. The difficulty with both is to get international agreement on the form and severity of controls when countries' banking practices and methods of financial control differ. The British official attitude still seems to be that expressed by the Governor of the Bank of England in 1972: 'As many of us have learned from our experience in domestic regulation, restrictions which bite at all severely on financial intermediaries lead quite quickly to disintermediation or to the rapid growth of new intermediaries not subject to the same strictness of regulation' (BEQB, June 1972: 237). There is, however, a Standing Committee of Experts, set up by the BIS in 1975, for the exchange of information and to develop cooperation in methods of control; and it has been agreed that parent banks should be held responsible for all overseas banking operations in which they have a direct stake (as they are already explicitly in the UK) and that adequate last resort finance could and would be made available by central banks.

Another danger is that flows of funds can interfere with or neutralise domestic monetary policy. Eurocurrencies can, like other holdings of foreign currency, be converted into sterling by sale to the EEA, which increases the banks' cash reserves. The EEA can, in principle, neutralise these flows by the sale of securities to pay for the foreign exchange, if these securities are sold to the non-bank private sector. Heavy sales of securities are likely to push up interest rates or keep them high, and relatively high interest rates are a major reason for inflows. An inflow may run into several hundreds of millions of dollars. In 1973, for example, the Bundesbank bought in $6 million in a few weeks, and eventually closed the foreign exchange market until the situation quietened. It is difficult to sell government debt quickly on this scale. The Bank of England's view appears to be that these flows can be neutralised (McMahon 1976). Nevertheless, after British companies had borrowed $500 million in the three months to January 1971, when the money supply was rising 10% p.a., the authorities tried to stem the money-creating inflow with a regulation that there should be no further borrowing for terms of less than five years. This made little difference until domestic rates of interest fell below the rates on Eurocurrency loans.[3]

With a 'clean' float, the strain is taken by the exchange rate, which will rise (fall) with an inflow (outflow). But, to repeat, inflows and outflows of funds did not originate with the Eurodollar market and would continue if it disappeared. There are other ways of dealing with this problem. One is direct and autarchic exchange controls, for example on the placing of funds in, or borrowing from, the Euro-markets, or on the conversion of Eurocurrencies into the domestic currency, but governments are reluctant to impose these because of the damage they inevitably do to the free flow of trade and desirable payments. Another which is only practicable within fairly narrow limits is forward intervention in the exchange markets. Most exchanges of foreign currency for sterling are covered by buying foreign currency (selling sterling) forward; the authorities can make this expensive if they sell sterling forward themselves.

The inter-bank market

As its name implies, this is a market in which banks lend to each other. The traditional method of topping up a deficient reserve ratio is to call in money from the discount market or sell bills or bonds. The immediate origin of the inter-bank market was the Eurodollar market. Here, banks on-lent foreign currencies to each other, and this broke the tradition that banks do not borrow from each other.[4]

The inter-bank market has many similarities with the Eurocurrency market. It is, like all the parallel markets, entirely a *wholesale* market. Deals are arranged, for sums as low as £50,000 or £100,000, but £250,000 is a common minimum, £500,000 or £1,000,000 are typical, £2 million is quite normal, and deposits of £20 million have been made. Loans are unsecured. Deposits are often on-lent several times within the market before finally passing to a non-bank borrower.[5]

Transactions take the form of deposits placed by one institution with another, for fixed terms ranging from overnight to five years, but most are short-term. Business is conducted by telephone, mostly through thirty-odd money brokers. They charge $\frac{1}{32}$% p.a. commission to each party. Most of the brokers are also Eurocurrency and/or foreign exchange brokers; they organise the market, telephoning banks at intervals through the day to ask if they have any funds on offer or on demand, at what rates, and then telephoning other banks to try to arrange a transaction.

The market grew rapidly in the late 1960s, the sums borrowed rising from probably less than £400 million in 1965 to over £2,000 million in 1971. Clearing bank participation in the market was stimulated by the new system of credit control instituted in 1971 (see Ch. 13). The relevant change was that, whereas previously deposits with other banks were not counted as liquid assets, they were now set off against deposits from other banks in calculating the liabilities against which a bank holds a minimum ratio of reserve assets. Borrowing/lending on the inter-bank market almost trebled within two years to more than £11 billion. In June 1976 the gross figure was $10.4 billion, by the end of November 1983 the figure was $23.2 billion; there is no net figure taking account of on-lending.

Operators in the market

The participants in the market are much the same as those in the Eurocurrency market: merchant banks, overseas and foreign banks and, since 1971, the clearing banks (they previously participated through their subsidiaries). The discount houses began to borrow from the market in 1968 and they have recently made increasing use of it for overnight and 'short money'. More than 200 banks and discount houses operate regularly.

The American banks in London have been important members from the start. Indeed, they were largely responsible for the initiation and early development of the market, whose function in the early days was the same as that of the federal funds market in the USA, namely to even out day-to-day cash surpluses and deficits between banks. The merchant bank subsidiaries of the clearing banks also played an important part in developing the market. Institutions outside the banking system – finance houses, insurance companies and pension funds, savings banks and large companies – can also be regarded as participants when they deposit money overnight or for a fixed term and the deposit is on-lent to other banks.

For example, a firm with £500,000 surplus to its requirements for the next seven days pays a cheque drawn on bank A into bank B as a seven-day deposit. B then receives a clearing bank deposit from A (if it is a non-clearing bank) or cash at the Bank of England (if it is a clearing bank). If it does not need this addition to its reserves it will make its own deposit in bank C, and so the deposit is passed on. Euro-currencies switched into sterling are another source of outside funds. Some banks – for example, the American banks – tend to be persistent net borrowers on the market; others – for example, the clearing banks – have usually been net lenders.

Uses of the market

The original function of the market was to provide a means whereby the non-clearing banks with surplus balances at the clearing banks could place them at a better yield than they could get from the discount market, and others could 'balance their books' at the end of the day; that is, achieve their desired reserve ratio at a lower charge than by borrowing from the clearing banks. The discount houses stood aloof from the market in the early days and lost much business in consequence as the non-clearing banks switched out of discount market assets into loans in the inter-bank market and to the local authorities.[6] It soon developed into a market offering a wide variety of maturities and a wide variety of uses of funds. Most deposits are still for short periods – overnight to seven or fourteen days – but there is a large trade in three months' and six months' deposits. The borrowing/lending facility is now used not only to balance daily receipts and payments but also to meet prospective surpluses and shortages of reserve assets. The flexibility of maturities means that inter-bank lending and borrowing can be used to fill gaps in the maturity structure of either side of the balance sheet for banks who follow the 'Christmas tree' practice of matching the maturities of assets and liabilities. Thus a bank which anticipates a shortage of funds in two months' time can take in, say, three months' deposits today and on-lend them for two months. If it expects a surplus it can lend longer and cover any resultant immediate shortage with short borrowings.

There is a good deal of forward trading; that is, the arranging of loans to be made at a future date. Flexibility of maturities also enables banks to speculate on future interest rates by time arbitrage, lending long at the current high rate and borrowing short if they expect rates to fall, and vice versa if they expect rates to rise or if short-term rates are higher than longer-term rates and are expected to remain high. They can speculate both in the spot market – the market for immediate loans – and in the forward market.[7] There are, obviously, bigger profits to be made by speculating than by simply on-lending deposits at similar term, but losses are also possible. The bigger banks can also make use of their size and reputation, taking large deposits and on-lending profitably for a similar term in smaller sums to less well-known banks. The return for lending on 'matched maturities' is small, $\frac{1}{16}$% p.a. with probably a broker's commission to be deducted from this.

Interest rates

Interest rates are generally higher than in the traditional market, for example, London clearing banks call money or CD rates, for three reasons:[8]

1 All loans are unsecured. Further, while in the traditional market most advances go direct to the final borrower and are for the most part put to a short-term, self-liquidating use, in the inter-bank market no lender knows how many times, nor to whom, his funds will be on-lent, nor who the final borrower will be, nor to what use the final loan will be put. There can be a long chain of on-lendings between the original depositor and the final borrower and the chain is only as strong as its weakest link. The common practice is to set limits on the sum one will deposit with any particular bank, the limit depending on several considerations: the size and reputation of the bank or of its parent bank, its capital, its total assets, and perhaps its liquidity; or the limit may be set only after a thorough examination of its whole balance sheet. If a bank is a persistent heavy borrower in relation to its size, word gets around and brokers may set their own limits for the bank or refuse to do business with it for a time. But knowledge can never be perfect, and no lender can know for certain what funds any given borrower is raising elsewhere. The liquidity crisis of 1974 showed the dangers.

2 There is no lender of last resort. If a bank is over-committed it can only turn to the market itself for help and pay whatever rate it must for short money. Normally the rates for one month or longer carry a differential of $\frac{1}{4}$% over the

rate on traditional market paper (bills and bonds) of similar maturity, but inter-bank rates are more volatile, especially so in the case of very short rates, where the differential can vary quite widely. In times of exceptional general tightness of money, these rates can be very high indeed; the overnight rate has on occasion been as high as 200%.

3 After 1971, call money placed with the discount market counted as a reserve asset under the 1971 regulations; money placed in the inter-bank market did not. Deposits with other banks were, however, deductible from borrowings on the inter-bank market when computing the 'eligible liabilities' against which a 12% reserve ratio had to be maintained. (See p 332.)

Rates are subject to many influences. They tend to be high, for example, for maturities which overlap the monthly and annual making-up days when the banks have to submit their balance sheets to the Bank of England and want to show a comfortable reserve ratio. Changes in expected rates pull the current rates up or down with them; so does Stock Exchange activity. For example, if a large issue of shares is heavily oversubscribed, the issuing house will hold, temporarily, some millions of pounds from unsuccessful applicants for shares and it may put them into the market for a few days until it can complete the administration of allotment of shares and repayment. Funds also flow between the market and the Stock Exchange with changing expectations about the future course of share prices. Nevertheless, there is a link between the inter-bank market and the traditional market, and rates have come closer since the traditional market dropped its cartel rate in 1971. Operaters can switch from one market to the other, for example a bank can obtain reserves by selling bills to the discount market or by borrowing on the inter-bank market, and its choice will obviously depend on the relative rates. The discount houses also move funds into and out of the parallel markets according to whether call money from the clearing banks is easy or tight. The movement of funds between the private and public sectors will also affect the market via its implications for clearing bank liquidity.

Inter-bank market rates have a strong influence on the banks' lending rates: indeed, the clearing banks' base rates follow closely the inter-bank three months' rate. One reason is that some banks draw substantial reserves from the inter-bank market. Another is that if the differential is wide enough, some of the banks' bigger customers will use overdrafts to lend in the wholesale markets. Conversely, if inter-bank loans were cheaper than overdrafts, the clearing banks would lose business.

The certificate of deposit market

Closely linked with the inter-bank market, and in some ways competitive with it, is the market in *certificates of deposit*.

The *certificate of deposit* is a document issued by a bank, certifying that a deposit has been made with the bank, at a stated rate of interest, which is repayable to the bearer on surrender of the certificate on a specified day. It is therefore associated with a deposit at the bank issuing it for a definite period – 'a term deposit' – and is a negotiable bearer security. The maturities of CDs range from three months to five years from the date of issue though the deposit is, of course, renewable at maturity. A CD originates with the deposit, either direct or through a broker, of a multiple of £10,000 ranging from a minimum of £50,000 to a maximum of £500,000. (This is a limit on the size of a single certificate, not on the size of the deposit.) The interest rate on a certificated deposit is usually within $\frac{1}{8}$% of the current rate on inter-bank deposits of the same maturity, because it has become an instrument of borrowing/lending between banks; but, like any other rate, it depends on supply and demand and can go higher if a bank is particularly anxious to secure a deposit of a particular maturity, perhaps to replace a maturing deposit, or to match a prospective or recently granted large loan of similar maturity.

The reason for its inception was basically to attract medium-term deposits. Traditionally in London, there was only one class of time deposits in the clearing banks, the deposit at seven days' notice, and only one rate of interest on the bank rate minus 2%. They did not accept deposits at longer term, and did not pay higher rates on large deposits, although the cost per £100 of handling deposits is lower for larger deposits than for small. The clearing banks could not, therefore, match their medium-term loans with deposit liabilities of similar maturity; they had to 'borrow short to lend long', and there are always dangers in this practice. First, since loans are made at a fixed rate, the lender borrowing at a shorter term than he lends stands to lose money on outstanding loans when interest rates rise. Second, he cannot rely on a continuous supply of deposits; there is always the risk that they will not be renewed. (As we saw on pages 42–3; this is not a problem for the banks as a whole; deposits are only withdrawn *from the system* if the public's desired ratio of cash to deposits increases. But it *is* a problem for each individual bank.) In the increasingly popular field of medium-term credit, banks were losing out to the secondary banks and other institutions who were not bound by their conventions and would adjust their rates to attract longer-term deposits. The idea of certificated deposits was, indeed, first mooted in Britain in the early 1960s in the course of the burgeoning debate about the desirability of the clearing banks competing for deposits, which in a climate of monetary restraint and an increasing demand for fixed medium-term loans were, unlike overdrafts, subject to recall.

Uses of CDs

Some forty-odd banks – the accepting houses, overseas and foreign banks, and some subsidiaries and affiliates of the clearing banks – were allowed to issue sterling certificates of deposit in October 1968. After a fairly slow start, the practice grew rapidly, especially after September 1971 when the clearing banks themselves began to issue and deal in this security. By mid-1973, about 150 banks were issuing certificates, and the total of certificates outstanding rose from £463 million in January 1970 to £3,600 million in June 1972, and more than £5,000 million in June 1973; by July

1984 this figure had increased to over £11,300 million. The discount houses made a market in certificates from the start; it was a discount house (Allen Harvey and Ross) which initiated the market with dollar CDs in 1966, and they were soon joined by the secondary banks and deposit brokers and, after 1971, by the clearing banks. All these institutions stand ready to buy and sell certificates on behalf of clients and on their own behalf; they hold CD assets. At 15 July 1984, they comprised about 6% of the total assets of all banks in the UK and about 30% of the assets of the discount houses.

It is perhaps surprising to learn that banks both issue and hold CDs, but there are good reasons for them doing so. (1) Banks lend to (deposit with) each other, and much of this lending is by CDs. (2) A bank can match anticipated receipts and payments by issuing certificates which mature in a period of expected cash surplus and holding certificates which mature in a period of expected cash shortage. (3) A bank may wish to hold certificates of a particular maturity as a kind of insurance against a heavy outstanding issue of its own CDs of the same maturity. There is, therefore, now an efficient and active 'secondary market', i.e. a market for outstanding CDs, where they can be sold cheaply and quickly either by the original buyer, the 'primary holder' who actually made the associated deposit, or by anyone who bought the certificate from him.

The CD is therefore an excellent credit instrument. The banks can obtain fixed-term deposits, yet the depositor is not 'locked in'; he can repossess his funds or part of them (CDs can be split into units of £10,000) at any time by selling his certificate on the market. The device thus provides a liquid asset to the holder of a CD (the depositor), while the bank's obligation to repay is deferred to the maturity date of the deposit. The liquidity of a CD, however, is not perfect. The liquidity of an asset is a function of its market price as well as of the ease and cost of selling it. The nominal value of a CD is equal to the original deposit plus accrued interest (interest on CDs of up to one year is paid at maturity, on longer-term deposits it is paid annually to the current holder of the certificate), but there are several competing assets of varying degrees of liquidity, and the price of a CD must be such as to give the buyer a competitive future rate of return. When rates of interest rise, a holder of a CD will suffer a capital loss if he sells it. Against this, however, we must set the fact that a holder who correctly anticipates a rise in interest rates can sell his CD before rates rise and move back into CDs or some other non-money asset after they have risen. Thus, although his deposit was accepted at a fixed rate of interest, the depositor is not tied to that rate for the term of the deposit. A similar risk faces the large holders who make the market, especially the discount houses. When there is a general expectation that interest rates are about to rise, they are likely to find themselves holding virtually unsaleable CDs financed with very short-term call money from the banks.

The issue and use of CDs is closely regulated by the Bank of England. Only banks who are authorised dealers in foreign exchange (approx. 300) are allowed to issue them. They can only be sold for foreign currency with the specific consent of the Bank. It was the Bank who decided the denominations in which they are issued and fixed the range of maturities. Each issuer must make a monthly return of the amount of his CD liabilities outstanding and the Bank can thus use its influence to discourage an excessive issue. Holdings of CDs could not be counted as part of the 28% liquidity ratio in the pre-1971 system, nor have they been classed as reverse assets; they could, however (at least up to 1981), be set off against the bank's own issued CDs in the calculation of eligible liabilities (see page 331). The banks will accept short CDs as collateral against call money, but they are not eligible securities at the Bank of England. A bank is expected not to buy, nor accept as collateral against loans to the discount market, CDs issued by itself or any of its subsidiaries.

In spite of these restrictions the CD has been a very useful innovation for the banks. It has allowed them to tap sources of large deposits for quite long fixed terms at fixed rates and so enabled them to meet more fully demands for medium-term credit. Certificated deposits are a little cheaper than other deposits of similar maturity. Not only are they quite liquid, they also carry a higher return than most reserve assets and they are better than assets which count neither as reserve assets nor as offsets to eligible liabilities. As we saw above, the certificate of deposit began as a device for attracting time deposits from outside the banking system issuing them, but it has developed into an instrument of inter-bank lending/borrowing. More than half the sterling CDs issued are held by other banks. Net borrowings by the issue of CDs issued are held by other banks. Net borrowings by the issue of CDs, like net borrowing on the inter-bank market, counted as eligible liabilities under the 1971 arrangements. As assets, they have the advantage over inter-bank deposits that they are marketable, and are thus a highly liquid source of reserves. This may be potentially important for a 'matching' bank; it can adjust the maturity structure of assets to deposits more quickly; it does not have to wait for certificates to mature. The rates payable on certificated deposits are closely related to inter-bank rates; usually, but not invariably, lower. Contracts can be made to buy or sell forward, for example, to sell a one-year certificate in two years' time, or to sell equal amounts of one-year certificates at the end of each of the next six months. The rate is agreed at the time the contract is made.

The discount houses are still important in the certificate of deposit market. They hold certificates briefly as investment; short-dated CDs are eligible collateral for call loans from the clearing banks, though at higher rates than loans secured on bills, but they are not eligible for loans from the Bank of England. They also act as jobbers, holding a variety of maturities for sale to meet the differing needs of clients with funds to invest. As stated above, the banks also buy CDs, both to hold themselves and on behalf of their customers. Much of the trade in CDs is done through brokers, usually firms who also operate in the inter-bank market. They are in close touch with both the issuing banks and other operators in the parallel markets and know where the lowest prices, or the best terms, can be obtained for a given maturity. All the operators deal with each other as well as with outside holders and primary buyers of CDs from the issuing banks. The minimum deal in sterling CDs is £50,000 and the average is probably about £500,000. In dollar CDs, the size of transactions in the secondary market is much larger: large American dealers rarely trade in less than £1 million, and around £30 million is not uncommon. Brokers often take the initiative in asking issuing banks to issue CDs to meet the needs of their clients. The bigger brokers also speculate in response to distortions of the maturity/yield pattern and on their expectations of future changes in rates. Any holder of CDs who sells a certificate stands to gain or lose, of course, from a change in rates after he has bought or sold. That is true of any security.

Both markets were set back by the fringe bank crisis of 1973–74; lenders became more cautious and terms shortened. At the height of the boom, funds could be raised for periods of two years with ease, with CDs being dealt for as long as five years and five years ahead: in effect, a forward market extending up to ten years. Nowadays the norm for wholesale money is three months, with six months relatively long; beyond that there is relatively little on offer. However, this may be a temporary phenomenon.

The inter-company market

During the credit squeeze of the late 1960s some large companies began to lend to each other, usually through brokers, sums ranging from £50,000 to a few million; the most common unit was $250,000. Revell (1973) dates the market back to the spring of 1968, when importers were obliged to deposit with the Treasury, for six months, 50% of the value of their imports. The regulations stated that this money must not be obtained by loans from the clearing banks. Firms who could not pay the deposit obtained the money from two sources, first their suppliers, and second a few import deposit brokers '. . . whose function was to obtain money in bulk from certain banks and to break it down into smaller units, often of as little as £250' (Revell 1973: 283). The term 'inter-company market' was coined in 1969. The lenders are companies with either surplus cash or unused overdraft facilities at the banks. Loans are usually at short-term, overnight or at two to seven days' notice; but some are made at terms ranging from three months to five years.

Although a true inter-company loan by-passes the banks, they have been involved since the earliest days. One of the drawbacks of lending to another company is that there is no secondary market in the deposits involved, and the lender's money is therefore locked into the loan for its full term. Moreover, the shorter-term loans are unsecured. The banks help by guaranteeing loans, for a commission. They have also been able to put surplus spenders and deficit spenders into touch with each other; the reward for this service is the goodwill it generates, which is especially important if the borrower is a customer whose request for an overdraft has been turned down because credit is tight. A large part of so-called inter-company loans now, in fact, comes from the banks, with the brokers acting as intermediaries between bank and company, finding borrowers for the one and the cheapest source of a loan for the other.

Estimates of the size of the market have varied widely, ranging from £100 million to £300 million in the early 1970s and we do not have an accurate figure, if only because the loans arranged directly between firms are not divulged. What we do know is that the market was smaller than the other parallel markets and appears to have contracted in the late 1970s and early 1980s.

The significance of the parallel markets

The growth of the complementary markets has changed the face of the City. They brought into existence a money market and sources of credit not directly controlled by the authorities which, in terms of both the size of the pool of funds involved and the volume of daily trading, eclipsed the traditional market consisting of the clearing banks and the discount market. Whereas in the mid-1950s the pattern of interest rates in 'the' – that is the traditional – money market was based on bank rate, by the late 1960s the bell-wether of interest rates was the sterling inter-bank rate. Perhaps the most explicit recognition of this was the decision of the Finance Houses' Association in September 1970 to base their charges and deposit rates on the monthly average rate on three-month inter-bank deposits, rounded up to the nearest $\frac{1}{2}$%. The post-1971 clearing bank base rate was also geared to this rate: the non-clearing banks were already basing their rates on the inter-bank rate. Another influence on London rates is the Eurodollar rate, since a large proportion of Eurodollars finally leave the network of Eurobanks in London. For example, the huge repatriation of dollars by American banks in 1969–70, in response to a credit squeeze at home, raised domestic rates of interest not only in the UK but throughout the world.

The new markets helped to maintain London's position as a financial centre and contributed significantly to the UK's invisible exports at a time when sterling's role as a reserve currency was in decline. They have also brought foreign funds to London, as well as foreign banks. When Eurocurrency deposits are switched into sterling, and overseas residents build up credits in London, for lending to banks on certificates of deposit or to local authorities or finance houses or to industry and commerce, most of the corresponding balances of foreign currency go into the national reserves. Previously, the main use of these foreign-owned sterling balances had been the purchase of Treasury bills and the Treasury bill rate, and hence bank rate, and consequently most other domestic rates had to be kept high enough to attract such funds during the frequent periods of balance of payments difficulties and downward pressure on sterling. With the new and more profitable outlets provided by the parallel markets, the authorities had rather more freedom to fix interest rates at the level deemed appropriate to the domestic situation. Note again, however, that the help to sterling was usually temporary; the effect was reversed when the holder switched back into another currency.

On the other hand, of course, the lending of foreign funds switched into sterling allows the borrowers to evade a credit squeeze, as happened in the UK in 1969–70, unless the authorities can neutralise it. The inter-bank and inter-company markets can also be said to impair monetary control; the surplus liquidity of the lender is used to build up the liquidity of the borrower. What reserves of money or credit are available are more fully used. From October 1971 to June 1973, inter-bank lending and CD issues increased nearly 200%. The London clearing banks were major borrowers, and these borrowed reserves fuelled a massive increase in the money supply. The answer, in principle, is a tighter squeeze. A slippage of control at the periphery must be counteracted by tighter control at the centre. The authorities can control the volume of credit by restricting clearing bank credit, if they are prepared to take the necessary steps; that is, sell securities to the non-bank private sector. The markets are not completely separate, and controls in the traditional market have repercussions in the complementary markets. If the discount houses are put under pressure, they will lend less on the inter-bank market and take up fewer certificates of deposit. If bill rates and call money rates in the discount market rise, the secondary banks will be less inclined to sell bills to the discount houses or withdraw call money from them to lend in the parallel markets and this restricts the supply of funds in those markets. It is in such ways that changes in the primary money market affect the parallel markets, quite apart from the general psychological effect on all markets of 'tight money'.

The emergence of competition from the new markets and the secondary banks not inhibited by controls forced the clearing banks and discount houses to reconsider their role and their activities. The discount houses entered the market in dollar CDs in the mid-1960s and created the market in sterling CDs. They invested more in local authority bills and bonds and some of them acquired, or bought a share in, money broking firms, some of whom operate in all the complementary markets. The clearing banks did not deal in the wholesale markets directly before 1971, but they participated through their subsidiary merchant banks and finance houses, and through the consortia. More recently, the building societies have become actively involved in the market (see Ch. 5).

The clearing banks, more than any other institution, felt the cold blast of competition from the new free markets, and especially from the American banks, and slowly roused themselves to fight back. Moving into the new markets with their subsidiaries, who were not subject to their parents' cash and liquidity ratios and cartel rates, was one answer. Another was massive advertising campaigns (higher rates for larger deposits) and new services such as credit cards, cash lines and personal loans. But some of the old oligopolistic attitudes remain: they still keep to their short and inconvenient opening hours and, unlike other retailers, have not found a way of combining six-day opening with a five-day week for their staff.

After 1971 the two halves of the market moved closer together. The new arrangements imposed the same reserve ratio on all banks. The discount houses began to deal in all the types of paper – Treasury bills, commercial bills, local authority bills and short bonds – which make up reserve assets. Call money lent to the discount houses was also a reserve asset and this brought the secondary banks back as large lenders to the traditional market. Both the discount houses and the clearing banks began to operate directly in the parallel markets. The clearing banks engaged on a large scale in term lending and some have brought in new schemes to attract term deposits up to five years' maturity; they have moved into factoring and leasing and insurance broking. Similarly, the exploration and exploitation of North Sea oil, requiring enormous sums, makes demands on the clearing banks for medium-term finance carrying a degree of risk which would have horrified them in the 1950s.

Notes

1   This 'net' figure measures the flow of credit from the market to final borrowers; it excludes inter-bank redepositing. The gross figure for European deposits reported by the Bank for International Settlements was $1,852 billion by the end of September 1983.

2   There was a temporary shortening of the average term of bonds and, indeed, of Eurodollar loans in general in 1975; few issues had maturity dates beyond 1982.

3   It should be noted that this effect on the money supply presupposes fixed exchange rates or central bank intervention to moderate changes in the rate. Alternative possible methods of neutralisation are the imposition of a 100% reserve requirement on these deposits or calls for equivalent interest-free special deposits to be placed with the central bank. Japan adopted this device in March 1978. Similarly, in 1977–78, Switzerland, in an attempt to stop the inflow of dollars, imposed a negative interest rate on a proportion of non-resident Swiss franc bank deposits and put a ban on foreign purchases of Swiss domestic securities.

4   In fact, of course, they did so indirectly. When a discount bank borrows from one bank to repay call money to another, it is issuing the surplus reserves of one to relieve a cash shortage in the other.

5   Many inter-bank loans do not leave the banking sector; for example, when a bank borrows to meet its own liquidity requirement or in pursuit of 'matching'.

6   See Table 13 on page 80 of Shaw (1975).

7   Only rarely does a clearing bank thus speculate on the future course of interest rates.

8   Though they are usually lower than the local authority and finance house deposit rates.

PART B

Monetary theory

CHAPTER SEVEN

Money in Classical economic theory

One extreme view of the contribution of money to economic welfare would be that 'money does not matter', a phrase which can have several interpretations. For example, we could say that money is not wealth. It is true that any one person would be better off if he had more money, but this is because it would give him a bigger claim on goods and services produced by the rest of society, who would therefore in that sense and to that extent be made worse off. If everyone's stock of money were doubled, nobody would be better off. The wealth of a community lies in its *real* resources. Money is not such a resource; it cannot be eaten or drunk or worn, it cannot provide shelter, and it is not productive. Double the quantity of money and you do not add one iota to the community's natural resources, or its capital, or the skills and energy of its people. Similarly, if we think of prosperity as a flow of income rather than a stock of wealth. It is *real* income that matters, not money income; not the size of the wage-packet but what one can buy with it. If all money incomes and prices double but the output of goods and services remains the same, nobody's lot is improved.

We could go on to argue from this that there is another sense in which money does not matter. Money may not be wealth, but it is nevertheless useful because with it we can avoid the inconvenience of exchange by barter. Money can, admittedly, thus be a powerful aid to economic efficiency (and hence to economic welfare) because it makes the business of exchange easier and less time-consuming and in so doing also encourages specialisation and all the economic benefits which follow from it. But that is all. Money is nothing more than a lubricant of trade: it has no effect on the economic system other than this. To change the metaphor, money is a *veil* behind which the economic processes of earning and spending, production and distribution, buying and selling go on much as they would if there were no money. The only difference is that they proceed more smoothly. So when we use the phrase 'money does not matter' in this second sense, what we mean is that money and the use of money do not disturb or distort the patterns of economic activity. Money does not affect the so-called 'real sector' of the economic system.

It is this view of money which we now attribute to the classical economists. Their economic analysis did in fact tend to be dichotomised into two distinct parts: the real sector and the monetary sector.

The real sector – 'general equilibrium'

Study of the real sector of the economy is concerned with the analysis of real wealth and real income and what causes them to grow, and of the determination of relative prices and relative incomes. Perhaps the main achievement of the Classical school was the grand concept of 'general equilibrium', a statement of the conditions under which the pattern of all relative prices (including the prices of factors of production as well as goods and services) will be such that the whole system is in equilibrium; a situation in which the economic activities of all the participants in the system, each trying to maximise his own rewards and satisfactions, are consistent, or in harmony, and every participant is 'in an equilibrium situation', i.e. nobody is being induced to change the type or amount of economic activity he is currently undertaking. But general equilibrium thus defined is not a complete model of the economic system. It is concerned with relative prices only, leaving absolute prices undetermined. Suppose that, starting from such a position of general equilibrium: *(Situation I)* The wages of carpenters and clerks rise because for some reason the demand for their services increases, or the rate of interest falls because people become more thrifty, or the price of steel falls because a new and more efficient method of producing steel is discovered. Then equilibrium will be disturbed. Some people will want to leave their present jobs and become carpenters or clerks, investors will want to invest more, or steel users will want to buy more steel. *(Situation II)* The system would no longer be 'at rest'; some people will be changing, or planning to change, one or more of their economic activities because relative prices have altered. The effects will be felt not just in the steel industry or the carpenters' trade union or the capital goods industries, but in every other industry which was even remotely competing or complementary with them. The repercussions will almost certainly spread through the whole system, and when all the adjustments have been made and equilibrium restored *(Situation III)* the pattern of production and employment and of relative prices will be different from that of Situations I and II. In short, given the underlying determinants of relative demands and supplies (the 'parameters' of the system), only one set of relative prices is consistent with any equilibrium: the model is 'determinate in relative prices'. But it is indeterminate in absolute prices. If, starting from Situation I, *every* price went up by the *same* percentage, or if *every* price fell by the *same* percentage, then equilibrium would not be disturbed. Nobody would be any richer or poorer; nobody would be induced to do more, or less, work; to save or invest more or less; to produce more or less of anything, or to buy more or less of anything: simply because every price paid, and every price received, would have changed to the same degree. The microeconomic general equilibrium system can be in equilibrium at any level of absolute prices. It therefore leaves absolute prices indeterminate, i.e. it cannot explain why any given level of absolute prices is what it is. The explanation comes in the other part of 'the Classical system', the monetary analysis.

The monetary sector: the quantity theory of money

This said, in effect, that absolute prices − the general price level (P) − are determined solely by the quantity of money. Their monetary theory also answered the question: What happens if we increase or reduce the quantity of money (M)? The answer was simple: All prices rise (fall) proportionately with the quantity of money. Double M and P (the price level) rises by 100%; reduce M by 5% and P falls 5%. The monetary theory thus rounds off their analysis, makes the system completely determinate. There is a unique pattern of relative prices, given the real parameters of the system. Similarly, there is only one possible general price level, given the quantity of money.

The equation of exchange

But M is not the only monetary parameter. It is obvious that money only affects P if it is spent. The flow of spending in any period, the total offer of money against goods, is measured not just by the quantity of money in use, but by that quantity of money multiplied by the number of times it is spent: the speed, or velocity, of circulation of money (V). Set this total spending in any period (M × V) against the total volume of transactions (T) in the same period and we arrive at the price level.

This relation between our variables M, V, T and P is summarised in the identity:

$$MV \equiv PT \qquad [7.1]$$

This 'equation of exchange' is a truism: it expresses a tautology, since the two sides of the equation are by their definition necessarily equal. It is not an equation, but an identity. Total expenditure on goods and services (MV) over a given period of time is really only another way of expressing the total value of goods and services sold (PT) in that period. The equation is, strictly speaking, non-operational; it cannot be tested by measuring the actual value of each separate item to ascertain if M × V does in fact equal P × T. One cannot measure 'the volume of transactions', because there is no single standard of measurement into which we can convert other diverse standards like gallons and tons. There is only one way in which we can add together, say, a kilo of oranges, a metre of cloth, and two hours' entertainment at the theatre; that is, by measuring them in terms of their money values, i.e. their prices. Money-value is the only yardstick common to them all. We could therefore measure PT, but not T alone. It is, however, possible to measure, *roughly*, changes in P and T separately by the technique of weighted index numbers.

It is impossible to measure transactions' velocity directly, if only because there is no record of most transactions. Any research designed to test the validity of MV × PT would be futile (see Shackle and Phelps-Brown 1938; Welham 1969), for even if all the terms in the equation were perfectly operational and we could measure them all directly, and accurately, failure of the equation to meet an empirical test would not disprove it. Rather, it would indicate either that our measurement had been inaccurate or that we had misinterpreted the terms of the equation and so had been measuring the wrong things.

The equation of exchange is, then, not itself a theory of anything; it explains nothing. It becomes a theory – or, rather, the expression of a theory – if we insert into it some sequence of cause and effect derived either from a priori reasoning or from observation of events. The causal sequence affirmed by Classical theory was that the prime mover is the quantity of money. It is changes in M which *initiate* changes in the value of MV and PT. The most rigid form of the theory states further that the consequential change in PT which keeps it equal to MV is a change in P alone. V and T are thus assumed, or asserted, to be constant terms in the equation. This was *not* meant to imply that they never alter, that they are constant through time, but that they are reasonably stable, i.e. that they only change slowly; more important, that they are independent of changes in M and P.

This expression of the Quantity Theory of Money, in terms of M, V, P and T, is known as the *Transactions Velocity* version. It is particularly associated with the American economist, Irving Fisher, who gave us the most detailed and comprehensive statement of the Quantity Theory of Money in his book, *The Purchasing Power of Money*, published in 1911.[1] He was not, however, the originator of the Quantity Theory, nor even of the Equation of Exchange. In fact, according to Hegeland (1951: 35), 'The most elucidating account of the essence of the original quantity theory is furnished by David Hume' (1711–76) and that John Locke (1632–1704) 'gives the most clear-cut statement of the quantity theory'. While Marget (1942) says that the 'type of reasoning' which gives the quantity of money a place in the determination of prices 'goes back at least as far as the time of Jean Bodin' (1530–96). The transactions-velocity approach had been put into an algebraic form, similar to Fisher's, a century earlier, and Fisher himself acknowledged an earlier (1886) virtually identical equation enunciated by Simon Newcomb, to whom he dedicated *The Purchasing Power of Money*.

Fisher, however, set out to demonstrate the particular relation between money and prices summarised above. As we have seen, this relation presumes that V and T are not affected by changes in M. He listed the determinants of T and V and in neither of these lists was there any mention of the quantity of money. Moreover, his determinants are characteristics of an economic system which are likely to change only slowly – e.g. resources, techniques of production and habits of payment – the fact that some incomes are traditionally paid in weekly and others in monthly instalments, some goods are paid for as they are bought and others on monthly accounts, and so on. Fisher did not regard these determinants as constant: indeed, he thought they had changed in the long run, in ways which had tended to increase T (and so reduce P) and also V (and so increase P). But they are independent of M. To quote Fisher (1911: 154–6):

No reason has been, or, so far as it is apparent, can be assigned, to show why the velocity of circulation of money . . . should be different, when the quantity of money . . . is great, from what it is when the quantity of money

148

is small ... The stream of business depends on natural resources and technical conditions, not on the quantity of money. The whole machinery of production, transportation, and sale is a matter of physical capacities and technique, none of which depend on the quantity of money ... a change in the quantity of money will not appreciably affect the quantity of goods sold for money.

Hegeland argues repeatedly that there is a *non sequituré* in proceeding from the proposition that the value of money is in inverse proportion to its quantity, so that the price level is in proportion to the quantity of money, and real wealth and income are independent of the quantity of money, to the assertion that *changes in* the quantity of money *cause* proportional changes in the price level. It is one thing to say that levels of output and the velocity of circulation are not related to the quantity of money in existence, that two communities with similar resources, similar techniques of production, similar habits of payment etc. but different quantities of money, would differ only in their general levels of prices. It is another thing to say that in the process of changing the quantity of money we will not change V and/or T, as well as P. To repeat, a truism, or a simple arithmetic relation between P and M does not imply a simple, direct causal link between them. Fisher also repeatedly stresses that the proportionality of ΔP to ΔM is only valid provided that V and T remain the same. He devoted a whole chapter to an analysis of the 'periods of transition' when the quantity of money is changing. He there recognised that rising prices may increase V as people try to get rid of money quickly because its value is falling; that prices are pushed up by increased purchases, i.e. T will tend to increase; and rising prices mean that more money is needed to finance the same real output so that firms will try to increase their borrowings from the banks, i.e. to increase the quantity of money. But these other effects will disappear when the increase in M and P ceases; V and T will then revert to the levels fixed by the basic determinants: 'the strictly proportional effect on prices of an increase in M is only the normal or ultimate effect after transition periods are over' (Fisher 1911: 159). Fisher's quantity theory, then, is essentially a long-run theory as the transitional period could extend to ten years.

The Cambridge equation

An alternative approach is the *Cash Balances* theory in which the V of the transactions–velocity approach is replaced by 'the demand for money'. The concept of a demand to hold money-balances, and the analysis of the motives which give rise to that demand, have a long history. It is to be found, for example, in Henry Thornton's *An Enquiry into the Nature and Effects of the Paper Credit of Great Britain*, 1802. But this version of the quantity theory was developed mainly in the twentieth century by a succession of economists at Cambridge, notably by Marshall, Pigou, Keynes and Robertson. Their various equations are therefore referred to as the Cambridge equations, of which the one most frequently cited is:

$$M = kPR \text{ (see Pigou 1917)} \qquad [7.2]$$

M is the quantity of money, P is the price level, k is the proportion of R over which people wish to hold command in the form of money. R is 'real resources', but has different meanings in different versions of the equation. It is variously defined as the total stock of wealth, the prospective flow of income, or a mixture of real income and real wealth, or of real income and real transactions.

The two equations compared

There is an obvious similarity between the Fisher equation and the Cambridge equation. Holding money is the opposite of spending it. Let us suppose that R were identical with Fisher's T (total transactions) and P stands for the average of the same set of prices in both cases. Whether money is held against transactions, or as a proportion of wealth or income, or for any other motive, the average value of actual money holdings could be *expressed* as a proportion of PT. Next, suppose that M = 100. It must be held by someone. If k = $\frac{1}{3}$, the Cambridge equation tells us that PR = 300. Since PR = PT, PT also has a value of 300. Since MV = PT, V = PT/M = 3. So the value of k would be simply the inverse of the value of V.[2] Some of the determinants of k, as stated by Robertson, are very similar to the determinants of Fisher's V; in particular, the frequency and regularity of payments. Others are the return on assets alternative to holdings of money, the degree of vertical integration of industry (the amalgamation of two successive stages of production eliminates the need to hold money against payments between them), the existence of partial substitutes for money, and 'the degree of certainty and confidence with which consumers and producers are making their plans' (Robertson 1965:336). Are these two versions then virtually identical?

T is the total value of goods and services bought and sold in a given period of time. It comprises *all* transactions. One should include 'financial' transactions such as the making and repayment of loans, the purchase of shares on the Stock Exchange, and so on. Purchases and sales of second-hand goods are also transactions requiring the use of money. 'Intermediate' transactions are also included: sales of 'intermediate' goods, those which are assembled or processed or manufactured into 'final' goods. It follows that PT will be some multiple of the value of the 'final goods'. V is *transactions-velocity*, the relation between M and the total value of all transactions. As we have seen, R has been given different meanings. The value of k will differ as the constant of R differs; the proportion of desired money holdings to wealth is probably different from the proportion of desired money holdings to income. But none of the suggested versions of R is identical with T. It follows that k is not simply the inverse of V, but if we define R as income, k is the inverse of *income-velocity* of circulation, which is the relation between the value of output and sales of *final* goods and services and the quantity of money. PT will always be bigger than PR, hence transactions velocity will always be higher than income velocity. If the structure of production and distribution – i.e. the number of money-transactions required to transform raw materials into final goods in the hands of the ultimate purchaser – does not change, then the ratio of transaction velocity to income velocity will not change: but they are not identical.[3]

Though we can assimilate the two equations by assimilating definitions, there is still an important difference between the two approaches.

The superiority of the Cambridge version

The transactions-velocity analysis is concerned with the flow of spending. The cash-balances approach is a 'stock analysis' concerned with money held rather than money being spent. In Sir Dennis Robertson's phrase, one looks at 'money on the wing', the other at 'money sitting'. This brings us to a frequently asserted superiority of the cash-balances approach over the transaction-velocity approach. The Cambridge equation is a tautology, a mere arithmetic relation, no less than the Fisher equation. But when we come to use it as the framework of a theory, its taxonomy has greater explanatory power. The concept of 'demand for money balances', it is suggested, has three distinct advantages over the velocity concept.

1 It is one explanation of V itself. Velocity of circulation is the result of decisions to spend money rather than hold it; that is, decisions as to the size of k. The latter is thus a more fundamental explanatory concept than V.

2 The Cambridge economists were members of what has been called the Neo-Classical school, whose main contribution to economic theory was the explanation and enunciation of the 'equi-marginal principle'. The concept k was essentially an application of this principle to monetary theory. Just as the consumer equates relative marginal utilities of goods with their relative prices, just as producers equate marginal revenue productivities of factors with their marginal costs and overall marginal cost with marginal revenue, so does the holder of money balances equate the marginal utility of those balances with the cost of holding them. Robertson (1965: 22) tells us that 'we must picture the individual distributing his real income between the uses of immediate consumption, of adding to his income-bearing property, and of adding to his store of ready value in such ways as to make equal the marginal utility derived from each use'. In thus extending the marginal utility theory of value to money, applying the same technique to the analysis of 'the monetary sector' and of 'the real sector', the cash-balances approach begins to close the Classical gap between them and represents a step towards the integration of monetary theory into the general framework of economic theory. In substituting 'demand for

money' for 'velocity of circulation', it treats money as a good which, like other goods, possesses utility. Money is useful because it satisfies the desire for 'liquidity', it is 'a store of ready value', and the demand for money therefore is analogous to the demand for other goods.

3   There may be little or no 'volition' or real decision-taking in the demand for money to hold against transactions. We *need* a certain amount of money to finance our expenditure between one pay-day or receipt of revenue and the next, and that is that. To keep less money in hand than we think we shall need is foolish, and there is nothing to be gained by keeping more. But the very idea of a 'demand for money' sets us looking for motives, reasons why people and corporations should really wish, rather than merely need, to hold money. It is only a short step from this to two important questions:
(a)   Are there any reasons for holding money other than the need to finance day-to-day payments?
(b)   Is the demand for money stable: might not it change because of those other motives? If so, in what circumstances is it likely to be high or low, and in what circumstances is it likely to rise or fall?

The earlier work of the Cambridge School did not pursue these questions very far, but they opened up the path along which Keynes moved to his final rejection and refutation of accepted monetary theory.[4] It was he who eventually produced a coherent answer, with a new theory. In his early work, he adopted the cash-balances theory, but as early as 1924 he was moving away from the Classical view of money; e.g. on page 75 of his *Tract on Monetary Reform* he suggests that 'when people find themselves with more cash than they require' for day-to-day purposes, 'they get rid of the surplus by buying goods or investments, or by leaving it for a bank to employ or, possibly by increasing their hoarded reserves'. A change in M, especially if people expect further changes, 'may produce a more than proportionate effect on P' because 'there will be some reaction to the value of k ...' and in trade cycles, k tends 'to diminish during the boom and increase during the depression' (pp. 81–83). His major work, *The General Theory of Employment, Interest and Money*, published in 1936, can be viewed as an extended attack on the Classical theory.

How the quantity of money determines the price level

Although the two approaches were different, their notions of the mechanism by which the quantity of money influences the price level were remarkably similar. The logic of the cash-balances theory is that people wish to hold a certain amount of money which is related to their real income (or wealth, or a combination of the two) and the price level. If the quantity of money increases so do their money balances, since all money in existence must be owned (held) by somebody. So if money balances were at their desired (i.e. equilibrium) level before, some people (if not all) must now have bigger balances than they desire. They therefore try to spend the surplus. Now any one person can get rid of the excess by spending it, but in so doing he passes the money on to other people, which increases *their* surplus. If nothing else changes, the community as a whole cannot rid itself of this unwanted money. But other things do change. The increased spending – i.e. increased demand for goods and services – must push up prices, or call forth a bigger output, or both. In short, the increase in M leads to an equal proportional increase in PR (the rigid quantity theory would assert that the increase is wholly in P); k is thus restored to its equilibrium level. Compare this with the following quotation from Fisher (1911: 152–4):

> Suppose, for a moment, that a doubling in the currency in circulation should not at once raise prices, but should halve the velocities instead; such a result would evidently upset for each individual the adjustment which he had made of cash on hand. Prices being unchanged, he now has to double the amount of money and deposits which his convenience had taught him to keep on hand. He will then try to get rid of the surplus money and deposits by buying goods. But as somebody else must be found to take the money off his hands, its mere transfer will not diminish the amount in the community. It will simply increase somebody else's surplus. Everybody has money on his hands beyond what experience and convenience have shown to be necessary. Everybody will want to exchange this relatively useless extra money for goods, and the desire so to do must surely drive up the price of goods. No one can deny that the effect of everyone's desiring to spend more money will be to raise prices. Obviously this tendency will continue until there is found another adjustment of quantities to expenditures, and the V's are the same as originally. That is, if there is no change in the quantities sold (the Q's), the only possible effect of doubling M and M' will be a doubling of the P's; ... In short, the only way to get rid of the plethora of money is to raise prices to correspond.

Note the emphasis here on the impact of *aggregate* behaviour.

Determination of aggregate output in Classical theory

Obviously the Classical view of the role of money in the economy is closely tied up with Classical approaches to output and employment. Without entering into a full discussion of these views, it is sufficient to note that, in Classical theory, total output is determined by 'real' factors, such as land, capital, technology and labour (see Hagen 1971). The operation of market forces in the labour market and the Classical predilection for 'full employment equilibrium' meant, quite simply, that the equilibrium levels of employment and wages must always be at some point on the supply curve of labour. The intersection of the demand and supply curves meant that workers are prepared to supply exactly the amount of labour currently demanded at the going real wage. They are being offered as much employment as they wish to supply at the current real wage. If anyone is unemployed, his unemployment is

153

voluntary in the sense that he could get work if he were prepared to accept a lower real wage. This may seem a harsh definition of 'voluntary unemployment'. It is also a definition of 'full employment' very different from the one we are accustomed to. We take 'full employment' to mean 'a low level of unemployment'. What percentage of unemployment is regarded as 'low' is a matter of opinion. There is no a priori limit to the level of unemployment consistent with Classical 'full employment'; *any* point on the supply schedule is potentially a 'full employment' position.[5] Interestingly, Keynes in the *General theory* expressed views not too dissimilar from these when he said 'apparent unemployment . . . must be due at bottom to a refusal by the unemployed factors to accept a reward which corresponds to their marginal productivity' (p. 16). This concept of unemployment excludes 'temporary' unemployment 'between jobs'. Together with all the other Classical notions such as the Law of Diminishing Marginal Productivity, the conclusion to be drawn from this analysis is that output and employment are determined by the willingness to supply labour and the quantity and quality of the other resources on which, and with which, men/women work. Output is not affected by changes in the quantity of money, the whole effect of which is, therefore, expended on changing the price level.

How does this square with the obvious truth that employment depends on spending, that men will only be employed if someone is prepared to spend money on the product of their labour? Last week's spending provides the revenue to pay this week's wages, salaries, interest and profits, but will this week's spending necessarily be enough to pay for the same amount of labour and output next week? If not, if some of this week's output is not sold, will there not be some unemployment next week because of 'deficiency of effective demand'? The Classical answer was that any such unemployment would only be temporary. Normal market forces would quickly bring the economy back to full-employment equilibrium. Persistent unemployment was ruled out by two fundamental tenets of Classical economics: their acceptance of Say's law and their assumption that prices and money wages are flexible.

Say's law

The simplest expression of this law, first stated by the French economist Jean Baptiste Say (1767–1832), is that 'supply creates its own demand'. Set in the context of a barter economy, this is a statement of the obvious. Goods are brought to market only to be exchanged for other goods: the supply of one good is a demand for another good. In a money-using economy, goods are supplied in exchange not for other goods, but for money. If supplies of goods are to be necessarily equal to the demand for other goods, it must therefore be assumed that all the money received by suppliers of goods is used to demand other goods, i.e. is spent. This does not imply that every good produced must always be sold, certainly not at the price expected by the producer. There can be overproduction of some goods (as, indeed, there can be in a barter economy); there is no presumed compulsion on anyone to buy something he does not want to buy at the price at which it is offered. But since the value of total output is paid out as incomes for producing that output, if the demand for some goods is less than their outputs, either some part of those incomes must have remained unspent or else the demand for some other goods must be bigger than their output. If we eliminate the first alternative (unspent income), any deficiency of demand in one industry implies an equal excess demand elsewhere; there can be no *general* over-production. The consequences of overproduction of some items is obvious; some prices fall and others rise; some prices received, and hence profits earned, are lower while other prices and profits are higher than the producers anticipated, and production will be switched from the unpopular to the popular goods.

The world of Say's law is, apparently, a world in which money is not wanted for its own sake, but only as a medium of exchange. We exchange goods, or our services, for money and then money for other goods or services 'Money performs but a monetary function in this double exchange; and when the transaction is finally closed, it will always be found that one kind of produce has exchanged for another' (Say, quoted by Skinner 1967: 159). But Say did *not* aver that all incomes will be spent on consumption. Indeed, he did mention the possibility that money may be hoarded, i.e. held as idle balances, and noted that this would lead to lower prices, losses and 'calamity widely diffused'. But he thought that hoarding is improbable, and that any money saved will rather be 'in all cases expended and consumed'. Money hoarded is 'barren', it earns nothing. In the Classical view, rational men will not hold money idle when they can earn income on it, and such income can be earned by using one's savings to buy either capital goods, or bonds or shares.

The Classical theory of interest

This was part of the 'real' analysis. Interest, in Classical thought, is a real phenomenon, not a monetary one. It is, of course, the price paid for the use of money, but it is deter-mined by the 'real' forces of productivity on the one hand and thrift on the other. Interest is a function of the demand for, and the supply of, money capital. The demand for finance arises from the productivity of capital, the fact that the use of capitalistic or 'roundabout' methods of production increases the productivity of other resources by more than the depreciation-cost of the capital goods employed. Capital, like other factors, is subject to the Law of Diminishing Marginal Produc-tivity, hence the demand schedule for finance has a negative slope. The supply of finance comes from savings. People accumulate savings by 'abstaining from consump-tion', and interest is their reward. Moreover, saving is interest-elastic; a higher rate of interest will call forth more saving. So the determination of *the* rate of interest[6] can be shown by the usual demand and supply 'curves' (see Fig. 7.1).

The equilibrium rate of interest r_0 is arrived at in the usual way; if the rate were set at a level above r_0, say at r_1, the supply of finance would exceed the demand for finance, and the rate would fall. The market for finance is only in equilibrium when the quantity demanded at the current rate of interest equals the amount being saved at the current rate. It was assumed that this equilibrium rate of interest will always be positive; saving and lending always earns a positive reward, because there will always

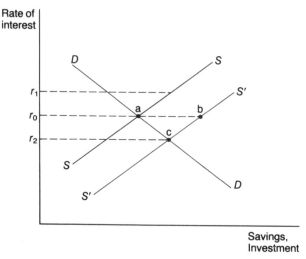

Fig 7.1   The Classical theory of interest

be enough profitable avenues of investment to warrant a positive demand price for finance. An excess of thrift – a desire to consume less and save more at any given rate of interest – is represented by a shift to the right of the supply schedule. This creates an excess supply of finance (savings), which causes the rate of interest to fall, which discourages savings and stimulates investment, and the market gradually moves to a new equilibrium with $r = r_2$. We can see this adjustment as a movement from position a to position b to position c. Investment, therefore, takes up any deficiency of total demand caused by the community failing to spend all its income on consumption. If the community's intended saving ever differs from its intended investment, saving and investment will be brought back into equilibrium by a change in the rate of interest. Moreover, when we couple this analysis of saving, investment and interest rates with the concept of a given total output, determined essentially by the parameters of supply, we see that consumption and investment are true alternatives; indeed, competitors. Investment depends on saving: the community can only invest in so far as it is willing to abstain from consumption. The function of the rate of interest is to act as a price, both to savers and investors, which equates desired saving (= supply of finance) with desired investment (= demand for finance). The distribution of the given total output between consumption and investment is thus determined by the market forces of demand and supply, operating through the price mechanism (the price in this context being the rate of interest).

So far, Say's law, or Say's identity, does not guarantee full employment, but only that any given level of output, employment and income will be maintained. With flexible wages, however, involuntary unemployment will give rise to competition for jobs, which forces money wages down. With flexible prices, competition between firms for sales will force prices down, and with a constant MV aggregate, real demand increases proportionally with the fall in prices. Prices must not, however, fall as far as money wages; an increase in output brings a fall in the marginal productivity of labour and must be accompanied by a fall in real wages if it is to be worthwhile for employers.

Hoarding and quantity theory

Say's law appears to imply that there will be no hoarding, no desire to hold money idle. If some money *is* taken out of circulation, total demand, represented by MV, declines. The consequent competition between producers for the smaller total revenue will induce a fall in prices. If money wages do not fall, real wages will now be higher. But if real wages rise, employment falls and competition between workers for jobs will then push money wages and real wages down. Prices and money wages will fall until the smaller MV is sufficient to buy the output produced at full employment (on the Classical definition). Goods and services not bought by the hoarders will be bought by the non-hoarders, whose (constant) money expenditure will buy more as prices fall. Any decline in MV will be matched by a decline in P, leaving employment and real wages unchanged. Prices are then a function of MV, not of M. The validity of the quantity theory hypothesis that the price level is a function only of the total supply of money requires either that all money is active (the Classical assertion) or a constant distribution of money holdings between active and idle balances.

Why should people want to hold a constant proportion of M as an asset? It would be a very unusual kind of demand function which produced this result. Indeed, a priori reasoning suggests that the demand function would not be like this. Remember, the Classical hypothesis that money is barren and therefore no rational man will hold it as an asset when he can earn a return from lending or investing it. We are now suggesting that it is not barren: money has a utility of its own; the possession of a money asset gives satisfaction to the holder. The general theory of choice surely suggests that decisions to hold money idle will be 'choice at the margin' decisions; people will determine their money holdings by marginal comparisons of the satisfaction derived from money assets with that derived from lending or investing, or from consumption. That much was suggested by the Cambridge School. 'Idle balances' then will probably vary inversely with the reward for lending or investing, i.e. inversely with interest rates.

Suppose, then, we insert into Classical theory a demand for money as an asset which varies directly with the price level and inversely with interest rates. The 'pure' quantity theory result could be maintained by a mechanism such as the following: Suppose that the quantity of money doubles; the first effect is to leave the public with more 'active' balances than they need at the current price level and/or more idle balances than they wish to hold at the current price level and rate of interest. One effect will be a fall in the rate of interest; just as excess transactions balances 'spill over' into demand for goods, so do excess asset balances spill over into a demand for bonds, shares and other financial assets, so raising their prices. A rise in the price of securities is a fall in the rate of interest, i.e. the yield on them. So, assuming that the rate of interest was in equilibrium at the outset, it will now be below the marginal productivity of capital goods. The consequences are as follows: (1) Firms will be disposed to buy more capital goods. This increased demand for capital goods is not accompanied by a reduced demand for other goods and services. Indeed, if transaction balances are larger, demand for goods of all kinds will be higher. But output as a whole is determined by 'real' forces, so the only result of this increase in demand originating in 'the monetary sector' is to push up prices all round. Hence firms spend more on capital goods, even though they may not actually buy more of them. (2) As prices rise, real wages fall. So money wages must rise equally with prices if the supply of labour, and hence output, are to be maintained. (3) To buy the same quantity of capital goods at higher prices, firms will need more finance, i.e. will issue more securities. Thus the supply of bonds will increase, reversing the decline in interest rates.

The system will gradually move to a new equilibrium, whose main features are easily predictable, given the Classical assumptions. The quantity of money has doubled and so have all prices. Money wages have doubled and real wages are unchanged. Total real output is also unchanged but its money value is doubled. Nominal money balances have doubled and real balances are unchanged, since all prices are twice as high as before. The cost of investment goods has doubled, but so have the money returns from investment. The profitable level of real investment by firms will therefore be the same as before but investment in money terms will be twice as high as before, requiring twice as much finance. The supply of bonds will therefore have doubled.[7] Since the demand for bonds will have doubled also, the rate of interest is the same as it was originally, and 'real' holdings of bonds – i.e. their value in terms of goods – will be unchanged. The money supply is distributed between active and idle balances in the original proportions. The demand for asset money will be in equilibrium with doubled holdings of money and of bonds, at the original interest rates.

The Classical dichotomy

A major criticism of the Classical analysis is that there is a logical error in 'the Classical dichotomy': the separation of the real analysis and the monetary analysis. The main task of the real analysis was to explain *relative* prices and outputs, why apples cost 40p a pound and potatoes 20p, not vice versa, and why the outputs of apples and potatoes are what they are. The explanation was entirely in terms of real determinants: essentially, the community's preferences (including the choices between income and leisure and between present and future income) on the one hand and production functions on the other. It is *relative* prices which establish equilibrium. The assertion that an equal change in all prices leaves demand and supply unchanged is called the homogeneity postulate: supply and demand are *homogeneous of degree zero in absolute prices*. The function of money is to determine absolute prices, and therefore the task of monetary theory is to explain how it does so, and the quantity theory of money states that the price level will change proportionally with changes in the quantity of money. Here, then, we have the dichotomy: a theory of value to explain relative prices and a monetary theory to explain absolute prices. The two theories, and the two aspects of the economy, the real and the monetary, are quite distinct and independent. Demand and supply of goods are functions of relative prices only. A change in the quantity of money will only change the general level of absolute prices; it will not affect outputs, nor relative prices.

Say's law, Walras' law, and the Classical contradiction

Suppose we begin with the barter economy, and then try to make barters easier by instituting a system of pricing goods in terms of some common object or abstract unit. There is no medium of exchange, but there is a unit of account. We can, if we wish, apply the name 'money' to this unit of account, this yardstick by which all values are measured, but remember that it is performing only one of the functions we normally associate with money. The Classical dichotomy is then valid. If we 'double the quantity of money' by a decree that the unit of account shall have twice its previous value, say 'ten pence' instead of 'five pence', all that happens is that prices are also doubled. If this seems too fanciful, we can assume that there are two 'moneys': a unit of account in which prices are expressed, and a supply of token coins, each given a certain value in terms of the unit of account and having no use except as a medium of exchange. We can then 'double the quantity of money' simply by doubling the face value of every coin. Exchanges will continue exactly as before, because the terms on which one good or service exchanges for any other will be exactly the same as before. An equal change in all absolute prices does not alter supply and demand for goods. Supply and demand are homogeneous of degree zero in absolute prices. Relative prices and absolute prices are determined by two quite separate processes, the former by market forces of supply and demand, the latter by arbitrary decree.

Once we think of money as a medium of exchange, embodied in tangible objects such as notes and coins, these objects would appear to be a useful possession: they avoid the difficulty of 'double-coincidence of wants' and so on. Suppliers of goods will not necessarily demand other goods in exchange; they will accept money instead of goods. At this point we introduce another well-known identity, *Walras' law*. Since every supplier of goods demands other goods, or money, to the value of the goods supplied, and every buyer is prepared to give goods or money to that value, 'Every demand is thus matched by an equal supply (in dollar terms) of some other items and vice versa. It follows at once that the total money value of all items supplied must equal the total money value of all items demanded' (see Baumol 1965: 341). In equilibrium, the total supply of money-plus-goods equals the total demand for money-plus-goods.

Next, we recall Say's law, which asserts that the supply of goods alone necessarily equals the demand for goods alone. It implies that suppliers accept money for their goods only in order to use it to buy other goods; money has no value except as a unit of account and a medium of exchange. Walras' law by itself allows for a disequilibrium in one sector balanced by an equal and opposite disequilibrium in another; e.g. if there were an excess supply of goods, there would be an equal excess demand for money. But if there must be equilibrium overall (i.e. the aggregate of all demands necessarily equals the aggregate of all supplies) and if there is also a necessary equilibrium in the real sector (i.e. total demand for goods equals total supply of goods (Say's identity)), then by a simple subtraction of the 'real' set from the total set of demand and supply equations, there must also be equilibrium in the money market. Acceptance of the homogeneity postulate – that the real sector remains in equilibrium at any set of absolute prices so long as relative prices do not change – now implies (by Walras' law) that an equal proportionate change in all absolute prices cannot disturb an equilibrium of supply and demand for money either. The 'money market'[8] also can be in equilibrium at any level of absolute prices. The general price level is thus left quite indeterminate; full equilibrium of both the real and the money market is equally possible at any price level. A change in the price level will not affect demand for goods, even if the quantity of money is constant. Only a change in relative prices can affect the demand and supply of goods. A change in the money supply will have no effect on the price level since there can be no excess demand for, or supply of, money. The condition of equilibrium that the demand for money equals the supply cannot be used to determine the price level. All this clearly contradicts the quantity theory, that the quantity of money determines the price level. For any given quantity of money there is one, and only one, equilibrium level of absolute prices; it is through changes in the general price level that the demand for money is brought into equality with a changed supply of money.

Resolving the contradiction

Money as wealth and the real balance effect

This approach is particularly associated with the work of Patinkin (1965). In a world in which the volume of transactions is assumed constant, the real balance version of the demand for money is, Patinkin argues, a logical corollary or implication of the assertion that money is held only against transactions.

First, we need the hypothesis, which seems reasonable, that demand for goods depends not just on tastes and incomes, but also on wealth. The greater our wealth, the more we can afford to spend out of a given income or in excess of our income. Money is one form of wealth *for the individual*; because it 'gives command over' real resources, it is a possible asset as well as a medium of exchange. So in a money-using economy, holdings of money are one of the determinants of demand for and supply of goods and services. The quantity of money, and the proportions in which it is distributed between different holders of money (e.g. spendthrifts and misers), will therefore affect demand for goods and services. There is now no longer a dichotomy between the real and the monetary analysis, between the determination of relative prices and of the general price level. Patinkin integrated monetary and value theory in two ways. First, he brought the quantity of money and its distribution (which are the concerns of monetary theory) directly into the analysis of supply and demand for goods and the determination of their prices (which are the subject matter of value theory). In effect, he introduced money balances and absolute prices (in the form M/P) into demand functions alongside tastes, incomes and relative prices. Second, since by implication we are now treating money as a good in its own right, with a utility of its own, we have destroyed the distinction between relative and absolute prices. Absolute prices have become simply another relative price; they are the exchange ratio, the money-per-unit-of-goods ratio, between money and other goods. They can be explained in much the same way as other relative prices, allowing for any peculiarities in the nature of money as a good; as, for example, if we say that the utility of money derives wholly from the fact that it is a source of ready purchasing power, it 'gives command over' other goods.

In this analysis, the quantity theory solution that all prices change in equal proportion with the money supply rests on a *real balance effect*; the demand for money is a demand for money balances of a certain purchasing power. Assume an increase in the quantity of money, and let us suppose that there is complete *money illusion.*[9] If people feel wealthier because they hold more money, they will spend more. Prices therefore rise, but if we interpret 'complete money illusion' rigidly, nobody realises that this is reducing real wealth and so everyone continues to demand more goods. Prices and income rise without limit because there is a permanent state of excess of supply over demand in the 'market' for money and, therefore, a corresponding excess of demand over supply in the market for goods and services. Money illusions would surely disappear eventually, but we cannot say how far prices must rise before it does so. If there is less-than-absolute money illusion, prices will rise more than proportionally with the quantity of money; people realise that their real wealth is declining as prices rise, but are not fully aware of the connection between prices and real wealth. One could also argue, again as a matter of pure logic, that if money is regarded as just another good, with no peculiarities, the effect on the economic system of an increase in the quantity of money is similar to the effect of an increase in the supply of any other good: it will throw out ripples through the whole system, changing other relative prices as well as its own, and there is no a priori reason why the new equilibrium should be a replica of the old, with all prices changed by the same percentage.

Only if the demand for money is a demand for real balances, only if money is wanted solely for its *general* real purchasing power (subject to previous discussion of the possible demand for money as an asset) do we get the results predicted by quantity theory. With no change in aggregate relative preference for real money balances as compared with any other good, an increase in the quantity of money gives an excess supply of money; people therefore spend the excess uniformly over all goods, and all prices rise until real balances are as before, i.e. until the change in P is equal to the change in M.

The real balance effect destroys the homogeneity postulate and the Classical dichotomy. If the community has less money than it wishes to hold, if there is an excess demand for money, this will reduce the demand for and increase the supply of goods, creating an excess supply of goods. It is eliminated by a fall in the price level which increases real balances: demands and supplies of goods are not independent of

161

the price level. (If everyone's money holdings changed in exactly the same way as prices, of course, demand and supply of goods would remain the same.) A change in the monetary sector — i.e. in the demand for, or supply of, money — does affect the demand for goods, it does affect the real sector; indeed, that is the logic of the quantity theory.

One way of resolving the contradiction, then, is to eliminate the dichotomy and deny the homogeneity postulate. Is it possible to preserve the dichotomy without contradicting the quantity theory?

The transactions-balances requirement

The Fisher analysis resolves the problem quite simply. In the real world, where money must be held as an asset between pay-days and between transactions (if only because it would not be profitable, or even feasible, to switch into and out of non-money assets for very short periods and/or small sums), there is an upper limit to the velocity of circulation. With a fixed T and a constant V, both determined by non-monetary factors, there is a determinate price level set by M and whatever V happens to be. In other words, there is no contradiction between Say's law and quantity theory.

The assumptions of real-balances theory

There are certain conditions necessary for the validity of the real-balances analysis.

1 If money is to be counted as an asset, and if an increase in the quantity of money is to be a net addition to the wealth of its holders, it must not be accompanied by an equal increase in their indebtedness. This means that it is *outside* money, not *inside* money, to use the current jargon. Outside money is created or produced outside the system, and simply flows into it: paper currency printed and spent by the state. Inside money is money created against private sector debt or the surrender of private sector assets. Bank deposits created by bank loans are the most obvious example; this money is not a net addition to the wealth of the holders, because when they are credited with the bank deposits they also accept an equal indebtedness to the bank. Other bank deposits are created when they buy bills and bonds, but again the customer who acquires the deposits is not thereby made wealthier; he has simply exchanged one kind of asset (bills or bonds) for another (the bank deposit). In neither case is the money holder made worse off by a rise in prices or better off by a fall in prices, simply because he holds money. The borrower's bank balance is worth less in real terms when prices rise, but so is his debt to the bank; and the seller of bonds or bills is no worse off than he would have been if he had held on to the securities, for their real value also falls when prices rise.

In an inside money economy, according to Patinkin, the Classical dichotomy is valid. Suppose the quantity of money increases as a consequence of an open market operation by the central bank. There is no wealth effect, hence no immediate increase in demand for goods; but there is an increase in the ratio of money balances to holdings of bonds, and the holders of the 'excess money' therefore exchange money for bonds. The demand for bonds reduces interest rates, which stimulates investment and so raises prices. The rise in prices increases the quantity of money required for transactions balances and the amount of finance required by firms. The demand for money thus rises proportionally with prices, and in turn reverses the fall in interest rates. In the new equilibrium, prices and the demand for money will have risen equally with the supply of money, as has the nominal value of bonds held. The real value of bond holdings and of money balances will be the same as before, as will interest rates. The price level is still determinate, in spite of the fact that changes in the quantity of money have no direct (i.e. real balance) effect on demand for goods. If prices rise, more money will be required to finance production, interest rates will therefore rise, hence demand for goods will fall, pushing down prices. Holdings of money and bonds, the rate of interest, and demand and supply of goods will only be in equilibrium again when the price rise has been completely reversed.

The crucial difference between this and the outside money analysis is that the force which generates the adjustments to a new equilibrium is a *substitution effect* between money and bonds, not a real balance effect. It is not indisputable that the dichotomy is validated. The quantity of money and the price level are seen to affect demand for goods, the difference being that it is now an indirect effect, via changes in interest rates; further, since investment is a function of the *real* rate of interest, one real quantity is presumably affected by changes in the monetary sector.

2 It assumes that there are no *distribution effects*. If the stock of money doubles, the increase is evenly distributed; everybody's stock of money doubles. Otherwise the result would be 'higher relative price for those goods favoured by individuals whose money holdings have more than doubled and lower relative prices for those goods favoured by individuals whose holdings have less than doubled' (Patinkin 1965: 298). Not all prices would increase proportionally with M. If there are any debts in existence fixed in money terms, then the debtors who gain (lose) by a rise (fall) in prices, must increase (reduce) their spending by exactly the same amount as the creditors, who lose (gain), reduce (increase) theirs. Similarly, if there are any incomes fixed in money terms, e.g. pensions, interest on debentures, we must assume that the payers of those incomes, who presumably gain when prices rise unless their own incomes are fixed in money terms, increase their spending by exactly as much as the recipients reduce theirs, and vice versa.

A further conclusion to be drawn is that we can demonstrate the interdependence of the real and the monetary sectors of the economy via the possible distribution effects of a change in the price level, which can change both the sum and the pattern of demand for goods and services, without need to appeal

163

to the real balance effect. If there are both gainers and losers from a rise in prices, and if the expenditure patterns of those who gain differ from those of the losers, then a monetary change which alters the general price level will affect relative demands, relative prices and hence relative supplies of goods, and will probably affect aggregate demand.

3 A major criticism of real balance theory is its neglect of *expectations*. A fall in prices stimulates spending because it raises the real value of money balances. But if people expect prices to fall still further they have an obvious incentive to spend less now and wait until they think prices have reached rock-bottom. So we have a depressing effect (on expenditure) of expectations to set against the stimulating effect of the fall in prices which has occurred already.[10] Conversely, expectations of further price increases can feed on inflation. Rising (falling) real balances are, however, likely to impose an increasingly strong brake on the expectations effect, especially in an inflation, as Patinkin (1965: 311) states: 'in the absence of adequate real money balances, they just do not have the means by which they can indefinitely increase their demands in accordance with their expectations'. Eventually, the inflation will stop, the expectations effect will disappear, and prices will then fall back to the level dictated by the real balance effect.

There is, however, one rider to add. Any demand for money as an asset may change during an inflation (deflation). A continuous fall in the real value of an asset reduces its desirability as a form of wealth, and vice versa. Alternatively, we can view a prospective fall in its real value as a cost of holding money. People may become accustomed to a lower (higher) ratio of money balances to expenditure, or of money balances to other assets. Is it inevitable that they will revert to the original ratios as the inflation (deflation) ceases? If they do not, the new equilibrium price level will be different from that indicated by the real balance effect.

Criticisms of quantity theory equations

Some criticisms of the quantity theory have been stated, or implied, in the exposition of the theory: the fact that the $MV = PT$ identity is non-operational; the fact that the T of the Fisher equation covers a heterogenous collection of transactions of all kinds; the difficulty of dealing with the index-number problem; and the point that the money payments of a given period (which are the basis of V) are not identical with the value of R or T in that period because many goods and services are either paid for in advance or in arrears. However, perhaps the main defect of the vigorous theory based on these equations is that it is too simple. The direct proportional relation between M and P is only achieved at the cost of highly restrictive assumptions. First there is the implication that the demand for money is a demand for real balances. Second, there is the assumption that all the terms of the equation except P are independent variables: i.e. that a change in one of them does not change the others, the assumption that V and T are constant. All these assumptions are questionable. It is debatable also whether M is always and entirely exogenously determined. A large part of M is created by the banks when they lend to their customers and its creation depends on willingness to borrow as well as willingness to lend, and the willingness to borrow depends largely on 'the state of trade', i.e. on the volume and value of transactions which constitute PT. It is true that variations in interest rates can be used to persuade customers to borrow more, or less, or to sell or buy bonds to/from the banks; but they may not be effective. The banking system can certainly set an upper limit to the quantity of money, irrespective of the pressure of demand for loans, but not a lower limit. The monetary authority may allow, indeed has allowed, M to respond to changes in P and T. A rise in P may, via the expectations effect, reduce the demand for money, whose value is falling, i.e. may increase V. It follows that V, T and M are not independent quantities. A modern capitalist economy does not, left to itself, gravitate to a full employment equilibrium and changes in M can be one of the forces determining output, and hence T. Finally, it is a matter of historical fact that V and T are not constant, and P is not passive and flexible, responding freely to changes in M. Prices and wages are notoriously 'sticky'. More important is the fact that some are more sticky than others; a change in prices or wages is not spread evenly throughout the economy. It follows that changes in prices do have 'distributional effects'; some prices change more than others, some money incomes rise (fall) more than prices, some less, so that some people gain from a change in prices while others lose. Since we earn our incomes from different goods and services, and spend them differently, it follows that a change in the price level will also change the relative demands for and supplies of goods and services. Contrary to the Classical hypothesis, therefore, money is not neutral. Money does matter, and it does affect relative prices and quantities in the real sector.

These criticisms do not imply that the quantity theory is hopelessly wrong, neither is it useless. There have been periods in which we could see a rough relation between secular changes in P and in M. The quantity equations are at least a useful piece of taxonomy. They do list the immediate determinants of P, and everything in monetary theory can be stated in terms of M, V, P and T if we so wish. But M, V and T are not themselves basic economic phenomena; we have to ask what determines M, V and T before we can claim to have a satisfactory theory. As Marget (1938: 81) put it: 'The "quantity equations" themselves are nothing more nor less than shorthand expressions designed to indicate the nature of the variables whose operation can be shown to influence prices'.

This concludes our review of the theory of money, output and prices which is now commonly termed 'the Classical theory'. It is now time to admit that this theory is probably a travesty of the writings of any of the scholars whom we refer to as 'the Classical School' and 'the Neo-Classical School' of economists. For just as there is a problem in defining what Keynes actually meant in his *General theory*, so also with the Classical theory (see Hegeland 1951; Becker and Baumol 1952). Though every part of the analysis can be traced back to one or other of these economists, in none of them would we find the whole analysis presented here, certainly not in this rigid form. In fact, every author who propounded some part of this theory will be found to

165

have qualified his assertions. For example, John Stuart Mill (1852) said that money can affect the real side of the economy when it gets 'out of order' and saw that 'the proposition (that changes in the quantity of money change the price level) is only true other things being the same'. Thornton (1802) argued that the neutrality of money is valid only in the long run; changes in the quantity of money will have 'real' effects in the short run. Hume (1825) recognised that if the quantity of money increases, there will be an 'interval or intermediate situation' during which trade will increase; only the final change in prices will be in proportion to the increase in money. James Mill (1826), after discussing changes in the quantity of money, said 'Similar changes are produced by any alteration in the rapidity of circulation'. Cantillon (1755) objected to the assumption of a constant velocity of circulation and to the assertion that all prices will increase in exact proportion with the quantity of money. Thomas Tooke (1838) denied that the quantity of money is the sole determinant of the price level and, indeed, argued that the quantity of money is determined by prices, rather than prices by the quantity of money.[11] This also seems to have been the view taken by Adam Smith (1776). Later on Marshall (1923) suggested that if the quantity of money were vastly increased, confidence in the currency might be shaken and the velocity of circulation would therefore rise, and he criticised the quantity theory for neglecting the factors which it supposes to remain constant when the quantity of money is changed. We have already noted that Fisher spent a whole chapter on the analysis of 'the transition periods' during which the change in the quantity of money occurs, and concluded that the proportional effect on prices is the ultimate effect, after the transition period (which may last for years) is ended. He had a monetary theory of the trade cycle, emphasising changes in interest rates as a source of fluctuations in economic activity. They did not all assume that hoarding is irrational; indeed, some of them saw a connection between the quantity of money and the rate of interest; several were concerned with the problem of unemployment. Spattered through the pages of the quantity of money theorists are such qualifying phrases as 'other things being equal', 'in the long run', 'the normal case', 'the ultimate effect', 'in equilibrium', and so on. It has to be stressed that the rigid model set out in this chapter has its origin in pre-Keynesian writings, but it has been constructed by post-Keynesian economists for comparison with models based on Keynes' work, which was written in refutation of classical economics. This Keynes makes abundantly clear on page 3 of the *General Theory*: 'I shall argue that the postulates of the classical theory are applicable to a special case only . . . Moreover, the characteristics of the special case assumed by the classical theory happen not to be those of the economic society in which we actually live, with the result that its teaching is misleading and disastrous if we attempt to apply it to the facts of experience.'

Notes

1   Fisher's M comprises currency only, and his equation is $MV + M^1V^1 = PT$, where M^1 and V^1 refer to bank deposits.

2   This shows that k can also be interpreted as the average length of time each unit of money is held. If, on average, money is spent three times in a year; it must be held unspent by each successive holder for one-third of a year.

3   We could, of course, make the two equations substitutable by confining T and V to income transactions only, i.e. transactions in final goods and services and letting R stand for income, i.e. total output of final goods and services.

4   Hudson (1976) has shown that the Cambridge theory as presented by Cassel, Marshall and Pigou denied the 'ceteris paribus' clause of the quantity theory, the assumption of constant V and T, and saw the complication that there is no necessary proportionate relationship between ΔM and ΔP. Both Marshall and Pigou used the technique of choice at the margin to explain the demand for money, which is then a function of, among other determinants, the opportunity cost of holding money, i.e. the return from holding non-money assets. However, they did not explicitly relate the demand for money to the interest rate, nor see the interest rate as a monetary phenomenon.

5   It is noteworthy that modern 'monetarist' analysis, which emphasises the 'natural' rate of unemployment and 'rational' expectations, is in the Classical vein here. Indeed, it is often referred to as 'New Classical' (see Chs 10 and 11).

6   It almost goes without saying that there is not one rate of interest, but several: the rate can be expected to vary with the length of time for which money is lent and with the risk incurred in the loan.

7   There is an underlying assumption here that firms borrow money for one production period only, or that all their capital equipment must be replaced during the period in question; in short, that a doubling of prices necessitates doubling of the nominal supply of bonds.

8   The term does not, of course, have the same meaning here as that in Chapter 2.

9   A situation where people see a given quantity of money as constituting a given value, regardless of the price levels.

10   The same point applies, as the author recognised, to the 'Pigou effect' which states that falling prices will stimulate spending, via the wealth effect, by holders of money and other assets of fixed money value.

11   Congdon (1980) draws a parallel between the current 'monetary base' debate and a similar controversy of the 1840s between the Currency School and the Banking School. The Currency School, propounded by such people as Lord Overstone and Colonel Torrens, argued that the note issue should be closely controlled in order that the currency could behave as if it were a metallic commodity, an approach not far removed from the modern 'monetary base' idea. The Banking School, on the other hand, led by Thomas Tooke and John Fullarton, adopted a stand close to the modern-day neo-Keynesians by arguing that the note issue as such was not responsible for price inflation or commercial crises but, in fact, the reverse: commercial crises were responsible for excessive increases in the note issue. Tooke, in his *History of Prices and the State of the Circulation* advocated, on the basis of evidence over the period 1792 to 1856, that fluctuations in the note issue come after, rather than before,

CHAPTER EIGHT

Keynesian monetary theory

Keynes versus the Classical school

The economic doctrines which are now commonly termed 'the Classical system' may have been appropriate to the nineteenth century. That was a century of growth, of development of new techniques, new products, new lands and, consequently, of expanding trade and production. Growth was not smooth and continuous; there were periods of economic depression and unemployment, but by and large the economic problem was scarcity of supply rather than deficiency of demand, and economists had some justification for accepting full employment as the norm and departures from it as temporary aberrations.

The economic history of the first four decades of the twentieth century, by contrast, was dominated by the trade cycle, the alternation of boom and slump which made it increasingly apparent that full employment is not the natural state of a capitalist economy. There were critics of orthodox economics among professional economists, but the first to provide a coherent and satisfactory explanation of this period of chronic unemployment was John Maynard Keynes, in *The General Theory of Employment, Interest and Money*, published in 1936. This book was a major event in the history of economic thought. Keynes tells us on the first page that the title of the book was intended to 'contrast the character of my argument and conclusions with those of the classical theory of the subject'.

The *General theory* was a revolutionary book. Because it was revolutionary – and because much of the new theory was badly expounded – it was both widely criticised and widely misunderstood (see Hicks 1937, 1974; Shackle 1967, 1972, 1974; and Leijonhufvud 1968, 1981). Yet 'the Keynesian Revolution' became 'the new orthodoxy' with remarkable speed. What is more remarkable, Keynes saw his theory become the foundation of economic policy in his own lifetime. Four years after its publication, he was a member of the Chancellor of the Exchequer's Consultative Council, helping to formulate policy.

Neither the theory nor the practice of Keynesianism are quite so revolutionary as was at first thought. Inevitably, critics have compared him with his predecessors and pointed out that he did not destroy the Classical structure and build afresh. Some have argued that, contrary to what he claimed, 'the Keynesian system' is no more than a variant, a special case, of the Classical system. It is certainly true that some of the basic concepts of Keynesian economics are pre-Keynesian. The possible divergence of saving from investment, the Keynesian relationship between saving and income, the deflationary nature of saving, the multiplier; all these are to be found in the literature before 1936. Keynes' achievement was to bring together a number of separate concepts and analyses, including some of his own, and build them into a theory not just of interest, or of employment, or of money, but a *general theory* which embraced all three. In so doing he made two major contributions to economic science: first, he integrated monetary theory and value theory, and clearly demonstrated some important reciprocities between the monetary sector and the real sector; second, his theory could explain the instability of a capitalist economy, and showed that persistent unemployment is as natural to it as full employment, and more to be expected.

The first difference between Classical and Keynesian economics is the latter's emphasis on demand as the determinant of income, employment and prices, and its comparative neglect of supply.[1] The flow of goods and services is produced only because there is a known or anticipated demand for them. Men remain in employment only so long as the community is prepared to spend money on the product of their labour. Nobody would deny this. But the Classical analysis puts supply first, and then asserts that the incomes earned from production (supply) will all be spent, thus creating a demand which is always sufficient to take up the supply.

Keynes divides aggregate expenditure into two categories, spending on consumption goods ('Consumption') and spending on capital goods and stocks ('Investment'). It is now customary to classify spending rather differently, and in rather more detail. There are three groups of spenders: the private sector of the economy (roughly, firms and households), the public sector (i.e. the Government and local authorities) and foreign spenders (who buy our exports). Some part of 'domestic' spending, which is that of the private and public sectors combined, goes on imports, and this must be deducted from the total to arrive at the spending which constitutes the total demand for the products of our own industries, that which creates employment and income in our own economy. Private expenditure is then classified as consumption and investment. Hence aggregate income- and employment-creating demand equals consumption plus investment plus government spending,[2] plus exports minus imports, or in symbols:

$$Y\text{(income created)} = C + I + G + X - M \qquad [8.1]$$

Of course, G, X and M can in turn be classified into consumption and investment, so that our simple classification would embrace all spending, by all three groups, and a simple equation, $Y = C + I$, is still correct.

Government expenditure is determined administratively, on political and social as well as economic considerations; the economic purpose of fiscal policy is to act as a stabiliser, offsetting large fluctuations in other expenditures. The balance of exports and imports is a function of domestic prices and incomes relative to those of other countries. Relatively high levels of domestic expenditure and prices cut exports and attract imports, and vice versa. Keynes' contributions to consumption theory and investment theory are well documented elsewhere (Morgan 1979; Hines 1971).

Here, we shall be concentrating on Keynes' monetary theory. However, another major difference between Keynesian and Classical economics is that the former lays far less emphasis and reliance on price-and-wage flexibility: changes in quantities (i.e. output and employment), rather than changes in prices, are the macro-economic equilibrating mechanism.

Keynes thought that complete price flexibility would be destructive: it would probably lead to 'a great instability of prices, so violent perhaps as to make business calculations futile' (p. 269). If people are to use money as a means of payment and, more particularly, as a store of value (the basis of Keynesian monetary theory), its value must be reasonably stable. Price flexibility would not guarantee full employment:

(a) The basic determinants of expenditure are not responsive to changes in the relevant price. Consumption, and hence saving, is a function of income rather than the rate of interest; shifts in MEC (the marginal efficiency of capital), especially those arising from reversals of expectations, are more important determinants of investment than are changes in interest rates. Changes in interest rates cannot therefore be relied on to equate saving and investment; saving could exceed investment even with a zero rate of interest. In any case, the rate of interest is not a reward for saving but for saving-and-lending. Savers can hoard their savings. Savings can be absorbed into the financial circulation where they will affect interest rates. The rate of interest is the cost of hoarding; it is a monetary phenomenon which equates the demand and supply of money. Savings and investment are brought into equilibrium by changes in the level of income, the size of the necessary change being a function of the marginal propensity to consume and its associated *multiplier*.

(b) Falling money wages are unlikely to restore full employment for a number of reasons. First, to cut money wages is to cut a major source of demand; expenditure (MV) would not remain constant. Second, if a wage reduction leads to expectations of a further fall in wages and prices, the effect is likely to be a fall in demand, especially in investment demand (investing at today's prices to sell the product at tomorrow's lower prices), rather than an increase. The best hope is the monetary effect, a fall in transactions demand for money and a consequent spill-over of money into idle balances, leading to a reduction in interest rates, which may stimulate expenditure. But this chain of events may be broken, as we shall see.

Prices do not, in fact, have the downward flexibility which, in Classical analysis, is crucial for the maintenance of full employment. Goods prices are inflexible because wages are inflexible, and for an institutional reason. Wages cannot 'except in a socialised community where wage-policy is settled by decree' (p. 267), be cut uniformly all round. Wage reductions occur piecemeal, each reduction applying only to one group of workers. In these circumstances, a cut in money wages is inevitably a cut in real wages also, since the prices of all goods except those produced by this group of workers will remain unchanged. Further, the workers concerned also suffer a cut in their wages relative to those of other workers, and this 'is a sufficient justification for them to resist it'. The rate of interest is relatively inflexible downwards for two reasons: first, as it falls it comes increasingly under the influence of the concept of a 'norm' or 'safe' rate; and, second, there is a floor to the rate of interest.

Keynes' monetary theory

Clearly the role of *expectations* is crucial to Keynes' contribution to macro-economics. This is especially so with his monetary theory. Whereas early critics of Keynes seemed pre-occupied on the issue of whether 'money matters' in Keynesian analysis, nowadays that debate is largely irrelevant (see Kaldor and Trevithick 1981) and economists now seem more concerned about fully understanding Keynes' treatment of expectations. Some (Begg 1982) have tried to outline the evolution of the modern 'rational expectations' approach. Inevitably, Keynes plays a leading role in that evolution, though it is doubtful whether, if he was alive today, he would ascribe to some of the more extreme versions of that approach. Nevertheless, to Keynes, expectations were vital.

Keynes analyses the demand for money under the title 'liquidity preference'. Money possesses, to the last degree, the quality of liquidity: 'immediate command over goods in general'. A commodity is money only insofar as it possesses this quality, i.e. only insofar as it is immediately acceptable in payment of a debt of any kind. It is this quality of liquidity which makes money a desirable possession. The motives for liquidity preference are stated on page 170 of the *General Theory* and elaborated in the following pages of this chapter: they are the transactions, precautionary and speculative motives.

(1) The transactions motive: 'the need for cash for the current transaction of personal and business exchanges'. There are two motives for this demand for money:

(a) The income motive, which 'will chiefly depend on the amount of income and the normal length of the interval between its receipt and its disbursement' (p. 195).

(b) The business motive, to bridge the interval between expenditure and receipts, which 'will chiefly depend on the value of current output and the number of hands through which output passes'.

With the business motive, the receipts could occur at short intervals. We could take the example of a professional practice, taking £100 a day and paying its accounts and salaries on the last day of each month. In many businesses, of course, the payments interval will be longer than this. Nor is it customary to make all payments on the same day or at the same intervals, and it would be more realistic to think in terms of a firm's average payment interval.

When an income receiver pays money out of his instalments of income, he releases it to a trader who can then use it to finance other payments. It is already clear, therefore, that if everyone received his income in very frequent instalments and spent it quickly, a small amount of money could finance a large annual flow of output and incomes. It is also clear that what we are discussing is the determination of Fisher's V, the velocity of circulation, and the Cambridge k. The greater the velocity of circulation – i.e. the more frequently a unit of money comes into and goes out of our pockets – the smaller is the quantity of money needed to finance a given national income (PT or PR).

The transactions-balance requirement

We may now try to determine the minimum requirement of money. To do so, we must put the analysis into the context of the whole economy and bring in Keynes' final determinant of transactions demand, the number of hands, or stages, through which output passes.

The minimum conceivable quantity of money required in an economy is, of course, equal to the maximum payment which is made in that economy. If somebody, sometime, somewhere, has to make a payment of £50,215.30, then there must be at least that sum of money available if money is to do its job. If an economy had 100 final income receivers being paid £56 each every Friday, then it would be possible – though extremely unlikely – to run the system with a money stock of £5,600, but not with less. If they were paid £224 a month, we would need at least £22,400 to finance the same flow of income. In what circumstances would the actual requirement of money be equal to this minimum requirement? The essential condition can be stated quite simply: it is that the money required to pay final incomes shall have passed through all the exchanges necessary to create the flow of income within the payments interval of the final incomes. A flow of payments of this kind can be illustrated thus:

Saturday	Sunday	Monday	Tuesday	Wednesday	Thursday	Friday	Saturday
$D \rightarrow A$		$A \rightarrow B$		$B \rightarrow C$	$C \rightarrow D$		$D \rightarrow A$
£56		£56		£56	£56		£56

This represents a *payments circuit*, the flow of money from a final-income receiver (a) through all stages, e.g. retailer (b), wholesaler (c) and manufacturer (d), back to the final income receiver.[3] The important feature of this particular example is that the money passes through all the stages within the week and is therefore available for paying the next instalment of income. The money requirement is then solely a function of income and the payments interval.

The kind of 'payments-complex' in which this timely replenishment of funds would *not* occur is illustrated by our next example:

Saturday	Sunday	Monday	Tuesday	Wednesday	Thursday	Friday	Saturday
$D \rightarrow A$		$B \rightarrow C$	$A \rightarrow B$		$C \rightarrow D$		$D \rightarrow A$
£56		£56	£56		£56		£56

Here B sends £56 on its way round the circuit on Monday. He then receives £56 from A on Tuesday and this he holds until he makes his next payment on the following Monday. There is, therefore, a total of £112 in the circuit. The money requirement has doubled because one stage in the circuit has to make his payment before he receives payment. Hence the condition for minimisation of the quantity of money required to finance a given income flow is that each member of every payments circuit in the economy receives payment from the previous stage before he has to make payment to the next stage. This condition is known as *perfect synchronisation* of payments or, to use Newlyn's term, *perfect articulation* (1971: 48).

The analysis can also be conducted in terms of the concept of *overlapping*.[4] Overlapping is perfect when the maximum payments interval encompasses ('overlaps') all the income-expenditure periods. We may use our previous examples in illustration, although they assume only one payments interval. (The significance of the maximum interval is similar to that of the maximum payment on page 173; if any of the 'stages' pays out only once a quarter, for example, there must be sufficient money in the system to finance that payment.) In our first example, A's income-expenditure period is 2 days (Saturday to Monday) and the sum of all the income-expenditure periods is 7 days, which is exactly covered by the (maximum) payments interval. In our second example, the sum of the income-expenditure periods is 14 days, while everybody's payments interval is still only 7 days. As articulation becomes imperfect, so does overlapping, and vice versa. Synchronisation and overlapping are quite different concepts, but overlapping can only be perfect so long as synchronisation is perfect, and vice versa. (If this assertion does not seem obviously true, construct a few different payments complexes to see if one is possible without the other.)

So long as perfect articulation and overlapping are maintained, the number of stages through which money passes is of no consequence for the requirement of active money. Suppose that in our first example we insert another stage (X) between B and C. For perfect articulation to continue, this new member of the payments complex must receive payment before Wednesday, when he pays C. Let B pay him on Tuesday. We now have an extra income-expenditure period – that of X – of 1 day (Tuesday to Wednesday), but at the same time B's income-expenditure period has been reduced from 2 days to 1 day. The sum of the income-expenditure periods is still 7 days; overlapping is still perfect.

If overlapping and articulation are less than perfect, the number of stages in the circuit does matter. If one stage has to pay before he receives, we need an extra £56 in the circuit. If two stages have to hold money over until the next week, we would need an extra £112, and so on. Hence the greater the number of stages with imperfect articulation, the more money will be required to finance a given flow of income. The money requirement would be at its maximum if everybody had to pay just before he received payment (i.e. no money is released to finance other payments). In that situation, everyone would need to hold his money receipt through his payments interval, and from this we draw two conclusions about the maximum money requirement. The first is that the maximum requirement is equal to the minimum requirement multiplied by the number of stages in the circuit. The second is that it occurs when the sum of the income-expenditure periods is equal to the sum of the payments intervals. Perfect articulation and perfect overlapping are a limiting case. They are never likely to be found in the real world, where a further determinant of the money requirement, therefore, to be added to the two stated on p. 172, is the number of stages through which money passes in the very many payments circuits in operation in a modern economy.

Economising on money

If there is a shortage of money to finance the volume of payments which people wish to make, the above analysis indicates the ways in which they could economise on money. They are:

1 Shorten their payments intervals or the time pattern of payments in general, e.g. pay salaries weekly instead of monthly.
2 Reduce the number of stages in the payments circuits by integrating the stages at which articulation is imperfect. Reverting to the example on p. 173, we see that if stages B and C were brought into common ownership so that payments from B to C were book-keeping transactions only, not requiring the use of money, the Monday payment from B to C which doubled the money requirement of that payment circuit would no longer be necessary.
3 Improve the synchronisation of payments. This, of course, is much easier said than done. The likelihood is that in synchronising payments and receipts for one transactor we would desynchronise them for another. Only a co-ordinated and immensely complicated retiming of a mass of payments could achieve any substantial economy. But if one firm's pattern of payments and receipts is such that for most of the time it has a large money balance, it could help others to economise in their money balances by paying them earlier than is the custom, e.g. paying in advance of delivery, or by giving trade credit to its customers, i.e. allowing them to defer payment. The same kind of help could, of course, be extended to firms with whom it did not have trading relations if it were prepared to lend out its temporary surpluses.

There is now an organised market for inter-company loans, but it only accepts large sums and does not appear to be widely used. Firms with very large balances also place them on the money market for periods as short as overnight, and the higher the rate of interest the smaller the sum it is worthwhile to employ in this way; but the shorter the period the less effect does a given change in the interest rate have on the sum earned from the loan. This overnight and short money is used to 'balance the books' of HP finance houses, discount houses, and others who have lent to other participants in the industrial circulation. It is generally agreed that since the war there has been a growing realisation that it pays so to economise on one's transactions balances; we do not know what scope there is for a further expansion of this use of money by company treasurers. Hire purchase can be seen as a money-economising device; the surplus balances of depositors are used to meet the deficits of borrowers, who do not then have to accumulate money balances gradually before they buy the goods. The banks also perform this kind of financial intermediation, of course, in their business of accepting deposits and making loans, and the inter-bank loan markets and the discount houses perform this function for banks.

Reviewing these suggested ways of economising on money requirements, we can see why the velocity of circulation of transactions money is likely to be stable, why the ratio of transactions demand to income changes only slowly. Probably the only large and *quick* adjustments to changes in the supply/demand ratio of transactions money outside the financial sector are those which can be achieved by variations in hire purchase and trade credit.

(2) The precautionary motive: 'the desire for security as to the future cash equivalent of a certain proportion of total resources'. This 'desire for security' creates a demand for money:

(a) 'To provide for contingencies requiring sudden expenditure.'
(b) 'For unforeseen opportunities of advantageous purchases.'
(c) 'To hold an asset of which the value is fixed in terms of money to meet a subsequent liability fixed in terms of money.'

It appears that the transactions demand is for money to meet day-to-day payments which are well and clearly anticipated, while the precautionary demand is for money to meet unforeseen emergencies (e.g. illness or accident), to take advantage of unexpected bargains, or to meet known but infrequent payments (e.g. school bills, insurance premiums paid annually).

It is today customary to categorise the total stock of money into *active money* and *idle money*. Active money is that which circulates, more or less continuously, from hand to hand or bank account to bank account to finance transactions. But the transactions concerned are 'income-creating transactions', those conducted for the purchase and sale of newly created goods and services. Money used for dealing in securities on the Stock Exchanges and the money markets — the 'financial circulation' — is not classed as active money. Neither is money used only to buy second-hand goods. (If a man who sells his piano uses the proceeds to buy a new radio, or to take a holiday, or to pay a dentist's bill, it would then, of course, become active.) This is a quite arbitrary definition of 'active', chosen no doubt because the practical purpose of monetary theory is to show the connection between money and the national income, and the only money which *directly* affects national income is that which is 'active' in this restricted sense. At any particular time, all money is idle in the sense that it is at rest, held (i.e. owned) by somebody. The distinction between active and idle money therefore involves a time element: whether a unit of money is to be classed at any time as active or idle depends on how long it is being held by the same holder. Newlyn suggests that 'idle money is simply that part of his money balance into which the individual does not need to dip in the course of his normally recurring transactions' (ibid. p. 44). That part (probably the major part) of idle money which is included in that category because it is in the financial circulation does, of course, circulate in payment for securities and other evidence of debt. It can be 'activated' at any time by passing into the 'industrial circulation'; this occurs when it is transferred to corporations or persons who use it to buy goods and services. Transactions balances are clearly active, but what about precautionary balances? Some will be held by the same owners for a few days only, some will be held for months as, for example, when a person accumulates a balance gradually through the year to pay an annual subscription. Keynes does not help us here, because he does not use the terms 'active' and 'idle'. But he does divide money into two 'compartments' which he labels M_1 and M_2. M_1 is money held to satisfy the transactions and precautionary motives, and M_2 is money held to satisfy the speculative motive. Writers on monetary theory usually identify idle money with Keynes' M_2. We therefore include precautionary balances in active money, and suggest as a further justification for doing so the fact that they are definitely held against possible and, in the long run, probable future expenditure on goods and services, but many speculative balances are not and can remain in the financial circulation indefinitely.

The alternative to holding money is, in Keynesian economics, the holding of bonds, and there is an opportunity cost of holding money: namely, the interest we could have earned on bonds. This is not a significant factor in the demand for transactions balances; any unit of transactions money is likely to be held for only a matter of days or weeks, and the interest which a household could earn on holding a bond for a few days is not worth the trouble and cost of buying and selling them. Bonds are a more realistic alternative to precautionary balances, and Keynes argues (p. 170) that the existence of an organised market (which makes the buying and selling of bonds easier and cheaper than it would otherwise be) reduces the precautionary demand for money. But the money value of bonds is not fixed; it varies with the rate of interest. Anyone who puts his precautionary balance into bonds, therefore, runs the risk of loss if he has to sell them quickly to meet an emergency payment, or has to sell them on or before a certain date to meet a payment due on that date. There is also, of course, the possible embarrassment that the money obtained from the sale will not be sufficient to meet the payments. To meet a liability fixed in terms of money, the only safe asset is one whose value is fixed in terms of money, and that (if bonds are the only alternative) is money itself.[5] There is another alternative: one could borrow money to meet these payments as they occur, and Keynes tells us (p. 196) that 'the strength of all three precautionary motives for holding money' will partly depend on the cheapness and reliability of obtaining cash, when it is required, by some form of temporary borrowing. His conclusion, however, is that the rate of interest is not a significant factor in the transactions and precautionary demand; they are 'mainly a resultant of the general activity of the economic system and of the level of money income' (p. 196).

So far, there is no major difference between Keynesian and Classical monetary theory. The demand for money is a function of money income. Since money income is a compound of real income and the price level, the demand for money will be partly a function of prices; it is a demand for real balances. Keynes' innovation was his statement and analysis of the speculative motive. It is this which has since provoked most of the debate on monetary theory. And it is with the speculative motive that the rate of interest comes in as a determinant of the demand for money.

(3) **The speculative motive**: 'the object of securing profit from knowing better than the market what the future will bring forth'. A speculator is someone who tries to buy at a low price and sell at a high price. He buys when the price is, in his opinion, relatively low, i.e. he expects it to rise; but if his opinion were shared by the market in general, everyone would want to buy and the price would be forced up. He sells when he thinks the price is relatively high and, again, he only gets the high price so long as the market in general is not selling. A successful speculator, therefore, must 'go against the market', and his opinion on market trends must be correct; he must know better than the market what the future will bring forth.

The price trend which the speculative holder of money balances looks at is that of bonds.[6] The price of a bond is, as we know, the inverse of the yield, or rate of interest, on that bond. We can therefore equally well say that the speculative holder of money is concerned with future trends in the interest rate. Since interest rates on different classes of bonds tend to change simultaneously and in the same direction, we can here use the term '*the* interest rate', signifying the average or 'representative' rate or any rate which concerns a particular speculator at a particular time. At one point, Keynes asks the Classical question: 'why should anyone prefer to hold his wealth in a form which yields little or no interest to holding it in a form which yields interest?' (p. 168). His answer is, 'uncertainty as to the future course of the rate of interest is the sole intelligible explanation of the type of liquidity-preference L_2 which leads to the holding of cash M_2' (p. 201). In other words, all holders of idle balances are speculators, and they have a single choice, to hold money or to hold bonds. In a footnote to p. 170, Keynes does admit equities as a third alternative, but does not discuss it further. In an article in the *Quarterly Journal of Economics* in 1937, he considers another alternative: the purchase of real capital assets. If the rate of interest changes (because of a change in the quantity of money or a change in liquidity preference, which he here terms 'the propensity to hoard') the first effect will be on the prices of capital assets; a fall in the rate of interest will raise the price of an existing asset offering a given prospective income, and vice versa. Since 'the scale of production of capital assets' (i.e. investment) depends on their cost of production in relation to the prices they are expected to realise in the market, a fall in the rate of interest will, other things being equal, stimulate investment, and vice versa. Here is a clear link between the monetary and real sectors of the economy.

Money offers liquidity but no income; bonds offer income, but their future money value is uncertain. Anyone who buys a bond runs the risk that the rate of interest will rise, i.e. the price of his bond will fall, while he is still holding it. If for any reason he needs to sell the bond when its price has fallen, he suffers an actual, realised capital loss: if he had waited, he could have bought the bond at a lower price and thus obtained a better yield on his outlay. In waiting he would, of course, have lost the interest he has earned on the bonds in the meantime. Suppose the rate of interest (the yield) on a particular bond is 4%. This means that if the 'coupon rate' is 4% – i.e. a bond of £100 face value yields £4 p.a. – the bond can be bought for £100. A year later its market price falls to £96. There is then no penalty for buying early (apart from tax considerations), since the £4 capital loss is exactly balanced by the £4 of income gained. With the price at £96, the yield is 4.16%, i.e. the rate of interest has risen by 4%. The holder of a bond suffers a net loss, therefore, if the rate of interest rises at an annual rate which is greater than the current rate of interest at the date of purchase. One's 'bonds versus money' choice will therefore depend not only on whether or not one expects a change in the rate of interest, but also on how far, and when, one expects the rate to rise. Conversely, of course, a fall in the rate of interest brings a capital gain to bond-holders, but since this supplements their income from the bonds, no calculation of the timing and extent of the change is involved.

It appears, then, that the only reason why anyone should hold money as an asset, denying himself the income from the bonds he could hold instead, is that he expects the rate of interest to rise to a certain degree, within a certain time. In that situation, he will hold no bonds at all. If, on the other hand, he expects no change in the rate of interest, or expects it to fall, he will hold no asset money. However, if everyone had the same expectations, the expected rate could never differ from the current rate and there would be no purchases and sales of bonds. Suppose, for example, that the rate of interest were 5%, and everyone expected it to fall to 4% a week hence and then stay at that rate. Everybody would rush to buy bonds, but nobody would sell at a price less than that which gave a return of 4%, hence the prices of bonds would immediately rise to that level without any sales actually taking place. If the rate of interest were expected to rise, everybody would want to sell bonds but nobody would be prepared to buy at the current price, and the price would fall immediately.

There are two things wrong with this scenario. First, asset-holders do not as a rule keep all their wealth in money or all in income-earning assets. They may sometimes hold reasonably firm and confident expectations about the future performance of interest rates, but this confidence can never be absolute; they never know for certain what the future will bring. So they hedge their bet, diversify their portfolios, hold some money and some income-earning assets, varying the proportions as their expectations change.[7] Second, the expectations of asset-holders are not uniform. The market nearly always contains some 'bulls' (people who expect the price of bonds to rise) and some 'bears' (people who expect the prices of bonds to fall). Bulls buy bonds and bears sell them, and without this difference in expectations – this 'market-uncertainty' – there would, as we have seen, be no market, no buying and selling. The prices of bonds are fixed by the weight of opinion (which means the weight of expectations) in the market. Rising prices imply that the weight of opinion is bullish, and bonds are being offered for sale out of the smaller bear holdings, and vice versa. If prices are steady, the weight of opinion is that the rate of interest will remain where it is, and either the bulls and bears together are in a minority, or else the market consists largely, or entirely, of bulls and bears whose operations cancel each other out.

The interest rate 'norm'

When the rate of interest is high, one would expect desired speculative balances to be low, for two reasons. First, the rate of interest is the opportunity cost of holding money rather than bonds, and the higher the cost of holding money the smaller the quantity of money people will wish to hold. Second, the higher the rate of interest the more likely is it to fall than to rise further, so there is a sound speculative reason for holding bonds rather than money; vice versa when interest rates are low. But 'high' and 'low' are relative terms like 'tall' and 'short' or 'rich' and 'poor'. This fact is particularly relevant in the present context, for otherwise why should a 'high' rate of interest lead people to expect the rate to fall? The answer Keynes gives is that they have some concept of normal or 'safe' rate of interest, based on past experience. In deciding how much idle money they wish to hold, 'what matters is not the *absolute* level of r but the degree of its divergence from what is considered a fairly *safe* level of r' (p. 201). This concept of the safe rate is an important element in liquidity preference theory. It is because people have at the back of their minds some concept of a norm to which the actual rate will sooner or later return that their confidence in the persistence of the current rate diminishes as the rate rises above or falls below this norm. In the jargon of economics, they hold *inelastic* or negatively elastic expectations. In Keynes' words, this concept of the safe rate means that, since 'its actual value is largely governed by the prevailing view as to what its value is expected to be, the rate of interest is a highly conventional . . . phenomenon' (p. 203).

This concept of the safe rate and its significance, do, however, create a logical difficulty. The experience on which the safe rate is based is a common experience, shared by all holders of speculative balances. Does this not mean that everybody will regard a given rate as too high, or too low, to be maintained? If so, the rate could never diverge far or for long from the normal rate and we would approach the absurd market portrayed above in which no dealings ever take place. One would suggest two answers to this problem. One is that there may be differences of opinion about the expected timing of a rise in the rate, and the profitability of bond-holding depends on this timing. But this does not apply when the rate rises above normal and one expects it to fall. The second is that while everyone may expect the rate to revert to its 'safe' level sooner or later, there can be wide differences of opinion about what will happen to it in the meantime. Thus if the rate is currently 6%, and the safe rate were 5%, we might all agree that the rate will eventually fall to 5%, but there will be bears who expect the rate to be higher six months hence and bulls who expect it to be lower. It is on different views of this interest rate, 'the appropriate rate in particular circumstances' (Newlyn 1971: 58) that the market operates. This is not to deny that a generally accepted norm for the interest rate would affect all decisions, preventing the wild fluctuations of the rate which would result from untrammelled expectations. It is a plausible explanation of the comparative short-term stability of interest rates.

At very high rates of interest, one would expect the bears to disappear from the market completely – i.e. the cost of holding money is so high and the risk from holding bonds so low that the speculative demand for money is zero – a situation which has been described as 'the liquidity gate'. At lower rates of interest there will be a positive demand for idle money, which grows as the rate of interest falls not only because the market becomes more bearish and the opportunity cost of holding money falls, but also perhaps because the rising prices of bonds increase the wealth of their owners, who may wish to hold part of the increment of wealth as money.

Money and the rate of interest

At any given rate of interest, therefore, the public will wish to hold a certain quantity of idle money. The market does not, however, decide how much money is available to be held. Money in existence must be held by somebody, and the quantity of idle money the public must hold is the total quantity of money minus transactions and precautionary money. It follows that the public cannot determine the quantity of money they will hold as an asset. But they can determine the terms on which they willingly hold any given quantity; those terms are, of course, the rate of interest.[9] This, according to Keynes, is how the rate of interest is determined. The rate of interest is a monetary phenomenon, determined not in the real sector of the economy but in the monetary sector, by the demand for and supply of money. The rate of interest 'is the "price" which equilibrates the desire to hold wealth in the form of cash with the available quantity of cash ... the quantity of money is the other factor which, in conjunction with liquidity preference, determines the actual rate of interest in given circumstances' (p. 167). For any given quantity of money, therefore, and any given income plus institutional factors (structure of industry, payments intervals etc.) which together determine holdings of active money, there will be a certain equilibrium rate of interest; the public willingly hold that quantity of money at that rate of interest. It does not necessarily mean that everyone is content with his current portfolio of money and other assets. Since expectations differ, there will probably be bears in process of selling bonds, but if so there will also be bulls willing to buy exactly the quantity of bonds offered at the current prices. Bullishness and bearishness will cancel out, and the market as a whole will be in equilibrium. Assuming for the moment the exogenity of the money supply, if the quantity of money increases (say through open-market operations) the market will move to a new equilibrium at a lower rate of interest. As the ratio of money to bonds in the market rises (note that an open-market operation increase in M also reduces the supply of bonds), the prices of bonds will rise (interest rates fall) and this will make the increased holdings of money acceptable for three reasons suggested previously: (1) a lower rate of interest is a lower cost of holding money; (2) a fall in the rate of interest makes a further fall less probable and/or a rise more probable; (3) the rise in the prices of bonds enriches the holders of bonds, hence they may wish to hold more money to preserve the balance between the values of their holdings of money and of bonds.

This analysis is illustrated in Figs 8.1 to 8.4.

In Fig. 8.1, LP is a liquidity preference curve or schedule, the schedule of demand for idle money originating in the speculative motive for holding money.[10] At the rate of interest r_0 ('the liquidity gate') demand is zero, below r_0 it is positive, increasing as the rate of interest falls. The supply schedule of idle money is the vertical line M_2, and the fact that it is vertical implies that the supply of idle money is independent of the rate of interest; the supply is the same at all rates. The equilibrium rate of interest is fixed by the intersection of these two schedules. With idle money = M_2, the equilibrium rate of interest is r_1; at that rate, and only at that rate, the public willingly hold

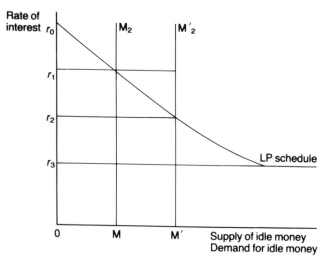

Fig 8.1 Liquidity preference schedule

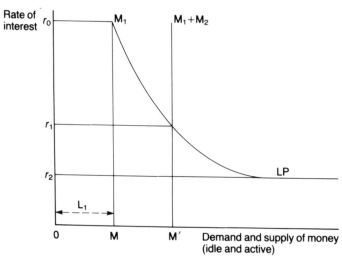

Fig 8.2 Demand and supply of money (idle and active)

182

the existing quantity of idle money. If the quantity of idle money increased to M'_2, the equilibrium rate of interest would fall to r_2.

We now add the supply and demand for active money, i.e. transactions and precautionary balances (see Fig. 8.2).

The demand for, and supply of, active money is OM, leaving $M-M'$ asset money out of a total supply of money OM'. The distance $M-M'$ is equal to the distance OM in Fig. 8.1 and the equilibrium rate of interest is thus again r_1. LP is now the schedule of total demand for money, consisting of a demand for active money OM, which we assume to be independent of the rate of interest, and a demand for idle money which varies inversely with the rate of interest. With a given quantity of money, the rate of interest depends on the shape and the position of the total liquidity preference schedule.

The shape of the liquidity preference curve

The negative slope of the curve has already been explained. The other significant characteristics are:

1   The schedule is convex to the origin. The change in the amount of idle money demanded in response to a given absolute change in the rate of interest is smaller at high rates of interest than at low rates; the interest elasticity of the demand for money increases as we move down the curve. The lower the current rate of interest, the smaller is the prospective *absolute* rise in the rate needed to make it seem more sensible to hold money than to hold bonds. At the same time, the lower the current rate the further does it diverge from the 'normal' rate, and the greater the prospective increase in the rate is likely to be. Hence a given absolute fall in the rate of interest will 'bring in more bears', induce a bigger shift out of bonds into money, the lower the rate is already. The precise shape of any section of the curve will depend on the size of what one might call 'marginal funds' and on the dispersion of expectations.

Perhaps the following example will clarify these points. Suppose that when the rate of interest is 6%, the quantity of money is increased by £5 million; our vertical supply schedule of Figs 8.1 and 8.2 moves that distance to the right. How far must the rate of interest fall to reach a new equilibrium, i.e. what is the slope of the liquidity preference schedule between the old and the new points of intersection of the M schedule and the LP schedule? There will be some holders of bonds who are – to coin an ugly phrase – 'on the margin of bearishness'; if the rate of interest fell by the merest fraction, they would sell bonds. Others would sell bonds only if the rate fell by, say, $\frac{1}{2}$%; another group would become sellers of bonds if the rate fell by $\frac{3}{4}$%; and so on. Clearly, these different groups have differing expectations concerning the interest rate, i.e. there is a dispersion of expectations. Bond-holders on any given day can be divided into a large number of groups, each group reaching the 'margin of bearishness' at a different rate of interest, and each group holding some quantity of bonds. A given fall in the rate of interest would therefore induce a willingness to sell a certain quantity of bonds, and the change in the rate of interest necessary to induce the sale of a given quantity of bonds as a direct measure of the dispersion of expectations. We can apply the analysis to holdings of asset money. Whether the rate of interest must fall to $5\frac{1}{4}\%$ or $5\frac{13}{16}\%$ or some other level to persuade the market to hold the extra £5 million of asset money depends on the degree of dispersion of expectations and the sizes of different holdings of bonds. The lower the rate of interest falls, the nearer is the market likely to approach to a consensus that the next change will be in the opposite direction, i.e. the smaller becomes the degree of dispersion of expectations.

In this connection we may mention Newlyn's interesting concept of *speculative fixation* (1971: 66–7). This occurs when there is no dispersion of expectations, when 'there is a consensus of opinion that the current rate is the "right" rate in the given situation'. There is 'a sufficient body of speculators prepared to release securities and absorb money whenever there is a tendency for the rate to fall, and to release money and absorb securities whenever there is a tendency for the rate to rise'. In this situation a change in the quantity of money would have no effect on the rate of interest (except insofar as a change in the quantity of money alters expectations); the liquidity preference schedule would be horizontal at the current interest rate. An important difference between Keynesian and Classical economics is Keynes' belief that changes in the quantity of money influence the national income via their effect on the interest rate, and 'if we are to control the activity of the economic system by changing the quantity of money, it is important that opinions should differ' (p. 172).

2   At a low rate of interest (r_3) the schedule becomes horizontal, i.e. the interest elasticity of the demand for idle money becomes infinite. This horizontal section of the schedule is known as *the liquidity trap*, a term coined, not by Keynes, but by Sir Dennis Robertson. Keynes suggests two reasons for its existence: (a) 'after the rate of interest has fallen to a certain level, liquidity-preference may become virtually absolute in the sense that almost everyone prefers cash to holding a debt which yields so low a rate of interest' because 'unless reasons are believed to exist why future experience will be very different from past experience, a long-term rate of interest of (say) 2 per cent leaves more to fear than to hope, and offers, at the same time, a running yield which is only sufficient to offset a very small measure of fear' (p. 207). The rate is so low that few, if any, speculators expect it to fall further. Hence the chances of a speculative gain from holding bonds is low; any speculative gains will arise from holdings of cash. In short, the nature of expectations concerning the rate of interest, based on the 'safe' rate, not only restrains fluctuations in the rate but also sets a floor to the rate.

Keynes' statement that 'almost everyone prefers cash' is misleading. There will be a certain existing quantity of bonds and they, no less than the existing quantity of money, must be held by someone. Nor must there be a general expectation that the rate will rise in the near future since, if there were, the rate would rise immediately. The liquidity trap situation must be a particular case of speculative fixation; the market is indifferent to whether it holds money or bonds at the current rate, and the monetary authority can buy or sell securities on the market without affecting their prices.

(b) The purchase or sale of securities costs money in commission and stamp duty, and the rate of interest must be positive to compensate for this. Keynes also mentions a possible risk of default by the borrower. His second reason for the floor to interest rates, therefore, is 'the intermediate costs of bringing the borrower and the ultimate lender together, and the allowance for risk, especially for moral risk, which the lender requires over and above the pure rate of interest' (p. 208).

Shifts in the liquidity preference schedule

The liquidity preference schedule is not stable; it does not remain in the same position for all time:

1 It is obvious that a change in the national income – i.e. a change in real income, or in the price level, or both – will shift the schedule to the left or the right, because a fall (rise) in national income reduces (increases) the requirement of active money. Unless the total quantity of money increases as income rises, people will sell securities to provide the money they need to finance the increased value of transactions. The price of securities will therefore fall (the rate of interest will rise). There is thus a different liquidity preference schedule for every level of national income. A change in the ratio of active money to income would also, of course, cause a similar shift in the M_1 schedule without any change in income.

2 The speculative demand for money is a function of expectations, and expectations are notoriously changeable. Any event which significantly affects the general economic climate can increase or reduce the demand for money, i.e. shift the liquidity preference schedule. A threat of war can increase the demand for money; increased profitability of real capital assets will reduce the demand for money, and perhaps for bonds. It will, however, also increase the profitability of investment, and firms who plan investments are likely to try to accumulate money balances in advance of the actual investment. The change from optimism to pessimism which can kill off a boom is defined by Keynes as a 'collapse of the marginal efficiency of capital', and 'the dismay and uncertainty as to the future which accompanies a collapse in the marginal efficiency of capital naturally precipitates a sharp increase in liquidity-preference'[11] (p. 316). The 'safe' or conventional rate of interest also changes over time. If a given rate can be maintained by the authorities for some time, one would suppose that it will gradually come to be accepted as the normal rate. A large

volume of government bonds was pushed on to the market in each of the two world wars, but it has been said that 'the 1914–18 War was financed at 5%, the 1939–45 War at 3%'. A simple announcement of government policy – e.g. that monetary restriction is going to be used to combat inflation – can change the market's view of the course of interest rates over the next few months.

3 A change in the quantity of money may cause not only a movement along the schedule but also a shift of the schedule. Suppose, for example, that an increase in the quantity of money reduces the rate of interest. If this stimulates investment, income will rise and with it the demand for transactions balances; thus the liquidity preference schedule will shift to the right. Changes in the quantity of money may also be taken as indicators of a change in government policy and so change expectations concerning business activity and the rate of interest (see Fig 8.3).

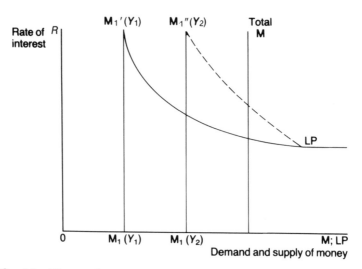

Fig 8.3 Liquidity preference and changes in money supply

In Keynesian analyses, monetary policy influences economic activity via the effect of changes in the quantity of money on interest rates and the effect of changes in interest rates on expenditure, especially on investment. The remaining significance of Keynesian monetary theory is its introduction of a demand for money as an asset which is a function, but not a stable function, of the rate of interest. In a liquidity trap situation, changes in the quantity of money are completely ineffective, being neutralised by contrary changes in velocity. It is Keynes' speculative demand for idle balances which breaks the Classical unique link between the quantity of money and money income.

The Keynesian analysis presented in this chapter can be illustrated by Fig. 8.4.

Figure 8.4(a) is the monetary sector diagram, while Fig. 8.4(b) is a partial representation of the real sector, in which the level of investment is shown as a function of

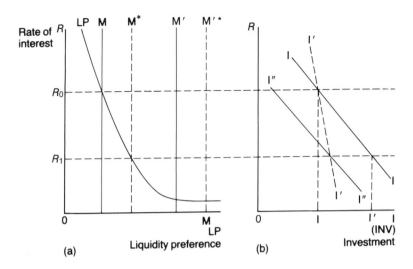

Fig 8.4 Liquidity preference and investment effects

the rate of interest. Suppose the quantity of money is increased from M to $M\star$. The rate of interest falls from R_0 to R_1, and the rate of investment consequently increases from 0I to 0I'. There is an equal primary increase in the level of income, and a secondary increase via the multiplier effect.[12]

There are four possible reasons why an increase in the quantity of money may have little or no effect:

1 If the original quantity of money is M', i.e. the economy is in a liquidity trap situation,[13] an increase in M will not change R and will therefore have no effect on I.

2 The increase in M could, possibly, arouse an uncertainty about the consequences of the change of policy which shifts the LP curve so far to the right that, again, R is unchanged (see *General theory*, pp. 172–3 and 203).

3 Investment may be very interest inelastic, (schedule $I'I'$, hence ΔR has little or no effect on I and, hence, on Y).

4 The effect of ΔR may be largely or wholly neutralised by a change in MEC (e.g. pessimistic expectations) which shifts the investment schedule to $I''I''$.

Loanable funds theory of interest

The Keynesian theory of interest-rate determination appears to stand in complete contrast with Classical theory. The rate of interest is a purely monetary phenomena, determined by the demand for money and its supply; there is no place for the Classical determinants, productivity and thrift. In fact, liquidity preference theory does implicitly allow for them. In equilibrium, the rate of interest will be equal to the marginal efficiency of capital, which is partly a function of the productivity of capital; if they differ, there will be net investment or disinvestment until they are equal. A rise in the marginal productivity of capital will, other things being equal, induce investment, and investment increases the demand for money, shifts the liquidity preference schedule to the right and (probably) raises the interest rate, first to acquire funds for investment and then to provide extra transactions balances to 'finance' the income created by the investment. An increase in saving, other things being equal, reduces income and hence the demand for transactions balances and so shifts the liquidity preference schedule to the left. In the fully-developed Keynesian system, investment, saving, income and the rate of interest are all interdependent, influencing each other.

A more clearly realistic picture is, perhaps, presented by an earlier theory which explains interest rates as a price which equates the demand for and supply of loanable funds. The potential supply of loanable funds, over any given period of time, comes from four sources: first, current savings out of income; second, money which has been saved in the past and has so far not been lent out but hoarded by the savers; third, money which has been tied up in capital goods − either fixed equipment or stocks − and is now available as funds set aside out of profits for depreciation reserves, or as proceeds from the sale of stocks; fourth, newly created money. The demand for loanable funds also has four sources: first, some people want to borrow money for consumption, e.g. through hire purchase; second, funds will be wanted for the replacement of fixed equipment, or to renew stocks of goods in the warehouses or on the shelves; third, there are the firms who want money to finance net investment; fourth, people may want money to hold, i.e. to satisfy their liquidity preference.

Not all these loanable funds will come on to the market, since it is obvious that the 'lender' and the 'borrower' are often the same person or firm. A saver who hoards his savings can be said to be supplying loanable funds and also demanding them to satisfy his liquidity preference. Similarly, most funds released from depreciation reserves or from the proceeds of sale of stocks will normally be used to renew capital equipment or rebuild stocks. In other words, a good part of the total demand and supply cancel each other out. The rest is made available for lending, if the rate of interest is right. In a free market, the rate of interest will be such that the quantity of loanable funds which lenders are prepared to lend at that rate is equal to the quantity which borrowers are prepared to borrow at that same rate.

This theory includes explicitly the influence of saving and the productivity of capital (which, we may suppose, will determine the price which borrowers are prepared to pay for loanable funds for replacement and expansion). Yet it also emphasises the fact that interest is paid for lending, not for saving as such. And it states quite clearly that part of the supply of loanable funds does not come from saving as we normally understand it, but from supplies of new money created by banks or by the state. The inclusion of the desire to hoard money as one source of demand for funds also seems to bring us close to the liquidity preference theory.

The two theories are, however, easily reconciled:

1   The demand for and supply of loanable funds are the supply of and demand for evidence of debt; call them all 'bonds'. Now divide the whole economy into three markets: for goods, for money, and for bonds. By Walras' law, excess demands in the whole economy must sum to zero. Given equilibrium in the goods market, equilibrium in the money market implies equilibrium also in the bond market, and vice versa. The rate of interest which equates the demand and supply of money also equates the demand and supply of bonds. The two theories amount to the same thing.

2   A change in any of the relevant variables – income, the supply of money, the demand for idle balances (the hoarding of loanable funds theory), investment, saving – changes the rate of interest in the same direction in both theories.

3   Full equilibrium requires equilibrium in the goods market (the real sector), which is achieved in Keynesian analysis when ex ante S (savings) = ex ante I (investment) and the money market (the monetary sector). It can be expressed thus: that savers are satisfied with their present rate of saving, investors are satisfied with their rate of investment, and owners of wealth are satisfied with the distribution of their wealth between money and other assets. For a static equilibrium, this means that M must be constant and there must be no desire to hoard or dishoard. (We could conceive of a dynamic equilibrium in which hoarding (dishoarding) is proceeding at the same rate as the quantity of money is increasing (decreasing), but in that situation people would not be satisfied with their current holdings of money.) Hoarding (H) is zero, and so, of course, is dishoarding (DH). Using the terminology of loanable funds theory, and concentrating on the major items, there is equilibrium in the market for money when $S + \Delta M = I + H$. But with an equilibrium of income, $S = I$, therefore $\Delta M = H$. But since $H = 0$, $\Delta M = 0$, a full equilibrium is only possible when the supply of money is fixed and the rate of interest is such that the demand for money equals the supply ($H = 0$). But this is also the equilibrium of liquidity preference theory.

This analysis is the source of the assertion that the loanable funds theory is distinguishable from liquidity preference theory only in a disequilibrium situation, e.g. when $S \neq I$; that it is a dynamic theory with no equilibrium significance.

There is, however, a difference between the mechanism implied by the two analyses. In loanable funds theory, there is a direct connection between saving, investment and the rate of interest. In liquidity preference theory, apart from the demand for money to finance planned investment, the effect on interest rates operates via changes in income, and saving and investment are brought into equilibrium by changes in income rather than by changes in the rate of interest. Interest rates are determined in the money markets and are subject to very many day-to-day influences. To take a few examples. The supply of funds on to the market falters during 'the tax season' and recovers soon afterwards. The weight of new issues of equities affects the supply of money in the market. One source of supply is inflows of funds from overseas, which are the product of many influences, the most important being interest rates relative to those ruling abroad, and the present and expected future exchange value of the currency. It seems to be generally agreed by the financial press that the anticipated rate of inflation affects interest rates, but the econometric evidence is mixed. (See, for example, Gibson (1972), Pyle (1972) and Carlson and Parkin (1975) (in favour), and Ball's study of the long-term rate in the UK 1921–61 (1965) (against), and Foster and Gregory (1977).)

However, one thing is clear: the relationship between the quantity of money and interest rates is not all one way. If the banks have excess reserves (as they have had since 1971), a fall in interest rates, however it originates, can swell bank deposits by increasing the demand for bank loans. The Government's monetary and fiscal policy will obviously affect this (see Ch. 13).

Notes

1   Keynes justifies this as follows: 'the aggregate supply function . . . which depends in the main on the physical conditions of supply, involves few considerations which are not already familiar' (p. 89).
2   In this context, government spending includes only central government and local authority expenditure on goods and services. It does not include payments such as pensions, subsidies, social security benefits, student grants and the like, which are not payments for goods produced or services rendered.
3   In reality, of course, retailers do not pay all their receipts over to wholesalers. They take out their own profits and put out another fraction in wages and other expenses. Similarly for the wholesalers. So a considerable part of the £56 will be returned to consumers from these intermediate stages and some will be sent on its way round other circuits (see Newlyn 1971: 50–1).
4   We owe this term to Professor Angell (1937); see also Ellis (1938).
5   As the reader will no doubt soon deduce, precautionary motives (b) and (c), and perhaps even (a), are often particular cases of the speculative motive.
6   The speculative motive could be extended to money held as an alternative to goods – e.g. primary raw materials – whose prices are unstable. The similarity to precautionary demand (b) would, in that case, be very obvious.
7   This does not appear in the *General Theory*, although on page 172 Keynes does say 'every fall in the rate may . . . increase the quantity of cash which certain individuals will wish to hold because their views as to the future of the rate of interest differ from the market views'. The explanation there is the one which follows. On page 171 he writes: 'each increase in the quantity of money must raise the price of bonds sufficiently to exceed the expectations of some "bull" and so influence him to sell his bond for cash and join the "bear" brigade'.
8   'If the elasticity of expectations is unity, a change in current prices will change expected prices in the same direction and in the same proportion: . . . changes

190

in prices are expected to be permanent ... The elasticity of expectations will be greater than unity, if a change in current prices makes people feel they can recognise a trend, so that they try to extrapolate: it will be negative if they make the opposite kind of guess interpreting the change as the culminating point of a fluctuation' (Hicks 1946: 205).

9   The speculative demand for money is largely independent of the price level; it is a demand for nominal balances, not real balances. If it were a demand for real balances, that would make a difference to the Keynesian analysis and bring it closer to the Classical analysis.

10   There is no liquidity preference curve in the *General Theory*. The diagram and the derivation of the shape of the schedule are the work of followers of Keynes.

11   On the changes in demand for money, bonds and real capital assets (or equities) in the different phases of the trade cycle, see Hansen (1953).

12   There are feed-back effects. The rise in income will increase the demand for active balances and shift the LP curve to the right. This raises the rate of interest, which will reduce investment, income will fall, and thereby the demand for transactions balances will fall, which shifts the LP curve to the left, and so on.

13   Keynes says, 'whilst this limiting case might become practically important in future, I know of no example of it hitherto' (p. 207). Yet he also says: 'but the most stable ... element in our contemporary economy has been hitherto, and may prove to be in the future, the minimum rate of interest acceptable to the generality of wealth-owners. If a tolerable level of employment requires a rate of interest much below the average rates which ruled in the nineteenth century, it is most doubtful whether it can be achieved merely by manipulating the quantity of money' (p. 309).

CHAPTER NINE

Post-Keynesian developments in monetary theory

There has been no attempt to demolish the Keynesian structure comparable to his own attack on Classical theory, and it was one of the most forceful critics of Keynes who said 'we are all Keynesians now'. But inevitably, there have been criticisms, modifications and extensions of his analysis.

The speculative motive and the liquidity trap

The essence of the speculative motive is that elasticity of expectations regarding the rate of interest is low or negative; this is what gives the liquidity preference curve its parabolic shape. Asset-holders have constantly in their minds the concept of a normal rate, and the desire to hold money rather than bonds increases to a greater degree with every successive fall in the rate of interest below this normal level, culminating in the liquidity trap. But there is no suggestion that any given normal rate remains fixed for all time: it can change with changing circumstances, and 'conventional expectations' can be 'modified'. Does it not follow that if a previously 'abnormal' rate can be held for some time, it will come to be accepted as the norm? Hence it is argued that if a low rate persists long enough, it will come to be generally accepted as the normal rate, and the public will gradually become more willing to hold assets yielding this low return. If the low rate could be held long enough, speculative demand for money might disappear.

Empirical studies of the demand for money do not, for the most part, support these two elements in the concept of the speculative demand for money. There is a conflict of evidence on the question of whether some concept of a 'normal' rate has any effect on the demand for money. The interest elasticity of the demand for money does not appear to increase as interest rates fall; the weight of evidence is that the liquidity preference schedule does not gradually 'flatten out' at low rates.[1] Though the empirical studies fail, in the main, to come to any firm conclusion about the shape of the speculative demand schedule, we need not suppose that the rate of interest could fall to zero, even if the speculative liquidity trap has to be rejected, as there remains the second stop on falling interest rates, the costs of buying and selling securities and the 'moral risk' to the lender. It is, further, worth noting that interest rates on long-term securities which involve no moral risk (e.g. government bonds) have never yet fallen to the level which is only just sufficient to compensate for the costs of switching between money and bonds except within a short period.

Near money and liquidity preference

More serious is the argument that in a fully developed financial system the speculative motive is no longer adequate to explain the demand for money and the determination of interest rates. The Keynesian demand for money is the consequence of a choice between liquidity and an interest income involving a risk of capital loss. The choice between money and bonds, the rate of interest, which is the opportunity cost of holding money, is the long-term rate, and liquidity preference is the demand for money. But, as we have seen earlier, there is a wide variety of short-term near-money assets available as alternatives to money on which there is a nil, or minimal, risk of loss, e.g. time deposits, Treasury bills nearing maturity, and deposits with financial intermediaries. There is also at least one class of long-term asset available, though only in small amounts, which is riskless: National Savings Certificates and Bonds. All these can be exchanged for money easily, quickly and cheaply; they are good substitutes for money as an asset.

The existence of near-money assets, and the ease and speed with which they can be exchanged for money, means that the 'money versus bonds' choice of liquidity preference is unrealistic. This fact has various implications:

1 The demand for liquidity is not synonymous with the demand for money. Liquidity preference can be satisifed almost as well, and in many circumstances (i.e. where the need for a means of payment is not immediate) equally well, by these non-money assets. Since their money values are stable – in most cases as stable as that of money itself – the potential speculative losses from holding them are either minute or zero. In a well-developed market, the cost of switching in and out of these assets is very low. The interest on *large* holdings of some of them (e.g. bills, or day-to-day deposits with local authorities or financial institutions such as discount houses) will pay for the costs of switching between them and money even if they are held for only a few days or even overnight. There thus seems to be little point in holding large money balances for speculative purposes. Indeed, it has been suggested by Fleming (1964) and Tucker (1966) that the demand for idle money can be regarded as a particular kind of transaction and precautionary demand, one related to payments 'on capital account' as opposed to day-to-day payments. It arises mainly from uncertainty about the size and timing of such payments and when the interval between the receipt of money and its investment at long-term is so short that it is not worthwhile to switch between money and liquid income-earning assets in the meantime.

2 The choice between liquidity and interest income is not clear-cut. Near-money assets provide both. If we follow Keynes precisely and treat the choice as one

between liquidity and a long-term rate of interest, it still is not necessarily a choice between money and bonds. It is likely to be largely between the relatively high-yield, high capital-risk long-term assets and relatively low-yield, low (or zero) capital-risk short-term assets. Speculative activity can thus take the form of switching not between money and bonds, but between long-term and short-term assets. Thus expectations concerning the rates on bonds need not affect the demand for money. If people expect bond prices to fall, they will sell bonds and buy short-term securities and deposits. A large shift out of bonds into bills will cause long-term rates to rise and short-term rates to fall, and vice versa. Speculation would then change the structure of interest rates rather than the average rate overall.[2]

The consequences for liquidity preference theory are as follows:

1 If these assets are good substitutes for money, an increased availability of such substitutes will reduce the asset demand for money, i.e. will shift the liquidity preference schedule to the left.

2 The rate of interest may be determined by the demand for and supply of 'liquidity', but this is not the same thing as the demand for and supply of money. The liquidity preference theory of interest is too simple. This need not be taken as a criticism of Keynes; after all, on page 166 he identifies 'liquid command over goods with money or its equivalent', and in a footnote to page 167 he suggests that in discussing the choice between holding 'money' and holding 'debts' we can draw the line between these two at whatever point is most convenient for handling a particular problem. 'It is often convenient in practice to include in *money* time-deposits with banks, and occasionally even such instruments as (e.g.) treasury bills.' The next sentence, though, reads: 'As a rule I shall . . . assume that money is co-extensive with bank deposits.'

3 Similarly, the demand for liquidity may be sensitive to the long-term rate of interest, but this is not the same thing as the demand for money.

It would seem to follow from this that the demand for money is likely to be interest inelastic in a highly developed financial system. Money is less likely to be imprisoned in a liquidity trap unless the rates on quasi-money are very low indeed, and when rates are higher than this there is unlikely to be a large pool of idle balances which can be activated as rates rise further. If, on the other hand, near-money assets are thought to be a good substitute for money as an asset, but not nearly a perfect substitute, their existence is likely to increase the interest elasticity of demand for money. A small rise in the interest rate on them will induce a large movement of funds out of money into near money, just as a small decline in the price of, say, one brand of canned fruit would induce a large switch of demand from other brands. A possible escape from this contradiction proceeds thus: as financial intermediaries develop and gradually become more widely accepted as a means of employing savings or temporarily idle balances, they increase the interest elasticity of demand for money (see Chick 1979). If and when their advantages to the lender become universally known and recognised, when they have fully exploited their sources of funds, they reduce the interest elasticity of the demand for money; idle balances are at, or close to, their minimum. There is a difference of opinion and of evidence on the actual degree of substitutability between these assets and money (see Ch. 12).

We must not exaggerate these modifications of liquidity preference theory. Changes in the quantity of money will still exert an influence on interest rates, and an expected change in *all* rates will still affect the demand for money. If we are confident that all rates of interest are about to rise, it will clearly pay to hold money (but including deposits at short notice or at a variable rate in the term 'money' in this context) rather than other assets, even short-term assets, whose price will fall.

Non-speculative demand for money and the rate of interest

Another development in monetary theory has been the introduction of motives for holding money other than the speculative motive which, it is suggested, can account for the observed interest elasticity of the demand for money.

Demand for active money

Hansen (1949: 66–8) suggested that at high interest rates we would try to economise on active balances. With a given quantity of money, the first consequence of rising income and transactions would be an activation of idle balances, and interest rates would rise as the quantity of money available to satisfy them and for idle balances fell. When all money held idle has been transferred to active balances, further increases in the flow of payments are only possible if the velocity of active money (which now comprises the total quantity of money) rises. Thus, even in the transactions sphere the demand function for money can become interest-elastic.[3]

The Baumol–Tobin formula

Formulae have been devised which would give a *continuous* inverse relationship between the rate of interest and holdings of transactions balances. There are two versions:

1 This is expressed in terms of the minimum worthwhile period of a loan. The exchange of money for a non-money asset, or vice versa, involves a cost. There is usually an actual money cost, e.g. broker's fee and stamp duty, and there is also the time and effort expended in the consideration of the relative merits of alternative assets, the clerical work of documentation, and so on. Let us call the total cost a, and assume that it is a fixed percentage of the sum transferred. Then a 'round trip', a switch out of money into a non-money asset and back again into money, costs $2a$. If r is the annual yield on the non-money asset,

then the minimum 'break even' period of a loan, that for which the income would equal the cost, is given by the fraction $2a/r$. If, for example, $a = \frac{1}{2}\%$, it costs £10 to buy and sell an asset costing £1,000. If r is 6%, £1,000 will earn £10 in $\frac{1}{6}$th of a year (i.e. $2a/r = \frac{1}{6}$). It therefore pays to lend out transactions balances only if one is certain that they will not be required for transactions for at least two months. If the rate of interest were 12%, one could profitably lend money which will be needed a little over a month from today. More money will be available for lending, less money will be necessarily held in transactions balances, the shorter the period required for a loan to be profitable, i.e. the higher the rate of interest on the loan. The transactions balances of a profit-maximiser will therefore vary inversely with the rate of interest.

2 This is expressed in terms of the number of times it pays to switch between money and income-earning assets within a payments interval (Baumol 1952 and Tobin 1956). The analysis here is analogous to that used to determine the optimum size of stocks of goods held by a trader or manufacturer. Suppose a person is paid a monthly salary (or a firm's accounts received are settled monthly). He receives £200 each month and spends it evenly through the month. Much of that £200 is held idle for all or part of the month. Why not put the £150 to work as soon as he receives it (keeping £50 to meet his expenses for the first week) and withdraw £50 at the end of each of the first three weeks of the month? He would thereby earn interest on £150 for one week, on £100 for two weeks, and on £50 for three weeks. Two alternative answers spring to mind: first, if he bought securities, he would incur a risk of capital loss for the sake of a very small return; there is a strong precautionary reason for holding cash; second, the market for deposits, no less than the market for securities, is not geared to deal in such small sums held for such short periods.

The essential fact in both cases is that the cost of administering such small deposits or purchases and sales of securities outweighs the return, to either the lender or the borrower, over such a short period. But when large sums of money are involved, it does pay to keep the money at work even for very short periods. A firm handling sums running into six figures can lend money overnight at a net profit. But suppose there were no cost, and no 'diseconomies of small-scale' in handling small sums. It would then pay to put all the £200 to work, withdrawing a small sum, say, each day. His average holding of bonds would then be £100 (just as his average holding of money, if he kept all his monthly receipts in cash, would be £100), and his return would be the interest on £100.

Put as a formula, the return is $cr/2$,

where r = the rate of interest
            c = monthly receipt

The general formula for the return (R) is:

$$(R) = \frac{n - 1}{2n} cr \qquad [9.1]$$

where n = number of transactions (purchases or sales) in non-money assets in the course of the month

If he withdraws money weekly, he will use $\frac{3}{4}$ of his income to buy bonds initially, and sell these in three instalments, i.e. four transactions in all; if he keeps enough cash in hand to last one-third of a month, he would put $\frac{2}{3}$ of his income into non-money assets initially and withdraw it in two instalments, three transactions in all, and so on. In each case, his initial holding of bonds is given by the formula, $(n - 1/n)c$; his average holding of bonds throughout the month is one half of this, i.e. $(n - 1/2n)c$, and:

$$(R) = \frac{n - 1}{2n} cr \qquad [9.1]$$

Suppose the cost, a, of each transaction is a fixed sum (not, as in the previous analysis, a fixed percentage of the value of the transaction), then the total cost of n transactions is na. His net profit (P) in his holdings of income-earning assets is therefore:

$$(P) = \frac{(n - 1)}{2n} cr - na \qquad [9.2]$$

The optimum figure for $n(n^\star)$, that which maximises his net return, is formed by differential calculus. The procedure is to differentiate the above equation with respect to n, and set the resultant derivative equal to zero:

$$(P) = \frac{ncr}{2n} - \frac{cr}{2n} - na \qquad [9.3]$$

$$= \frac{cr}{2} - \frac{crn^{-1}}{2} - na \qquad [9.4]$$

$$\frac{d(P)}{dn} = \frac{n^{-2}cr}{2} - a = 0 \qquad [9.5]$$

$$= \frac{cr}{2n^2} - a = 0 \qquad [9.6]$$

$$\therefore \quad 2n^2 = \frac{cr}{a} \qquad [9.7]$$

$$n^2 = \frac{cr}{2a} \qquad [9.8]$$

$$n^* = \sqrt{\frac{cr}{2a}} \qquad\qquad [9.9]$$

His average cash balance will, of course, vary universely with n. As shown above, if he makes four transactions, he holds one quarter of his income in cash at the beginning of each week, and zero cash at the end of each week, hence his average holding is equal to one eighth of his monthly income, or $c/2n$. The formula for his optimum holding of transactions balances, M_T, is:

$$M_T = \frac{c}{2n^*} \qquad\qquad [9.10]$$

$$= \frac{c}{2\sqrt{\dfrac{cr}{2a}}} \qquad\qquad [9.11]$$

$$= \sqrt{\frac{ca}{2r}} \qquad\qquad [9.12]$$

This analysis assumes a smooth, stable rate of expenditure. The resultant demand for money takes no account of precautionary balances. M_T in the above equation should, therefore, be regarded as the minimum holding of money.

The payments interval, which was significant in the earlier analysis because the possibility of lending part of the initial transactions balance was ignored, is no longer important because, for a given annual income, r increases equally with c. If, for example, our salary-earner were paid £600 per quarter instead of £200 per month, c would be £600 and the relevant r would be the rate of interest per quarter.

The important results of this analysis are, first, that the demand for transactions balances is inversely related to the square root of the rate of interest and, second, that it is a function not of income but of the square root of income, i.e. it increases less than proportionally with income. There are *economies of scale* in money holding. This has the implication that one determinant of the demand for money is the distribution of income; the bigger the proportion of aggregate transactions money held in large balances, the smaller will be the amount of transactions money associated with a given aggregate income.[4]

The Baumol–Tobin analysis does not cover all the possible determinants of transactions demand: (1) it assumes that the pattern of receipts and payments is fixed; it does not consider the possibility of adjusting them so as to economise on transactions balances (see page 175). Clearly, the rate of interest is one incentive to do so. (2) The only rate of interest considered is that earned on loans. In deciding what stock of cash to hold, this is compared with the cost of buying and selling non-money assets and, presumably, with the 'cost' of running out of cash before the next planned 'monetisation' of the asset. But persons, and more especially firms, often have overdraft facilities at their bank, and the cost of holding inadequate stocks of money is not the embarrassment of running out of money but the cost of taking up the overdraft facility. The important comparison in this case is that between the interest earned on the non-money asset and the interest charged on the overdraft.

These rates will tend to be closely correlated and in such cases the interest elasticity of the transactions balance will therefore be greatly reduced: the reward and the penalty rise and fall together. Banks also make a charge for servicing accounts but will waive the charge if the customer keeps a certain minimum credit balance in his account. Here, therefore, is another motive for holding transactions balances. (3) Transactions costs are either fixed or vary linearly with the sum transferred. In fact, they often consist of a fixed plus a variable charge.

(4) It has also been shown (Sprenkle 1969) that the minimum size of annual receipts required for *any* switching (i.e. one purchase and sale within the payments interval) to be worthwhile, now depends on the payments interval as well as on the (fixed) cost of switching and the rate of interest earned. For example, with the cost of purchase or sale at £20 and the rate of interest 5% p.a., the minimum *annual* receipts required for minimum switching to be profitable would be £12,800 if they were received at six-monthly intervals. (The 'minimum switch' would be one half of his six-monthly income, for three months. The 'break-even' sum for this would be £40 × $(100/1\frac{1}{4})$ or £3,200.) It would be £460,800 if they were received at monthly intervals. Sprenkle compared the actual cash holdings at the end of 1966 of 465 of the 500 biggest US companies with the cash holdings which could have been predicted by the Baumol–Tobin analysis, assuming a cost of transfer of £20 and a rate of interest of 5% p.a. The mean percentage of cash holdings explained was only 3% and, for the fifty largest firms, it was only 1%. The study found no evidence of 'economies of scale' in money holdings.[5] The author concluded that these firms held cash for purposes other than transactions, and suggested that they were held to avoid bank charges. The obvious other possibility, of course, is that firms also hold precautionary and/or speculative balances.

Demand for idle money

The Tobin analysis

One weakness of the Keynesian analysis of the demand for money as an asset is that it logically implies that any one person or corporation will hold either asset money or bonds, but not both. This is unrealistic; probably few investors behave in this way. At most times their wealth is likely to consist partly of money and partly of income-earning assets, held in variable proportions. Tobin (1958) explains this type of behaviour, and without recourse to inelastic expectations concerning the rate of interest. Assume that the investor's expectations are neutral: that is to say, he regards a rise or a fall in the interest rate as equally probable. He sees an equal likelihood of gain from appreciation of the value of any securities he holds or of loss from depreciation. These neutral expectations are assumed to be independent of the current rate of interest; he 'considers a doubling of the rate just as likely when the rate is 5% as when it is 2%, and a halving of the rate just as likely when it is 1% as when it is 6%' (p. 71). If wealth is, as we believe, subject to diminishing marginal utility, the utility lost if

£100 were deducted from one's wealth is greater than the utility gained if £100 were added. Psychologically, therefore, there is a net risk of loss from holding bonds, and the return on bonds is compensation for this risk. This is the only risk; there is assumed to be no risk of default on interest payments nor, if it is a terminable bond, on repayment of the principal. The return is the interest paid plus capital gain or minus capital loss. The degree of risk is assumed to be measured by the standard deviation of the return; since the interest payment is fixed, the risk is the capital value risk multiplied by the number of bonds held. The degree of risk increases, of course, with the quantity of bonds held; but so does the income earned from the portfolio.

In choosing a particular combination of money and bonds, the investor is balancing income against risk.

He acts according to his own preferences, a situation which Tobin presents as an indifference curve analysis, with each investor having his own individual indifference map. Some may be *risk-lovers*: to them, risk affords utility, as does income, and they would accept a lower income in order to take on higher risks (and, of course, the accompanying chance of a higher capital gain). Since bonds give them both more income and more risk than money, such people would hold all their assets in bonds. The majority of investors, however, are more likely to be *risk-averters*, at least with most of their assets, and will only accept more risk along with a higher income. Some risk averters are *plungers*; they will keep their wealth entirely in bonds at or above some given rate of interest, and entirely in money at rates lower than this. Others are *'diversifiers'*: they tend to hedge their bets by holding both money and other assets.

For risk averters, the choice between income and security is, says Tobin, subject to diminishing marginal substitutability; increasing increments of income are required to compensate for equal successive increments of risk. Income is subject to diminishing marginal utility, and risk is probably subject to increasing marginal disutility. Their indifference curves are therefore positively inclined and convex downwards (see Fig. 9.1). A rise in the yield on bonds (a shift of the 'opportunity locus' from OD to DE) has three effects:

1 *A substitution effect* (the move from position A to position B). The higher the running yield for a given risk, the greater is the incentive to hold non-money income-earning assets, and vice versa.

2 *An income effect* (the move from position B to position C). If the rate of interest rises by, say, one fifth, the investor can reduce his bond holdings by, say, one tenth and still enjoy a higher income. He is, in effect, being offered a higher income and/or more security. If the demand for income is satiable, which is unlikely, the income effect, *taken alone*, could induce him to reduce his bond holdings proportionally with the rise in the yield. If, over the relevant range of income, security is an inferior good, which is certainly possible, he will accept more risk and the income effect will reinforce the substitution effect. If the income elasticity of demand for security is 'normal', i.e. positive, the income effect, taken alone, will lead him to demand more security, i.e. buy fewer bonds. The net effect then depends on the relative strengths of the

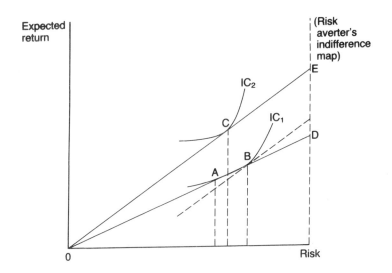

Fig 9.1 Risk averter's indifference map

substitution effect and the income effect, which in turn depends on the configuration of his indifference map. So far, we can say nothing a priori about the shape of the liquidity preference curve.

3 *A wealth effect.* This applies only to those who already hold bonds when the interest rate rises. A rise in the rate of interest is a fall in the price of bonds, and so reduces the wealth of bond-holders. This could conceivably change drastically the distribution of wealth between money and bonds (it can be analysed in terms of positive and negative effects, as in the case of the income effect above), but assuming 'normal' reactions, it would reduce the demand for both money and bonds. But since the reduction in wealth would be borne entirely by the value of bonds, we may presume that the major part, if not the whole, of this effect will fall on the demand for money; vice versa in the case of a fall in interest rates. This effect, taken alone, thus gives a demand for money varying inversely with the interest rate. Its importance depends, of course, on the size of bond holdings as compared with money holdings at the time. The absolute effect on wealth of any given proportional change in the interest rate increases rapidly as the rate falls. Take the case of a £100 bond with a 4% coupon rate. A rise in the interest rate from 6 to 12% reduces the value of the bond from £66.6 to £33.3; a rise from 1 to 2% reduces it from £400 to £200. A given absolute change also has a bigger absolute effect at lower interest rates. There is no income effect on any current bond holdings; a rise in the interest rate cannot affect the yield-on-purchase-price of bonds already held. Finally, since the risk of bond holding is always positive, there will be some minimum rate of interest necessary to persuade individuals to hold the existing supply of bonds, and at which any increment of wealth will be held as money. On balance, it seems

likely that the liquidity preference schedule emerging from this analysis will bear a strong resemblance to the Keynesian schedule, in an economy holding bonds.

This analysis is similar to Keynes in envisaging a single choice, that between one riskless asset, money which earns nothing, and interest-yielding assets which carry a significant risk of capital loss. If there is a variety of non-money assets available, the search for greater security when interest rates fall may take the form of a switch out of risky, high-yielding securities into safer, low-yielding securities. Tobin does mention the existence of a variety of assets, but says 'the argument is not essentially changed' by introducing them; we can 'describe the investor's decisions as if there were a single non-cash asset, a composite formed by combining the multitude of actual non-cash assets in fixed proportions' (p. 70).

The analysis, however, differs from Keynes' in three distinct ways. First, Tobin's argument could account for the undoubtedly widespread practice of holding both money and bonds, not one *or* the other. Second, the demand schedule he envisages is much more stable than the liquidity preference schedule. Its shape and position depend only upon relatively stable characteristics of economic structure (e.g. the size distribution of individual wealth holdings and the costs of buying and selling securities) or of basic attitudes (e.g. the degree of aversion to risk). Third, it does not invoke the concept of a norm of interest rates and the consequent inelasticity of expectations as to movements of the rate.

It can, if we wish, easily be adapted to incorporate inelastic expectations. If expectations concerning the rate of interest are dominated by a 'norm', the higher the current rate lies above this norm the greater will be the expected capital gain from bonds, and the lower the rate the greater is the prospective capital loss. Expected capital gains will then not be independent of the current rate of interest, as assumed above, but positively related to it. They are an added incentive to buy bonds at high current yields; at some (high) rate the risk factor will be eliminated and the investor will wish to hold all his wealth in bonds. Conversely, they are a deterrent to the holding of bonds at low rates of interest and make it more likely that the desired portfolio will consist entirely of money. To generalise, 'the stickier the investor's expectations, the more sensitive his demand for cash will be to changes in the rate of interest' (Tobin 1958: 86).

How important neutrality of expectations may be is a matter of opinion. How often is it reasonable to suppose that 'a doubling of the rate is just as likely when the rate is 5% as when it is 2% . . .?' Granted that in trying to predict an unknown future we tend to fall back on our knowledge of what happened in the past. Can the rate considered appropriate to a particular situation at times be very different from the 'norm' of the recent past? Or does the norm colour even our views of the temporary rate appropriate to a particular situation? Crouch (1971) tested this, using weekly quotations of the yield on consols 1962–66, and Bohi (1972) used rates on short-term and long-term government bonds in eight countries, 1960–70. Both found that interest rates followed a course described as a *random walk*, i.e. successive changes in them were uncorrelated. These results support the Tobin view that the probability of a rise in interest rates, or of a fall, is independent of the current rates. Other studies come to different conclusions. They all adopt a weighted average of past interest rates as the 'norm'. Ball (1965), Ford and Stark (1965) and El-Mokadem (1973) found it significant in the explanation of the demand for money and/or the current interest rate. Starleaf and Reimer (1967) found it unimportant.

Attitudes to risk

The theory of portfolio selection, then, classifies investors into three broad groups: risk lovers, risk averters and risk-neutral investors. The latter take no account of risk, but opt for the asset with the highest expected rate of return. A risk lover, as we have noted on p. 200, will prefer a high-risk to a low-risk portfolio. Of two assets with the same expectations of return, he will choose the one with the larger standard deviation. The risk averter, on the other hand, prefers the less risky asset. Moreover, he will demand successively larger additions to the expected return in compensation for equal successive increments of risk. These different attitudes to returns and risk are usually associated in the literature with different schedules of marginal utility of income (return). To the risk-neutral investor, the marginal utility of income is presumed to be constant: each successive equal increment of income affords the same utility. To the risk lover, the marginal utility of income is presumed to increase as his income rises. The risk averter, however, is subject to diminishing marginal utility of income. It is because the prospect of losing £100 is a bigger deterrent than an equal chance of gaining £100 is an attraction that he is a risk averter.

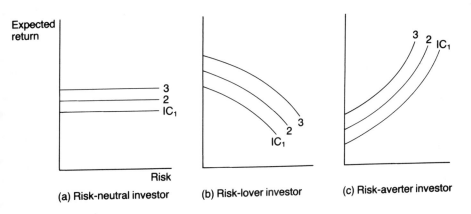

Fig 9.2 Investor responses to risk

The 'trade-off' between expected return and risk for each of these classes of investor can be represented by indifference curves. They are constructed in the usual way; each curve connects a series of points, each point representing a particular conjunction of expected return and risk, between which the investor is indifferent, and he prefers the situation represented by any point on a higher indifference curve to that represented by any point on a lower indifference curve. These indifference curves will be horizontal, concave from below, or convex from below (see Fig. 9.2).

The purpose of diversification, of holding a 'balanced' portfolio of assets, is to reduce risk. Diversification therefore appeals only to the risk averter, and it is with this category of asset-holder that we are concerned in the following section.

How diversification reduces risk

Whether or not risk can be reduced by diversification depends on the way in which, and the degree to which, returns on different assets are correlated, if at all.[6] The essential point is that the combined standard deviation of two returns with a perfect positive correlation is equal to the sum of the standard deviations of each return, whereas in the case of negative correlation or independence it is less than this sum. A perfect negative correlation between the returns on two assets would mean that the returns always change inversely by the same proportion. It is obvious that in this case one could reduce the overall risk to one's portfolio by holding both assets instead of one only. Indeed, there would be some proportionate holding of the two which would eliminate risk, the perfect hedge. If the returns were independent, i.e. if the correlation were zero, so that any of the anticipated returns on one might be accompanied by any of the anticipated returns on the other, diversification would reduce the risk: there would be *some* likelihood that a low return on one asset would be compensated by a high return on the other. But if there were a perfect positive correlation between the returns, if the returns were subject to the same influences, affecting them in the same way, so that they always changed in the same direction by the same proportion, then diversification clearly would not reduce the variability of the total return on one's portfolio. If the returns are positively correlated, but not perfectly so, diversification can still reduce risk. There will be a slight possibility that a low return on one will be associated with a high return on the other.

The returns on securities tend to be mildly positively correlated since they are usually all affected in much the same way by changes in the general economic climate. But the correlation is not the same for all portfolios. It is surely obvious that the stability of the return on a portfolio is improved by not investing it all in the shares of firms in the same industry, or firms selling in the same geographical market area, or firms dependent on, say, military expenditure or the fortunes of the building industry. However, the profits of firms operating even in the same industry or the same market area are not always positively correlated; it often happens that one or more firms do well when the industry as a whole is depressed, and vice versa.

One important conclusion to be drawn from this discussion of correlation is that the effect on the riskiness of a portfolio of adding another item to it depends on whether, and how, the return on the new item is correlated with that on the existing portfolio. One can improve the security of an already fairly safe and diversified bundle of assets by adding a relatively risky asset so long as the returns on the new asset have a low, positive, zero, or best of all, a negative correlation with those of the assets already held.

The benefit from diversification, and the best mix of assets, can be demonstrated on a single diagram.[7] First, we show the effects of diversification (see Fig. 9.3).

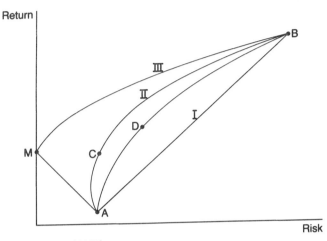

Source: Moore (1968)

Fig 9.3 Effects of diversification

We assume that there are two assets in the portfolio, *A* and *B*, which offer the returns-cum-risk indicated by points *A* and *B* respectively. The mathematical expectation of return for *B* is higher than for *A*, but so is the risk incurred. If the return on *A* and *B* were perfectly and positively correlated, the possible combinations of risk and return obtainable from a mixture of the two would lie along the straight line *AB*. His aggregate return/risk is a weighted average of the two individual returns/risks, with the weights equal to the proportions of *A* and *B* in the portfolio. The *opportunity frontier* III illustrates the case of perfect negative correlation, with perfect hedging at point *M*. Note that to move along this frontier from *A* towards *M* brings a bigger return and less risk. A risk averter would never hold a portfolio which gives a combination of risk and return along the line *AM*: if the situation *M* is possible, he will not opt for any situation which is both below and to the right of *M*. Hence any efficient portfolio must offer a combination of return and risk indicated by a point somewhere along the *M*–*B* section of this frontier. Frontier II is the intermediate case in which the correlation between returns is neither perfectly positive nor perfectly negative. Again, it is assumed that there are some mixed portfolios which offer a bigger return and less risk than *A* alone, with the limit at point *C*. This is not inevitable; the opportunity frontier could be a line such as *ADB*. But if *ACB* were the opportunity frontier, the efficient frontier would be *CB*. Comparing II and III with I, we see that they offer a bigger return for a given risk, or a lower risk for a given return, than points along *AB*: in all cases except the perfect positive correlation case, a diversified portfolio is superior to one consisting entirely of asset *A* or entirely of asset *B*.

We then combine the opportunity frontier (the one chosen here is appropriate to an intermediate case, the type most likely to be found in the real world) with the risk averter's indifference map of return and risk (see Fig. 9.4).

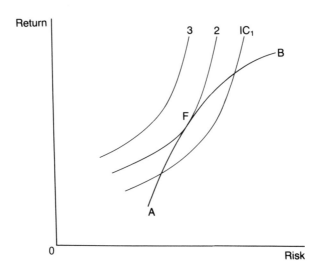

Fig 9.4   Opportunity frontier and risk averter's indifference map

He will choose the portfolio which gives the return/risk indicated by point *F*, where his marginal rate of substitution between return and risk (= the slope of the indifference curve at *F*) is equal to the marginal trade-off (the appropriate technical term would be marginal rate of transformation) between risk and return which the market offers him (= the slope of the opportunity frontier at *F*). A risk lover or risk-neutral investor would choose the portfolio represented by point *B*. The relative amounts of *A* and *B* in the portfolio at *F* are given by the proportions in which *F* divides the vertical distance between *A* and *B*. Different investors, all being risk averters, would hold different portfolios both because they have different attitudes to return/risk opportunities and because their estimates of prospective returns and risks differ; remember that the expectations on which *AB* is based are 'subjective probabilities'.

There are some costs of diversification to set off against the gains. First, there is often a fixed element in the money cost of transactions in assets. Second, there is the time and effort required to obtain information on prospective returns and to monitor changes in the prospects of different assets. These costs vary with the number of assets held, but not with the sum invested in each asset, and are therefore a smaller deterrent to diversification, the larger the total wealth holding concerned.[8]

The demand for money in portfolio balance theory

What place is there for money in a diversified portfolio? Money is distinguished from other assets by the fact that it is perfectly liquid: its money value is certain because it is itself the unit of account and it affords immediate command over other assets. One could only achieve the same security of money value from other assets by perfect hedging, which is probably as impossible in the real world as any other perfect thing, and may in any case require such a wide spread of one's portfolio, and such frequent changes in its composition as the prospects of different assets change, that transactions costs would wipe out the benefit. A sufficient degree of risk aversion, then, would justify holding some money in one's portfolio. Second, there is the speculative motive for holding money: a portfolio may at certain times include a high proportion of money awaiting a favourable opportunity for investment. Other possible motives have been mentioned in earlier pages of this book. There is, for example, the fact that the investment of small sums is either not possible or not worth the trouble and cost incurred, hence less wealthy personal investors will tend to accumulate money gradually until they have enough to invest and will thereafter repeat the process; but this motive applies only to small asset holders. We can also apply the precautionary motive to money in the financial circulation. Firms may hold money because they are uncertain about the size and timing of future payments, e.g. for stocks. Money may be held briefly to meet a known commitment, e.g. to pay for shares already bought on the Stock Exchange. Firms accumulating reserves for internal investment may eschew any form of external investment and hold these reserves only in very liquid form.

However, most of the above requirements could be met by holding highly liquid but income-earning assets, in particular deposits at short notice of withdrawal with local authorities, merchant banks, building societies, or hire purchase finance houses. They are sufficiently liquid for most purposes; most assets do not have to be paid for immediately. So there appears to be little place in an efficient portfolio for money defined as cash plus demand deposits. On the other hand, demand deposits can be said to be an income-earning asset in as much as the banks will usually waive the service charge on the account if the balance does not fall below a specified minimum. Taking everything into account, however, the definition of money as an asset probably ought in most cases to include at least time deposits at the banks and deposits with other financial institutions.

Granted that risk averters do have good reason to hold money as an asset, the amount they hold will presumably be a function, in part at least, of their total wealth. It may or may not change proportionally with their wealth. One could argue that liquidity at the expense of earnings is a luxury of which we can afford more as our wealth increases, and that money holdings are likely to increase more than proportionally with wealth. On the other hand, one could argue that the wealthy can afford to put a bigger proportion of their assets at risk, and hold a smaller proportion of the total in the safe asset, money. One could ignore these possibilities and say there is no a priori reason why the demand for money should not rise or fall by the same percentage as total wealth. Finally, there is, of course, the possibility that the demand for money is satiable, that there is an upper limit to the amount of money a person, or a corporate body, will wish to hold even though total wealth continues to increase. The evidence so far available on the relation of money holdings to total wealth is both meagre and conflicting; we cannot yet say which, if any, of the suggested relationships is the one which most frequently exists in the real world.

The proportion of total wealth held in money will vary from one holder to another according to their differing opinions, circumstances and − in the case of persons − their differing temperaments. First, some are more cautious than others; their aversion to risk is greater. This may apply not only to the risk of loss on an investment, but also to the risk of being embarrassed by illiquidity. In calculating his money requirement, the cautious man will try to be prepared for all eventualities. Second, investors differ in their estimates of the degree of risk attached to particular assets, in their projections of future changes in interest rates (which affect their speculative holdings of money), and in their expectations concerning future prices (which, as we shall see, may also influence demand for asset money). Third, some face greater uncertainty than others as regards their future expenditure, both the size and the timing of future payments. It is the possibility of a need for cash in the very near future which is really important here. If I am confident that my expenditure over, say, the next six months or the next twelve months will not exceed my income, then a non-money asset which will mature six months, or twelve months, hence is, for me, as liquid as money itself.[9]

In the final analysis the demand for money, in an aggregate sense, will depend on the relative strengths of the speculative as opposed to the risk motive, and the proportion of risk-conscious individuals who can be classified as risk averters.

Some differences between the Keynesian and balanced portfolio analyses

Clearly there are some obvious differences between the portfolio-balance analysis and Keynesian theory.

1 The Keynesian choice is between liquid money and illiquid bonds. It is true that on pages 170 and 212 of the *General Theory*, and in his article in the

Quarterly Journal of Economics, 1937, Keynes refers to the ownership of money and debts as an alternative to the ownership of equities or real capital assets. He does not, however, discuss the differing degrees of liquidity of different financial assets (although he does so in his *Treatise on Money*). In his chapters on liquidity preference (15) and on the theory of interest (13), there is a simple choice: money versus bonds. Perhaps his reason for here ignoring the alternatives is to be found in Chapter 11, 'The Marginal Efficiency of Capital', where he emphasises that in a free market the yields on real capital and on bonds will be equal. Perhaps we can say that the bonds of Chapter 13 are used as the representative non-money asset. The concept of a diversified portfolio, on the other hand, implies that the investor considers, and chooses between, a wide variety of assets, probably including real assets such as land, industrial capital and durable consumer goods. It extends the Tobin analysis by disaggregating bonds into a variety of non-money assets. There is, however, a sense in which the portfolio balance analysis can be said to be a continuation and development of the Keynesian tradition: it simply introduces more alternatives to money.

2 As we have seen, the logic of Keynesian liquidity preference theory leads one to the conclusion that the investor will hold either money or bonds, but not both. The later theories show that any investor who is a risk averter has good reason to hold both money – in its wider definition, at least – and a variety of other assets, except in a period of high inflation.

3 The price level is supposed not to enter significantly into the determination of Keynesian demand for money as an asset. As has so often been said, there is a money illusion in the speculative demand for money.[10]

If, however, asset money is seen as one of several different forms of wealth holding, and if we take it that people are interested in the *real* value of their wealth, then we may presume that the demand for money as an asset, like the demand for transactions money, is a demand for real balances rather than nominal balances. At higher prices, therefore, people will wish to hold more money (unless they expect a substantial further rise in the price level). The demand for money will not, however, necessarily change proportionally with prices as in Classical theory, for two reasons. First, to the extent that the wealth-holder's portfolio includes money and other assets of fixed money value, its real value will fall as prices rise and this will tend to reduce the demand for real balances. Second, if the elasticity of expectations is greater than unity, this is also likely to reduce demand for all assets of fixed money value.

Notes

1 For surveys of the evidence, see Bain (1980), Laidler (1977), and Smith and Teigen (1965).
2 There is a large literature on the term structure of interest rates (see Meiselman

1962; Modigliani and Sutch 1969; Rowan and O'Brien 1970; and Michaelson 1973). Some of that literature emphasises the significance of the 'preferred habitat' theory as an explanation of the term structure of interest rates. Karakitsos (1977) uses this approach to explain the term structure of interest rates in the UK, and reaches the conclusion that, though expectations may exhibit both extrapolative and regressive elements, they do influence the term structure of interest rates in a reasonably 'stable' manner (see also Ch. 12).

3   In the Hansen analysis, transactions demand only becomes interest elastic after all the money has been activated. It is not clear why this condition is necessary. Is it not conceivable that some holders of active balances will be induced to speed up their 'rather leisurely velocity' by rates of interest which are not high enough to induce some other holders of the balances to activate them?

4   It is currently fashionable to argue that money is required only in a world of uncertainty: uncertainty as to future receipts and commitments, as to future interest rates (the particular uncertainty with which Keynes seemed to be concerned), uncertainty as to the credit-worthiness of purchasers offering evidence of debt in exchange for goods and services, uncertainty as to the relative prices of goods sold now and goods desired in the future, and so on. But even if all future transactions were known, the time gaps between receipts and payments or between exchanges would necessitate the holding of a medium of exchange. Certainty alone would not remove the need for money: a further condition is simultaneous payments and receipts and/or simultaneous mutual clearing of credits and debits. It is significant that the world without uncertainty usually envisaged in these discussions is a Walrasian world, in which all transactions occur simultaneously (see Goodhart 1973; Leijonhufvud 1981).

5   Empirical studies of firms' holdings of cash in relation to sales, or total assets, have so far produced conflicting results. See for example Meltzer (1963), Brunner and Meltzer (1967), Vogel and Maddala (1967), Kavanagh and Walters (1966), and Sprenkle (1972).

6   The degree of diversification possibly also depends on the size of the portfolio; the bigger it is the more diversification is feasible. Tobin does not take account of this. For the mathematics of correlation and risk and arithmetic illustrations, see Tobin (1965: 22–5) and Stapleton (1970: 89–96).

7   This diagram has been adapted from the diagram in Moore (1968: 45).

8   Goldsmith (1976) argues that the number of different assets it is profitable to hold will increase as the square root of total wealth.

9   For an analysis of liquidity in terms of maturity and encashment needs, see Newlyn (1971: Chs 1 and 13).

10   On page 266 of the *General Theory*, Keynes writes: 'if the quantity of money is virtually fixed it is evident that its quantity in terms of wage-units can be indefinitely increased by a sufficient reduction in money wages; and that its quantity in proportion to incomes generally can be largely increased'. A wage-

unit is 'the money wages of a labour unit'. This extract could therefore be taken as a recognition of the real balance effect applied to *all* money balances. But from the context, especially the following paragraph, it seems more likely that he was referring back to page 263, where he states that lower prices reduce the need for transactions balances, and hence leave more of the total stock of money to be held as idle balances, thus possibly reducing interest rates and increasing investment, the *Keynes effect*.

CHAPTER TEN

The new quantity theory and modern monetarism

Perhaps the most controversial, certainly the most widely discussed, of the theories which link the demand for money to wealth is that developed by Professor Milton Friedman and his colleagues at the University of Chicago. The comprehensive statement of the basic theory is to be found in his opening chapter of *Studies in the Quantity Theory of Money*, published in 1956. He begins his exposition of the theory with the assertion that 'the quantity theory is in the first instance a theory of the *demand* for money. It is not a theory of output, or of money income, or of the price level. Any statement about these variables requires combining the quantity theory with some specifications about the conditions of supply of money and perhaps about other variables as well'. Nevertheless, he also asserts later in the chapter that the demand function for money plays 'a vital role in determining variables . . . such as the level of money income or of prices' (p. 4).

The new quantity theory and Classical theory

The Chicago theory has an obvious affinity with Classical monetary theory, and is usually referred to as the new quantity theory. It is, however, much more sophisticated than the 'old' quantity theories, and is in fact more in line with the Cambridge and Keynesian traditions than with the classical equation of exchange or the 'Chicago tradition' of the 1930s. Although Friedman insists that his theory is in the Classical tradition, he does not argue the Classical equality between changes in P and changes in M. Friedman (1971: 49) also writes: 'It seems plausible that the division of a change in nominal income between prices and output depends on two major factors: anticipation about the behaviour of prices . . . and the current level of output or employment'. In an article in the *AER* 1975, he suggests that for the first six months, an increase in ΔM has no effect, except possibly on interest rates. After six to nine months, the rate of growth of GNP will increase. Some eighteen months later (two years after the increase in ΔM began), the main effect will have shifted to prices. After another year or so, the rate of growth of output will fall back to, or below, its 'natural' level and in the long run prices will rise faster than nominal income. So we can see that the effect gradually switches from output to prices; but we are not told why the switch begins, when and why expectations change. He appears to find a close relationship between changes in the quantity of money and changes in nominal income, and the 'price level is then a joint outcome of the monetary forces determining nominal income and the real forces determining real income' (1971: 50). Friedman has not yet devised a satisfactory theory of the distribution of changes in nominal income between prices and output, as he would probably be the first to admit. Indeed, there is as yet *no* satisfactory theory to explain how firms decide whether to increase output, or prices, or both.[1] He seems to envisage chiefly a situation of continuous growth of the money supply, and equilibrium is produced not by a stable level of money income but by equality between the actual and the expected rate of change of money income; the level of real balances demanded at any given level of money income will then be stable.

The determinants of the demand for money

Monetarist theory does not see the demand for money – and its inverse, the velocity of circulation – as a simple function of transactions, or of income, a 'physical datum' determined by institutional factors such as methods of payment, the degree of integration of industry, and so on. Rather it is a function of a number of variables, as is the demand for goods, and can be analysed in a similar way. Money, however, is not consumed, like bread and butter. It is an asset, which people wish to hold because it yields a flow of services arising from its peculiar characteristic that it is a 'readily available source of purchasing power'; in short, from its liquidity: 'money yields its return . . . in the usual form of convenience, security, etc.'. The first determinant of demand for money, therefore – the *budget constraint* which sets the upper limit to demand – is wealth rather than income: 'Thus the theory of the demand for money is a special topic in the theory of capital.' There is, of course, an obvious close link between the two;[2] the value of wealth is the present discounted value of the future income which it will produce. The second determinant is 'the price of and return on this form of wealth and alternative forms'. The opportunity cost of holding money is the forgone anticipated income from earning assets, including expected capital gains.[3] The third determinant is, of course, 'the tastes and preferences of the wealth-owning units'.

A particular feature of the theory is that it includes in wealth not only the usual components – money, other financial assets, and physical assets – but also 'human wealth', the productive capacity of human beings. The value of this component of wealth is, of course, the present discounted value of expected future earnings. However, human wealth differs from non-human wealth: it cannot be bought and sold on a market. In general, the only way in which one can substitute the one form of wealth for the other is by disinvesting in one form in order to invest in the other, e.g. by selling non-human assets to buy training or education. Non-human assets, on the other hand, can be freely exchanged for each other on a market. Now since changes in the composition of one's portfolio are an important part of any monetary theory incorporating choices between money and other assets, and since substitution between assets is a crucial element in the suggested mechanism by which changes in the monetary sector of the economy are transmitted to the real sector, this difference between the two kinds of wealth is important. Hence he includes the ratio of non-human to human wealth as a separate determinant of the demand for money. One might ask how human wealth affects the demand for money if we cannot substitute between it and money. The answer, it appears, is that the two different forms of wealth generate different income flows, and with them are associated different demands for money.

The demand for money is a demand for real balances; naturally so, since money is wanted for the services it renders and since these services derive from the fact that money is a source of purchasing power. Holdings of money and other assets are subject to a diminishing marginal rate of substitution: the more units one holds of any one of them, the less of any other asset one would give up in exchange for a further unit. The wealth-holder's portfolio of assets will be in equilibrium, i.e. it will be his 'desired' portfolio, when the services from another unit of money – say, one pound – have the same anticipated value as the expected income lost by giving up another asset whose market value is one pound.

To summarise, the equation expressing the demand for money is:

$$\frac{M}{P} = f\left(r_b, r_e, \frac{1}{p}\frac{dP}{dt}, w, \frac{Y}{P}, u\right)$$
[10.1]

where

P = the general price level. (The demand for money is a demand not for nominal balances, M, but for real balances, M/P.)

r_b = the expected return on a unit of wealth held in the form of bonds, including anticipated capital gains/losses.

r_e = the expected return on a unit of wealth held in the form of equities, including anticipated capital gains/losses.

$\dfrac{1}{P}\dfrac{dP}{dt}$ = the return, in services rendered, on a unit of wealth held in the form of physical goods, whose 'nominal value' varies directly with the price level, plus the change over time in the money value of the goods themselves dP/dt, the equivalent of capital gains/losses on b and e. Both are denoted by the rate of change of the price level.

w = the ratio of non-human to human wealth.

Y = the return to all forms of wealth other than money.

u = any factors which affect tastes and preferences for the different forms of wealth.

The determinants of business demand for money are similar. The main differences are that wealth is not a constraint because firms can obtain additional capital through the capital market, and that the division of wealth into human and non-human forms is irrelevant. For wealth he substitutes the 'scale' or size of the firm, but 'it is by no means clear what the appropriate variable is: total transactions, net value added, net income, total capital in non-money form, or net worth' (Friedman 1970: 203).

214

Income, interest and the demand for money

The essence of Friedman's theory is that the demand for money is not a stable absolute theory, as in Classical theory, but a stable function of the determinants enumerated above. So, for example, the velocity of circulation can rise during an inflation because anticipated further inflation reduces the expected return on money, which is its expected real purchasing power. Expectations are a vital element in the demand for money: expected income yields, expected capital gains, the expected rate of change of the price level. The conclusion he draws from empirical studies is that the main determinant of demand for money is permanent income, i.e. expected future income. This may appear to contradict the assertion above that wealth, rather than income, is the determinant. Not so: 'What comes out as income originally entered as wealth ... the "income" relevant to this equation is not income as measured in the national accounts but income conceived of as the net return on a stock of wealth, or wealth measured by the income it yields.' 'Permanent income can be regarded as a concept closely allied to wealth and indeed as an index of wealth' (Friedman 1959: 137). Note that there are no separate transactions, precautionary and speculative demands for money. Money is simply a 'temporary abode of purchasing power', an asset of perfect liquidity. The current income which determines Keynesian transactions demand, and partly determines precautionary demand, is not included as a determinant variable. The income variable is permanent income, which is really a wealth variable. He thus emphasises the store of value function of money.

In view of the importance which the monetarist theory attaches to substitution between assets, and in the light of our knowledge of portfolio balance theory, we would surely expect rates of interest, the returns on non-money assets, to be an important determinant. But apparently they are not. His empirical tests show that the interest rate does, indeed, have a systematic effect on demand for money, and it operates in the 'right' direction: demand for money moves inversely with the rate of interest; but the effect is small.[4] In an article in the *Journal of Law and Economics*, October 1966, and his articles in the *Journal of Political Economy*, April 1970, Friedman is at pains to deny the assertion, which he says is attributed to him, that interest rates have no effect on the demand for money. His position is simply that income, or wealth, is much more important. Friedman and Schwartz, in their *Monetary History* (1963), use an estimated interest elasticity of demand for money of − ·15.

Cyclical and secular changes in the demand for money

The measured velocity, actual measured income divided by the quantity of money, fell over the period covered in Friedman and Schwartz (1963) from about 4.6 p.a. to 1.7 p.a. The peak velocity was 4.97 in 1880, whence it fell to a low of 1.16 in 1946.[5] But this change, large in total, only amounts to 1% p.a. on average, and the year-to-year change in velocity exceeded 10% (a change from 3 p.a. to 3.3 or 2.7 p.a. would be a 10% change) in only 13 years, and the largest change was 17%. The demand for money was therefore reasonably stable along a long-term upward trend over this period. It was a period of rapidly rising income, and Friedman sees this as the main explanation of the decline in velocity; money is a luxury good, of which the community chooses to hold more, in proportion to its incomes, as incomes rise. They ignore other possible explanations such as changes in the timing of and frequency of income payments and retail payments, and so on. And it is unlikely that businesses regard money as a luxury good. He estimates the secular income (measured) elasticity of demand for money at 1.8.[6] Price (1972), covering the years 1956–70 for the UK, showed a lagged income elasticity of demand for money (M_3) by persons of 2.0 or more; the figure for companies was more than 1.0. While Hacche (1974) found elasticities (M_3) for both sectors close to 1.0 for the period 1963/IV to 1972/IV (for M_1 it was 0.7). For the US, Peterson's (1974) cross-section study of demand for 'broad money', 1960–62, found a permanent income elasticity of 1.88.

The cyclical relation between income and velocity was the reverse of this secular relation; that is to say, the income velocity of circulation increased as real income rose during cyclical expansion, and decreased as income fell in the cyclical contractions. Velocity also changed in the same direction as the money supply, and the changes in V and M were of about equal importance in accounting for cyclical changes in nominal income. There is a further important difference between secular and cyclical experience: over the period under study, there were a number of 'long swings' in money income, long fluctuations around the rising trend. During these fluctuations, the quantity of money and velocity changed inversely, and the changes in the quantity of money were much greater than the changes in velocity. How can we explain these contrasts between the long-run and short-run behaviour of these relationships?

Cyclical experience could be the result of a shift of the demand schedule relating desired money balances to income, due perhaps to changes in interest rates; when interest rates rise, people demand smaller money balances at any given level of income; vice versa when they fall. But, says Friedman (1959: 138), observed cyclical changes in interest rates 'seem most unlikely to account for the . . . cyclical pattern in velocity'. His explanation is that the demand schedule for money is stable, but demand is related to permanent income rather than measured income. Permanent income is more stable than actual measured income. Over the cycle, 'measured' (i.e. actual) income fluctuates more widely than permanent income, because this year's permanent income is a weighted average of this year's measured income and the higher/lower measured incomes of recent years. Hence measured income velocity, Y_m/M, can rise during an expansion while permanent income velocity, Y_p/M falls; vice versa in a slump. 'If money holdings were adapted to permanent income, they might rise and fall more than in proportion to permanent income, yet less in proportion to measured income as is required by our cyclical results' (1959: 120).[7]

This conclusion is reinforced if we bring in price changes as a separate consideration. If money holdings depend on 'longer term price movements – permanent prices, as it were – rather than current or measured prices', people will hold smaller real balances when prices, like measured incomes, are temporarily high, and bigger real balances when prices and measured incomes are temporarily low: money holdings will be geared to the expected longer-term price level rather than the relatively high/low current price level. The ratio of real cash balances to measured income will then fluctuate more widely than their ratio to permanent prices and incomes. Thus measured velocity Y_m/M rises in expansions, when prices and the stock of money are also likely to increase, and falls in contractions, and this is not incompatible with opposite changes in the fraction Y_p/M, which relates demand for money to permanent income.[8] Changes in velocity over the cycle will also be greater than over the long, secular swings, for which 'the income figure we used . . . is an average value over a cycle, which may be regarded as a closer approximation to permanent income than an annual value' (Friedman 1971: 42). In short, the data used for the secular estimates ironed out cyclical fluctuations.

The basic Friedman thesis then is that the demand function for money is stable. One would, of course, expect it to be more stable than the more simple Keynesian function, which contains fewer determinant variables. It will be obvious to the reader that the more determinant variables one includes in an equation, the more stable a function of them the dependent variable will be. One can predict the demand for pears better from the behaviour of the price of pears, the prices of substitutes, and incomes than from the behaviour of any one of these determinants alone. But he also says that a demand schedule which relates demand for money to only one variable, permanent income, also shows a high degree of stability.

These major determinants of demand for money are stable; they change comparatively slowly. (We would therefore expect the demand for money and its inverse, the velocity of circulation, to be stable also. The supply of money is much less stable than the determinants of velocity.) It follows from these relative stabilities that changes in the value of money are likely to be caused by changes in supply rather than by changes in demand as we see later.

The money multiplier versus the expenditure multiplier

A more important conclusion for theory and for policy which Friedman and Meiselman (1963) drew from their study of US data over the period 1897 to 1958 and Friedman and Schwartz (1963) from their study of business cycles 1867–1960, is that consumption expenditure is more a function of the quantity of money than of 'autonomous expenditure'. Friedman and Meiselman ran a comparative empirical test of money and autonomous expenditure as determinants of consumption expenditure: the 'money multiplier' versus the 'investment or income-expenditure multiplier'. The two multipliers tested were as follows:

$$Y = b_0 + b_I I + u \qquad [10.2]$$
$$\text{and} \quad Y = d_0 + d_I M + v \qquad [10.3]$$

where Y = money income
       I = autonomous expenditure, basically $I + G + X - M$
       M = money supply and
       u, v = error terms

Or, in terms of consumption, using $C = cY$

$$C = k_0 + k_1I + u \qquad\qquad [10.4]$$
$$C = h_0 + h_1M + v \qquad\qquad [10.5]$$

where C = consumption
       c = marginal propensity to consume

(Note that the permanent income concept rather than the current income concept was used in this transformation.) Except for the post-1929 depression, they found the following: (a) the correlation between money and consumption is significantly higher than that between autonomous expenditure and consumption. (b) The partial correlation between money and consumption (i.e. an attempt to answer statistically the question: if we eliminate any effect from autonomous expenditure in a multiple correlation by holding it constant, what is then the relation between money and consumption?) was much the same as the simple correlation, while the partial correlation between autonomous spending and consumption was sometimes positive and sometimes negative and in neither case diverging far from zero. (c) If, having measured the relation between money and consumption, we then bring in autonomous expenditure as a possible further 'explanatory variable', the explanation of consumption is not significantly improved. (d) If *changes in* the stock of money, or in autonomous expenditure, are correlated with *changes in* consumption, there is a similar, and even sharper, contrast between the results. The results were essentially the same when the variables were put into real terms by taking price changes into account.

These conclusions were broadly confirmed by Friedman and Schwartz. Correlating the variability of annual changes in gross investment and money with the variability of annual changes in consumption, they found a higher correlation for money-consumption variability than for investment-consumption variability, and the partial correlation was also higher. The conclusion was that the money multiplier is a better explanation, and predictor, of consumption than the expenditure multiplier. The money in question is money 'broadly defined' to include time deposits as well as current accounts; but they tried other definitions of money and the correlations were high in every case.[9] However, Friedman and Schwartz do say that the case for a monetary explanation is not nearly so strong for minor economic fluctuations as for major fluctuations. If they had evidence only for minor fluctuations, they could not rule out 'the possibility that the close relation between money and business reflected primarily the influence of business on money'. Correlation is, of course, simply a statistical association between variables: it does not itself imply that changes in one variable are the *cause* of changes in another. It is theory, preferably supported by other evidence, which puts the causal links into equations. In their mammoth *Monetary History*, Friedman and Schwartz present evidence in support of two important assertions:

1 'The changes in the stock of money can generally be attributed to specific historical circumstances that are not in turn attributable to contemporary changes in money income and prices. Hence, if the consistent relation between money and income is not pure coincidence, it must reflect an influence running from money to business' (1963). The quantity of money is, as we saw in Chapter 3, determined by: (a) the actions of the monetary authority which create currency and bank reserves; (b) the ratio of banks reserves to deposits; and (c) the public's absolute and relative demands for currency and deposits. Of these (a) may be, but is not necessarily, autonomous, while (b) and (c) are likely to be subject to many influences, including actual or anticipated interest rates and income. They argue that (a) has in fact been autonomous and that (b) and (c) have 'played a roughly constant role over the whole period'.

2 'Appreciable changes in the rate of growth of the stock of money are a necessary and sufficient condition for appreciable changes in the rate of growth of money income . . . this is true both for long secular changes and also for changes over periods roughly the length of business cycles' (1963). For the years 1870–1963 the correlation between year-to-year changes in the quantity of money and changes in nominal income was 0.7; the similar correlation between money and wholesale prices was 0.54, for retail prices it was 0.58 (Friedman 1969: 148).[10]

Their conclusion is stated on p. 695 of *A Monetary History*: 'Apparently the forces determining the long-run rate of growth of real income are largely independent of the long-run rate of growth of the stock of money, so long as both proceed fairly smoothly. But marked instability of money is accompanied by instability of economic growth.'

This must not be taken to imply that the quantity of money is always and completely exogenous, nor that it is the only influence at work. Friedman (1969: 266) himself says, 'undoubtedly there can be and are influences running both ways . . . the changes in the stock of money producing changes in business that produce changes in the stock of money that continue the cycle . . . there can be and almost certainly are factors other than money that contribute to the cycle . . . The question at issue is . . . whether money exerts an important independent influence, not whether it is the only source of business fluctuation and itself wholly independent of them'.

The transmission mechanism

Granted that there is a firm and predictable link between money and money income, the statistical correlations which demonstrate that link do not tell us anything about the chain of reactions and economic decisions which produce the correlation. We would be better satisfied if we could understand the mechanism by which changes in the stock of money are transmitted to changes in expenditure and income.

Suppose there is an increase in the rate of growth of the stock of money, say, by open market operations (OMO). If the securities bought by the central bank are sold by the commercial banks, then the latter receive in exchange an addition to their cash reserves. If the securities come from non-bank holders, the proceeds from the sale will sooner or later appear as equal additions to bank deposits and to the banks' cash reserves. The first consequence, then, is that the public and/or the banks are left with fewer securities and more money. The addition to bank reserves is primary or *high-powered* money on which they can now build up a multiple of bank deposits, or secondary money.

The essence of the transmission process is that this leaves portfolios in disequilibrium; they contain too much money and too few securities. One can easily accept this in the case of the banks; cash is the base on which they build an *inverted pyramid* of earning assets. They react by increasing their non-cash assets, to reduce their cash ratio to its original level. In the case of the non-bank public, however, one might point out that sales of securities to the central bank are voluntary, and ask: if portfolio holders were in equilibrium before the OMO, will they deliberately put themselves into disequilibrium by changing the money/securities composition of their portfolios? The very concept of equilibrium makes this seem nonsensical. The answer is that 'the bank offered them a good price, so they sold: they added to their money balances as a temporary step in rearranging their portfolios' (Friedman and Schwartz 1963a: 60). They are persuaded to sell by a 'good price', which must mean a higher price than that at which the securities in question were standing before the OMO occurred. The central bank, in effect, disturbs the original equilibrium by reducing the yield on the securities it buys, and the sellers prefer the money to the (now lower) yield on the securities sold. As far as the ratios between money and *these* securities are concerned, their portfolios are still in equilibrium, but a different one. But the yields on other assets are not, at this first stage, reduced. People have more liquidity than they want in view of the income obtainable from non-money assets; so they set out to buy prospective income with the excess money. They will probably turn first to the securities similar to those they have sold, safe fixed-interest securities. Their demand pushes up the prices of these securities. It is a basic law of economics that there can only be one price in any one unified market for any particular good. Yields on this whole class of securities therefore fall, whoever holds them. So *every* holder is left with an unbalanced, inefficient portfolio: in view of the decline in their yield, he is holding a bigger proportion of this class of security than he wants. So now the effects begin to spread out from the participants in the OMO to the market in general. The next adjustment of portfolios is a purchase of some other class of asset, perhaps fixed-interest securities carrying higher yields (and, presumably, higher risk), or equities. This increased demand reduces the yields on *this* category of assets, so the process of adjustment is repeated ... and so on. The series of adjustments originated from a situation of excess liquidity, and the general aim is therefore to reduce liquidity. This portfolio holder can do not only by increasing the proportion of assets of less certain capital value in their portfolios, but also by increasing the average length of life of redeemable assets held. So the ripples of portfolio adjustment spread out not only from safe to less safe assets but also along 'the liquidity spectrum', from the short to the long end of the bond market.

It is at this point that one effect on the real sector appears. We know that a rise in the prices of debentures and equities is synonymous with a fall in their yields, the returns on them: but the return to the holder is identical with the cost of this form of finance to the issuer. Since existing securities compete on the market with newly issued securities, they must offer comparable yields. So the cost of new finance falls as yields on existing securities fall, which stimulates investment financed by the issue of new debentures and equities. Meanwhile, as we noted above, the banks will have been expanding their loans and overdrafts – probably at lower interest rates – and these will also be spent. The fall in interest rates will probably have spread also to the mortgage and hire purchase finance markets, increasing expenditure on housing and durable goods.

To return to the holders of portfolios of assets: the 'monetarist' school argues that they have an interest in real assets as well as financial assets: we should 'regard the relevant portfolios as containing a much wider range of assets, including not only government and private fixed-interest and equity securities . . . but also a host of other assets, even going so far as to include consumer durable goods, consumer inventories of clothing and the like and, maybe also, such human capital as skills acquired through training, and the like' (Friedman and Schwartz 1963: 231). As the prices of financial assets rise, they become expensive relative to real assets and this induces further adjustments of portfolios by the purchase of real assets. These purchases raise the prices of real assets. The rise in the prices of existing real assets pulls up the prices people will pay for similar new assets, since new and existing assets are sold in roughly the same markets. So the improvement in the markets for existing assets improves the market for new assets, and more are produced: investment increases.[11]

Apart from the direct effects of changing interest rates on spending, there is a *wealth effect*. As the prices of assets rise, the holders of assets are made wealthier. They therefore feel free to spend more: on consumers' goods in the case of personal asset-holders, on investment of all kinds if they are firms.

There is also a more direct *portfolio adjustment effect*. Since portfolios include real assets, any early reaction of at least some wealth-holders to excess money will be to buy real assets as well as, or instead of, financial assets. A deficiency of real assets in portfolios is one counterpart of an excess of money. The effect on real assets, no less than that on financial assets, is an interest-rate effect. Real assets yield services which can be regarded as the yield on money spent on them; real assets carry an implicit *own-rate of interest*. According to Friedman, the inclusion of these implicit and unmeasured rates of interest is one of the major differences between Keynesian and monetarist analysis:

The difference between us and the Keynesians is less in the nature of the (transmission) process than in the range of assets considered. We insist that a far wider range of assets and interest rates must be taken into account – such assets as durable and semi-durable consumer goods, structures and other real property. As a result, we regard the market rates stressed by the Keynesians as only a small part of the total spectrum of rates that are relevant. (Friedman 1971: 28)

The above adjustments are what has become known as the 'real balance effect'. However, movement to a new equilibrium may be cyclical. The initial demand for real balances is based on the initial price level. As excess balances are spent, prices rise and so do desired, or necessary, real balances. Meanwhile, the real value of existing balances is falling. Moreover, the fall in interest rates will tend to increase the demand for money: the effect may, as Friedman believes, be only small; nevertheless, the likelihood is an increase in desired real balances in a portfolio of given total real value. The attempt to rebuild real balances puts a brake on expenditure and prices, which reduces the anticipated need for money balances, which stimulates expenditure again . . . and so on; there can be a repeated 'over-shooting'.

At some point a further consideration comes into the picture: namely, that expectations may reduce the demand for money as a proportion of total wealth. A rise in the actual price level increases the real-balance requirement; a rise in the expected price level increases the cost of holding money and so reduces desired holdings. Desired holdings are stabilised by stability in the expected rate of price change, which is usually taken to occur when the actual rate of change equals the expected rate of change. There is evidence that a serious inflation does reduce the demand for money, but not a mild inflation (Allais 1966; Cagan 1956; and Bain 1980). The overall consequence, however, according to Friedman, is a 'reverse feed-back' effect on the demand for money and for other assets, with consequent reverse effects on interest rates.

Money and the rate of interest

Interest rates are, he says, also strongly influenced by price expectations. Lenders demand an 'inflation premium' in nominal (market) rates to maintain a satisfactory real rate of return, and borrowers will be prepared to pay a higher nominal rate. So within a year interest rates will rise again. Like spending and the demand for money, they may overshoot and move to a new equilibrium cyclically. Taking into account inflationary expectations, monetary expansion is likely to bring higher, not lower, interest rates eventually.

The interest rate is not the true price of money (that is given by increases in the price level), but the price of loanable funds, although the supply of loanable funds is probably linked with the supply of money. Friedman presents a theory of the determination of nominal interest rates which, briefly, runs as follows. He begins by asserting that, because of the actions of speculators, the current market rate will tend to equality with the expected rate: that we can accept. The nominal rate is equal to the real rate plus an allowance for expected changes, if any, in the price level. Anticipated changes in the price level are the difference between expected changes in nominal income and in real income. The rate of growth of real income changes little in the short or medium term and the expected real rate, he believes, changes more or less in step with the rate of growth of real income. The real rate is a function of basic 'real' variables such as the supply of savings and productivity of capital, and is comparatively stable. The market rate of interest is therefore determined largely by anticipated changes in nominal income, in particular by expected changes in the price level. It is the 'inflation premium' which accounts for most of the variation in market rates.[12]

Friedman's hypothesis can be expressed mathematically as follows:

$$r = p + \left(\frac{1}{P}, \frac{dP}{dt}\right) \qquad\qquad [10.6]$$

where r = the nominal rate of interest
        p = the real rate of interest
        P = the price level
        t = time

If $r_c = r_e$ $[10.7]$

i.e. the current rate of interest = the expected rate,

then $r_c = P_e + \left(\dfrac{1}{P}, \dfrac{dP}{dt}\right)e = P_e + \left(\dfrac{1}{y}, \dfrac{dY}{dt}\right)e - \left(\dfrac{1}{y}, \dfrac{dy}{dt}\right)e$ $[10.8]$

$$= P_e = g_e + \left(\frac{1}{Y}, \frac{dY}{dt}\right)e \qquad\qquad [10.9]$$

where Y = nominal income
           y = real income

           g = anticipated rate of growth of real income $\left(\dfrac{1}{y}, \dfrac{dy}{dt}\right)e$

With p_e and g_e determined outside this system of equations by stable real forces, and the difference between them being constant, or nearly so, the nominal rate of interest becomes a function of $(1/Y,\ dY/dt)e$, the anticipated rate of growth of nominal income. If this is the whole truth, one wonders how interest rates can change significantly from week to week.

He similarly derives a *monetary theory of nominal income*: let the demand for money, a function of income and the interest rate, be kept equal to the supply of money.

Then $M = M_s = M_D = F(rY)$ [10.10]

$$Y = F \cdot \frac{1}{(r)} \cdot M$$ [10.11]

But $$r = P_e - g_e + \left(\frac{1}{Y}, \frac{dY}{dt}\right)e$$ [10.12]

So $$Y = F \frac{M}{p_e - g_e + \left(\dfrac{1}{Y}, \dfrac{dY}{dt}\right)e}$$ [10.13]

With $p_e - g_e$ constant, nominal income is a function of the expected rate of change of nominal income and the quantity of money. The anticipated rate of change of nominal income is, Friedman suggests, determined by the past history of nominal income, hence current Y is a function of M and of Y in past periods. But Y in past periods is a function of M in past periods, as indicated by our equation $Y = f(1/(r))M$ above. Thus nominal Y is a function of current and past levels of M, *if* we accept all the assumptions in the analysis.

In the short run, monetary change can influence output and employment, but in the long run they, and real wages, are determined by real forces such as the size of the population and its skills, the stock of natural resources and capital, technology and industrial organisation. There is a 'natural' level of real wages and a 'natural' level of employment at which real wages are such as to equate the demand and supply of labour. The economy will in the long run tend towards these natural levels; a monetary policy which tries to keep unemployment below its natural level will necessarily be maintaining an excess demand for labour and will be inflationary. To keep down real wages (or interest rates), the supply of money would have to grow at an accelerating rate. Conversely, any attempt to keep interest rates or unemployment higher than their natural levels will generate an accelerating deflation (see Ch. 11). Monetary policy can control nominal quantities: money income, the nominal quantity of money, market rates of interest; but it cannot 'peg a real quantity – the real rate of interest, the rate of unemployment, the level of real national income, the real quantity of money, the rate of growth of real national income, or the rate of growth of the real quantity of money' (Friedman 1969: 105). We are, it appears, back to the Classical dichotomy. As we saw earlier, in recent publications Friedman suggests that an increase in the rate of growth of the stock of money will in the long run reduce the level and rate of growth of real output, and prices will therefore rise more than nominal income.

The several ripples of adjustment of portfolio composition, prices and output will end when prices, income, real wealth and ratio of real money balances to wealth are once more in an equilibrium relation to each other.

What is new in the new quantity theory?

The new quantity theory has some obvious similarities with Keynesian theory and, more particularly, with portfolio balance theory. Friedman himself has admitted that his reformulation of the quantity theory was 'much influenced by the Keynesian analysis', and that 'its emphasis is on what is called "portfolio analysis", analysis of the structure of people's balance sheets, of the kinds of assets they want to hold', whereas the quantity theory of Irving Fisher 'put major emphasis on transactions and on money as a mechanical medium of exchange' (1911: 73). Like Keynes, he sees the demand for money as a choice between different ways of holding wealth; but like the portfolio balance theorists, he envisages a wide range of assets. A statement of Keynes' own 'portfolio balance' view is to be found in his article in the *QJE*, 1937. In equilibrium, loans and capital assets 'must offer equal advantage to the marginal investor in each of them'. One may deduce that Keynes would have raised no objection to much of the transmission mechanism suggested by Friedman and Schwartz that the adjustment spreads through a range of financial assets (Keynes' 'loans') to real assets via changes in their relative prices and yields. In both analyses the final link between money and nominal income can be seen as the sensitivity of expenditure to changes in the prices and yields of assets. Friedman himself has asserted that the main difference between them is the range of assets considered and the policy implication of the two schools.

Whether the differences between Friedman and Keynes are theoretical or empirical is still a subject of burgeoning debate. Stein (1976: 2) writes: 'Monetarists are policy oriented. Their major propositions are a series of empirical observations ... rather than a theory in direct opposition to neo-Keynesian analysis ...' And Friedman (1976: 315) himself asserted: 'I continue to believe that the fundamental differences between us are empirical and not theoretical ..'. There are, however, some important differences of emphasis and of basic theory. Keynes regarded money as one of a number of competing forms of wealth, one of which is real assets. He also recognised the 'windfall' wealth effect on spending of changes in interest rates. Nevertheless, in his discussion of liquidity preference, and of the determinants of output and money income, he ignores these themes; he concentrates rather on the demand for money alone.[13] If the stock of money increases, there occurs a movement down the liquidity preference curve until money holdings are once more in equilibrium, at a lower rate of interest: the fall in interest rates stimulates investment, and the increase in investment induces a larger increase in money income via the multiplier. Insofar as changes in the stock of money are transmitted to income, this is the transmission mechanism. The subsequent feedback, reversing the fall in interest rates, comes via the income effect of rising output and/or prices on transactions demand for money, not via a wealth effect. The (speculative) demand for money as

225

an asset is not a function of total wealth. Put into portfolio balance terms, i.e. introducing specifically a margin of substitution between money and other assets, the assets which are substitutes for money would be financial assets. It would be the rising prices and falling yields on bonds which persuaded people to hold a bigger proportion of money in their portfolios.

Friedman, on the other hand, emphasises wealth and demotes interest rates as determinants of demand for money. His concept of income is really a measure of wealth. In his article in the Journal of Political Economy, *1972*, he writes,

> I . . . pay no attention to "the effects on the rate of interest" of shifts in the demand function for money. I . . . tend to minimise changes in market interest rates as the primary channel through which changes in the quantity of money effect spending, output, and prices. To go further, in the "Restatement" I do not even consider the effect of changes in the quantity of money on interest rates.

He agrees with the Classical assertion that the interest rate is 'determined by saving and investing or lending and borrowing. Monetary changes affected the interest rate by producing inflation (or deflation)' (p. 944), e.g. inducing an inflation premium in nominal rates. The monetarist approach does not concentrate on, nor even emphasise financial assets as alternatives to, substitutes for money. They are no nearer substitutes for money than are real assets.

This difference of emphasis in the transmission process derives logically from differences between the two theories of the demand for money. In Keynesian theory, there is a largely income-determined demand for transactions and precautionary balances, and an interest-determined demand for speculative balances. It is the fall in interest rates which disposes of the excess in holdings of money; once rates have fallen sufficiently to persuade the community willingly to hold the new money in their portfolios (less that part, if any, required to supplement transactions balances in view of the rise, if any, in income resulting from the decline in interest rates) the direct effect of an increase in the quantity of money is complete. Moreover, the transmission process is uncertain and imperfect. The monetary authorities, he says, usually operate in the short-term market only, leaving 'the price of long-term debts to be influenced by belated and imperfect reactions from the price of short-term debts' and there is a limit to the decline of the long-term rate, set by the liquidity trap. If this minimum rate is higher than the marginal efficiency of capital, there is no effect on purchases of goods; the transmission process stops before it reaches the real sector. The monetarist does not make the same sharp distinction between 'transactions' and 'speculative' balances, between 'active' and 'idle' money: 'dollars of money are not distinguished according as they are held for one or the other purpose. Rather, each dollar is, as it were, regarded as rendering a variety of services' (Friedman 1969: 61). The interest elasticity of demand for money is low, and there is no liquidity trap. And the demand for money as an asset, as well as the demand for money in its medium of exchange function, is a demand for real balances.

Expenditure, on the other hand, both on financial and on real assets, is interest elastic. When the prices of financial assets rise (yields fall), the relative yields on real assets rise, so we buy goods up to the point at which 'own rates of interest' are the same for all assets. It is for these reasons that the excess money balances are not mopped up by a fall in measured interest rates (except via the wealth effect) and the chain reaction continues until it reaches the real sector. It is the rise in the value of assets, and (particularly) rising output and/or prices of goods, which eventually bring the ratio of real balances to total assets back to their equilibrium level. Friedman (1971: 29) says that the Keynesian analysis assumed that short of full employment, prices of goods are fixed; hence the portfolio adjustment transmission process, which operates through changes in relative prices of assets, had to stop short of the goods market. It was forced to concentrate on 'a narrow range of marketable assets and recorded interest rates'. This explanation is wrong. Keynes made no such assumption (see Ch. 21 of the *General Theory*, especially p. 296).

In Keynesian economics, V (the inverse of the demand for money) changes directly with interest rates, *vide* the shape of the liquidity preference schedule. Furthermore, the liquidity trap can be seen as a situation in which changes in M are completely neutralised by inverse changes in V. Friedman, on the other hand, argues that velocity is relatively stable (if measured as a relation between permanent income and real balances) and, more important, predictable. Further, the *cyclical* changes which do occur are in the same direction as changes in the quantity of money: changes in velocity do not thwart monetary policy, they reinforce it. Money is therefore an important regulator of expenditure, and monetary policy a powerful weapon of control. There are obviously as many theoretical differences as there are empirical differences between the two schools: 'the differences are almost all theoretical . . .' (Hahn 1980: 15).

Some criticisms of the new quantity theory

The publications of the monetarists have caused more controversy than any other work in this field since Keynes' *General Theory*. The dispute between the Keynesians and the Friedmanites is far from settled, and equally eminent economists are to be found in both camps. The eventual outcome is of more than purely academic importance; it has obvious implications for policy. Much of the criticism relates to the statistical methods and procedures employed by Friedman and his colleagues; some of it is highly technical and beyond the scope of this book.[14] This apart, the critics have attacked both the theoretical models and the choice of, and interpretation of, data. The major objections are as follows:

The definition of autonomous expenditure

The Friedman–Meiselman confrontation of the Keynesian model (changes in consumption as a function of changes in autonomous expenditure and the multiplier) with the quantity theory model (changes in consumption as a function of changes in the quantity of money) rests on a mis-specification of autonomous expenditure. They define it as net private domestic investment (including investment in stocks), the Government deficit, and the net foreign balance (exports minus imports). But these items are not entirely autonomous. Imports, for example, are partly induced by the level and rate of growth of domestic income, and exports are not independent of them. Inventory investment depends closely on sales, which are related to income and consumption. Fixed investment is related to income (to be precise, the growth of income) by the acceleration effect. Tax revenues which, together with government expenditure, determine the budget surplus or deficit, fluctuate with income and expenditure. In short, a significant part of the expenditure which, in their supposed Keynesian model, determines C or Y is, in fact, partly determined by C or Y; it is not autonomous. Investment, a major component of A, is not independent of M. An increase in M may influence I via the interest-rate effect, the real balance effect (firms spending excess balances) and the acceleration effect coming from the wealth (real balances) effect on consumption (Gramm and Timberlake 1969). Private investment is financed by bank loans, which increase deposits before the effect on production; exports are also financed partly by bank borrowing; Government expenditure is related to the public sector debt, which may be financed by borrowing from the banks, which in turn increases the quantity of money. In short, the supposed alternative multiplicands are not completely unrelated.

Friedman and Meiselman are well aware of these facts. They do not assume *a priori* that the Government deficit and the foreign balance are autonomous. Instead, they chose their autonomous items by statistical tests as follows: (1) If two categories of expenditure are autonomous (A), a shift between them, with no change in their total sum, will not affect consumption (C). (2) If expenditures are induced, a shift between them which does not alter their total sum will not change the ratio of that total sum to A. (3) In each case, the correlation between each separate item and C or A as the case may be, will be lower than the correlation between the total of the items and C or A.

It would, indeed, be difficult to find any kind of expenditure which is consistently and unequivocally autonomous; but the results of a test are likely to depend significantly on what items are chosen for inclusion in the category. Friedman and Meiselman have admitted (1965: 754): that 'However useful "autonomous expenditure" may be as a theoretical constraint, it is still far from having any generally accepted empirical counterpart.'

Some tests of the multiplier

Several further confrontations of the two theories have appeared since the Friedman–Meiselman article, using different definitions of autonomous expenditure and, in some cases, different definitions of money, and covering different periods. Some found money to be the better predictor of consumption or income, others concluded that the Keynesian model works better. For empirical investigations whose results favour the investment multiplier, see Hester (1964), Ando and Modigliani (1965) and De Prano and Mayer (1965) (the last two of these conclude that both A and M are significant determinants of C, as does Chow (1967)). Support for the money multiplier comes from Bronfrenbrenner (1963), Phillips (1969) and Anderson and Jordan (1968).

Anderson and Jordan found that about half the variances of ΔGNP in the years 1952–68 were explained by changes in the money supply (M_1). The money multiplier was both high and fast, with a once-for-all increase of $1 billion in the money supply, raising GNP by $6.5 billion within a year. The fiscal multiplier was virtually zero. De Leeuw and Kalchenbrenner (1969) substituted the reserve base of the banks (H) for the money supply (as more likely to be exogenous), and found a similar explanatory power, but they also found that fiscal policy had a significant effect on income. Davis (1969) presents other 'St. Louis-type' equations, using rather different statistical methods, and omitting the fiscal variables. ΔM explained 62% of ΔGNP 1960–68, but only 18% 1952–60. Christ (1973) has a reduced form model in which both ΔG and ΔH had a substantial effect on GNP 1891–1970. Breaking the whole period down into six sub-periods, the effects were not stable from one sub-period to another. Poole and Kornblith (1973) tested the Friedman–Meiselman, Hester, Ando–Modigliani, De Prano–Mayer and Anderson–Jordan equations over the period 1959–70. While some of the equations, using one or other of eleven different definitions of autonomous expenditure, performed quite well, in general their performances were poor. None of these single equations models predicted the future very well; neither the simple Keynesian nor the simple quantity theory models provide an adequate understanding of business cycle fluctuations. Fisher and Sheppard (1974: 235) presented an analysis of twelve econometric models of the USA and concluded:

> We only note that most of the models which aim at any disaggregation at all show that *both* fiscal *and* monetary policy measures make a significant contribution to the determination of major macro-aggregates, such as output and employment. The major difference appears to be in the channels of influence, the speed of response, and in the sectoral impact of different policies. The proper approach is to try to determine what combination of the two would be most effective for the achievement of a given objective in particular circumstances.

For the UK, Barrett and Walters (1966) compared the stability of Keynesian and monetary multipliers in the period 1878–1963.[15] Comparing the two theories, the monetary explanation of changes in consumption performed better before 1914, although adding autonomous expenditure improved the explanation significantly, and for the period 1878–1938, while the Keynesian explanation was better for the inter-war years and for the whole period 1878–1963. The explanatory power of the two hypotheses combined was not particularly high; changes in the money supply and in autonomous expenditure together explained 44% of the variation in consumption expenditure over the whole period, 54% for the period 1878–1939, 68% in the inter-war years. For the post-war period to 1963, neither determinant nor the two together were statistically significant.[16] They suggest a number of reasons for this, which have been echoed by other commentators: increasing importance of the Government as a taxer and spender, government interference in the terms and availability of credit, the development of more, and a bigger variety of, assets which are good substitutes for money. However, they conclude that 'Our results suggest that both money and autonomous expenditures have been important features in the determination of aggregate consumption.' Artis and Nobay (1969: 49) reported the results of an investigation of British experience 1958–67: 'In general, the level of statistical explanation was not high'; but the results suggested that fiscal measures are more powerful, and act more quickly, than monetary measures. However, they placed little reliance on these results, chiefly because of their strong doubts about the exogeneity of either monetary or fiscal changes; the results are, they suggest, 'more correctly interpreted simply as measures of association'. Sheppard (1971) found changes in autonomous expenditure (exports plus government expenditure plus gross fixed capital formation) in the same year more important than changes in the money supply as a determinant of consumption in the years 1881–1939. He found that neither appeared to have any relation with consumption 1948–62. The contribution of changes in the money stock was unimportant in all three periods, pre-1914, inter-war and post-1945.[17] But when he put all the variables into real terms, i.e. in constant prices, he got a different picture. $\Delta A/P$ had a correlation coefficient with $\Delta C/P$ in the same year of 0.24 in the early period, 1882–1914, but the lagged relationship ($\Delta C/P$ lagged six months behind $\Delta A/P$) was 0.02. Thereafter, 'the contribution falls sharply', and there was no significant correlation in the later periods. But both real money balances and real encashable assets (encashable assets = money + savings bank deposits + National Savings instruments + life assurance funds + building society shares and deposits + Government securities as recorded in the Post Office register) made a surprisingly potent contribution in each period. But the relationships he reports were unstable, and the lagged values show small or insignificant results in the first and last periods, and in three cases the relationship was the opposite of what one would expect.

Taking correlations with total private expenditure (equal to consumption expenditure plus gross fixed domestical capital formation plus value of physical increase in stocks and work in progress), the results 'suggest that the percentage change of the money stock has been of some significance, but the standard errors of its regression coefficients in all periods are too large to place much confidence in them' (p. 83). The correlations for equations including log A_t were twice or three times as high. Neither A nor M was significant in 1948–62. Expressing the variables in constant prices, changes in real money balances and in real encashable assets were significantly correlated with changes in real private expenditure in the first and last periods, but not in the inter-war period. He does not test for the effect of changes in real autonomous expenditure.

Starleaf and Floyd (1972) made an international comparison in thirteen countries of the stability of the growth of the money supply and the stability of the growth of national income over the years 1952–67. Their results showed a positive relationship between them. They also found a highly significant positive inter-country relationship between the rate of growth of the money supply and the rate of growth of GNP, and that deviations of GNP from its trend rate of growth were significantly correlated with deviations of the money supply from its trend rate of growth. 'None of this evidence conflicts with the implications of Friedman's hypothesis' but 'like any set of empirical findings, they are consistent with more than one hypothesis' (p. 722).

This is a mixed bag of results (see also Artis and Lewis 1984). If there is one generalisation we can make, it is that further work has shown that money is, or at least has been, much more important than was thought, say, twenty years ago: it has not, however, borne out the monetarist contention that autonomous expenditure has little or no effect on income. Whether it is more or less important than the money supply is not clear.

The demand for money

If money is defined strictly as a means of payment, which gives immediate command over goods and services, then it consists of currency plus demand deposits. The Friedman–Meiselman–Schwartz definition includes time deposits also. They give a number of reasons for this. First, there are no reliable data of demand and time deposits separately before 1917. Second, time deposits 'are such close substitutes for money that there is less error in including them than in excluding them'. Third, it may be that a better concept of money is that it is 'a temporary abode of purchasing power, enabling the act of purchase to be separated from the act of sale'. That there is a difference between the interest elasticities of money 'narrowly defined' and money 'broadly defined' is confirmed by several studies of the demand for money, most of them relating to the USA, but a few based on UK data. More important is the fact that nearly all the above studies find a significant role for interest rates in the determination of the demand for money on either definition. Friedman's conclusion that the interest rate is insignificant cannot, therefore, be explained by his particular definition of money (see also Stein 1976, and Modigliani 1977).

Contrary to the assertions of the monetarist school, then, there does appear to be a significant relation between the demand for money and rates of interest on alternative assets. Further studies indicate that income is more important than interest rates as a determinant of the demand for money, although the relation between changes in the quantity of money and changes in income is not nearly as strong, especially since the Second World War, as would appear from the findings of Friedman, Meiselman and Schwartz. The evidence on permanent income versus measured income is mixed. In view of the concept of permanent income employed, what is presented as a relation between demand for money and permanent income may in fact be simply a lagged relation between money and measured income. Permanent income is, as we have seen, a particular concept of wealth. The more usual concept is what Friedman would term 'non-human wealth'. Whether one version is superior to the other in this respect is not yet clear.

Is the money supply exogenous?

It is part of the monetarist explanation of history that changes in the stock of money were 'exogenous' not 'endogenous', that is, they were determined 'outside the system' by the monetary authority in pursuance of an autonomous, deliberate policy and not as a passive response to changes in the demand for money arising from changes in business activity. Only then can money be said to be 'the primary source of change and disturbance'. Their evidence for the assertion that this was the case over the period 1867 to 1960 is of three kinds. First, the fact that changes in the quantity of money usually preceded changes in business activity. Second, their detailed study of monetary history showed that most major changes in the stock of money were in fact autonomous in the sense stated above. Third, the relation between money and economic activity has been stable in spite of changes in the arrangements which determined the quantity of money, whether it was linked to gold reserves as under the Gold Standard or 'managed', and despite changing criteria of control by the monetary authority. The statistical case for the predominance of the money-to-income causation appears to rest on two further pieces of evidence. First, the length of the $\Delta M \rightarrow \Delta Y$ interval in cyclical changes is more uniform than the length of the $\Delta Y \rightarrow \Delta M$ interval. Second, a steep contraction of income is usually followed by a steep expansion, but a steep expansion is not usually followed by a deep contraction. The same is true if we substitute 'mild' for 'steep' or 'deep' in the last sentence. This is also the case with the (prior) changes in the quantity of money: 'the pattern for business is a reflection of the pattern for money'.

The first kind of evidence has been criticised as a *post hoc, propter hoc* argument. This is related to the 'leads and lags' problem (Sims 1972). Firms and individuals may arrange loans *before* they spend, and the first result of increased purchases is likely to be a fall in stocks. It may be some time before actual production increases. An increase in the quantity of money might, therefore, be demand-induced rather than autonomous even if it occurred before the increase in expenditure or output (see Kaldor 1970). The important question here is: how do these lags between financing and spending, and between spending and economic activity, compare with the observed lag between changes in the quantity of money and changes in economic activity? We do not know the answer. The first is probably short, if only because people are unlikely to pay interest on loans for longer than is necessary, or forego interest by building up large money balances of their own. The Friedman–Schwartz estimates of the money-activity lag have been disputed.[18] Some have suggested a much shorter lag; most estimates lie between six months and one year, but at least one contribution to the debate argues that the lag between peaks and troughs in the money supply and peaks and troughs in GNP has fallen as low as three months in the post-war period (Davis 1968). If the lag were, generally, so short, it might be held to support the above argument for an endogenous supply of money.

Of the three determinants of the supply of money – the quantity of currency and bank reserves ('high-powered money'), the banks' reserve ratio, and the public's desired ratio of currency to bank deposits – only the first can be purely exogenous.

Within the limit set by the supply of high-powered money and the controls on ratios or total deposits, the deposit/reserve and currency/deposit ratios are what the banks and the public wish them to be. They are 'behavioural ratios', subject to many influences. The public's demand for holdings of cash (which, together with the total cash issued, determines the amount available for the banks' reserves) as compared with deposits depends on such things as confidence in the banks, methods of payment, perhaps slightly on the interest paid on deposits or the free banking services offered to depositors, and perhaps on income. The monetary authority can always cancel out an expansionary effect on the total money supply of any change in this desired ratio by altering the total supply of currency. The banks' cash ratio may be above the minimum if the return on earnings assets is very low or, more importantly, if there is an insufficient demand for loans and overdrafts. The demand for bank loans is, surely, a determinate, not a determinant, of the level of business activity. A study of the data on determinants of the supply of money in *A Monetary History* shows that changes in these ratios were largely responsible for the major contractions in the stock of money, and that they also contributed to expansions. For example, between August 1929 and March 1933, changes in these ratios 'converted the $17\frac{1}{2}$ per cent rise that high-powered money would have produced into a 35 per cent decline in the stock of money' (see Ch. 12).

The supply of 'high-powered money', the monetary base, may have been exogenous over most of the period covered by *A Monetary History*, but this does not mean that it is necessarily so at all times. A change in the supply of 'high-powered' money is only exogenous if it is initiated by the authorities autonomously, not in response to one or more of the presumed endogenous variables such as income or the rate of interest. Monetary policy in the UK, and to some extent in the USA, in recent years has been dictated by the external balance, by the need to finance fluctuating government deficits and by the general aim of policy to avoid large fluctuations in interest rates. This last aim meant that when there was a shortage of money to finance expenditure, the authorities supplied it. If holders of the large outstanding government debt wished to dispose of their securities (perhaps to spend the money received), the central bank stepped in and bought them to avoid a rise in interest rates. Similarly, the money supply would be increased to accommodate large issues of debt to the public (Kaldor and Trevithick 1981). A surplus on the balance of payments also tends to increase the supply of money. In all these cases, the increase in the quantity of money is likely to be associated with an increase in money income. But it was not the increase in the money supply which caused the increase in income.

There are two answers to many of these criticisms. The first is that the monetarist case for the exogeneity of money does not rest simply on statistical associations, but on the study of actual changes in M. Their assertion is that they were, as a matter of historical fact, not passive reactions to demand; they were deliberate and autonomous, not related to income or expected income. The second is that the admitted feedback from income to money does not invalidate the money multiplier (see Frost 1977). Friedman and Schwartz are aware of these 'influences running the other way, particularly during the shorter run movement associated with the business cycle'

(1963: 695), i.e. from income to money, and in their 1963 article they write that the changes in these ratios 'bespeak a rather complex feedback mechanism whereby changes in business activity react on the stock of money' (pp. 265–6). But even if this year's money supply is a response to the demand for money, it may still determine future nominal income; if the supply had not increased, future nominal income would have been that much less.

The behaviour of velocity

Many studies exist showing the relationship between interest rates and real wealth and the decline in velocity before 1900 (Meltzer 1963 and Brunner 1965). Indeed, only for the periods 1880–1914 and 1929–46 is there clear evidence of a downward trend in velocity, and there has been a clear upward trend since 1946. Tobin (1965) asserts that '. . . the annual percentage change in the money supply explains only 31 per cent of the variation in the annual percentage change in money income over the period 1869–1959. So the relationship between the quantity of money and income is not so stable, and neither it appears has velocity been a stable function of "permanent income" (p. 472). But perhaps the most serious problem posed for the permanent income theory of demand for money is the post-Second World War rise in velocity. Permanent income has been rising, but so has velocity. Indeed, both the long-run and the short-run movements of velocity have been the opposite of what this theory would predict. Friedman and Schwartz devote a whole chapter of the *Monetary History* to this problem, rejecting the explanations which have been suggested. The rise in interest rates, the growth of monetary substitutes and inflationary psychology could together only account for less than half the post-war rise in velocity. Their own explanation lies in 'one possible common root' of the pre-war and post-war periods, which is 'changing patterns of expectations about economic stability' (p. 673). Just as the economic instability and uncertainties of 1929–42 were, in their opinion, responsible for the sharp increase in demand for money in that period, so was the 'growing confidence in future economic stability' of the post-war period, whose high level of employment and only mild recessions contrasted sharply with pre-war experience, responsible for the decline in the demand for money. They cannot support this opinion with quantitative evidence, and they advance it tentatively, claiming only that it is plausible. They do not really establish its superiority over the rejected explanations.

Another reason they suggest for the post-war rise in velocity to 1960 is that it was a reaction to the sharp fall during 1942–46, and the rise from 1932 to 1942, interrupted from 1937 to 1940, was a reaction to the 'collapse' of velocity 1929 to 1932. Gould and Nelson (1974) say we can draw no such statistical inferences nor perceive patterns and trends from the Friedman–Schwartz data on velocity. The series has the character of a 'random walk', a 'simple summation of uncorrelated shocks'; they find no evidence of correlation, or pattern, in successive changes in velocity, which would enable us to predict velocity from its past history.

Friedman and Schwartz (1982) have published another version of their *Monetary*

234

Trends, this time comparing trends in the US with those in the UK for the years 1867–1975. In that volume, they say (p. 624):

> The broad survey of our basic time series with which we begin our empirical analysis is sufficient to demonstrate that the simple Keynesian view can be rejected: the movements in the level of income and its rate of change parallel extraordinarily closely for more than a century the contemporaneous movements in the quantity of money and its rate of change and this is equally true for the United States and the United Kingdom.

They do, however, admit that either could be 'cause' or 'effect', and somewhat harmlessly argue that 'the two magnitudes are clearly not independently determined'. Their assessment of the pattern for velocity is that its variation was far less than either that of nominal money supply or nominal income, this of course being understood in 'permanent income' terms. Similarly, in comparing changes in velocity in the US with those in the UK, they found very little difference. They did, however, find that the two countries displayed a different pattern when it came to price changes. In the UK, price changes accounted for a larger percentage of the fluctuation in nominal income and output changes a smaller proportion than in the USA.

This recent publication by Friedman and Schwartz has not gone unnoticed in the literature. Indeed, a special panel paper (No. 22) written by the Bank of England Panel of Academic Consultants, published in October 1983, was devoted to it. In two separate papers, Professor Arthur J. Brown and Professor David J. Hendry, along with Neil R. Ericsson, produced convincing evidence that Friedman and Schwartz' analysis is of dubious quality. Hendry and Ericsson, in particular, in a paper which examines the econometric methods adopted in the book, were extremely critical. They criticise the procedure adopted of averaging the 108 annual observations to 36 phase averages, which although it did not seriously reduce the serial correlation in such a long data set, because it wasted much information with regard to business cycle behaviour, did lead to the use of equations which were 'badly fitting'. Hendry and Ericsson were also sceptical of Friedman and Schwartz' finding on the relative constancy of velocity which relied on the inclusion of a dummy variable selected after examination of the data sample, and not on theoretical grounds, which is the normal econometric approach. Hendry and Ericsson were, however, at pains to stress that they were not attacking the monetarist position on theoretical grounds, nor in terms of the basic model adopted by Friedman and Schwartz, but merely that with the econometric approach they adopted, the evidence for the UK was not convincing.

The panel's overall conclusion on *Monetary Trends* was that the estimation of economic relationships which extend over such long time periods is an extremely complex task and that Friedman and Schwartz had failed to convince. For though it is possible to estimate long-run coefficients, even where the process of causation changes, this is best achieved by comparing results for sub-periods with those for the whole period. The panel concluded in general terms, that Friedman and Schwartz' work was uninformative on the short-run mechanisms involved in money–income relationships, and that this was a serious limitation of their analysis, given the importance of short-run effects for stabilisation policy.

The inadequacy of monetarist models

The theoretical models used to compare the monetarist and Keynesian hypotheses are, it is suggested, too simple. Empirical tests of policy relationships are of two kinds. First, there are small, single-equation studies in which a particular kind of expenditure – e.g. consumption, housing, private fixed investment – is regressed on one or more variables, one being a monetary instrument, e.g. a change in base money.

The second, more ambitious, but technically much more satisfactory, approach is to try to construct a model of the whole economy. Such models take two forms: the large-scale structural models and the so-called reduced-form models favoured by the monetarists. A structural model consists of a series of interlocking equations intended to replicate as closely as possible the real world. They are, necessarily, based on theories and an actual knowledge of what variables should be included in the equations and the quantitative values to be attached to them, the lags in reactions and so on. The underlying theory has, so far, invariably been the Keynesian system. These equations express as many as possible of the supposed basic economic relations and interactions which exist in the real economy, such as, to take two simple examples, the relationship between consumption and income, or investment and the supply of credit. Since several of the variables appear in several equations, a change in one or more values in one equation will change one or more values in several of, if not all, the others. A structural model is, in fact, a set of interdependent simultaneous equations. Early versions of one of the best-known American models, the Federal Reserve Bank – Massachusetts Institute of Technology – University of Pennsylvania (FMP) model, had 200 variables in 110 equations. The current (1984) UK Treasury model has about 800 equations. With such a model, one can conduct a 'policy simulation', introducing an actual value of, say, money supply into the model, then a supposed or actual change in that variable, and trace the consequences for the solutions of the equations. Insofar as the variables and the relationships between them are correctly specified, one can use the model to predict the effects of changes in one or more strategic determinant variables. In spite of the incomplete knowledge on which these models are based, some of them have been remarkably successful. It has been estimated that the American models had a mean error of only about 1% in the early 1970s in forecasting GNP four quarters ahead, although they were less successful in predicting the values of the intermediate endogenous variables (Brainard and Cooper 1975).[19] The record of the British models is rather less encouraging.

The monetarists reject this type of model on the grounds that the channels of transmission are too diverse and complex to be covered by any model. No model can comprehend all the relevant relationships, many of which we are probably unaware. Some of the important elements in the transmission mechanism – implicit interest rates, real rates of interest, expectations – are, in any case, not observable. If our main concern is the prediction of some large and particularly important variable or target, such as consumption or GNP, knowledge of the detailed mechanism is not necessary. In view of the inevitable defects of structural models, a better method is to regress this final variable on the control instrument, such as the money supply, or autonomous expenditure. The several stages and reciprocal reactions of cause and effect between the policy change and the target are telescoped. The Anderson–Carlson model, for example (1970), has only three exogenous and eight endogenous variables, and eight equations and identities. This may be justified; but consumption, or GNP, is not the sole target of policy: the price level, the level of unemployment, real output, the balance of payments are equally important. And it is often important to know which sectors in the economy will feel the impact, or most of the impact, of policy; will it be house-building, or engineering, or consumer goods, or will the impact be on all sectors? It is also frequently important to be able to judge the differential timing of these effects. Such models are also unsatisfactory in that there is no underlying theory. What we get is not an explanation of the behaviour of the real world, but only a macro-statistical association; we have to take the causation on trust. The channels of transmission are not specified; the monetary change disappears into a 'black box', out of which emerges the change in the target variable. What happens inside the black box is a mystery. If the results produced by the models are different from what theory would lead us to expect, we are left in the dark about the reason for this (Stein 1976).

The significance of the source of money

The monetarists have also been criticised for their failure to differentiate between different sources of money. There are five:

1 Money created by the Government to finance a public sector deficit.
2 Money earned or borrowed abroad and converted into domestic deposits (assuming no offsetting action by the central stabilisation fund).
3 Deposits created by borrowing from the banks.
4 Deposits created by the sale of assets to the banks.
5 Deposits created by open-market purchases from the non-bank private sector.

The immediate consequences are unlikely to be the same in all five cases. Money acquired from the first and third sources are directly associated with expenditure; that acquired from the first two sources is *outside money* with a direct wealth effect on private expenditure. Money acquired in the last three ways is *inside money* which is not an increment of wealth; if its creation is associated with lower interest rates it may have a *valuation effect* on wealth, but its main consequence will be a *substitution effect* on portfolios. In the first case, the new money originally accrues to firms and persons who have sold goods or services to the Government. Their new money balances are also an accrual of income.

Money earned by net exports is also current income. Part of the wealth-income receipts from these first two sources may be saved, part may be spent on securities, while a large part is likely to be used to further swell aggregate demand for goods and services. Money borrowed abroad or from the bank is destined to be spent; it is unlikely to be held idle. Deposits received from the sale of assets to the banks or to the central bank may be held idle or used to buy securities or goods and services. It appears, therefore, that the immediate effect on the goods markets of the first two methods, and to a lesser extent (because of the absence of a wealth effect) of the third, is probably greater than that of the fourth and fifth methods. It is strange that Friedman should virtually ignore this difference, since his transmission mechanism includes specifically a 'direct' effect on the goods market.

His reply (1972: 921–3) is that the difference exists only in the first round or two: as the 'new' money spreads through the economy, any first round effects will tend to be dissipated. 'The "new" money will be merged with the old and will be distributed in much the same way.'[20] He doubts the relative importance of this 'first round' or *impact effect*. Theory cannot settle the matter; it is an empirical question, and

> It has long seemed to me that the apparently similar response of income to changes in the quantity of money over a long span of time in different countries and under different monetary systems established something of a presumption that the first-round effect was not highly significant. More recently, several empirical studies designed explicitly to test the importance of the first-round effect have supported this presumption.

There is a danger that we may take too simple a view of what Friedman is saying; some of his opponents, in particular, seem to think that he is asserting that velocity is constant, that interest rates are irrelevant, that 'monetary policy' is all we need. This is wrong and, for that reason, unfair. Perhaps his only unqualified assertion is that large changes in the rate of growth of the quantity of money have induced large changes in the rate of growth of income. He does not deny that other forces are at work in the trade cycle, especially in mild cycles. But these other cyclical influences change from one period to another; the one constant factor in all the major cycles, the single thread running through history, has been the influence of money.

The crowding-out effect

It should be stated at the outset that the 'crowding-out' concept is not a new mechanism. At the time of Keynes, the prevailing 'Treasury view', which Keynes himself tried to challenge, was based on a mechanism similar to the modern concept.[21]

Certainly the modern 'crowding-out' effect is explained in more complex terms, and divergent formulations abound. The basic premise is that, if the supply of goods and services in the economy is fixed and resources fully employed, the Government can claim more of the economy's output only by taking it away from the private sector. There are two mechanisms at work here: (i) 'resources' or 'physical' crowding-out, and (ii) 'financial' crowding-out (B M Friedman 1978). (i) is similar to the Bacon and Eltis (1976) thesis; when the Government places orders for more goods and services, this only leads to an increased wages and capital bill, which in turn has to be financed by higher taxation. The private sector is unable to meet these higher bills and ultimately resources are shifted into the public sector.[22] (ii) is perhaps the more important component. The essence of the argument is that a bond-financed increase in the budget deficit cannot have any significant impact on real income and inflation, because of the effect of the policy on interest rates. If the deficit is financed by sales of gilt-edge stock, and the money supply remains unchanged, the private sectors' demand for relatively illiquid financial assets becomes more fully satisfied. Unless the level of borrowing falls, there will be a consequent increase in the interest rate which, *ceteris paribus*, will reduce investment. This mechanism, indeed, lies at the very heart of the 'monetarist' criticism of fiscal policy as a 'pump-priming' tool.

The Keynesian response is to suggest that where there are unemployed resources, even a bond-financed budget deficit can actually 'crowd-in' private expenditure. There are, in fact, two distinct issues here: the first is whether financial crowding-out takes place at all; the second is whether a financial crowding-out leads inevitably to real crowding-out or resources crowding-out (see Wilson 1979). Despite this, the theoretical debate has tended to concentrate on financial crowding-out (see Stein 1976; Burton 1982), to the exclusion of resources crowding-out.

On its own, financial crowding-out can occur through a change in the demand for money for transactions purposes, or through wealth effects on portfolio behaviour. Whatever the source, financial crowding-out can take place even if the economy is at less than full employment. But even if we ignore, for the moment, the possibility of real crowding-out (which means more than assuming that there are unemployed resources in the economy, as the monetarists believe that even with these real crowding-out can still occur), some doubt exists as to the processes necessary for financial crowding-out.

The monetarist contention has traditionally been viewed in terms of the slopes of the LM curve in an IS–LM model. More sophisticated approaches also deal with 'portfolio' crowding-out effects (BM Friedman 1972; Blinder and Solow 1973; Tobin and Buiter 1976). In the context of the simple IS–LM model, one contention is that the extreme version of financial crowding-out in the short run fails to make a clear distinction between the many different interest rates that may influence the model. Let us, first of all, discuss the simple version of 'crowding-out'.

The IS-LM system is a set of equations which show equilibrium both in the money market and the goods market, and between these markets.[23] These equations postulate certain relationships regarding the propensities to spend, to save and to hold money balances. The system is reduced to two equations. One shows various

If the LM curve is steeply sloped as in Fig. 10.1, the increase in government spending which is reflected in a movement to the right of the IS curve will cause a sharp rise in interest rates, and little or no change in income, $Y1$ to $Y2$. The marked increase in interest rates may also have a significant adverse effect on private sector investment. Only if the increase in government expenditure is financed by an increase in the money supply, i.e. there is a rightward shift of the LM curve, will income rise by a significant amount (from Y_1 to Y_3), though in the long run this may prove to be of zero benefit because of the potentially inflationary consequences of the increased money supply. Similarly, if the increase in government expenditure also has an adverse effect on liquidity preference, the LM curve may actually shift to the left (LM − LM ') and income will increase only slightly from $Y1$ to $Y2$ (see Fig. 10.2).

If, in addition, the marginal efficiency of capital is adversely affected, the IS curve will shift back to IS '' and once again the outcome is a small increase in income (from Y_1 to Y_2).

In terms of the transactions 'crowding-out' element, the Government deficit financed by issuing non-monetary claims leads to an increase in the demand for money for transactions purposes, and if the money supply is to remain fixed and yet the money market is to clear, some offsetting decrease in money demand must occur. But, if the public's demand for money balances is interest-sensitive, this required offset for money demand must be brought about by an increase in the rate of interest earned by non-monetary claims. And, because aggregate private spending varies inversely with the rate of interest, the interest rate that clears the money market nullifies some of the expansionary effect of the initial fiscal action.

How significant the transactions crowding-out effect is likely to be in practice is an empirical question, relating to the steepness of the LM curve. If the LM curve is relatively steep − that is, a relatively small interest sensitivity of money demand − the transactions crowding-out effect is likely to be large. However, this result depends on the types of non-money claims being considered. Although the simplified LS-LM model usually refers to the interest rate on non-money claims, in fact the yields earned on different claims behave differently. Additionally, the interest elasticity estimated for the money-demand function depends on which interest rate(s) the equation includes. Most empirical studies show, in fact, that money demand has a small elasticity with respect to short-term interest rates, such as the yields on time deposits and commercial paper, or the yield on Treasury bills, but a large elasticity with respect to long-term interest rates, for example, the yields on long-term government bonds and equities (see BM Friedman 1977; Goldfield 1973; Hamburger, 1977).

Nevertheless there seems little doubt that transactions crowding-out will offset some part of the fiscal policy on income, if not all of it. Only when the LM curve is vertical will it offset all of it, while if the IS curve is vertical it will offset none of it. Differences will exist between the short-run and the long-run effects, and because of the different income elasticities of the public's demand for time and demand deposits. On the whole the offset is likely to be greater if monetary policy controls M_2 rather than M_1 (see Chs 12 and 13).

As far as the 'portfolio' crowding-out effect is concerned, most studies use just three assets, *money, government bonds* and *real capital*. If 'transactions crowding-out' does not dissipate the intended impact of the fiscal policy, portfolio crowding-out may do so. Ever since Pigou's (1917) pioneering work, wealth effects have long been recognised to operate. However, the portfolio effect is more than a simple wealth effect.

We can, in fact, explain this mechanism by using the equation of the IS curve:

$$Y = Y_0 + Y_1 G + (1 - Y_1)T + Y_2 r + Y_3 W_1$$
$$(Y_3 > 0 > Y_2, Y_1 > 1) \qquad\qquad [10.14]$$

where Y = national income
      G = government expenditure
      T = taxation
      r = rate of interest
      W = wealth variable

Assume that wealth consists of three distinct components,

$$W = M + B + k \qquad\qquad [10.15]$$

where M = the money stock
      B = the outstanding stock of interest-bearing government bonds
      k = the outstanding stock of real capital

In a static equilibrium analysis the budget constraint emphasised by Christ (1968) and Silber (1970) is as follows:

$$G - T = dM + dB \qquad\qquad [10.16]$$

It is assumed that k is fixed and that the expression is in nominal terms.[24]

This equation states that the change in the budget deficit dG equals the private sector impact that finances it (or $dM + dB$).

The crucial thing to explain is, of course, behaviour in the assets market, and the many inter-relationships that may exist between them, even when linear combinations of assets can be assumed. Ultimately the existence and size of the portfolio crowding-out effect will depend on assumptions regarding the portfolio, investors' objectives and their assessments of the risks and rewards associated with each asset. The usual assumption made is that investors are risk averse, whereby the effect of the increased budget deficit is:

$$\frac{\delta Y}{\delta G} = Y_1 + Y_3 \qquad\qquad [10.17]$$

where Y_1 is the traditional multiplier effect of a fiscal action, and Y_3 the goods-market wealth effect of financing the deficit, which reinforces the multiplier effect.

The additional income generated by the goods-market effect increases the transactions demand for money, and if M remains fixed, either or both the rate of interest on B or k must rise to clear the market. If both M and B were to remain fixed, these rates of interest would rise, and given that $Y_2 < 0$, the increase in rk would offset some part of the income effect in the goods market. However, the final outcome will depend on the degree of substitutability between the various forms of wealth holding. If there is bond financing of the deficit, M will remain unchanged but total wealth, $M + B + k$, will increase. If $Y_3 > 0$ (which is an empirical issue) in the money market, the wealth effect will reinforce the transactions effect causing a larger net excess demand for money, so that an even greater rise in either or both rb and rk would be necessary to clear the money market.

However, the issue of whether the portfolio effect offsets or reinforces the income effect of fiscal policy is not as simple as determining whether what clears the money market is a rise in both rb and rk, or in only one of them. The reason is that the entire increase in wealth resulting from financing the deficit consists of an increase in the outstanding stock of bonds. So the increase in rb not only helps eliminate excess demand in the money and capital market, it also helps to reduce net excess supply in the bond market. The opposite applies for an increase in rk, which would reduce real investment and help clear the money market. Similarly the decrease in rk, which would stimulate real investment, helps clear the bond–capital market.

Therefore, it is impossible to say *a priori* whether rk rises or falls, and because the effect of interest rates in the goods market depends on rk, it is impossible to say whether the portfolio effect (or the sum of the portfolio effect and the transactions effect) will offset or reinforce the income effect of fiscal policy. In essence, what this means is we don't know whether the portfolio effect taken by itself is one of crowding-out or *crowding-in*.

Inevitably, the question of whether or not the portfolio effect of bond-financed deficit spending crowds out or crowds in private investment reduces to the old question of whether bonds are closer portfolio substitutes for money or for capital. B M Friedman (1977) highlights the problem by referring to a *relative substitutability index*, the ratio of substitutability of bonds for money (and vice versa). There is likely to be portfolio crowding-out when the value of this index – the *interest rate coefficient ratio* – is smaller than the corresponding *wealth coefficient ratio*, but portfolio crowding-in when the index is greater than the wealth coefficient ratio.

The various possibilities can be presented in terms of the IS-LM framework, but it is sufficient for our purposes that we recognise that there are no *a priori* reasons for believing that the portfolio effect associated with bond-financed government deficits offsets or reinforces the income effect of fiscal policy. The only conclusion we can reach is that a portfolio effect depends on whether the ratio of the substitution coefficient between bonds and money to the substitution coefficient between bonds and capital, is greater or smaller than the ratio of respective wealth coefficients of the demands for money and capital. If the two ratios are identical, there is no portfolio effect, and the traditional IS-LM analysis would be adequate to describe bond-financed government deficits. However, if portfolio crowding-out does occur, it can (unlike the transactions effect) offset more than all of the standard income effect of fiscal policy.

The monetary approach to the balance of payments: international monetarism

So far the discussion has been conducted implicitly in terms of a closed economy. The 'monetary' approach to the balance of payments must now be discussed. Once again, this is not a new approach per se. Sometimes referred to as 'open-economy monetarism', it has antecedents in David Hume's price-specie flow mechanism. The classical price-specie flow mechanism was concerned with the automatic adjustment that should take place under the gold standard. A balance of payments surplus, because it causes an accumulation of gold and an expansion of the domestic money supply, would lead to an increase in prices and consequently a reduction of the balance of payments surplus; a deficit would lead to the opposite effect. The Classical theory assumed a system of fixed exchange rates vis-à-vis gold parities, the gold standard.

The modern 'monetary' approach, particularly that developed by Johnson (1958, 1972, 1977a, 1977b) and Frenkel and Johnson (1976) may also be viewed as an extension of the absorption approach of Alexander (1952, 1959). The approach hinges on the view that the balance of payments must be looked at as a whole. In analysing capital and current account trends, international monetary movements should be regarded as the outcome of a *stock* disequilibrium between the supply of and demand for money within a country. An excess demand for money will lead to a net inflow of international reserves and a balance of payments surplus, while an excess supply of money would lead to a loss of reserves and a deficit on the balance of payments. Johnson (1977a) puts it this way: 'balance of payments deficits and difficulties are essentially monetary phenomena, traceable to either of two causes: too low a ratio of international reserves relative to the domestic money supply, so that the authorities cannot rely on the natural self-correcting process, or the pursuit of policies which oblige the authorities to feed the deficit by credit creation . . .' (p. 218).

The main implication of this approach is a far-reaching one. It is that payments disequilibrium must be regarded as temporary, because in the final analysis the impact of the monetary response will be one of self-correction. If a country is suffering from a deficit which, under a fixed exchange rate system, means a loss of reserves, the appropriate policy is contraction in the money supply. Policies designed to alleviate 'structural' factors such as devaluation, tariffs and expenditure-switching policies in general will only improve the balance of payments to the extent that they increase the demand for money, perhaps through a *real balance effect*, the raising of domestic price levels.

Clearly, there is substance to the monetary approach (see also Coppock 1978; Hahn 1977; Currie 1976; and Congdon 1982a). A deficit, since it means an excess of payments over receipts by residents, must imply either a net purchase of foreign

244

exchange by the central bank or a reduction in reserves. By definition, the stock of privately held money must be falling, and if the monetary authorities do not increase the supply of money to compensate for this, a *stock deficit* will exist. This, however, would be ultimately self-correcting because interest rates will rise.

If the authorities, instead of allowing this process to proceed, try to fill the gap by adding to the money supply, the stock deficit will not be self-correcting, and the balance of payments deficit may persist, that is a *flow deficit*. If a distinction is made between the bond market and the money market, the reason for viewing the balance of payments as a totality will be clearly understood. Suppose there is excess demand in the goods market, there must, by definition, be excess supply in the money and bond markets together. If there is equilibrium in the money market, there must be an excess supply of bonds, which would lead to a surplus on the capital account of the balance of payments. What this means basically is that the current account is financed by a capital inflow.

All of the above, particularly the loss of reserves, applies to a fixed exchange rate regime. Under a flexible exchange rate arrangement, which has been the case since 1973, the mechanism would operate rather differently. To understand this we have to introduce the concept of Domestic Credit Expansion (DCE) (see Cobham 1977, 1982). Since any change in a country's domestic money supply must, by definition, be made up of changes in foreign exchange reserves *and* the level of domestic credit expansion, if there is a balance of payments deficit, the loss of reserves under a fixed exchange rate regime will actually reduce any increase in the domestic money supply that takes place. Therefore, the extent to which domestic monetary policy influences the economy and the balance of payments may be understated.

The Bank of England now calculates DCE separately and has done so since the late 1960s. The basic accounting identity is as follows:

$$\Delta R = \Delta Ms - \Delta D \qquad [10.18]$$

where Ms = the money supply
D = domestic credit expansion
and R = foreign reserves

If a DCE target is established, this implies that the money supply itself must vary positively with changes in reserves, i.e. expand when the balance of payments is in surplus and contract when it is in deficit. Crucial to the monetary approach is the notion that the money supply varies positively with the level of foreign-exchange reserves, and that under a fixed exchange rate system the authorities have great difficulty in *sterilising* the effects of reserve changes on the money supply. Hence the argument for a flexible exchange rate. Under a flexible regime, a deficit would not be accompanied by a loss of reserves, because in theory the exchange rate should depreciate, and the balance of payments would adjust accordingly. As far as the domestic money supply is concerned (or DCE), since ΔR would now be negligible, the official definition of the money supply, which in the UK is £M_3, would not diverge as much from DCE as it would under a fixed exchange rate.

Obviously there is much more to these questions than we have space to cover in this chapter. The monetary approach to the balance of payments produces valuable insights into a number of other issues, such as: the possible conflict between internal and external balance; the 'law' of 'one' price; and the 'assignment' problem.

However, as is true of all of monetary economics, 'international monetarism' is not without its critics (see Thirlwall 1978, 1980). The old question of causation reappears here also. What, after all, is the direction of causation whenever a balance of payments problem exists? Is it inevitably one way, or are their feedback effects in operation? What role is played by so-called 'structural' weaknesses in the economy, such as export instability or low productivity? These are all essentially supply-side issues. The 'monetary' approach to the balance of payments, it may be argued, conveniently sidesteps these questions.

Notes

1   Monetarists would say that an increase in the money supply (over and above the 'announced' increase) would lead to an increase in prices if two elasticities are positive: (i) the elasticity of aggregate demand with respect to changes in the quantity of money; and (ii) the elasticity of absolute prices with respect to aggregate demand: (i) depends on the elasticities of the liquidity preference function and the investment function; and (ii) depends on the degree of capacity to utilisation (full employment/natural rate of unemployment) (see Trevithick and Mulvey 1975).

2   In his Statement on Monetary Theory and Policy to the Joint Economic Committee, 1958, Friedman gave 'the level of income' as the budget constraint on the demand for money. Other members of the Chicago School, e.g. Cagan and Selden in their papers in 'Studies in the Quantity Theory of Money', also use income as a determinant of the demand for money.

3   Friedman says elsewhere that the main cost of holding money is anticipated inflation.

4   Note that it is the current rate, not the difference between the current and 'normal' rates of Keynesian economics, which affects the demand for money.

5   The decline was not, in fact, continuous; velocity was stable from 1915 to 1929 and rose from 1946 to 1960. In the 1960s it ranged between 1.69 and 1.76 and in 1970 was 1.73.

6   We are not told if there was a good 'fit' in the regression. Other estimates put it at about 1.0. Probably one reason for the discrepancy is that most studies measure the 'impact elasticity' by using annual or quarterly data. Friedman's data are averages over the cycle; if velocity of circulation is falling over the longer run, elasticity will be greater than the shorter run 'impact elasticity' (see Mason 1974).

7   Chick (1979: 39) points out that Friedman estimates permanent income as an average of current and recent past income, with current income given a weight of about one third. Since past income cannot change, the whole burden of adjustment of Y_p in the current period to a change in money supply falls on current income. She mentions Tobin's (1969) point that if income elasticity of demand for money is 1.8, Y_p must rise by 0.55% to create a demand for a 1% increase in the money supply. If the weight given to current income in Y_p is 0.33, current income must rise by 1.65% to equate supply and demand for money in the current period.

8   Friedman (1971: 42) suggests another explanation: '. . . if the rate of change of money equals the anticipated rate of change of nominal income, then nominal income changes at the same rate as money – we are in the simple quantity equation world. If the rate of change of money exceeds the anticipated rate of change of nominal income, so will the actual rate of change of nominal income which will also exceed the rate of change of money velocity in a "boom". Conversely, for a "contraction" or "recession", interpreted as a slower rate of growth in the actual than in the anticipated rate of growth of income . . .'

9   The size of the money multiplier-cyclical fluctuations in income relative to cyclical fluctuations in money is given as approximately 2.

10 Schwartz (1969) discovered that the correlation of rates of change for the UK between 1881 and 1967 was 0.79 for prices and 0.74 for money (nominal) income; for real income, omitting the war years it was 0.36.

11 The effect on investment will, of course, depend on the profit expectations of both actual and potential holders of shares, and of firms. Portfolio holders will not move into shares, raising their prices and reducing yields and the cost of equity finance, if they expect a fall in profits. A fall in the cost of finance will not induce firms to invest if they expect returns on real assets to fall. Changes in expectations during the lags in portfolio adjustment can stop a transmission process in its tracks. These expectations depend very much on whether shareholders and firms expect monetary policy to succeed.

12 Yohe and Karnasky (1969) concluded that changes in the price level in the US, rather than changes in the real rate of interest, had accounted for nearly all the variations in nominal rates since 1961.

13 This appears in Chapters 13, 15, 18 and 21 of the *General Theory*.

14 For discussions of these technical matters, and of the difficulties of empirical work in this field, see Edge (1967), Artis and Nobay (1969), Teigen (1965), Desai (1982) and Laidler (1975).

15 Their definition of autonomous expenditure was not quite the same as that used by Friedman and Meiselman. They considered public sector revenue as an endogenous variable M, so their A = private domestic investment + government expenditure + exports – imports.

16 Friedman and Meiselman obtained quite significant results for the period 1945–58.

17 A later test covering the period 1948–68 showed a strong relationship (Sheppard 1971: 107–8).
18 We saw earlier that the Friedman/Meiselman lag, though calculated in a different way, was much shorter than the Friedman/Schwartz lag.
19 For a survey, see Ash and Smyth (1973).
20 Keynes, incidentally, says something similar on page 200 of the *General theory*.
21 For a good discussion of some of the origins of the 'crowding-out' concept, see Spencer and Yohe (1972).
22 The Bacon and Eltis thesis itself has been subject to much criticism, particularly in the light of their particular distinction between 'marketed' and 'non-marketed' output.
23 It thereby does away with the need for a classical dichotomy where the real and monetary sides of the economy are considered separate. For those readers who require a simple exposition of the derivation of the IS/LM framework, see McKenna (1969).
24 This is perhaps a narrow approach: it would obviously be more pertinent to analyse the 'real crowding-out effect', one which assessed the effects of real interest rates.

PART C

Monetary policy

CHAPTER ELEVEN

Macroeconomic issues: inflation and unemployment

The definition of inflation

We normally assume that inflation is synonymous with rising prices, but not all price increases are necessarily inflationary. An increase in indirect taxes raises prices, but both its objective and its effects are deflationary. It takes money out of the income-and-demand-creating expenditure stream and – unless, of course, it is put back as Government expenditure or repayment of loans – sterilises it in the Government's coffers. The failure of a major crop will induce a rise in its price to ration out the meagre supply. Prices rise during the upswing of a trade cycle, but this can be seen as simply a recovery from the depressed prices of the slump. Both these price increases are short-lived and are likely to be reversed.

Similarly, an inflationary situation can exist without an increase in prices. If, for example, aggregate demand exceeds aggregate supply valued at current prices at full or near-full employment (which is another possible definition of inflation), the gap can for a time be filled by depleting stocks, increasing imports or diverting exports to the home market. Indeed, these are all probable initial consequences of excess demand. Inflationary pressures can also be contained by price controls, by rationing and by administrative controls on the purchase of key materials; this would be a situation known as *repressed inflation*. This is likely to be of temporary benefit only, for example during war-time.

We define inflation as a *chronic* or sustained increase in the general price level serious enough to create some of the problems discussed under the next section but one.

Recent UK inflation and unemployment: 'stagflation'

Apart from the post-Korean War inflation of 1951–52, the annual rate of increase of prices in the period 1950–67 ranged between 1.1% (1960) and 5.4% (1956) and the overall average was a little over 3%. From then on, the inflation accelerated almost continuously from 4.5% in 1968 to 26% in the year to September 1975. In the subsequent period, 1975–85, inflation initially stayed at a high level, but from 1981 on began to decline to a level of 5.1% by mid-1984 (see Table 11.1 and Fig. 11.1). This,

Table 11.1 Inflation and unemployment percentages at year end (1967–84)

Year	Unemployment*	Inflation**
1967	2.4	2.2
1968	2.4	5.6
1969	2.4	5.1
1970	2.6	7.7
1971	3.8	9.2
1972	3.4	7.7
1973	2.3	10.3
1974	2.8	18.2
1975	4.8	25.3
1976	5.5	15.0
1977	5.9	13.0
1978	5.5	8.1
1979	5.3	17.3
1980	8.4	15.3
1981	11.1	11.9
1982	12.5	6.3
1983	12.3	5.1
1984	12.4	5.3

* The percentages (of the working population) one year on (that is December to December) seasonally adjusted and excluding school-leavers.
** The percentages are given by the Retail Price Index and are year-on.

Source: Central Statistical Office, *Economic Trends*, various issues.

of course, was achieved against the background of historically high unemployment levels.

There is much debate about the early 1980s and the impact of government policy on the inflation and unemployment relationship. The fact that it took some time before the inflation rate began to fall, even with such a high level of unemployment, as well as doubts, as to whether the decline would persist, has tended to complicate analysis of this period. The Conservative Government, during its first term in office, repeatedly argued that its policies could only really be assessed from a long-term standpoint. Therefore, the outworkings of the Government's monetary and fiscal policies, whether truly 'monetarist' or not, are still being experienced (see Ch. 13).

Moreover, when analysing any particular factor in the inflationary process, such as earnings, the figures are not easy to interpret. During 1981, for example, while the average annual rate of wage increase was 9.9%, the annual rate of price increases measured by the retail price index (RPI) was 12%, suggesting that other 'exogenous' factors were contributing much to the inflationary process. Similarly, during 1982 and 1983, when the inflation rate halved between March 1982 and the end of the year, earnings did not fall by as much. In the period January 1982 to January 1983,

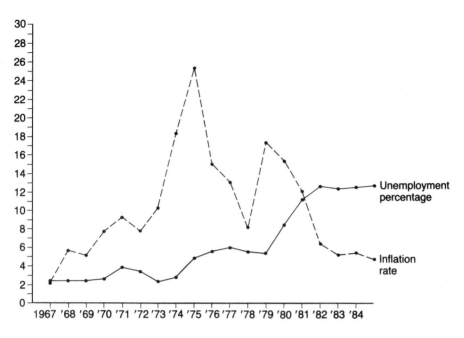

Fig 11.1 Inflation and unemployment trends, 1967–84 (%)

for example, while the retail price index rose by just 4.6%, earnings rose by around 8.2%. From December 1982 to December 1983, earnings rose by 7.75% while for the year ending December 1984 the increase was 7.5%, with the retail price index for that year rising by 4.9% (see Struthers 1984a). An additional point to note is that though the UK inflation rate by the end of 1982 was still higher than that of many of her competitors, the Government did take some comfort from the fact that the decline in inflation was greater than that for the major developed countries as a whole. In January 1983, for example, the UK inflation rate was 1.5% below the average for industrialised countries; the comparable figure for the same month in 1982 was 2.5% above that average.

In order to properly assess these trends it is essential to take a long-term view. In comparing the 1970s and early 1980s with the 1950s and 1960s, two particular features of the latter periods are discernible:

(a) While the inflation of the 1950s and 1960s could be described as a mild demand inflation with low unemployment, the inflation of the 1970s and early 1980s was, for the most part, more typical of a cost inflation. Unemployment was high by post-war standards and, with the exception of the period from the autumn of 1972 to the end of 1973, was rising.

(b) The other major industrial countries also experienced accelerating inflation, along with high unemployment. This suggests that some, at least, of the causes of the inflation were not peculiar to, and were probably exogenous to, the United Kingdom.

We have not far to look for exogenous shocks. The *first* was a consequence of the devaluation of sterling in November 1967, which raised import prices 11% in the following year and, coupled with the increase in the world prices of commodities, brought a 30% rise in UK import prices between 1967 and 1972. The fall in the exchange value of sterling after it was floated in June 1972, like devaluation, raised the domestic prices of imports. In 1972–73 there was a commodity-price boom, the product of inelastic supply and an upsurge of world demand probably caused partly by the big increase in world liquidity consequent on the introduction of Special Drawing Rights (SDRs) and the rapid growth of the Eurodollar market in the late 1960s and early 1970s (see Ch. 6). Finally, in late 1973, came the quadrupling of the price of oil, the first of a series of increases. British import prices in general doubled between 1972 and 1975, although a rise in the cost of imports is not necessarily inflationary. Indeed, insofar as more money is spent on imports there is less available, other things being equal, to spend on domestic output and the effect is demand deflationary. But the Government chose to maintain full employment and borrow abroad (from the IMF in 1976).

The *second* apparent source of accelerating inflation was the behaviour of the money supply of which more will be said in the next two chapters. Apart from a short burst in the second half of 1967, the increase in the quantity of money (M_1) in the second half of the 1960s was quite modest: about 4% p.a. 1963–68, 5% in 1968, and zero in 1969. The increase in 1970 was 9.3%, but it was in the second half of 1971 that the money supply really took off. From July 1971 to June 1972 M_1 rose 19%. Then there was a lull; the rate of increase over the previous twelve months fell in each succeeding quarter (with the exception of the second quarter of 1973) for the next two years. The supply of narrow money (M_1) actually fell about 3% between the second quarter of 1973 and the first quarter of 1974, the increase through 1973 was only 5.8%, and over the year to June 1974 there was no increase. But the money supply at the end of 1974 was nearly 11% higher than a year previously, and there was a further rise of 20% in the first three-quarters of 1975. In both years, however, the rate of increase was less than the inflation rate. The rate of increase of the broader monetary aggregate, M_3, diverged markedly from M_1 after the introduction of new methods of monetary control in 1971; in 1972 and 1973, for example, it averaged 28% p.a., and remained significantly higher than that of M_1 through most of 1974.

Monetarists see this behaviour of the money supply as the main, if not the sole, cause of the inflation. Cost increases arising internally – for example, from higher wages – were a reaction to excess demand and rising prices and expectations of further price increases. 'Correlating inflation with past monetary expansion provides an increasingly strong correlation as one increases the length of lag to about two and a half years . . .' (Parkin 1975: 10).

There is no place for trade union push or any other kind of cost inflation in the monetarist analysis. 'Inflation is always and everywhere a monetary phenomenon'

(Friedman 1970: 36).[1] However, there appears to have been little evidence of excess demand in the 1970s. Only in the boom of late 1972 and the first half of 1973 is there likely to have been a strong demand pull. Rising unemployment, sluggish investment and falling returns on capital are clear indications of cost inflation rather than demand inflation. From 1970 to the autumn of 1975, both wage rates and hourly earnings were rising faster than prices, and for most of the period, real Gross National Product was rising only slowly: 2% p.a. from 1969 to 1971, 4% in 1972, 6% in 1973, nil growth in 1974, and a fall of nearly 2% in 1975.

This was not, however, a spontaneous wage push. The wage explosion really began in 1970 with a 13.6% rise in wage rates, and was in all probability a defensive reaction to the rise in the cost of living caused by the 1967 devaluation and to the tax-generated squeeze on real disposable income and consumption in the second half of the 1960s. The wage and salary increases thereafter, both in the longer term and in particular periods, have been attributed to many causes. One is resentment at the attempts by the Labour Government in 1968 and the Conservative Government in 1971–73 to apply legal controls on the activities of trade unions. Another is the gradual realisation of the power of labour as one large union after another succeeded in enforcing its demands by strikes or strike threats. A third is the belated realisation that wage increases were being supported by fiscal and monetary policy. This quote from Phelps Brown (1971: 239) is illustrative here: 'For so many years before the war men had had it driven into their minds that rises in pay beyond a certain point would put jobs at risk, that many years' experience of the conjunction of cost inflation with full employment was needed to induce a new frame of mind; but it has come in the end'. In other words, a belated realisation of the fact of inflation and the gradual disappearance of money illusion, 'a sense that the purchasing power of money is something that is always falling' (Phelps Brown 1971); that increases were being quickly eroded by further inflation were, in themselves, factors responsible for the acceleration of inflation in the 1970s and 1980s. These forces, and the extent to which inflationary expectations fuel the fire of 'inflationary psychology', are more fully discussed in subsequent sections.

Some effects of inflation

(a) Anyone holding money, or claims to fixed interest or of fixed money value – for example, anyone who committed his wealth to long-term loans before the inflation really got under way – is bound to lose. Inflation could be described as a tax on money and bonds. How far all this constitutes a redistribution of wealth or income between persons is, however, an open question. Probably most people who hold fixed money claims also have some fixed money liabilities, and so gain on the swings at least something of what they lose on the roundabouts. I lose on my insurance policy, unless it is a good with-profits policy, and

255

on my debentures, but gain on the mortgage on my house. What does seem certain is that the less sophisticated savers, those who keep their money in the savings banks and building societies and do not venture into the world of property and the stock exchange, are usually people with comparatively few assets. They lose in comparison with the active investors in property and shares, who in the main are also wealthier.

(b) Rates on new loans do rise with inflation, but slowly: 'if we ask how long it takes for rates to change sufficiently to compensate fully for a change in the inflation rate, the answer . . . at least as far as the United States is concerned, is somewhere in the region of two decades' (Laidler and Parkin 1975: 789). A calculation of the real rate of return on medium-term government bonds by Barr (1975) showed that they yielded a positive return of less than 0.25% in the years 1955–69, but over the period 1948–74 as a whole they gave a negative real return, −1.11%, and in the decade to December 1974, the return was −1.89%.

It is worth noting, however, that the equity holder does not necessarily keep up with inflation. The index of share prices tends to fluctuate independently of the price levels of goods. Barr showed that, assuming that dividends were taxed at the standard rate, equities showed a positive real return of 0.13% in the years 1955–64, but over the rest of the period 1948–74 the return, including the capital gain over the period but not taking account of capital gains tax, was negative; in the decade up to December 1974 it was −3.13%.

(c) As inflation proceeds, especially if it accelerates, we are warned of the danger of a runaway inflation, a hyperinflation, causing a complete breakdown of the monetary system and a reversion to barter. This fear is probably ill-founded as economic disasters of this nature and magnitude are rare. The evidence of history is that creeping, moderate inflations usually either end in a stabilising monetary reform or wear themselves out and go into reverse. A moderate inflation will degenerate into a hyperinflation when asset-holders realise what is happening. The perceived cost of holding money becomes not the interest forgone but the anticipated depreciation in the real value of money; similarly with other assets and returns of fixed money value. They therefore try to turn their bonds into money and their money into goods and equities. Their rising expenditure on goods makes the inflation worse, and the flight from money becomes a stampede. Eventually prices rise so fast that it pays to spend even transactions balances as quickly as possible. The end comes when money is losing its value so rapidly that it is no longer acceptable even in day-to-day payments.

To see how improbable this story is, let us consider briefly what it implies. *First*, people sell assets of fixed money value because they expect the inflation to continue; real assets bought today are no protection against an inflation which has occurred already. A stampede out of money and bonds is the consequence of an almost universal expectation of further inflation and almost universal determination to avoid the consequences as far as one's own assets are concerned. In that case, who will buy the bonds? It seems more likely that, unless the Government stands idly by and lets the inflation rip, there will always be a substantial body of willing holders of money and bonds who expect the current package of anti-inflationary policies to succeed. Moreover, as we saw in earlier chapters, some large holders – for example, banks and insurance companies – have a large proportion of their liabilities also fixed in money terms, and many personal money balances and claims to money are held to meet fixed monetary liabilities. Such monetary assets are not affected by inflation; the liabilities against which they are held depreciate as fast as the assets. *Second*, there is a gap in this account of the decline in the use of money. It comes when all idle balances have been activated but money is still the accepted means of payment. It is, as we have seen (p. 175), much more difficult to economise on – i.e. increase the velocity of – active balances than to activate idle balances. It seems highly probable that if the inflation depended entirely on an increasing velocity of circulation of a fixed quantity of money, there would at this stage be a brake on prices. It is unlikely, therefore, that even a strong inflation will continue indefinitely, still less turn into hyperinflation, if it is financed solely by increases in the velocity of circulation.

This is borne out by studies of past inflation. If, as suggested above, the basis of the increasing velocity is that the cost of holding money is the anticipated inflation, one would expect changes in velocity to be well correlated with the rate of increase of prices. Brown (1955: 194) observed that '. . . in all economies in which there is no direct control of expenditure, there is usually some correlation between income velocity and price movements, but . . . the former is not very sensitive to the latter . . .' Several countries have experienced rapid inflations which did not end in hyperinflation and disruption of the monetary system. Brown concluded that, in countries where money is in general use by the whole population, there is no evidence that a widespread flight from cash (to the use of barter) has ever begun until prices have doubled in six months or less. In the same vein, Cagan's study (1956) of seven hyperinflations showed that some quite fantastic rates of increase of the price level – for example, 19,800% per month in Hungary in 1945–46 – did not provoke a flight out of money. Laidler and Parkin (1975: 748) also list a number of studies of rapid inflations which '. . . all confirm that the sensitivity of the expected rate to the actual rate are both small enough to rule out a self-generated flight from money'.

The responsibility for past hyperinflations rested not with the public's desire to get out of money into goods but with reckless increases in the supply of money. Cagan's conclusion was that none of the seven hyperinflations he investigated were self-generating: that is, due to increasing velocity. In every case, 'price increases remained closely linked to past and current changes in the quantity of money and could have been stopped at any time, as they finally were, by tapering off the issue of new money' (p. 88). It is these changes in the quantity of money which cause hyperinflation, 'an extreme rise in prices depends almost entirely on changes in the quantity of money' (Cagan 1956: 91).

(d) Finally, in an open economy – that is, one which engages substantially in international trade – with fixed exchange rates, inflation can cause a balance of payments problem. If our prices and income rise faster than those of our competitors, we are likely to incur a deficit on the balance of payments. This will serve to modify the domestic inflation. Part of the excess demand spills over into imports; the decline in our reserves is reflected in a fall in the domestic supply of money and in the potentially inflationary government domestic borrowing requirement. We thus, incidentally, also tend to 'export our inflation' by increasing the supply of money and the demand for exports in other countries. But our inflation will tend to be higher than the world rate because some goods are not traded internationally and there is thus no competition creating a check to the upward pressure in their prices. The Government must eventually take steps to correct the balance of payments deficit; with fixed exchange rates we must sooner or later adjust to the world rate of inflation, and the policies adopted are likely to be deflationary, hampering or even reversing growth.

Periodic balance of payments crises, and the resulting alternation of policy between 'stop' and 'go', have been one of the worst consequences of Britain's post-war inflation. Devaluation, or allowing the exchange rate to float down, can provide a temporary respite; we are no longer tied to the world rate of inflation but can choose our own. But both these relaxations of the constraint are themselves potentially inflationary. They make our exports cheaper and our imports dearer, thus increasing the volume of exports and reducing imports, which reduces the supply of goods to the home market while increasing the incomes which are the source of demand. Rising import prices raise industrial costs and the cost of living and are therefore likely to initiate a cost inflation. Again, the authorities must, sooner or later, adopt internal (deflationary) policies to stabilise the exchange rate.

These are just some effects of inflation. Many more, such as the effects on taxation, income distribution effects and the emergence of inflation accounting, might also be discussed, but space prevents this. But whatever the effects of inflation, rising prices are just a symptom of an inflationary situation. Some would prefer to define inflation in terms of its cause; for example, monetary inflation (caused by a large expansion of the supply of money), budget deficit-induced inflation, demand inflation, cost inflation. The merit of this approach is, of course, that it not only defines inflation but also indicates its source, and recognises that there are a number of possible explanations of a sustained rise in the price level. Most current analyses distinguish three basic forms of inflation: demand inflation, cost inflation and structural inflation.

The initiation of inflation

A demand inflation

This can be defined simply as a situation in which the community is trying to spend more than its current income at full or near-full employment or, in monetarist terms, the 'natural level of unemployment'. What are the possible sources of such an excess demand? Aggregate demand on the output of the economy consists of consumption, investment, government expenditure, and exports minus imports ($C + I + G + X - M$).

Consumption is largely determined by income itself, but if the public find themselves endowed with an abnormal level of assets, especially liquid assets, they will probably indulge in an abnormal level of consumption. This is one explanation of the widespread phenomenon of post-war inflation. People are encouraged to support the war effort by saving, and in any case rationing and price control and the general shortage of consumer goods close most avenues of spending, so that when the war ends they have a mass of accumulated savings and a dearth of consumer goods of every kind. Here we have all the ingredients for a massive and sustained spending spree. Similarly, an improvement in the trade balance, exports minus imports ($X - M$) is inflationary; exports create income at home but not supplies of goods for the home market.

The main sources of demand inflation, however, have been investment and government expenditure. A housing boom, a major capital-using innovation (for example, the railways in the nineteenth century), a rearmament programme, all these have in the past created a demand for investment goods bigger than the economy made room for by its voluntary saving or taxation. A budget deficit may be inflationary, more so if it arises from an increase in goverment expenditure rather than a reduction in tax collections. Whether or not the deficit is inflationary depends on whether it is financed by the creation of new money or the activation of idle balances on the one hand, or by the transfer of active balances to the Government and the consequent crowding out of private expenditure on the other (see Ch. 10).

Investment and/or government expenditure in excess of tax revenue and/or current saving must, of course, be financed by some form of activation of idle balances or money creation. But whatever the financial devices employed, we also know that, with a given total real output, extra resources for the investment and government sectors can only come from some other sector(s) of the economy. In other words, assuming no change in the balance of payments, investment plus government expenditure ($I + G$) must, *ex post*, be matched by saving plus taxation ($S + T$). If investors and the Government do succeed in spending more in real terms, consumers and taxpayers must spend less, whether the extra saving be voluntary or forced, and the extra taxation open or disguised. Thus consumers living on fixed money incomes are compelled to consume less eventually as prices rise; if consumers in general have a money illusion, their real consumption will fall as prices rise. If they dis-save, or insist on higher money incomes to match the higher prices, then some other expenditure – for example, private investment – must somehow suffer, in real terms if not in money terms. A progressive tax system abstracts a bigger proportion of income as incomes rise, even if rates of tax are unchanged.

Precisely how does excess demand bring about a *persistent* rise in the price level? Most prices are not determined by some invisible hand or impersonal market force, or by some other mechanism which eliminates excess demand by raising the price. Rather are they *administered*, determined by a deliberate managerial decision. The initial effect of excess demand, therefore, is not a rise in price but falling stocks and lengthening order books. Excess demand will pull up costs, for one or more of a number of reasons. At the outset, some firms are likely to have some excess capacity and can increase output; as they do so, costs eventually rise as a consequence of the operation of the law of diminishing returns, or because they have to bring in less efficient units of factors of production as aggregate demand for factors presses on the supply. The excess demand for final products passes back to the markets for raw materials, some of whose prices are more immediately sensitive to demand than the prices of manufactures. It is also reflected in the market for labour, where firms may offer higher wages, or overtime, or fringe benefits to attract labour, or the unions find employers more willing to negotiate higher rates of pay. Prices then rise because firms are adding their profit margins onto a higher cost base.

It used to be argued that all price increases in industry are triggered by these rising costs of production, but several studies (Laidler and Parkin 1975: 767–8) indicate that excess demand causes price increases independent of changes in costs.

Cost inflation

If prices thus tend to follow costs, can they not be pushed up by increases in costs even without an initial excess demand? Can we have a spontaneous cost inflation, as opposed to the 'induced' cost inflation just described, which is really a demand-induced inflation? If so, how and why is it likely to occur?

There are several components in the costs of the individual firms, but if we take any item of expenditure – for wages, materials, buildings and equipment, or services such as electricity and water and refuse disposal – and ask what happens to the money paid out, who gets it (the supplier) and what he does with it (it goes to meet his own costs and provide his profits), all the expenditure eventually becomes incomes. The only costs which do not eventually become domestic incomes are payments for imports. Taking the economy as a whole, therefore, costs comprise payments for imports, incomes paid to employees ('wages') and the incomes from ownership of firms ('profits'). It follows that a cost inflation will be due to higher import costs and/or higher wage costs and/or bigger profit margins.

There have been occasions when rising prices of imports set off an inflationary spiral. The acceleration of inflation in the early 1970s has been partly attached to the deterioration in the terms of trade. The 1967 devaluation raised import prices by about 15%. In the year to June 1973, import prices rose 28%. But a rise in commodity prices of this magnitude tends to be an isolated event, and may well be reversed.

Unless there is persistent inflation in the exporting country, import prices may initiate an inflation but are not likely to be responsible for sustaining it.

Similarly, a decision to hoist profit margins is likely to be a once-for-all decision. It is indeed doubtful whether an inflation will originate from a rise in profit margins. *First*, if firms are profit-maximisers, presumably their mark-ups (the percentage added to cost to arrive at the selling price) are at the optimum level already. *Second*, to raise prices, when there is no excess demand, invites competition from other firms and other products, loss of goodwill, and a consequent reduction in sales which may leave the firm worse off than before. There are other, safer ways of increasing profits than price manipulation: a bigger sales effort, for example, or higher productivity. This does not mean that profit margins are absolutely fixed and insensitive to the state of demand. There is some evidence that firms do respond to rising demand by increasing their margins: increasing prices by a rather bigger percentage than costs, giving fewer and/or smaller allowances and discounts to customers, and so on; vice versa when sales and costs are falling (Silberston 1970: 565–7). But such a distension of profit margins is a response to inflationary pressure rather than a cause thereof. Profits may, however, contribute to the perpetuation of an inflation, especially if the share of profits in total income and/or the rate of return on capital is increasing.

The other possible originator of cost inflation is wages. We envisage a situation in which there is no excess demand for labour, yet wages rise. If this is to occur, the labour market cannot be an atomistic competitive market. If it were, wages could only change in response to the market forces of supply and demand; starting from an equilibrium situation, wages could only rise if either the demand schedule or the supply schedule of labour shifted so as to create a situation of excess demand. We know that the labour market is in fact not like this; it approximates rather to *bilateral monopoly*, with a union which controls the labour supply facing a single employer or a unified (for this purpose) body of employers. Unions can obtain wage increases which their members would not otherwise have obtained. There is some evidence of bigger wage increases, in relation to the level of unemployment, to strongly organised than to weakly organised groups of workers (Vanderkamp 1966; Pierson 1968). Wages are fixed by negotiation; that is, they are an administered price. Further, for a wage increase to induce a price increase in the absence of excess demand, the prices of the products of labour must also be administered.

Two other factors, which can probably be best categorised as 'institutional', are at work in the labour market. The first is the practice of nationwide bargaining. The rates finally agreed then apply throughout the industry irrespective of differences in demand, or profits, or labour productivity, in the various sectors or firms within the industry. Hence a wage increase which can be met at current prices in some firms will, in some cases, compel other firms to raise prices. In some industries the basic nationally agreed rate is supplemented by special piece-rates, bonuses or local allowances negotiated at area or plant level. The consequence is that actual earnings rise more than negotiated rates, a phenomenon known as 'wage drift'. It has been argued that wage drift is demand-induced; the employer must be earning sufficient revenue to make the extra payments, and he makes them in order to maintain an adequate supply of labour. This is not necessarily the explanation; local wages, like national wages, may be pushed up by pressure from the shop floor. Some empirical studies do in fact show that wage drift is not solely due to excess demand.

The second institutional factor is the apparent importance attached by trade unions to maintaining differentials between their wages and those of certain other groups. Thus if wages rise in industry A – and it is important here to note that this rise may be supported by rising productivity of labour and hence not be inflationary[2] – workers in other industries demand similar increases simply to maintain differentials. Several studies support the hypothesis of wage leadership and a wage-transfer mechanism (Trevithick and Mulvey 1974; 1975: 103–4).

One further aspect is the analysis of inflation in game-theoretic terms. The concept of *prisoners dilemma* is relevant in this context (Sutcliffe 1982). In a trade union versus employers game, for example, the dominant strategy for the trade union is, of course, to ask for a high wage rise; while the dominant strategy for employers is to introduce large price rises. The outcome, therefore, would be both a high wage/high price rise. Yet, the paradox is that both trade unions and employers would likely prefer the low wage rise/low price rise outcome. The inflation which results may therefore be viewed as unwanted inflation and, strictly speaking, cannot be called wage push inflation because each player in the game is assumed to have chosen their strategy independently.

The essence of this approach is that unions or employers, acting independently, will not see their own particular strategy as one likely to induce inflation. But, when other agents jump on the bandwagon, the outcome is likely to be such. This process is summed up well by Phelps Brown (1971: 238):

> Whether or not monetary laxity promoted the pay explosion, monetary restraint is unlikely to be able to contain it . . . even if all employees understand that a general rising of pay against a limited increase in the stock of money is bound to result in unemployment, they will also see that it is only by the aggregate of pay rises that the sanction will be actuated: no one group will bring the sanction down upon itself by pressing its own claim, nor escape it by not pressing its claim if others go ahead with theirs.

This approach to inflation has yielded some valuable insights for economic agents and government alike. Government policies to curb inflation such as incomes policies or wage fixing (Meade 1982) can then be viewed as potential solutions to the prisoners dilemma problem. There is therefore a crucial role for government in this context in improving both the quantity and quality of information received by the respective agents in order that they more fully appreciate the significance of a particular course of action.

Demand inflation or cost inflation

It is usually impossible to identify the first impetus to inflation and therefore impossible to say whether a particular inflation is cost-induced or demand-induced.

It is almost as difficult to classify an on-going inflationary process. The apparent distinction would be in the timing of wage and price increases; if wages rise first and are followed by prices, this is evidence of cost-push, while if wages follow prices, that is evidence of demand-pull. But this is, in fact, a useless approach. It is vitiated by the fact that in a world of administered prices and wages the first effect of excess demand may be a rise in wages, and prices rise shortly after. If, on the other hand, prices rise before wages, the initiating factor may not be in excess demand but higher prices of imports.

If wages rise faster than prices, is this evidence of cost-push? It may be, but it may equally well be evidence of rising productivity of labour and/or of the fact that wage costs are only one component of prices. If wages constitute 50% of total costs, any one 20% wage increase, fully passed on, would raise the relevant price by 10%. If wages are rising faster than labour productivity, the reason may be excess demand for labour, or union pressures. If profits are rising faster than wages, is this evidence that excess demand is pulling up prices and profits, and wages follow later? Not necessarily; it may be evidence of 'mark-up' inflation, or of firms taking wage increases as an opportunity to raise their percentage mark up as well. A fairly clear case of cost inflation would be a situation in which wages are rising, profits are falling, and unemployment is also rising; or, if there is full employment, the excess demand for labour, as measured by 'unfilled vacancies', is falling. If, by contrast, prices are rising faster than wages but there is no independent evidence that labour productivity is declining, while at the same time there is increasing excess demand for labour, the inflation is demand-induced.

Some factors contributing to the rise of UK prices in the first half of the 1970s and the early 1980s are presented in Tables 11.2 and 11.3. Note the large contributions of import prices in 1973–74 and of wages in 1974, and especially in 1975. By

Table 11.2 Contributions to six-monthly percentage increases in index of market prices

Period	Calculated contributions					
	Employment income per unit of output	Gross profits etc., per unit of output	Net indirect tax rates	Import prices of goods and services	Residual error	Overall % increase over 6 months
(1) Q2 to Q4, 1972	+2.4	+1.5	−0.1	+0.9	−	4.7
(2) Q4, 1972 to Q2, 1973	+2.35	+0.25	−0.6	+2.2	−	4.2
(3) Q2 to Q4, 1973	+2.9	+0.8	+0.3	+2.8	+0.4	7.2
(4) Q4, 1973 to Q2, 1974	+4.7	−0.9	+1.35	+5.5	+0.65	11.3
(5) Q2 to Q4, 1974	+6.9	+2.0	−1.3	+1.6	−0.3	8.9

(Note that a pay freeze was in operation from November 1972 to April 1973 and a control on pay increases from April 1973 to July 1974.)

Source: Allen 1975: 610.

Table 11.3 Components of inflation (percentage changes from a year earlier)

	Weights (%) in total final expenditure in 1982 in italics	1980 Year	1981 Year	1982 Year	1983 H1
Domestic factor costs[1]					
Income from employment	45½	+22½	+10	+ 4½	+ 4
Profits etc.[2]	12½	+ 5½	+ 8½	+ 8	+22½
Other incomes[3]	11½	+18½	+11½	+ 7½	+ 6½
GDP deflator		+19	+10	+ 6½	+ 7
Other components of final expenditure					
Taxes on spending less subsidies[4]	12	+25½	+19½	+12	− 1½
Import costs[5]	19½	+10	+ 7½	+ 7½	+ 9
TFE deflator		+17½	+11	+ 7	+ 6
Deflators for domestic expenditure					
Consumer spending		+16½	+11	+ 8½	+ 6
Fixed investment		+19	+ 9½	+ 2	+ 3½

[1] Nominal amounts divided by an index of the volume of GDP. These are components of income; differences between the income and expenditure measures of GDP make for some inconsistency in the table.

[2] Company profits and trading surpluses of public corporations and government enterprises net of stock appreciation. Profits from North Sea operations are included.

[3] Income from rent and self-employment.

[4] The factor cost adjustment at current prices divided by the same at 1980 prices.

[5] The deflator for imports of goods and services.

Source: *BEQB*, Dec. 1983: 465

contrast, in the later period, both import prices and labour costs rose more slowly. Import prices, in spite of a depreciating exchange rate since 1981, have not risen much, and labour costs, though rising in the 1982–83 pay round by 7¾%, have been matched by production increases thereby reducing wage costs per unit of output. Profit margins also diminished until mid-1981, but thereafter increased.

There has been a wealth of econometric tests of the demand-pull and cost-push explanations of inflation. They assume, implicitly or explicitly, that prices are administered and are based on costs, in particular wage costs. The question at issue, therefore, is whether wages rise because the demand for labour exceeds the supply, or are pushed up by trade union pressure. To determine this, the tests try to discover how far changes in wage rates, or earnings, are correlated with other variables which can be taken to represent the forces of demand-pull or cost-push. For useful summaries see Challen *et al.* (1984), Heathfield (1979) and Hudson (1982). It may seem odd that in a situation in which anyone is unemployed, or in which there are more unemployed than vacancies, one can say that there is excess demand for labour. But remember that absolutely full employment is impossible: there will at best always be some frictional unemployment. A key indicator of cost-push appears to be the price level, or the cost of living index, on the grounds that this is the most likely stimulus to pressure for higher wages.

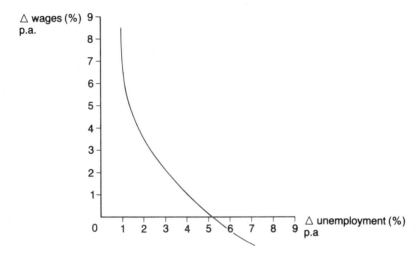

Fig 11.2   The Phillips curve

Phillips (1958) took up this relationship, using it as a test of the hypothesis that one factor influencing the rate of change of money wages 'might be the rate of change of the demand for labour, and so of unemployment' or that 'when the demand for labour is high and there are very few unemployed we should expect employers to bid wage rates up quite rapidly'. His investigation covered the period 1861–1957, and concluded that in the UK, for stable wage rates, the associated level of unemployment would be $5\frac{1}{4}\%$; that is, at this level of unemployment the labour market is in balance, with no excess demand or excess supply. To keep wages in line with productivity (assumed to be rising 2% p.a.) and so maintain stable prices, an unemployment rate of just under $2\frac{1}{2}\%$ would be required. He also noted that the rate of increase of wages associated with a given level of unemployment is higher when unemployment is falling, and lower when unemployment is rising. Employers are more willing to offer higher wages or agree to union demands when they expect rising revenues and tightness in the labour market. Further, each successive fall in the unemployment rate is associated with a bigger rise in wage rates; the *Phillips curve* is convex to the origin (Fig. 11.2).

The cost-push element – that is, changes in retail prices – only comes into the picture, he suggested, when prices rise faster than wages would have risen as a result of the demand-pull influence as measured by the level of unemployment. Thus, with $U = 2\%$, wages would rise 3%; only if prices rise more than 3% will they give an additional upward push to wages.

The current position appears to be that it is accepted that both in the UK and the

USA there is some relationship between unemployment and wage inflation, but that the statistics show a wide variation over time of the wage change associated with a given level of unemployment and of the unemployment associated with wage stability; the Phillips curve, in other words, is not stable. Prices and, perhaps especially, expected changes in prices have become significant determinants of changes in wages. The Phillips relation appears to have broken down about 1967; the rise in wages and prices has since then been much higher than would have been predicted by either the Phillips, the Lipsey (1960)[3] and Hines (1964) equations, and in the mid-70s the UK experienced both accelerating inflation and rising unemployment.

Various reasons for this apparent breakdown have been put forward, most of them suggesting that it was not a disappearance of the relationship but a shift of the Phillips curve. The abandonment of a prices and incomes policy, especially a wage freeze, will release a burst of pent-up wage claims, as in 1970 and 1974. With full employment, rising standards of living and higher social security benefits, people become both more willing to change their job and prepared to spend longer looking for a new one; the level of frictional unemployment will rise. A change in the distribution of employment can raise the average rate of increase of wages at any given overall level of unemployment; as unemployment falls in one sector the rate of increase of wages will rise, and as it rises in another the rate of increase of wages will fall, but the shape of the Phillips curve indicates that the former change will be greater than the latter. A third possibility is that the unions have become more militant as inflation has accelerated.

It has been argued, in defence of the Phillips relation, that the apparent shift of the curve is an aberration of a kind which has occurred before and will be temporary (Parkin 1971). However, an unstable function is a poor guide for policy unless the shifts are controllable or predictable. Taylor (1974) contended that the statistics of unemployment are inadequate because they cannot record variations in hoarding and under-utilisation of labour, and that hourly earnings (corrected for overtime) are a better measure of 'wages' than weekly wage rates. If the appropriate corrections are made to the Phillips data, the relation is seen to be much more stable. The debate continues (Sumner and Ward 1983).

Unfortunately, we cannot draw from the wealth of econometric studies (see also Desai 1975) any firm conclusions for the demand-pull versus cost-push debate. *First,* none of the proxies for excess demand or cost-push has completely explained the rate of increase of wages. *Second,* none of the determinants of wage – and price – changes is in fact a clear and ineluctable proxy for either demand-pull or cost-push. Rising profits may be both a symptom of the high demand which pulls up wages as employers compete for labour and a reason for trade unions to push for wages which would not have been given otherwise. Rising prices which induce higher wages may be due to excess demand for goods, which feeds back to the labour market, or they may be the consequence of rising wages caused by autonomous trade union pressure. In the latter case, the employers may have conceded the claim only because market prospects were such that they were confident that they could raise prices without a significant loss of sales. Prices are then pushed up by costs, but only because of

266

existing or anticipated excess demand. In the event, of course, an all-round wage increase is also an increase in incomes which will, to some degree, create the demand to sustain sales at higher prices. Unemployment may be an index of demand for labour, but there is some dispute about this. It is being argued that unfilled vacancies ought to be brought back into the analysis; that the recorded figures on unemployment are distorted by variations in the amount of disguised unemployment in the shape of labour hoarded by firms; and that the official statistics include an unknown number of unemployed people who are not genuinely seeking work and exclude another unknown number who are. We therefore cannot say, a priori, at what level of unemployment the demand and supply of labour are in balance, because the amount of frictional unemployment is bound to vary from one time and circumstance to another.

The strength and militancy of trade unions is another likely influence on wages, and a number of studies have concluded that it is, or has sometimes been, significant (Dicks-Mireaux and Dow 1959; Klein and Ball 1959; and Pierson 1968). Hines also argued in a series of articles (1964 and 1969) that trade union militancy, as measured by the level and the rate of increase of trade union membership, accounted for 82% of the variation in wage rates in the period 1893–1961, and 90% over the period 1921–61. Taking unemployment into account does not improve significantly the explanatory power of the equations. When tested against actual wage movements between 1962 and 1967, this cost-push model performed better as a predictor than either the Dicks-Mireaux (1961) model or the Lipsey version of the Phillips model.

Hines' results have been criticised, notably by Purdy and Zis (1973) who asserted that union membership can only account for a small part of wage changes since the Second World War. They pointed to the fact that after the mid-1950s, when there was little increase in unionisation, there was no slackening of the pace of wage escalation. A more crucial limitation of the Hines thesis is that union membership may not be a good proxy for union push; it is not apparent why there should be any precise relationship between the degree of unionisation and the degree of union militancy. Hines argued that militancy is evidenced by pressure on wages and by vigorous recruitment. But union membership is not due solely to active recruitment. It may be the consequence of successful wage claims rather than the cause or the result of an expansion of the unionised sectors of the economy relative to the non-unionised sectors. A more obvious and direct relationship would be between union militancy and some measure of strike activity, for example the number of strikes, numbers of workers involved, or the number of working days lost through strikes. Investigations of British and American experience in the 1950s, 1960s and 1970s found a highly significant relationship between the rate of change of wages and strike activity (Godfrey 1971; Taylor 1972).

However, strikes are not the only form of industrial action nor the only symptom of union militancy, and not all strikes are in support of a wage claim. Ward and Zis (1974) used the above-mentioned measures of strike activity in equations of wage determination in six European countries in the years 1956–71, and concluded that trade union militancy, if measured by strike activity, is not generally important, and certainly not in the UK (see also Knight 1972). All this must not be taken to imply that union militancy or bargaining power are irrelevant. The weight of evidence is that they do exert an inflationary influence in labour markets; but we do not know how significant that influence is.

Henry *et al.* (1976) tested four models against UK data of the post-war period up to the 1970s. They were the Phillips/Lipsey model (including the expectations hypothesis), the Hines model, a monetarist model, and a model developed by Sargan (1964). They found no support for the views that unemployment, or trade union membership, has an effect on the rate of wage inflation. The best results (coefficients of determination 0.279 for 1948–66 and 0.469 for 1948–74) were obtained with a variant of the Sargan model, a 'bargaining equation' based on the hypothesis that unions bargain for a level of real take-home earnings after allowing for expected increases in retail prices. Their results 'provide confirmation of the view that pressure for money wage increases from workers in order to reach some target for growth in take-home pay has been a decisive influence in the current inflation'.

Recent developments in the theory of cost inflation highlight particular institutional arrangements as having an influence on the inflation rate. Two, in particular, will be discussed here, if only briefly (for a useful review of these see Hudson (1982)). The *first* are 'Search' theories of inflation and unemployment, developed by Stigler (1962), but extended by Phelps (1968), Mortenson (1970) and Holt (1970). Referred to as 'the new micro-economic approach to macro-economics', these theories emphasise the role of imperfect information in the labour market. Put simply, they argue that individuals need to undertake search activities, in order to improve the quality of their information on the labour market. Holt's contribution stressed the significance of an *aspiration* or acceptance wage which normally declines with the length of search. If the offered wage is higher than an individual's aspiration wage, the job will be accepted; if not, it will be turned down. Two factors will determine the acceptance wage: wages in the previous job, and the tightness of the labour market itself. If the labour market is tight, workers will justifiably raise their initial aspirations. The wage at which the individual is employed will then vary positively with the acceptance wage, and inversely with the period of unemployment. Relating this to the Phillips curve, this implies that the average rate of change of wages between jobs will vary inversely with the average duration of unemployment. And, if it is assumed that the average duration of unemployment varies directly with the number of unemployed workers, the outcome is a Phillips-type relationship between the average rate of change of wages between jobs and the level of unemployment.

Much of the empirical work in this area has focused on the effects of unemployment insurance or benefits on the duration of search. Since these serve to reduce the opportunity cost of search, the prediction is that they should lead to an increase in the average time actually spent searching, as well as in the wage offer eventually accepted. On the whole, this is confirmed for the UK, as borne out in studies by Cubbin and Foley (1977) and Nickell (1979), as well as in a number of American studies.

The *second* theoretical development in this vein are the 'implicit contract' theories. These assume that firms may be willing to reduce the risk of lay-off to workers in return for a lower average wage. Particularly during a period of high unemployment, workers should be prepared to accept a lower wage in return for greater income security. This approach was developed in order to explain why wages do not always fall by enough to clear the market, whenever excess supply exists. It is suggested that *sticky* wages often prevail because of long-term contracts between employer and employee, elements of which guarantee to minimise wage variations. By separating wage movements from current economic conditions, implicit contract theories are a plausible explanation for the disappearance of the Phillips curve relationship during recent years.

At the empirical level, US studies tend to dominate. Feldstein (1978), for example, highlighted the effect of unemployment insurance on lay-off decisions. Using a regression analysis, he found that a 1% increase in the ratio of potential benefits to after-tax wages increases the probability of lay-off for a worker by 0.7%. This study, based on the March 1971 sample of the Current Regulation Survey, was followed by a number of others in a similar vein (see Hudson 1982: 39).

The weakness of these – and, indeed, of most econometric studies – is that they employ single-equation models, in which the supposed dependent variable (for example, wages, the price level) is related to, and presumed to be a function of, what would appear to be the more important determinant variables (for example, unemployment, the cost of living, the strength or militancy of trade unions, the money supply). They are, therefore, partial models only; they study only one market and concentrate on a few immediate determinants of prices and quantities in that market. We know that the economic system is not in fact segmented. All markets – the money markets, the markets for goods and services, and the labour markets – are interdependent, and prices and quantities in any one market are partly determined by events in the others. As Laidler and Parkin, in their 1975 survey article, repeatedly remind us, for an adequate analysis of inflation it is necessary to analyse these interactions between markets in a model of the whole economy. Work of such sophistication has not yet got very far.[4]

Structural inflation

Pressure to maintain differentials, as well as the impact of relative price changes, form the bases of this third type of inflation. In an economy with near-full employment, but no excess demand, suppose there is a shift of demand; sector A enjoys an increase in demand, sector B suffers a fall. Increased demand in A induces a rise in wages and prices; if prices and wages were flexible, they would fall in sector B. Given certain similarities between the two sectors – of size, elasticity of supply etc. – the overall price level would not change. But, in fact, wages and prices rise much more easily than they fall; the wage/price increase in A will be larger than the fall in B, and the general price level rises. Indeed, sector B will be compelled to pay higher wages to maintain differentials and retain the labour it still needs. If demand later shifted from B to A, the demand-shift inflationary impulse would be repeated, with B now initiating the increase. Structural inflation is then a mixture of demand inflation and cost inflation. It begins with an increase in demand in one sector, but there need be no excess demand overall; and it is cost-push – which may, however, take the form of resistance to a wage cut rather than pressure for an increase – which is responsible for the wage transmission to other sectors.

The inflation is sustained by repeated and alternating changes in the composition of demand coupled with the tendency of wages and prices to respond easily to an increase in demand but to be 'sticky' in the face of a decline in demand. It is this 'ratchet effect' which spreads a price increase in one sector to the other sectors of the economy. Each rise in wages and prices, of course, is the source of the higher demand, in money terms, which is necessary to sustain real demand when prices rise.

This theory could explain particular short periods of inflation, such as that in the USA in 1955–57 which gave rise to it. But it is unlikely to account for a continuous, smooth inflation. That would require a fairly regular series of alternating shifts of demand between different sectors of the economy: a series of shifts in the same direction would eventually produce a degree of unemployment in the declining sector(s) sufficient to halt the imitative price increases there. There is, moreover, some conflict of evidence on two important and related elements in the theory although, on balance, the evidence does add some support to this approach. The first is that prices rise wherever there is excess demand but do not fall in the sector(s) where demand is deficient (Silberston 1970: 565–7). The second is that wage increases occur in a 'follow-my-leader' pattern, with little difference between the percentage increases in different sectors of the economy (Minsky 1961; Snodgrass 1963; Eckstein and Wilson 1962; Hines 1969; Sargan 1964; Turner and Jackson 1970 and 1972; Brechling 1973; and Mulvey and Trevithick 1974). There are, in addition, a number of studies of this type of inflation in developing countries, where supply inelasticities and bottlenecks in specific sectors (typically the food sector) induce a strong independent inflationary pressure (Wachter 1976; Thorpe 1979; and Struthers 1981).

Expectations and inflation

There can be little doubt that the issue of expectations formation is a central one to both monetary economics and macro-economics. Ad hoc assumptions concerning expectations, while at one time acceptable, are no longer so. The fact is that much of the disagreement between the different schools of thought (see Chs 8, 9 and 10) seems to revolve around their divergent views on expectations. The problem is that once we introduce the element of *time* into monetary economics, we enter into the realm of uncertainty. Expectations are, by definition, subjective and therefore not directly observable. Therefore a *theory* of expectations formation, as such, becomes necessary.

Keynes, though he considered expectations important (particularly in his analysis of investment), treated them largely as exogenous, and therefore independent of current variables in any model.[5] The essential innovation of modern versions of monetary theory and policy is the attempt to absorb the expectations of individual economic agents explicitly in any model which is devised. A model of the economy which purports to take account of expectations can only do so by relating these unobservable expectations to variables that can be observed, and for which data exists. One possible approach is to undertake surveys on expectations formations. However, this approach is wrought with difficulties as some commentators have shown (Foster and Gregory 1977). The main difficulty lies in the fact that we cannot ask individuals what *they* at a later date will expect regarding a particular phenomenon at a *yet* later date. All we can really attempt is to model the *process* by which expectations are formed, try to forecast the variables on which these expectations are based, and thereby derive a forecast of what expectations are likely to be.

Because the model *specification* involves both an hypothesis about the underlying structural characteristics (for example, a function showing the relationship between the demand for real balances and the level of income and the rate of interest) *and* an hypothesis about the process of expectations formation, it is often difficult, in econometric terms, to decompose these two elements. If only the process of expectations formation could be accurately discovered, the information on aggregate behaviour could then be utilised to test whether the underlying economic theory and the basic model structure are acceptable or not. This, in fact, is a statement of the problem.

After Keynes, the first real attempt to model 'endogenous' and systematic expectations revision was the adaptive expectations hypothesis (Cagan 1956; Nerlove 1958). The analysis of expectations becomes endogenous when individuals are permitted to revise their expectations in the light of new information. The adaptive expectations formulation postulates that economic agents would utilise information on previous forecasting errors in order to revise their current expectations. For example, if $_{t-1}Y_t^e$ is the value of variable Y at time t which is expected by individuals forming expectations at the end of time $t - 1$, the hypothesis of adaptive expectations would appear as follows:

$$_{t-1}Y_t^e - {}_{t-2}Y_{t-1}^e = \lambda[Y_{t-1} - {}_{t-2}Y_{t-1}^e], \quad 0 > \lambda < 1 \qquad [11.1]$$

that is, having some forecast $_{t-2}Y_{t-1}^e$, which is based on information available at the end of time $t - 2$, economic agents make an ex-post decision on how accurately they have predicted the actual value Y_{t-1}, and thereby revise their forecast for Y one period later at time t by some fraction of the forecasting error at time $t - 1$. Rearranging the variables in the above equation:

$$_{t-1}Y_t^e = \lambda Y_{t-1} + (1 - \lambda)_{t-2}Y_{t-1}^e \qquad [11.2]$$

and given that the same formula would apply one period earlier:

$$_{t-2}Y_{t-1}^e = \lambda Y_{t-2} + (1 - \lambda)_{t-3}Y_{t-2}^e \qquad [11.3]$$

Then the unobservable expectations can be substituted out of this equation in a recursive fashion to produce the following equation:

$$_{t-1}Y_t^e = \lambda Y_{t-1} + \lambda(1 - \lambda)Y_{t-2} + \lambda(1 - \lambda)^2 Y_{t-3} + \ldots \lambda(1 - \lambda)^n$$
$$Y_{t-n-1} \ldots$$
$$+ (1 - \lambda)^{n+1}$$
$$t-n-Y_{t-n-1}^e \ldots \quad [11.4]$$

All the variables in equation 11.4, apart from the final one, are observable. Since λ is a positive fraction, $(1 - \lambda)^{n+1}$ becomes smaller as n is increased. If the value of this final expectation is finite, its influence on current expectations can be regarded as insignificant, as long as n is large.

The main merit of the adaptive expectations hypothesis was that unobservable expectations could be modelled in terms of past observations on the actual variable Y, so that there was no need to use any specific process of expectations formation. Since current expectations Y_t^e are based on an extrapolation of past actual values of Y in which the weights decline geometrically, this hypothesis is referred to as a 'geometric distributed lag' on past values of Y. Moreover, the hypothesis seemed to justify acceptance of extrapolative integration of expectations into model-building. Later, with the contribution by Almon (1965), a technique was developed to cope with more flexible lag shapes.

Nevertheless, though this hypothesis was viewed as an improvement on 'partial adjustment' models which had come before, its main limitation was that the particular weights chosen tended to be those which suited the data of which the model was trying to explain. It was also an entirely retrospective formula in which, because adjustment of expectations is a slow process, economic agents were permitted to make systematic errors.[6]

A diagrammatic exposition

The analysis is conducted in the framework of the Phillips curve, and has indeed been used to support the Phillips hypothesis in the context of the 'stagflation' (inflation-with-high-unemployment) of the 1970s and 1980s. But while Phillips was concerned with the relationship between the level of unemployment and the rate of increase in money wages, the expectations hypothesis begins by emphasising that the demand for and supply of labour are functions of the real wage, and that whether money will provide a given real wage depends on the price level in the period covered by the wage contract. Nobody knows what that price level will be, and wage bargains are therefore based on expected prices. If prices have been rising in the recent past people will, in general, and in the absence of any good reason to the contrary, expect them to continue to rise at about the same rate in the future. If the expectations are proved wrong, they will be revised. If, for example, inflation accelerates, so that prices rise 8% this year but were expected to rise only 5% because that is the rate at which they have been rising in recent years, then expectations will be revised upwards by some proportion of the error, and the greater the error the greater the proportionate correction of expectations. The expected rate of inflation thus depends on past inflation rates, especially those of the recent past; it is, in fact, assumed equal to a weighted average of the current and past inflation rates, with the weights declining for each successively earlier period, the weights summing to 1.

The consequence of bringing price expectations into the analysis can be shown by the following example (see Fig. 11.3). We begin with a situation in which prices are stable, the productivity of labour is not increasing, and unemployment is at its *natural* level, OX. This is the level 'which is consistent with the existing real conditions in the labour market'. It is determined by the 'structural characteristics of the labour and commodity markets, including market imperfections, stochastic variability in demands and supplies, the cost of gathering information about job vacancies and labour availabilities, the costs of mobility, and so on' (Friedman 1968: 8). It is 'the level which keeps supply and demand in the labour market balanced . . .' (Friedman 1975a: 24).

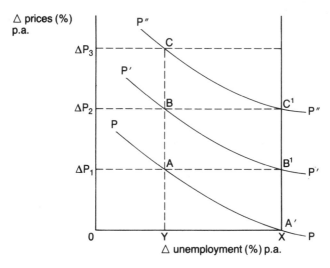

Fig 11.3 Expectations – adjusted Phillips curves

It would be determined by the way in which the geographical distribution of job vacancies was matched up with the geographical distribution of the unemployed; by the way in which the skill mix required to fill vacancies was matched by that among the unemployed; that is, by the rapidity of adjustment of supply to demand in the labour market. The age distribution of the labour force would influence it, as should the educational characteristics of the labour force. Barriers or subsidies to geographical mobility of labour and of jobs, such as trade union restrictions, council house subsidies, etc. as well as barriers or subsidies to the acquisition of new skills, such as professional examination standards, would also affect it. (Laidler 1975: 44–5)

It is synonymous with what is usually termed 'frictional unemployment'. 'Unemployment is zero – which is to say, as measured, equal to "frictional" or "transitional" unemployment, or to use the terminology I adopted some years ago from Wicksell, at its "natural" rate' (Friedman 1975a: 14).

The Government now set in train an expansionary policy to reduce the level of unemployment to OY. The consequence is a rate of inflation equal to ΔP_1; we move up the Phillips curve PP to point A. (The vertical axis of the original Phillips diagram measured the rate of increase of money wages, not prices.) The crucial feature of the curve PP in the Friedman analysis is that is assumed that workers expect prices to remain constant. One of two situations is possible. The first is that the increase in aggregate demand raises prices, but money wages lag behind prices, real wages fall and this increases the demand for labour. The implication is that workers operate, temporarily, under a money illusion. The more likely alternative is that employers offer higher wages to attract more labour, and more labour is supplied because workers see the higher money wages as an increase in real wages. But the higher labour costs are passed through to prices. When labour contracts are renegotiated, they take into account this increase in prices, and money wages rise further, but real wages are immediately eroded again as the money wage increase is passed on in yet higher prices. Thus the original price increase is transformed into a price–wage spiral, with prices rising at the rate ΔP_1. The next step in the analysis is to assert that this situation cannot continue. Essentially, the reason is that the real wage demanded for the supply of labour consistent with an unemployment rate OY is higher than employers are able, or willing, to pay: each wage increase, which workers intend to be an increase in real wages, in the event is passed on in higher prices. To restore equilibrium in the labour market, there must be a movement back down the curve PP to the level of unemployment OX. 'There is thus a *short-run* "trade-off" between inflation and unemployment, but no long-run "trade-off"' (Friedman 1975a: 21).

Let us return to the $\Delta Y/\Delta P_1$ situation. Wage earners realise that each increase in money wages is being eroded by the consequent price increase, and they therefore step up their wage demands to take account of these anticipated price increases. In terms of the Phillips relation, they demand bigger money wage increases at any given level of unemployment; that is, the Phillips curve shifts upwards from PP, which assumes expectations of stable prices, to $P'P'$. But this impetus to wages is reflected in prices; to keep unemployment down to the level OY will generate inflation at the rate ΔP_2, which is greater than the anticipated rate ΔP_1. Sooner or later, this higher rate of inflation will also become the expected rate, wage bargains will be based on it, the Phillips curve shifts further to $P''P''$, and now the rate of inflation associated with unemployment OY is ΔP_3. The attempt to reduce unemployment generates an accelerating inflation, and each 'trade-off' position between unemployment and inflation, indicated by A, B, C etc., is only temporary.

With prices rising, say 5% p.a., there is a wage increase of 9%, 4% because of the

Phillips relationship and 5% to compensate for the anticipated inflation; but a 9% wage increase raises prices 9% so the next claim is for 4% plus 9%, and in the next period prices rise 13%, and so on. The attempt to catch up with anticipated inflation repeatedly generates an actual rate higher than the anticipated rate, and the anticipated rate follows the actual rate upwards. Only when the 'Phillips element' in wage increases is eliminated will the actual and expected rates converge. The only long-term equilibrium is at positions such as A'B'C', where the expected rate of inflation is equal to the actual rate (remember that the curve P'P', for example, is based on an expected rate of inflation OP') and unemployment is at the 'natural' rate OX. Unemployment can be held below this natural level only at the cost of an accelerating inflation. Moreover, this equilibrium level of unemployment is compatible with any rate of inflation. Real wages, which determine the demand for and supply of labour, remain the same whatever the rate of increase of prices so long as wages are increasing at the same rate. In the long run, then, the Phillips curve follows the line A'B'C'; it is *vertical*; there is no long-run trade-off between inflation and unemployment. Once the given rate of inflation is generated, it can be constrained to that rate only by allowing unemployment to rise to OX. Further it can only be reduced by inducing, temporarily, an unemployment rate higher than OX. Suppose we are at position *a* (see Fig. 11.4), with unemployment OX and the rate of inflation OP. The authorities wish to reduce the rate of inflation to OP_1 and institute policies which restrain aggregate expenditure. But, currently, pricing and wage policies are based on expectations of an inflation rate OP. Aggregate expenditure is now insufficient to maintain sales and output at this rate of inflation. If firms hold to their planned prices, they will be left with unsold stocks. If they sell at less than planned prices, profits and cash flow will be reduced because wage costs are geared to the expected (planned) prices. In either case the demand for labour will fall; unemployment will increase to something like the level OZ (position *b*). As the actual rate of inflation is trimmed below its previously expected level, the expected rate of inflation will fall. Rising unemployment will reduce labour's bargaining power. Both will tend to reduce the actual rate of inflation further, which reduces expected inflation, which reduces actual inflation . . . and so on. Alternatively, the authorities could undertake a milder deflation, moving from *a* to *d* via positions *c* and *e* rather than *b*. Assuming that expectations change more quickly the greater the difference between expectations and the actual out-turn, we have a choice between high unemployment for a short period or not so high unemployment for a longer period. There is a trade-off between the degree and the duration of high unemployment. Although controls on prices and wages have not been particularly successful hitherto, we can see how they can, in principle, by operating on both the actual and the expected rate of inflation, help to reduce both the degree and the duration of the unemployment required.

Rational expectations

This approach is radically different from the above, and asserts that individuals do not make systematic mistakes in forecasting the future. The problem then is to

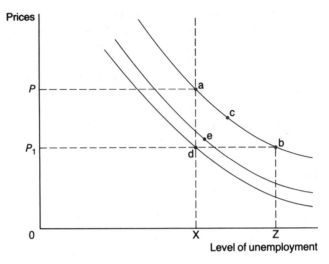

Fig 11.4 Inflation – unemployment adjustment paths

construct a model of the exogenous behaviour of those individuals who *on the average* get their expectations right. One way of interpreting this averaging process would be to argue that those who accurately predict the model dominate those who do not or that, even when errors are repeated, the size and impact of the errors will be reduced over time.

The most relevant context in which to discuss the empirical modelling of rational expectations is the unemployment/inflation trade-off. It is assumed that the monetary authority wishes to influence both the inflation rate P and the unemployment rate U, perhaps by adjusting the rate of growth of the money supply. From the outset, an 'heroic' assumption is required; it is assumed that the monetary authority faces a public which can somehow be regarded as monolithic; that is, there are no debilitating internal disagreements; the public responds in a homogenous fashion. The hypothesis then says that the impact of monetary policy on the (P-U) trade-off will merely depend on whether the actions of the monetary authorities are correctly anticipated by the public or not. Once again, there is a problem here: it is implicitly assumed that it is the monetary authority that is the decision maker, not the public. Certainly the public will form their expectations and act on the basis of these. Indeed, the formation of expectations and the action or response will usually occur simultaneously; the only way the authority can, in fact, gauge how efficiently expectations are being formed is to monitor policy responses. In reality, however, more is expected of the public than of the monetary authority. This point has been made by Frydman *et al.* (1982: 314) '. . . the public is the super being, whose ability to predict the monetary authority's action is summarised by the probability with which the monetary authority thinks that the public will correctly anticipate its policy choice . . .'

The most basic presentation of the rational expectations model is that of Lucas (1973):

$$y_t^s = y_t^\star + \alpha[P_t - P_t^e]; \qquad [\alpha > 0] \tag{11.5}$$

$$y_t^d = m_t - P_t + V_t \tag{11.6}$$

$$y_t^s = y_t^d \tag{11.7}$$

where y_t^s, y_t^d are logs of aggregate supply and demand, $y_t^\star$ is the log of 'full employment' or 'natural' level of output, P_t is the log of the price level, P_t^e is the log of the price level expected by the public, m_t is the log of the money stock, and V_t is the log of velocity (a constant). Equation (11.5) is the Lucas supply function. P_t^e is the price level expected by the public, given the assumption that labour supply decisions will determine the level of output supplied. Equation (11.6) is the simple *quantity theory*, and for simplicity $V_t = 0$.

Assuming that P_t will equate y_t^s to y_t^d, we have:

$$P_t = \left[\frac{1}{1+\alpha}\right] m_t + \left[\frac{\alpha}{1+\alpha}\right] P_t^e - \left[\frac{1}{1+\alpha}\right] y_t^\star \tag{11.8}$$

Since macro-economic models under a regime of rational expectations assume that individual agents do not make systematic errors as this would cause them to abandon the whole process of expectations formations completely, these models should therefore generate endogenous expectations without systematic errors by *simulating* a world in which individuals act *as if* they already know the *systematic* part of the equation, including the Government itself. From this, they form their expectations. Using the equation above, it is assumed that the public know the coefficients of the model and, in forming a rational expectation of P_t, equation (11.8) itself is used. Thus

$$P_t^e = \left[\frac{1}{1+\alpha}\right] m_t^e + \left[\frac{\alpha}{1+\alpha}\right] P_t^e - \left[\frac{1}{1+\alpha}\right] y_t^\star \tag{11.9}$$

Solving (11.9) for P_t^e,

$$P_t^e = m_t^e - y_t^\star \tag{11.10}$$

Clearly, from equation 11.10, the expectation of m^e is vital for the formation of rational expectations of P_t. Hence, forming rational expectations also involves adopting a rational expectation of the monetary authority policy action. Using (11.9) in (11.8):

$$P_t = \left[\frac{1}{1+\alpha}\right] m_t + \left[\frac{\alpha}{1+\alpha}\right] m_t^e - y_t^\star \tag{11.11}$$

Then, using (11.10) and (11.11) in (11.5) gives:

$$y_t = y_t^\star + \frac{1}{1 + \alpha} \, [\, m_t - m_t^e \,] \qquad\qquad [11.12]$$

If deviations $y_t - y_t^\star$ are related to unemployment, thus:

$$y_t - y_t^\star = K \, [\, U_t^\star - U_t \,] \qquad\qquad [11.13]$$
[where $K > 0$ is a constant]

Equation (11.13) assumes that when $y_t = y_t^\star$, unemployment is equal to the 'natural' rate $U_t^\star$. Again using (11.13), equation (11.12) can be rewritten as:

$$U_t = U_t^\star + B \, [\, m_t^e - m_t \,] \qquad \text{where } B = \frac{1}{K \, [\, 1 + \alpha \,]} \qquad [11.14]$$

$$\text{or } U_t = U_t^\star + B \, [\, [\, m_t^e - m_{t-1} \,] - [\, m_t - m_{t-1} \,] \,] \qquad\qquad [11.15]$$

In this framework, deviations between actual output/employment and the 'natural' rate are therefore proportional to the deviation between actual and expected inflation.

The rational expectations model thus asserts that the subjective expectations are exactly the mathematical expectations formed by using the model itself, conditional on information available at the date expectations are formed. In other words, expectations are stochastically self-fulfilling in the sense that ex-post forecasting errors cannot be predicted with the information available at the date expectations are formed. These expectations may be thought of as equilibrium in the sense that there is no incentive to revise the process by which they are formed, despite the fact that the expected value of any particular variable will be revised as new information does become available and is recognisable as useful.

Following the early work of Muth (1961), individuals, like economists, are assumed to think up stylised models of the economy and thereby understand the basic inter-relationships in the system. Paraphrasing Maddock and Carter (1982), 'they all have econometric models under the sink! . . .' As a result, they are enabled to analyse the main determinants of the variables in the equations of the model, including the government itself. Feedback effects are also considered and it is assumed that individuals are qualified to distinguish the major (namely significant and non-random) disturbances from the minor ones. A crucial requirement in all of this is that they are able to assess all the available *information* which is relevent to their model. If this information set is called I_{t-1} the following equation would apply:

$$_{t-1}P_t^e = E \left[\frac{P_t}{I_{t-1}} \right] \qquad\qquad [11.16]$$

All this says is that price expectations (for example) are the mean value of the expected probability distribution of the variable to be predicted when all the available information is absorbed into the forecast.

The theory of rational expectations therefore implies that these expectations are unbiased predictors of the actual event — the expectation and the actual event differing by a random forecast error only:

$$P_t - {}_{t-1}P_t^e = P_t - E\left[\frac{P_t}{I_t}\right] + U_2 \qquad [11.17]$$

[where U_2 is a random forecasting error]

This forecast error is uncorrelated with each element of the set of all information available in the previous period that was relevent for forecasting inflation (I_{t-1}). In econometric terms, there is no *noise* (or undiscernible randomness). This assumes that there is no change in the structural equation, where rational expectations could accommodate such a change.

Though the theory of rational expectations claims that individuals should not make systematic errors, this does not necessarily imply perfect foresight. Rather, in an uncertain world where random events are inevitable, the theory simply says that informed (and also perhaps ill-informed) guesses about the future must, on average, be correct; if, that is, we are to expect individuals to continue to form their expectations in the fashion they have become accustomed to. Given the existence of uncertainty, the crucial question is whether systematic influences are more important than random ones. Past values of the variables are not sufficient, because information is also required on future values of endogenous variables. In a stochastic framework, then, it is assumed that individuals will know the statistical properties of those random observations which affect *their* model.[7] This implies that the expectations factor will be the mathematical expectation which can be obtained by devising the correct model of the economy which includes these random terms. These mathematical expectations would be conditional on information available at the date at which expectations are to be formed. The hypothesis of rational expectations thus asserts that the unobservable, subjective expectations of individuals are identical to the true mathematical expectations implied by the model itself. Namely, that the behaviour of individuals in the aggregate 'seems' to indicate that they behave *as if* they know the parameters of the model and form their expectations accordingly. This response need be neither conscious nor deliberate. All that is required is that their behaviour displays characteristics which we might call consistent and which seems to indicate almost that they know the future exactly.

In forming expectations about the rate of inflation one period ahead, individuals must in fact look even further ahead than that. This is so because the actual inflation rate one period ahead will itself be a function of expected inflation in a later time period. Strictly speaking, the entire future path of the economy must be incorporated into the forecast.[8] Therefore, whereas in the adaptive expectations approach, steady-state growth or convergence is a mere fluke, with rational expectations convergence is certain and the past is only of interest to the extent that it conveys information about the future. Economic agents who are forward looking are assumed to solve the model over all future time in order to determine current expectations. These expectations need be neither unanimous nor correct for, in reality, individuals will have differential access to information. A complete model would thus require some assessment of incentives to acquire information, as well as (presumably) the costs incurred in destroying information that is deemed no longer useful or advantageous to retain. These, however, are complex issues and perhaps this is where the real contribution of rational expectations lies; namely, in aiding our understanding of the impact of information flows on the economy.

Most models, which utilise rational expectations, have assumed instantaneous market clearing (Muth 1961; Barro and Grossman 1971; Grossman 1980), and critics of the hypothesis question the validity of rational expectations on that basis. However, proponents of the hypothesis have also been quick to point out that instantaneous market clearing is not essential to the rational expectations approach. '. . . there is nothing in the Rational Expectations approach which asserts that individuals may not realise that markets may not clear, and form expectations accordingly . . .' (Begg 1982: 264).

Criticisms of rational expectations theory

(a) The concept of rational expectations seems to allude to a set of expectations which are somehow in equilibrium even when equilibrium may not exist in the economy as a whole and, indeed, may be both unachievable and undesirable. Moreover, by permitting errors on the part of rational economic agents, it sets in motion a disequilibrium process which itself provides incentives for individuals to acquire information of a better grade, which in cost-benefit fashion they can utilise to revise their behaviour (Hahn 1973). Hence the phrase, bygones are bygones are bygones! However, in highlighting gains and losses in the context of information gathering, it does not address itself to the question of differential access to information. Rather, it dismisses this complication by saying that the fact that one individual has better information than another can itself be viewed as another piece of relevant information to consider and respond to. But the question which must follow on from this is: Can expectations formation be difficult or non-rational even for individuals who may view themselves as being well-informed (commercial speculators in the foreign exchange market, for example, or operators in the stock market)? Can a cost-benefit analysis (incorporating information flows, the cost of information etc.) be seriously attempted in the context of revising one's expectations? These are questions largely left unanswered by the rational expectations paradigm.

(b) It is also a pure excess demand theory; there is no mention of cost-push. As in the Phillips analysis, higher wages are offered, or wage claims accepted, because employers are bidding competitively for labour. If its exponents were questioned about this they would presumably say that trade union pressure, by raising the supply curve of labour, would raise the 'natural' level of unemployment.

(c) It assumes that wage claims are based on price expectations, determined by the error-learning process, and that they are successful. The statistical evidence on this, however, is mixed. The evidence supporting the Phillips–Lipsey thesis of a trade-off between inflation and unemployment covers a very long period. Perhaps the 'no money illusion' case, with wages fully compensating for expected inflation, is associated with high inflation rates such as those of the 1970s. Some argue that recent evidence supports the 'vertical Phillips curve' hypothesis; others that it suggests a 'weak' expectations hypothesis, that is, that the long-run Phillips curve is much steeper than the short-run curve, but is not vertical; there is some long-run trade-off between inflation and unemployment (see Ch. 13).

(d) There appears to be some ambiguity in the specification of the 'natural' level of unemployment. It is not stated why the level of unemployment at which the 'real' demand and supply of labour are in equilibrium is necessarily that at which the only unemployment is frictional. Work at the University of Manchester suggested that it is probably about 2% in Britain, but could be higher. Britain had accelerating inflation in the 1970s with significantly higher rates than this. Therefore it is important for policy to have some idea of what is the 'natural' rate. For their part, the monetarists say that if the money supply is expanded at a rate equal to the rate of growth of output capacity, the economy will eventually converge on its natural rates of capacity utilisation and unemployment.

Some versions of rational expectations (Begg 1982) suggest that providing information regarding the structure of the economy and government policy remains unaltered, rational expectations formation will facilitate the achievement of a convergent path involving perfect foresight. When new information becomes available and seems relevant, the outcome is a leap on to a new convergent path, after which behaviour is consistent, unless new information again has to be absorbed, and so on.

However, to non-believers, the crucial issues are more fundamental than this. How is this steady-state path to be defined in terms of real variables such as output, employment and productivity? Where is this steady-state leading to; in other words, what is the economy converging towards?

The typical monetarist response to questions such as these that this path leads inexorably to the 'natural rate' of unemployment, where expectations regarding inflation are exactly fulfilled and the long-run Phillips curve is vertical, is, it is suggested, open to the criticism of circular reasoning, if not *mauvaise foi*. To postulate that expectations are rational, and then utilise this assumption to express views on policy options which in themselves are a function of a particular and positive view about expectations (that is that expectations are exactly fulfilled), is to have it both ways! (Struthers 1984).

Conclusion

How, and to what extent, the price level is linked with the money supply, and whether money has been a causal agent or merely permissive in the inflationary process, are unsettled questions and will probably continue so for some years. But all are agreed on one thing: that without an increase in the quantity of money an inflation will come up against a monetary barrier and, by the same token, an inflation can be stopped by monetary restraint. The consequent restriction of demand will cause unemployment: massive unemployment for a short time or moderate unemployment for a longer period, depending on the severity of the monetary restraint. The question: can we prevent (stop) an inflation?, then devolves into the question (given our present institutions): how much unemployment will be tolerated? The permissive nature of money supply policy up to 1975 was therefore largely the result of the primacy of full employment in government policy. Non-monetarists, at least, accept that other policies, such as fiscal restraint and prices and incomes policies, will help; an incomes policy will, if it reduces the expectations effect, have the additional advantage of reducing the level of unemployment associated with an anti-inflationary monetary policy. No policy can succeed in the face of an irresponsible expansion of the money supply. To abandon control of the money supply in an attempt to stabilise interest rates in the face of inflationary pressure arising from non-monetary causes, such as cost-push forces, will defeat its own object: the nominal interest rate includes a premium to allow for the expected rate of inflation, and the inflation made possible by monetary expansion will eventually raise interest rates. To avoid both the resultant high cost of 'genuine' borrowing from the public and a further rise in interest rates, the authorities are then tempted to borrow more from the central bank, and the money supply increases further, inducing more inflation, and so on.

Notes

1   It is, however, possible to detect a minor concession on this question in this assertion by Friedman (1975a: 33): 'I am not saying that the existence of strong unions may not be one of the factors that, by a variety of devices, affects what monetary policy is'.

2   Jackson et al. (1972) suggest one model of inflation in which wages rise in the sector with the highest rate of growth of productivity, and then spread to other sectors with lower, or zero, rate of growth of productivity.

3   Lipsey's (1960) results, based on the application of more sophisticated and rigorous statistical techniques to the Phillips data, refuted the Phillips suggestion that prices have only a secondary threshold effect on wages. Especially during the period 1948–57, prices had a far greater influence than unemployment on wages, a conclusion stated even more strongly by Hines (1964).

4   Laidler and Parkin (1975: 774–81) attempt to review some of this work.

5   In one sense this helps us to appreciate why Keynes and his followers regarded current income a more significant variable than either wealth or permanent income (see Ch. 8).

6   Similarly, there is no substantive economic theory which would indicate the magnitude of the adjustment factor λ.

7   In other words, if agents discover that their model is a poor predictor of events they will amend it and develop, through trial and error, a 'better' model; one which, in the Friedmanite sense, predicts the future more accurately.

8   Begg (1982: 31) refers to this as the 'Perfect Foresight Equilibrium Path'.

CHAPTER TWELVE

The theory of monetary policy

Monetary policy is part of macro-economic policy, whose other arm is fiscal policy. Fiscal policy can be defined as the manipulation of the size, form and timing of government expenditure and taxation. Monetary policy is concerned with financial variables: the supply of money, the flow of credit, and interest rates. The two arms of policy are not independent. It is a truism that one should support the other, and fiscal policy affects financial variables. All payments between the public and private sectors have monetary repercussions. The financing of a budget deficit, or the disposal of a budget surplus, infringes on one or more of the financial variables. Management of the national debt is part fiscal, part monetary policy: the size and composition of the debt are the outcome of past fiscal policy, while operations to change the size and composition of the private sector's holdings of existing debt are part of monetary policy, conducted by the central bank.

The instruments of monetary policy

The traditional weapons were bank rate and open market operations, by which the central bank can set an upper limit to the supply of money (but not a lower limit, since the actual supply depended in part on the demand for bank deposits) and this determined one set of interest rates. By operations in the gilt-edged market, the central bank is also able to change the maturity structure of government debt held by the private sector and so may be able to influence the pattern of interest rates on the debt. Another traditional weapon has been the manipulation of required reserve ratios. Both the supply of money and the administered rates of interest exert some influence on other rates.

Other instruments of monetary policy are specific rather than general. Their targets are the flow of particular forms of credit rather than the supply of money; they focus on particular types of lending, or lending by particular institutions. They are administrative controls; they do not rely on the market mechanism or on normal banking practice for their effects, but are direct requests or instructions to the institutions concerned to restrict their loans in general or particular kinds of loan. The direct controls employed in the UK have for the most part been 'moral suasion'; for example, requests to the banks to limit their advances and holdings of commercial bills, and controls on hire purchase finance. Others can be devised. The US monetary authorities, for example, have from time to time imposed ceilings on mortgage credit, on interest rates paid on time deposits, and on the margin between pledged collateral and loans for the purchase of shares.

Control of the money supply

In this chapter we ignore the debate on what constitutes the supply of money (see Ch. 13) and assume that it consists of notes and coins (C) plus deposits (D), on both current and deposit account, at the deposit banks.

Part of the cash supply is held by the bank as a reserve, part by the public:

$$C = C_b + C_p \qquad [12.1]$$

The banks' reserves of notes and coin are not in use; only those held by the public are an effective part of the money supply. 'The money supply' means 'money held by the public':

$$M = C_p + D \qquad [12.2]$$

Deposits are constrained by the banks' cash reserves (C_b + deposits at the central bank) often termed 'base money' or (in the US context) 'high-powered money'. The public's desired holdings of cash are probably related to their holdings of bank deposits, the precise relationship depending on several possible influences, but chiefly on the distribution of payments between cash and cheques. So the total supply of money appears to be related to the total supply of cash. The supply of money consists of bank deposits and the currency in circulation. If the banks maintain a fixed ratio of cash to deposits, the supply of money would be determined by the total supply of currency and by that fraction of the total supply which the public wish to hold. Given also a stable ratio of the public's desired holdings of currency to bank deposits, the quantity of money would be a unique function of the supply of currency, and the most simple and effective way to control the quantity of money would be to set a limit to the issue of notes and coin. This, presumably, is the logic of *monetary targets* (see p. 351). If, further, there is some stable relationship of currency or of money to income, we could influence income – and that is the ultimate purpose of controlling the quantity of money – by varying the issue of currency.

This argument is misleading, for three reasons. First, the cash base of bank deposits includes not only cash in the till but also the banks' balances at the Bank of England, and these can and do change without any change in the note issue or in the public's demand for cash. Any payment, by purchase or loan, by cash or cheque, from the Government or the Bank of England to the private sector, or vice versa, produces a change in bankers' deposits. Second, the supply of cash is a small, but necessary, part of the payments system. People would evade a limit on the note issue by changing their methods of payment, using cheques more and cash less. But their ability to do so is limited; there is a multitude of payments, such as single payments between strangers and payments of small sums, for which cheques would be inconvenient, administratively expensive or unacceptable. To leave the volume of transactions uncontrolled but then set a limit on the means of conducting one part of those transactions would at best cause much inconvenience and at worst be quite disruptive: the situation would be absurd. Third, as we shall see shortly, the fundamental relationships are not in fact rigid.

In practice, there is no direct control of the issue of currency, even though the Treasury and the Bank decide the size of the note issue. What happens is that the Government tries to influence the level of income by various means, both fiscal and monetary, including control of bank deposits, and supplies whatever cash is wanted to finance the day-to-day payments associated with the existing level of income. The authorities recognise that currency is only the small change of the monetary system, but an essential part of it. Bank deposits are the major part of the money supply and it is deposits which they aim to control.

The deposit multiplier

The supply of money is given by the equation:

$$M = C_p + D \qquad\qquad [12.3]$$

Total cash held outside the Bank of England (C) is held by the public and by the banks,

$$C = C_b + C_p \qquad\qquad [12.4]$$

D is constrained by C_b, according to the formula:

$$D = \frac{1}{r} C_b \qquad\qquad [12.5]$$

where r is the banks' ratio of cash to deposits. If this were the only determinant of D, then the relationship of changes in deposits to changes in the supply of cash would be $\Delta D = \Delta C / r$. But as the public's holdings of bank deposits increase, their desired holdings of cash increase. Let us assume provisionally that they have a desired ratio of cash to deposits, a: $C_p = aD$, and that a is constant; that is, the marginal ratio is equal to the average ratio: $C_p = aD$

Then: $\Delta C_b = r\Delta D \qquad\qquad [12.6]$

$\Delta C_p = a\Delta D \qquad\qquad [12.7]$

$\Delta C = \Delta C_p + \Delta C_b = (a+r)\,\Delta\cdot D \qquad\qquad [12.8]$

$$\Delta D = \frac{1}{a+r} \cdot \Delta C \qquad\qquad [12.9]$$

Further:

$$M = C_p + D \qquad\qquad [12.10]$$

$$= aD + \frac{1}{a+r} \cdot C \qquad\qquad [12.11]$$

$$= \frac{a}{a+r} \cdot C + \frac{1}{a+r} \cdot C \qquad\qquad [12.12]$$

$$= \frac{1+a}{a+r} \cdot C \qquad\qquad [12.13]$$

Another frequently used formula expresses the public's desired holdings of cash as a proportion of total money; instead of $Cp = aD$, it has $Cp = cM$. Total cash:

$$C = Cb + Cp \qquad\qquad [12.4]$$

$$= cM + rD \qquad\qquad [12.14]$$

Total money supply:

$$M = Cp + D \qquad\qquad [12.3]$$

$$= cM + D \qquad\qquad [12.15]$$

And

$$D = M(1-c) \qquad\qquad [12.16]$$

Therefore:

$$C = Cb + Cp \qquad\qquad [12.4]$$

$$= cM + r(1-c) \qquad\qquad [12.17]$$

And

$$M = \frac{c}{c+r(1-c)} \qquad\qquad [12.18]$$

This is also equivalent to another frequently used formula:

$$M = \frac{1}{1-(1-c)(1-r)} \cdot C \qquad [12.19]$$

The associated formula relating increases in deposits to increases in bank cash is:

$$\Delta D = \frac{1-c}{c+r(1-c)} \cdot \Delta C \qquad [12.20]$$

As the banks create money (bank deposits) by buying earning assets and by lending, part ($c\Delta M$) of the increment of deposits is withdrawn in cash; hence the increase in deposits is less (by the fraction c) than the increase in earning assets and loans which are the counterpart of the increase in the total supply of money. This formula is reconciled with the deposit expansion formula $1/(a+r)$ by deriving a relationship between c and a.
Thus:

$$Cp = cM \qquad [12.21]$$

And

$$Cp = aD \qquad [12.22]$$

and $Cm = aD$ $\qquad [12.23]$

But $M = Cp + D$ $\qquad [12.3]$

Thus:

$$aD = cM$$

$$= c(Cp + D) \qquad [12.24]$$

$$= c(aD + D) \qquad [12.25]$$

$$= c(1+a)D \qquad [12.26]$$

Therefore:

$$c = \frac{a}{1+a} \qquad [12.27]$$

Substituting [12.27] for c in [12.20]
Therefore:

$$\Delta D = \frac{1}{a+r} \cdot \Delta C \qquad\qquad [12.28]$$

Limitations of the deposit multiplier
For a number of reasons, these bank multipliers present an unrealistic, too mechanical, account of how the money supply is actually determined.

Constraints on deposit creation
The multiplier formulae state the *maximum* deposits and earnings assets which can be built up on a given Cb or Cp. There are circumstances in which the banks will be unable or unwilling to expand deposits up to this limit, for example:

(a) There is a limit to the quantity of deposits the public are wiling to hold. Deposits are a means of payment, the demand for which is a function of incomes and the level of economic activity and the accompanying value of transactions. They are also an asset, the demand for which is similarly a function of income, and of wealth, but which also must compete with other assets. The existence or the prospect of a serious economic recession will reduce the volume of safe lending the banks can undertake. Until 1971 the clearing banks were inhibited by their cartel agreement from reducing interest rates to stimulate demand for loans. But even in a free market, there is obviously a minimum rate below which the return on the loan would not give an adequate margin over the cost of administering loans and deposits. if the banks turn to deposit-creating purchases of other assets, they face similar problems. Wholesale purchases of bonds will push up their prices (reduce their yields), and also reduce the chance of capital gain from a further rise in the price and increase the risk of capital loss from a fall. There is no such inhibition on the banks' purchases of liquid assets; the risk of capital loss on bills is minimal, especially since they are held in *echelon*, and there is no risk on call money. Even at very low yields, they are a better asset than non-earning cash. The returns could, however, conceivably fall so low that they do not cover the cost of servicing the accounts (deposits) paid for them.

Another possible restraint is a shortfall in the supply of liquid assets. Suppose, however, that some sequence of events did leave the public with more deposits than they wished to hold. To say that there is an excess supply of deposits implies that some holders, at least, use them to buy non-money financial assets and/or real assets. To spend a deposit does not destroy it; it simply transfers ownership to the seller of the alternative asset. The economy as a whole cannot rid itself of deposits once they are created except by repaying loans or buying securities from the banks, and banks aiming to maintain deposits would try to reverse this by relending or buying more securities. The counterpart of an excess supply of deposits, therefore, is an increase in the demand for other assets. This raises their prices, which has further consequences, and these in turn affect the level of deposits.

First, the opposite side of the coin of higher prices (lower yields) on securities is a lower cost of finance for the primary issuer of securities. This may reduce the demand for loan-created deposits because the cost of the alternative source of funds has fallen, but is likely to stimulate the overall demand for finance. Spending out of these borrowed or invested funds and the increased demand for goods from owners of unwanted deposits increases output, employment and income, which increases the demand for deposits as a means of payment. On the other hand, it will also increase the drain of cash from the banks. Second, falling yields on non-money assets make money relatively more attractive and increase the demand for money as an asset. Third, the falling yields on bills and bonds reduce the banks' incentive to create deposits by buying them. Along these paths, then, we eventually arrive at an equilibrium situation in which both the banks and the public are satisfied with the existing level of deposits; but that level may be lower than the limit set by the banks' original cash reserves and our simple deposit multiplier.

(b) The transfer of deposits to intermediaries who hold the same kinds of reserves as the banks and are subject to minimum reserve requirements may cause some reduction in the banks' reserves and hence in their ability to create deposits. And, as we saw in Chapters 4 and 5, the lending of some intermediaries also competes with bank loans, thereby affecting the size of the deposit multiplier.[1]

The instability of a and r

The formula $1/(a+r)$, or its alternative $(1-c)/c+r(1-c)$, are a useful measure of the deposits/cash multiplier only if a and r, or c and r, are stable. They may not be:

1 We have already seen that the banks may be pushed into holding 'excess reserves' – that is, a cash ratio higher than the required minimum – because they are unable or unwilling to expand deposits to the limit set by the ratio.

All the determinants of the desired cash ratio, clearly, are likely to change over time, and will vary from one bank to another. At some times and for some banks the desired cash ratio is likely to be higher than the traditional or prescribed minimum. These divergences have never been large in British banks. From 1946 to 1971 the London clearing banks cash ratio varied only slightly around 8%; after 1971 it was usually within the range $4\frac{1}{2}$–$5\frac{1}{2}$%.

If the banks do not all observe the same cash ratio, r is an average of different ratios and can change with the distribution of deposits between different types of bank. Since 1963 our official definition of the money supply (until 1970, the only definition) has included deposits with the accepting houses and overseas, other banks and the discount houses as well as the clearing banks. Between 1959 and 1969, although the cash ratios of the London clearing banks was held close to 8%, that of the wider circle of banks varied between 9.4 and 10.5%.

Similarly, if banks are obliged to observe one cash ratio against current accounts but are allowed a lower ratio against deposit accounts, as in the USA, the overall ratio will change with changes in the 'mix' of the two types of account.

2 There are a number of reasons why the public's desired ratio of currency holdings to bank deposits might change: a wider spread of 'the banking habit' and use of cheques will reduce the need for currency. Such a change may result from advertising by the banks, the offer of new or cheaper services, the opening of more branches, a wider adoption of the practice of paying wages and salaries by cheque or credit to a bank account, or greater confidence in the safety of bank deposits. Similarly the development of new methods of payment out of bank accounts – notably credit cards – reduces the use of cash.

One would expect that the banks could attract more cash from the public by the offer of higher interest rates on deposits, but it appears that changes in the rate do not, in fact, have any significant effect on the public's cash ratio in the UK (Gibson 1967: 33). Such influences have only a long-term effect, and there have been significant changes in the value of a over the years (Sheppard 1971).

One possible reason for instability of the public's cash/deposit ratio is that desired cash holdings are a function of some other variable which is not itself closely related to bank deposits. The obvious candidate is income, and Newlyn (1971: 22) suggested that the rise in the Cp/D ratio during the 1950s and 1960s occurred 'because the relationship between the level of national income and cash holdings is close, but that between national income and deposits is not ...' In the 1970s, however, the ratio of Cp to income (Gross National Product) fell slowly but almost continuously, as did London clearing bank deposits.

The non-bank financial intermediaries hold deposits with the clearing banks as reserves. Total clearing bank deposits are therefore greater than those owned by 'the public', and the ratio 'a' depends on the public's desired ratio of bank deposits to deposits with other intermediaries and on the reserves/liabilities ratios of the non-bank intermediaries.

Other leakages

The simple multiplier formula $1/(a+r)$ includes only the most immediate and obvious leakages, the 'internal cash drain' (r) and the 'external cash drain' (a).

There are others. A leakage occurs whenever the banks lose cash to the rest of the private sector or their balance at the Bank of England is reduced.

1 Some deposits may be used to buy newly issued government securities – Treasury bills and bonds, National Savings securities – or be transferred to the savings institutions who put their funds into government securities – in particular, the National Savings Bank and the Trustee Savings Banks.

2 Some will be transferred to intermediaries such as building societies and

finance houses, who buy government securities either as a temporary investment of surplus funds or to hold as a reserve.

3　The banks themselves, of course, also buy government securities, both short term and long term. Any private sector purchase of newly issued government securities direct from the Government results in a transfer from bankers deposits to public deposits at the Bank of England.

Many of the purchases under (2) and (3) are likely to be 'second-hand' Treasury bills and bonds bought from holders in the private sector. They may, nevertheless, cause an indirect drain of cash as, for example, when discount houses sell Treasury bills to the banks and replace them with new bills bought at the next tender, or when people or institutions sell bonds to the banks and use the deposits so created to subscribe to a new issue of government bonds, because the new bonds are for some reason – for example, their maturity dates – more suitable for their current portfolios. We must emphasise that this indirect leakage is only a possibility, not a certainty. The cash drain through the discount houses will, of course, be reversed as the Treasury bills mature. Only as the market's holdings of Treasury bills increase is there a continued net drain of cash from the market. More generally and precisely, only as there is a *net* purchase of securities by the private sector from the public sector is there a drain of cash from the banks.

4　If the creation of more deposits increases aggregate expenditure, national income rises, and with it the Government's tax revenue. Payment of taxes also results in a transfer from bankers' deposits to public deposits. If there were a relationship between a given increase in deposits and the consequent increase in national income, and a further relationship between increases in national income and increases in tax revenue, we could add a further symbol to the denominator of the deposit multiplier formula. But such a leakage would probably be less stable over time than a or r. How far changes in national income are related to (previous) changes in the quantity of money is a matter of dispute between the main schools of monetary theory. The relationship between income and tax revenue depends on government policy, which changes frequently.

5　Some deposits, or bank reserves, may be used to buy existing 'second-hand' securities from the Bank. The proceeds are not, in this case, revenue for the Government and there is no likely corresponding government expenditure. The drain out of bankers' deposits is not reversed. But this purchase constitutes an open market operation.

6　Just as there is an 'asset drain' into purchases of government securities and an 'income drain' into taxes, so is there a possible asset drain into purchases of securities issued or owned in other countries, and an almost certain income drain into purchases of imports. For these the buyer needs foreign currency, which he may buy from the Exchange Equalisation Account (EEA) out of his bank account. The consequence of such a purchase, therefore, is again a transfer from bankers' deposits to public deposits. It seems unlikely that there is a stable *direct* relationship between these leakages and deposit expansion. There appears to be little reason why foreign securities should be a stable proportion of most portfolios, and imports are related to income, not to holdings of bank deposits. There may, however, be an indirect connection between deposits and inflows and outflows of funds, via interest rates. An increase in deposits (that is, in the quantity of money) is usually assumed to reduce interest rates temporarily at least. If rates abroad have not fallen, borrowing in London is encouraged and lending is discouraged. Hence there is an outflow of funds, and the EEA receives sterling in exchange for foreign currencies.

Therefore, the usual bank deposit multipliers have major limitations. This is so because they do not really explain the link between base money and deposits. As Goodhart (1978: 136) has pointed out, 'multipliers may reveal the result of rational choice, but they do not illuminate that process'. And, while there is a close long-term relationship between high-powered money and the money supply, as Sheppard (1971) showed, the relationship is not stable over shorter periods.

Can the authorities control the supply of money?

Returning to our simple formula for the money supply,

$$M = Cp + D \qquad\qquad [12.3]$$

$$C = Cb + Cp \qquad\qquad [12.1]$$

From [12.9]

$$D = \frac{1}{a+r} \cdot C \qquad\qquad [12.29]$$

$$\text{and } M = \frac{1+a}{a+r} \cdot C \qquad\qquad [12.13]$$

where $a = Cp/D$ and $r = Cb/D$.

From this we derive the necessary conditions for perfect control of the money supply. They are that:

1 The authorities control the supply of cash: 'high-powered money'.
2 The ratio of M to C is constant, or at least under the authorities' control. For this to be so, certain other conditions are necessary:

3   The general condition is that either (a) the authorities must be able to deter-
    mine directly the distribution of total cash (C) between the public (Cp) and the
    banks (Cb); this they cannot do. Or (b) the ratio between Cp and Cb is stable. In
    the formula above, the link is provided by D, which is taken to be a function of
    Cb, and Cp a function of D. These functions must be stable: that is, a and r
    must be constants. Stability of r implies that the banks always expand deposits
    to the limit set by their cash reserves; r is always equal to the minimum cash
    ratio.
4   An alternative condition to 3(b) is that changes in a and/or r are predictable,
    and that the authorities can quickly take steps to offset the effects of such
    changes on M.

We have seen several reasons to doubt the stability of a and r and their adequacy
as explanations of the 'money multiplier' which relates M to Cb. However, the
authorities can, in principle, always offset variations in the leakages out of the
multiplier by changes in Cb. Hence control ultimately turns on the authorities' ability
to control bank cash. Again, in principle, Cb is perfectly determinable by open
market operations. But there are various impediments to and inhibitions on the effective use of open market operations.

Goodhart (1973) has contested, on different grounds, the authorities' ability to
determine the supply of high-powered money. He first assumes a given public sector
deficit (PSD), and points out that it can be financed in three ways. First, by sales to
the private sector of securities, both marketable and non-marketable (S) in excess of
maturing securities (M). Second, by net receipts of sterling in payment for foreign
exchange, lent to the Exchequer by the EEA; that is, financed by a net deficit on
external transactions (ECF). Third, by borrowing from the Bank of England, which
increases bankers' deposits ('high-powered money') as the money is spent (ΔH).

Hence: $\text{PSD} = S = M + \text{ECF} + H$ [12.30]

$\Delta H = \text{PSD} - S + M - \text{ECF}$ [12.31]

PSD is determined by government expenditure and taxation policies which cannot
be changed quickly. Debt maturities depend on past loans and their length, and are
not subject to control except in so far as the owners can be persuaded to take up new
issues. The difficulty with ECF is that it reacts perversely to changes in interest
rates. A restriction of the money supply raises domestic interest rates and so
encourages borrowing abroad; it also attracts funds from overseas. Foreign exchange
is surrendered to the EEA for sterling; and the domestic supply of sterling is increased.

More directly, suppose the authorities sell securities on the open market to
restrict the money supply. How are the purchases financed? Some, perhaps, by the
sale of foreign assets; the sale of the foreign exchange received to the EEA neutralises
the open market operation; the effect is on foreign exchange reserves (increasing

them) instead of on the quantity of money. Sales of non-marketable debt such as Savings Certificates are also likely to respond perversely to changes in the general level of interest rates, because rates paid on them are sticky. In short, two of the flows affecting H are largely outside the monetary authority's control (PSD and M), while two respond perversely to changes in interest rates (ECF and sales of non-marketable debt); that is, an increase in interest rates will, as far as these two determinants are concerned, induce an increase in H. However, some of these flows are to some extent mutually compensatory. A large PSD is more likely to coincide with an external deficit than a surplus. A large inflow of foreign exchange usually stimulates sales of gilt-edged direct to overseas buyers, an additional ECF. When the public sector has a large deficit, either the private sector will have a large surplus or there will be a large deficit on the balance of payments.

The obvious answer to these uncontrollable or perverse influences on H is to *neutralise* them by compensatory changes in the issue of debt (S) or by open market operations. Goodhart's analysis highlights the authorities' dilemma between support and control, between budgetary policy, determination of the money supply, and control of interest rates. With a large PSD, monetary control is impossible unless the authorities are prepared to accept, if necessary, a drastic rise in interest rates, a large fall in the prices of gilt-edged. It is a question of priorities.

How monetary policy operates: the transmission mechanism

The monetary authority cannot operate directly on the quantities which policy seeks to control. The levels of employment and income and prices, and the balance of payments, are largely the consequence of expenditure decisions by firms and households; policy operates on variables which are believed to have some bearing on these decisions. The question therefore arises: what are the links between the financial quantities and spending decisions? Through what channels does monetary policy operate? The only agreement is that, in so far as financial variables do affect the economy, the effect is on aggregate demand; how monetary policy actually works is a matter of dispute. The source of disagreement is, of course, the conflict between the different monetary theories examined in earlier chapters; with each theory there is associated a particular view of the operation of monetary policy.

The Keynesian version

The direct interest rate effect
Suppose the central bank undertakes an open market buying operation. (The initial effect is an increase in idle balances.) Money thus created therefore has no immediate impact on expenditure and income. Since a bigger proportion of total M is now held

idle, (the velocity of circulation has fallen) But to persuade the public to hold more money, the rate of interest − that is the yield on the alternative asset to money, namely, bonds − must fall. It is this effect on interest rates which is the key link in the transmission process, because what is the yield on bonds on the one hand is the cost of borrowing on the other, and it is primarily via the lower cost of borrowing that spending is stimulated. Lower rates of interest induce an increase in investment, which raises the level of income both directly and via the multiplier. This effect of the increase in the money supply thus depends on:

(a) The interest elasticity of the demand for money. The lower this is, the larger is the decline in interest rates required to increase the demand for money equally with the supply.

(b) The interest elasticity of expenditure. The higher this is, the more spending will be generated by a given fall in interest rates. This is also affected by the size of the multiplier and the velocity of circulation of active money.

But, are interest rates effective? Keynes himself took a rather pessimistic view, for the following reasons:

(a) He said: 'The monetary authority often tends in practice to concentrate upon short term debts and to leave the price of long term debts to be influenced by belated and imperfect reactions from the price of short term debts' (1936: 206). Clearly, it is the cost of long-term borrowing which influences long-term investment.

(b) The dominance of the 'normal' rate of interest in market psychology means that successive increments of money have less and less effect on interest rates and eventually, in the liquidity trap situation, increases in the money supply have no effect on the interest rate.[2]

(c) Investment responds to changes in interest rates, but other factors are probably more important. 'New capital investment can only take place in excess of current capital disinvestment if *future* expenditure on consumption is expected to increase' (1936: 105). The 'state of confidence' is one of the major factors determining the expected return from investment (p. 149). Expectations 'play a dominant part' in the determination of investment and 'they are subject to sudden and violent changes' (p. 315).

The credit rationing effect

If the market for credit were unified, perfect and free, any difference between demand and supply at current rates of interest would be eliminated by a change in rates; they would rise (fall) to 'clear the market'. Moreover, a shortage (surplus) of credit in any part of the market would quickly spread to the rest of the market as borrowers (lenders) turned to other sources of credit (opportunities to lend). Finally, there would be a common rate of interest for all loans of given maturity and degree of risk.

In fact, the market is not unified, or perfect, and not all rates are perfectly flexible. Some important rates were not, until 1971 at least, determined by demand and supply but were fixed ('administered') by the lenders: some were 'sticky'; some still are because they change infrequently and so often bear little relation to the current state of demand and supply of funds. Rates on clearing bank loans, for example, were until September 1971 set at a fixed interval above bank rate, as were the rates charged and paid by the major finance houses until about the mid-1960s. (The building societies' borrowing and lending rates lag behind other rates.) The effect is that some of the most important credit institutions restrain lending by rationing rather than by price. Rationing is the normal method of allocating bank credit.

The consequence is shown in Fig. 12.1.

Suppose the supply curve of credit (in a free market) shifts from S_L to S'_L. With flexible interest rates, the charge for credit would rise from R_{L0} to R_{L1}, and the flow of credit would fall from L_0 to L_1. It is obvious that the decline would depend on the interest elasticity of the demand schedule for loans (D_L). But if the rate were fixed at R_{L0}, funds available would be L_2 only, and would have to be rationed out among the claimants.[3]

Two conclusions follow:

(a) Monetary policy may still be effective, even if expenditure is interest inelastic. However, it should be noted that the credit-availability mechanism operates

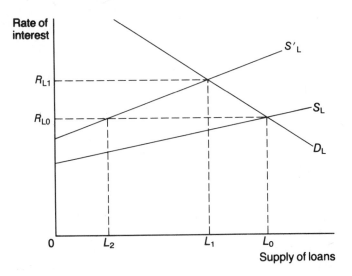

Source: Chick, 1979

Fig 12.1   The credit rationing effect

297

only in the case of a restrictive policy. Willingness to supply a bigger ration of credit will not increase the flow of credit unless there was previously an unsatisfied demand.

(b) Rationing leaves an 'unsatisfied fringe of borrowers'. If some lending institutions are not rationing credit, borrowers will turn to them, unless the market is completely segmented; that is, unless borrowers denied loans from one set of institutions cannot, or do not, seek other sources of funds.

As the Radcliffe Report stated in para. 319, 'There are, as it were, faults in the structure of the market which are difficult to cross, partly because of ignorance, custom or prejudice and partly because of the greater inconvenience or cost of using a different type of financial institution.' But these 'faults in the structure of the market' apparently were not particularly effective in restraining expenditure. Both lenders and borrowers are, it seems, prepared to switch at least part of their funds/ borrowing.

Credit rationing then works by maintaining an enforced disequilibrium between demand and supply in the market for finance. To be effective, it must cover the whole market, or the market must be segmented, or the rates charged in the unrationed sector must be intolerably high; this last restraint would be a cost-of-capital effect.

The locking-in effect

Stickiness of rates is an important feature of that particular cause of credit rationing known as the 'locking-in effect' or 'Roosa effect' (Roosa 1951). The Radcliffe Committee, although they doubted its efficiency and feasibility (see paras. 487 to 529 passim), thought it was the main effect of changes in interest rates; 'their chief influence lies in their repercussions on the behaviour of financial institutions' (para. 487). 'A rise in interest rates makes some less willing to lend because capital values (of assets) have fallen, and others because their own interest rate structure is sticky. A fall in rates, on the other hand, strengthens balance sheets and encourages lenders to see new business . . .' (para. 393).

The banks and other financial institutions could provide funds to lend by selling assets, in particular their holdings of bonds. A rise in interest rates dissuades them from doing so, for three reasons:

1 The rise in yields makes bonds a more attractive asset, as compared with loans, unless rates on loans are raised pari passu. That is the significance of stickiness of rates.

2 The sale of bonds at low prices brings capital losses (unless, of course, they had been bought at low prices) and weakens balance sheets; and any considerable sales would depress prices still further. Loan rates did rise with the penal rate, of course, and in this event losses could possibly be recouped in time. But suppose a bond standing at £80 showed a yield of 8%. A very small rise in the rate, to 8.5% would imply a fall in the price to £75.4. If it were sold to finance a loan at, say, 11% it would take $2\frac{1}{2}$ years to recoup the capital loss; and that assumes

that loan rates would not fall again within $2\frac{1}{2}$ years. Hence securities are 'locked into' the institutions.

3 The uncertainty about the future caused by deflationary policy also deters them from committing funds until stability is restored. Everybody – lenders, borrowers and spenders – becomes more cautious.[4]

In so far as the 'locking-in effect' operates, interest rates come back into the armoury of credit controls, influencing expenditure via their effect on lenders rather than on borrowers. There is, however, some doubt as to the validity or the strength of the locking-in effect.

Firstly, of the credit institutions whose operations are described earlier in this book, only the banks and building societies are intrinsically subject to the 'locking-in effect'. The building societies hold less than 10% of their assets in securities, only the longer dated of which will be seriously affected by changes in interest rates. The clearing banks hold their investments in *echelon*, and about one sixth mature each year, when they can be run off at their par values. Moreover, the capital loss to the banks, at least, is greatly reduced because they are recognised dealers in securities and can set off capital losses against taxes on profits. Many institutions – the finance houses, the merchant banks and foreign and overseas banks – keep only very small proportions of their resources in government securities. The insurance companies tend to expand their mortgage loans during a credit squeeze; the acceptance houses react by accepting bills of exchange; the finance houses lend deposits obtained from the public; the investment trusts switch out of bonds into equities; trade credit expands.

Secondly, if the higher rate were expected to hold permanently, and if the securities have a long life to maturity, the rational course would be to accept the capital loss if a better yield could be obtained on loans. However, any interest rate is, by the nature of things, temporary. The decision to sell or to hold therefore depends on interest rate expectations: what capital gain is to be expected on the present value, when it will appear, and how it compares with the expected differential in returns on the securities and loans in the interval. Meanwhile, there is still the possibility of lending by attracting more deposits from the public. The rise in interest rates which locks in assets is also an inducement to holders of idle balances to exchange them for the liabilities of financial institutions, who then activate them by lending to deficit spenders. How far the intermediaries can thus thwart a credit restriction, and to what extent they have done so, is a question to be considered later.

Thirdly, the lending institutions need to sell securities only in order to increase their lending. The Roosa effect will not actually *reduce* the flow of credit.

The evidence on the Roosa effect is mixed. Evidence from the Radcliffe Report suggested that it did not operate effectively in the 1950s. Chase (1967) looked at the security holdings of a group of New York banks through 1959 and concluded that they were reluctant to realise losses on bonds. But Tussing (1966) showed that US commercial bank holdings fell $13 billion and $10 billion respectively in the credit squeezes of 1954–56 and 1958–60, and rose $10 billion in the 1957–58 period of monetary ease. Entine (1964) showed that in the period 1954–62, the mutual savings associations and insurance companies sold more bonds and the savings and loan associations bought fewer bonds in periods of tight money than in periods of easy money. For the UK, Chant (1967) estimated that the banks lost £90 million in 1951–52 and £67 million in 1955–56 on the sales of gilt-edged stocks. They must have been willing to accept these losses. Econometric studies of commercial bank asset portfolios by Brechling and Clayton (1965) for the period 1951–63, and Sheppard (1971) for the periods 1920–39 and 1947–62, both support the view that a rise in the long-term rate of interest (the yield on consoles) induces banks to switch out of investments into advances. Parkin, Gray and Barrett (1970), on the other hand, in a study of London clearing bank portfolio behaviour, 1953–67, found that a rise in the rate on government bonds induced bigger holdings of them.

The portfolio balance version

The portfolio balance version of the transmission mechanism asserts that monetary policy operates via changes in the composition of asset holdings in response to changes in relative yields on assets. It describes in detail how and why these adjustments of portfolios occur and how and why they influence aggregate expenditure. There are differences of detail between different versions of the theory but, briefly, the transmission mechanism is as follows:

Money is just one of several assets, one form of 'capital'; hence the use of the term 'capital-theoretic' to describe portfolio theories of the demand for money. It has a place in portfolios because of its liquidity, the fact that it gives immediate command over goods and services.

Suppose all portfolios are in equilibrium; asset-holders are content with the composition of their portfolios at current relative yields. Then suppose an increase in the money supply via an open market operation. Once created, the money must be held in portfolios somewhere in the private sector. Some securities have disappeared into the central bank; and the commercial banks, with higher cash reserves, will probably have created some of their new deposits by buying bills and bonds. We now have a disequilibrium situation; the aggregate of portfolios contain 'too much money', given the prevailing yields on other assets.[5] The banks will also have increased their lending to the discount houses, to finance houses and local authorities and in the inter-bank market, and their overdrafts and advances. This increased flow of credit can be regarded as a portfolio adjustment by the banks, and their loans will have a direct and immediate impact on these other financial markets and on the markets for goods and services.

At this point we may recall from an earlier discussion (Ch. 9) that an increase in the money supply has both wealth and substitution effects on portfolios. The nature

300

of the wealth effect, how far it is a real balance effect and how far a valuation effect, and the comparative strengths of the wealth effect and the substitution effect, depend on the source of the increase in the quantity of money.

We now suppose that the banks' portfolios are in equilibrium once more, but those of the remainder of the private sector are 'long on money and short on other assets' in spite of the above-mentioned fall in some yields. So we get a 'ripple of adjustments' of portfolios through the bond and equity markets. Some of the excess money will no doubt flow into the financial intermediaries, to be on-lent by them.

For Tobin (1961, 1969), one of the leading members of the portfolio balance school, the rise in the prices of equities is crucial. An equity is a title to real assets, and he identifies a willingness to hold equities at lower yields as a willingness to hold existing real capital at lower returns. The value of any stock of capital is equal to the anticipated future return on it, discounted back to the present: reduce the rate of discount, and the present value rises. Once this value of real capital rises above the cost of producing new real capital, there is an incentive to invest. If existing assets, replaceable for £1 million, are valued at £1.25 million on the Stock Exchange, this is an inducement to invest.[6] Since a fall in the yields on existing equities means that new equities can be sold at lower prospective yields, an alternative way of describing the situation is to say that the cost of raising equity finance has fallen, and this encourages firms to raise new equity finance for investment. Tobin confines this part of his analysis to equities. He does not appear to consider the issue of new debt, since his argument proceeds from the concept of the equity-holder's willingness to hold real capital. A weakness of the analysis as he presents it is, of course, the assumption that the market price of a firm's equity is the market price of its real capital assets and that it is this 'excess price' of shares which motivates investment decisions. He takes no account of the effects of stock exchange speculation on share prices nor of the divorce of ownership from control of the firm.

The portfolio adjustments also extend to the goods market, raising the prices of existing goods and so inducing an increase in output. Equilibrium is restored when the supply of bonds and equities and their yields, real and income, and the price level have changed sufficiently to bring the demand for and supply of money back into equilibrium.

There is a rather complicated mechanism of feed-back on portfolios. For example, if there is a pronounced effect on investment and hence on the demand for finance, the price of loans and the yields on securities will rise, they will become more attractive as compared with real assets, and the readjustment of portfolios will attenuate the rise in the prices of real assets which was the initial stimulus to investment. This is additional to the feed-back effect on the demand for money caused by rising incomes. There will probably be a series of expansionary impulses and feed-backs producing a cyclical path to a new equilibrium.

Portfolio balance theory thus brings financial markets in general into the analysis. It is a stock model rather than a flow model; it is concerned with adjustments of stocks of assets rather than with flows of credit. However, it is difficult to see any real differences between the 'existing asset/new asset price' mechanism and the direct interest-rate effect of the Keynesian mechanism.

The monetarist version

The monetarist version of the transmission to the real sector of changes in the monetary sector is also a portfolio adjustment mechanism. Its peculiar features are:

1 Monetarist theory includes a particular specification of the demand for money. This is a function of several variables of which the rate of interest is only one. The interest elasticity of the demand for money is low. The main determinant is 'permanent income', which changes only slowly.

This has two implications:

Firstly, a change in the supply of money does not have an immediate significant effect on interest rates or on the demand for money. It simply leaves the economy with excess money balances. The effect on interest rates comes as the excess money causes portfolio adjustments which push up the prices of other assets. Since there is a wide variety of assets on which money is spent, the effect on the price of any one of them is probably small.

Secondly, any immediate impact of money on income will be on current income. But the current level of permanent income is a compound of current income and previous years' incomes which cannot be affected by current policy. A modest rise in current income would not eliminate the excess supply of money. Money therefore has a powerful effect on current income, and the velocity of circulation probably increases. This, coupled with the presumed small effect on interest rates because of the wide spread of portfolio adjustments, implies that expenditure is interest elastic. Later, as permanent income gradually rises, the demand for money increases and the measured velocity of circulation falls. Velocity is therefore not stable, but changes in a systematic way.

2 The monetarist portfolio includes, explicitly, real assets (the present value of future services of real assets) as well as financial assets. There are therefore two portfolio adjustment effects on the demand for goods and services. There are the usual wealth and substitution effects via a chain of repercussions through a variety of financial assets which finally impinges on expenditure by raising the prices of existing real assets and so making the production of new assets more profitable. But in addition, before or simultaneously with the rise in the prices of financial assets, portfolio adjustment will take the form of expenditure on real assets as well as on financial assets. The effect on real assets comes via implicit 'own interest' rates.

The main feed-back effect appears to be via changes in the price level and anticipated changes therein. Again, the path to a new equilibrium is cyclical.

The monetarist transmission mechanism is thus a portfolio adjustment mechanism. There is no mention of lending or borrowing, or the credit-availability effect.

The term structure of interest rates

Sympathetic changes in rates are to be expected in a fairly unified market when borrowers/lenders can switch easily from one course/use of funds to another: for example, finance by overdraft or by bills of exchange, holding a deposit at a bank, or a building society, or a finance house. In so far as the whole market for finance is fluid, changes in short-term rates will also 'spread to the long end of the market'. If short rates fall and long rates do not, some borrowers will switch from long-term to short-term loans and some lenders will switch funds from the short-term to the long-term market. Such movements increase supply and reduce demand at long-term, and vice versa in the short-term market, and these changes in demand/supply relationships will bring the two ends of the market into line.

However, the unity of the market as a whole is not nearly as complete as the internal unity of each of its parts. Lending/borrowing at long term is not nearly so close a substitute for any one form of short-term lending/borrowing as is another form of short-term lending/borrowing. Long-term rates are not so closely tied to short-term rates as is one short-term rate to others, and they react more slowly to changes in short-term rates.

There are several reasons for this. One is the 'segmentation' of the market by 'faults'. Short-term borrowing is rarely a safe substitute for long-term borrowing, and long-term borrowing is unnecessary for short-term projects. Many institutions try to match the maturities of their assets to those of their liabilities; previously, we have seen why. The banks have traditionally kept a minimum proportion of their portfolio in short-term assets and preferred short bonds; insurance companies and pension funds, on the other hand, are heavily weighted with long-term commitments and want both stable income and assured capital values at certain dates from a substantial proportion of their assets. Such institutions do not move easily between widely different maturities in response to changes in relative rates. 'Interest arbitrage', switching between assets to take advantage of changes in relative yields, costs time and money. It requires expert and continuous observation of the market to seize opportunities of profitable switching, and every switch costs a commission or a dealer's profit margin. Another reason, one would suppose, is that variations in relative supplies of different maturities can be expected to change relative rates; expectations influence the timing of issues of debt; and the effect of changes in supply may be reinforced by expectations concerning their effect.

Expectations are important. If the weight of opinion is that long-term rates are likely to remain stable, changes in short-term rates will have little or no effect on long-term rates. One theory asserts that the term structure of rates is determined entirely by expectations; the long-term rate is the average of expected short-term rates. It follows, therefore, that if short-term rates are expected to fall they will be lower. Especially if we couple this with the Keynesian concept of a 'normal' long-term rate do we see why, although long-term rates are usually higher than short-term because a long-term asset is less liquid and more subject to significant loss of capital value. Nevertheless, when interest rates in general are high (for example, at the top of a boom), short rates are likely to be higher than long rates, and short rates will fluctuate more widely than long rates. Another suggested explanation of these phenomena is that the short-term market is used for residual funds. Money is poured into this market when industry and trade are depressed and their financing requirements are low, and withdrawn from it in periods of high economic activity. Expectations theory also offers an explanation of inverse changes in short and long rates. If interest rates in general are expected to fall, there will be pressure to sell short-term assets and buy long-term, and vice versa, the more so because the effect on prices of a given change in yields is greater for long-term assets than for short-term.

One can criticise all the theories of the term structure of rates. For example, the market is not completely segmented; there are many asset-holders who bestride the markets and many arbitrageurs and dealers operating at the maturity margins. The strict expectations hypothesis assumes an unrealistic degree of uniformity and confidence in expectations, and ignores the hindrances to arbitrage. We can accept Keynes' assertion that the links between short-term and long-term rates are 'belated and imperfect'. Nevertheless, the evidence is that rates do tend to move in harmony, though not always simultaneously, and that changes in penal rates such as the now defunct MLR have some influence on rates in general.

The rationale of monetary policy

Monetary policy operates on its ultimate targets via changes in the quantity of money, changes in interest rates, and direct control of one or more forms of credit.

Suppose the objective is to control the level of money income (Ym); this is, in fact, the main general, persistent objective. If Ym were a unique function of some version of the quantity of money (M), any other influences on Ym being insignificant, then control of M would give control of Ym. This would be the position if the demand for money were a unique and perfectly stable function of money income, as Classical theory asserts.

If Ym were, on the other hand, a unique function of some interest rate, we could determine it if we could control that rate of interest. If that rate of interest were in turn a unique function of M, then again we could determine Y if we could determine M; the only difference from the first case would be that the effect of M on Ym would be indirect, via the interest rate. This would be the position if the demand for money were a stable and unique function of a particular rate of interest, and Ym were a stable and unique function of the same interest rate. The effect on Ym of a given change in M would depend on how low is the elasticity of the demand for money with respect to that interest rate as compared with the elasticity of the demand for goods and services.

In either of these two cases, the fact that the authorities may be able to control M, or interest rates, but not both, does not matter; we only need control of one. If the relevant interest rate were, or could be, determined by some means other than changes in the money supply, the operative monetary quantity (the intermediate target) would be that interest rate, not the money supply.

To be more realistic; if the demand for money is a function of other determinants as well as income and interest rates, and aggregate expenditure is a function of other determinants as well as M and/or one or more interest rates, we clearly lose any hope of precise control of Ym by monetary policy alone. It is possible that in this situation credit rationing may be a more effective instrument than traditional operations on M and interest rates; but credit rationing is an instrument of restriction only.

In fact, of course, nobody expects perfect and precise control by any policy or combination of policies. The simple Keynesian transmission mechanism proceeds via a long chain of repercussions and there is a weakness in every link. The generalised portfolio balance chain is longer still, running through a variety of financial markets before it affects expenditures on goods and services. There is no assurance that the M/Ym relationship will be very stable or predictable. The comparative strength claimed for the monetarist chain derives from their assertions that the demand for money is closely related to permanent income, rather than to interest rates; that although the latter relationship is weak, it is stable; and that portfolio adjustment includes a direct link between M and the goods market.

Targets and indicators of monetary policy

The instruments of monetary policy do not operate on their ultimate goals directly, but via the responses of economic decision-makers to certain intermediate variables such as interest rates or the supply of money or credit. There are several links in the chain of causation which runs from, say, a change in the central bank's discount rate to the level of employment; indeed, monetary instruments create repercussions in several different parts of the economy and, because the parts interlock, these cause further repercussions elsewhere, and there are many reciprocities. A web would be a better metaphor than a chain. Policy-makers can never be certain of the effects of manipulating any of the monetary instruments, for three reasons:

1 We do not know enough about the structure of the economy, the force and stability of responses to changes in monetary variables and the precise patterns, strengths and stability of the many reciprocal repercussions. There is, as we have seen, no universally accepted specification of the precise transmission mechanism.
2 The ultimate goals are subject to the (uncertain) effects of other policies – taxes and subsidies, controls on prices and wages, and so on – and to many influences other than government policy. And no policy, or combination of policies, can control them fully. Further, we cannot control responses to policy

in a free society, and in any case an open economy is influenced by events and policies in other countries.

3 The 'endogenous variables' on which the instruments operate respond for the most part to instrumental changes only after a lag. These lags differ from one instrument and one variable to another; for example, the response (if any) of the balance of payments to a change in interest rates is quick, the response (if any) of investment is slow. Moreover, the lags may be unstable, shorter at some times than at others. Because it takes time to collect and process statistics, there is a lag before the information from these observations becomes available. Signals arrive late; by the time action can be taken, it is overdue.

These problems have prompted the adoption of certain intermediate variables as *intermediate targets*, one stage or more back from the ultimate goals. Ideally, such a target will have the following characteristics:

1 It will be closely related, quantitatively, to the ultimate goal. A given value of the target variable will, ideally, be associated unequivocally with a given value for the ultimate goal. This reduces the uncertainty about the effect of policy.
2 To reduce the uncertainty arising from lags, the target should be quickly affected by one or more policy instruments, and should be observable easily, immediately and accurately.
3 It must, of course, be subject to control by monetary action. Monetary policy should be capable of reinforcing or offsetting any non-policy influence on the targets.

A rate of interest, or a selection of interest rates, appears at first sight to be a suitable intermediate target. It is immediately observable; it responds quickly to monetary pressure; and it may be presumed to affect income and output through various channels, the cost of capital effect, the valuation effect, the portfolio adjustment effect, and perhaps the availability of credit via some version of the Roosa effect. But all these effects are uncertain; there is no assurance that a given interest rate will achieve a given policy goal. And interest rates are subject to strong non-policy influences. Different rates are appropriate to different situations. That, in itself, is no barrier to the use of interest rates as the target; nobody would recommend rigid adherence to a fixed target: but it is difficult to know what is the appropriate rate at any particular time.

Further, the relevant rate for investment decisions may be the current or anticipated *real* rate of interest, and there is no knowing how this relates to the observable nominal rate, which is the one on which monetary policy operates, since we cannot observe expected changes in price levels. In an inflation, real rates may be falling when nominal rates are rising; we do not know what nominal rate produces a higher relevant real rate.

It is real rates which reward savers and lenders; it is real rates, and implicit rates at that, which measure the productivity of investment. But neither real rates nor implicit rates are observable; the only interest rates which can be incorporated into a working model of the economy and tested against available data are nominal rates, the rates charged and paid for the loan of money, and in the Friedman model, for example, nominal rates as such do not appear to have any influence on 'real' events. In fact, of course, nominal rates do influence expenditure if borrowers and lenders have different expectations about future prices. If borrowers expect a higher rate of inflation than do lenders, a given nominal rate will represent a lower prospective real rate to borrowers than to lenders, and this promotes borrowing-and-lending to spend.

Similar criticisms can be made of the choice of the money supply, or the rate of change in it, as the intermediate target. As we shall see later (Ch. 13) there is not a precise relationship between the quantity of money, or changes in it, and income. The authorities cannot determine the quantity of money precisely; they may be able to determine the supply of high-powered money (currency plus bank reserves), but this only sets an upper limit to the money supply, subject to the public's choice between cash and bank deposits. Further, the authorities cannot control the distribution of bank deposits between different kinds of account, and the effect on expenditure of a given total of bank deposits may depend on the distribution of that total between current and deposit accounts.

The dilemma of the authorities, faced with a choice between money and interest rates as targets, is illustrated by Fig. 12.2 (Poole 1970).

On Fig. 12.2, interest rates or the money supply will serve equally well as the target variable. The authorities can either fix the money supply to produce the curve

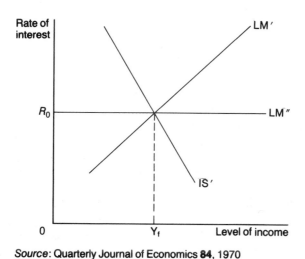

Source: Quarterly Journal of Economics **84**, 1970

Fig 12.2   Money or interest-rate targets

LM′, which intersects the IS curve at the desired level of income Y_f, or they can fix the rate of interest at R_0, and supply the quantity of money required at that rate.

However, the volatility of investment implies that the IS curve is not stable. It can be shown that if the demand for money is stable in interest rates and income, as the monetarists believe, so that the LM curve is also stable in the absence of action by the monetary authorities, a fixed rate of interest will produce bigger fluctuations in income. That is it will give less control over income than setting a money supply target (see Fig. 12.3).

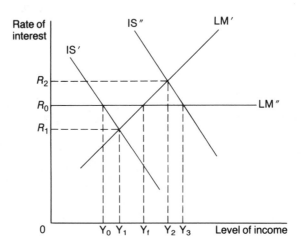

Source: Quarterly Journal of Economics **84**, 1970

Fig 12.3   Money or interest-rate targets: shifts in the IS curve

With a fixed LM curve LM′, a shift from IS′ to IS″ will raise income from Y_1 to Y_2, and the interest rate will rise from R_1 to R_2. But if the interest rate is held at R_0 and the money supply is increased to meet the demand for money at that rate (LM schedule LM″), income rises from Y_0 to Y_3. Now suppose, on the other hand, that the IS curve is stable, and it is the LM curve which shifts (see Fig. 12.4).

To hold the money supply constant in the face of a shift in the demand for money function, which has the effect of reducing demand at a given interest rate and level of income, will shift the LM curve from LM′ to LM‴, and income will rise from Y_1 to Y_2. To hold the interest rate constant at R_0 and allow the supply of money to adjust to demand (LM″) will hold income at Y_f. If both schedules are unstable, which target variables gives most control over the ultimate goal (taken to be the level of income) depends on which schedule is subject to the greater disturbance – that is, is least stable – and on the relative slopes of the two functions; in short, on investment and saving behaviour and the parameter of the demand for money.

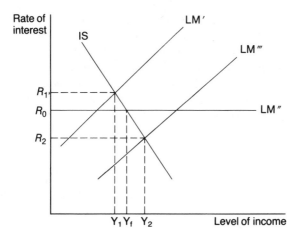

Source: Quarterly Journal of Economics **84**, 1970

Fig 12.4 Money or interest-rate targets: shifts in the LM curve

Perhaps bank advances and overdrafts would be a better target than the money supply; most of these are, after all, likely to be taken to finance expenditure on goods and services. This may be so, but in fact we do not know the exact relationship between overdrafts and spending. We know that a proportion go to 'the financial sector', most of which are likely to be used to finance holdings of securities. And bank advances are not the only source of credit; unsatisfied would-be borrowers from the banks can turn to other sources. The wider our definition of credit, the closer are we likely to come to the figure which is highly correlated with spending, but the more difficult does control become; and the tighter we draw the net, the greater the incentive for new institutions to spring up to evade the controls (see Ch. 13).

The conclusion to be drawn from the last few pages is that there is no perfect target. This being so, an eclectic policy, using a combination of targets, is probably the best. In practice, the authorities do not know the values of all the parameters which determine the position of the IS and LM curves, they do not know the quantitative relationships between changes in M and/or R and changes in Y, and they do not know whether any current change in R is due to a shift of the IS curve or the LM curve or both; and the parameters which determine IS and LM can change without warning, changing the levels of M and R which are consistent with the desired target level of Y. In short, the use of proximate targets probably adds little to the precision of monetary policy; its main value is that it shortens the information lag concerning the effects of monetary action (Ward 1973).

Since no target variable is likely to be uniquely related to the instrument variable, all are subject to changes other than those induced by policy actions; we also need *indicators* of monetary policy. The function of an indicator is to depict the effects of policy actions alone. The characteristics of an ideal indicator are, therefore:

1 It must be closely controllable by policy instruments.
2 Non-policy changes must not affect the indicators or, if they do, their effect must be small in comparison with the policy effect.
3 If the indicator always moves with the target, which in turn is affected by non-policy events, the indicator will not reveal the effect on the target of policy alone. It must, however, be related to the target and to the policy goals. It must be part of the transmission process.
4 Like the target variables, the indicator must be easily and immediately observable.

Indicators are, conceptually, quite distinct from targets. In practice the distinction is not so clear, and in the literature both terms are applied to the same monetary quantity; for example, the money supply, or interest rates. For example, with a single ultimate goal, full employment, and a simple 'structural hypothesis' that employment is a function only of aggregate expenditure, the latter could be the target variable, and the money supply or interest rates possible (if not very good) indicators. But denominating these latter variables as targets means that we must move nearer to the instrument of policy to find an indicator, and it can be difficult to find a measurable quantity which comes between the target and the instrument. Perhaps the rate on Treasury bills is one appropriate quantity; high-powered money is another.

The problem of lags

One of the major uncertainties in monetary policy relates to the time lag between the occurrence of the need for action and the effect of action on the ultimate targets. This lag has several parts, which are classified into 'inside lags' and 'outside lags'.'

There are two *inside lags*, each of which can be further sub-divided. First is the 'recognition lag', the time taken to decide that action is required. This is largely due, first, to the existence of an 'information lag'. The information which gives the authorities a picture of the state of the economy is statistical, and it takes time (at least a month, and in some cases a quarter or more) to collect and tabulate the statistics. The policy-makers are always working with out-of-date information; how serious an impediment this is depends, of course, on whether the situation is changing and, if so, how quickly. Second, the statistics may not all point in the same direction: for example, some sales may be rising and others falling, production may have risen a little but employment is still declining. Further, any short-run change of direction in a series of statistics may indicate the start of a new trend or may be only a hiccough in the trend. The policy-makers often need to see two, three or more successive sets of figures before they accept the need for action.

The second inside lag is the 'action lag', or 'implementation lag' or 'administrative lag'. This consists of the 'decision lag', the time taken to decide exactly what to do, and the 'action lag', the time taken to do it. The decision lag (if we keep it separate from the recognition lag) is probably short and, in the case of monetary policy, so too is the action lag. The monetary authority can change its stance on interest rates and the supply of money and/or credit from day to day. Changes in fiscal policy (that is, in government expenditure and taxation) take much longer to prepare and put into effect. This applies particularly to direct taxation; when changes in income tax are announced in the budget in March or early April, the effect on wage packets does not come until June. Changes in rates of indirect taxation can be made effective immediately, but frequent changes are impracticable because they would cause too much work and confusion in wholesale and retail pricing. The outside lag of fiscal policy, on the other hand, is shorter.

The *outside lag* is the period which elapses between the implementation of a policy change and the effect of that change on the ultimate targets of policy. It is the product of a number of delayed reactions. First there are various financial lags: for example, the lag of interest rates behind changes in the quantity of money, the time it takes banks and other financial institutions to adjust their portfolios, the lag in the response of the public's demand for money or for credit to a change in the rate of interest,[7] the lagged response of the new issue market to a change in interest rates and the general economic climate. These are sometimes termed the 'intermediate lag', the lag in the effects of policy on the intermediate targets such as interest rates or supply of money or credit. Next there are the lags in spending decisions by firms and households. Finally, there is the 'production lag', the time it takes for production to respond to changes in the intermediate targets and expenditure decisions and, clearly, this will vary from one industry to another.

The problem of lags is much more complex than would appear from the above brief description. Some of them, probably all the outside lags, are *distributed*: that is, the reaction is spread over a period; the effect of the policy action may then be cumulative, or it may reach a peak and then die away; the peak may come early or late in the process, or there may be more than one peak. In that case, how does one measure the lag? Is it the time taken to reach the peak effect, or to complete the effect, or to produce some percentage of the complete effect? The delay in response will vary from one intermediate variable to another (for example, short-term rates of interest are more flexible than long-term rates, the banks' rates are more flexible than, say, building society rates, less flexible than inter-bank rates) and from one ultimate target to another (for example, consumptions decisions and investment decisions, output of capital goods and output of consumer goods), according to technical conditions, the behavioural characteristics of the participants in the market concerned, the size of the response, and so on. And, of course, the lag in the response of any sector is likely to vary from time to time according to circumstance. The lengths of lags will vary with the form of monetary policy; for example, the lag in the effect of an increase in the quantity of money will depend on whether the increase comes by way of bigger advances to consumers or bigger advances to producers, and in which industries, by an open market operation, or as a result of a government deficit; and if the latter, it will depend on whether the money is paid out in pensions, or interest on the national debt, or on goods and services (of what kinds?) and so on. It also appears that, in the case of the USA at least, the length of the lag depends on the choice of the operative monetary variable: whether it is total bank reserves, the money base, or the money supply (which gives a short lag of four to five quarters) on the one hand, or unborrowed bank reserves (which gives a full-effect lag of $2\frac{1}{2}$ years) on the other.

Evidence on lags

Friedman and Schwartz, we remember, decided on the evidence of eighteen cycles that the outside lag alone is both long and variable, with peaks in the rate of change in the stock of money leading peaks in general business activity by about 16 months on average, but varying between 13 and 24 months, and troughs preceding troughs by about 12 months, but with a range from 5 to 21 months. Most other studies showed shorter and less variable lags than these. Mayer (1971: 332) tabulated the results of twelve studies in five countries: seven of them estimate lags lying between two and four quarters; another has a lag of six quarters for the maximum effect of a once-for-all increase in the interest rate. Kareken and Solow (1963) pointed out that it is a fact of statistics that if we regress the level of one variable on the change in another, the 'levels' always lag behind the 'first differences'. Regressing changes only, they find a much shorter average lag (one or two quarters) but very unstable; but their own methods and results were strongly criticised by Mayer (1971). They measured lags in investment only, of three different kinds, and only in one case (inventory investment) do they present a complete lag, which is in fact longer than Friedman's lag; so is their lag for producers' equipment. Kareken, and Solow also have an estimate of the inside lag, which varies from 0.5 to 10 months. Simulation exercises on the structural models also come up with long lags (for example, De Leeuw and Gramlich 1969). Single-equation studies and the reduced-form monetarist models, on the other hand, tend to show shorter lags: for example, Anderson and Jordan (1968) show the full effect achieved within a year, and according to Laffer and Ransom (1971) the whole effect comes within one quarter. Tanner (1969) said the full effect can occur within six months; Moroney and Mason (1971) found the peak effect occurring after six months, but the effects continue long after that.

Studies of the UK also tend to conclude that the outside lag is fairly short. Barrett and Walters (1966), Sheppard (1968), and Walters (1967) indicated that it is about six months, while Artis and Nobay (1969) put it at about nine months. Crockett (1970), on the other hand, detected a bi-modal lag, with one peak effect within three months and the other after about one year to fifteen months. However, on the whole there appears to be some room for optimism about the speed of operation of monetary policy, once action is taken.

Rules versus discretion
Lags in monetary policy create two different kinds of problem. The first is that if the lag is very long – say, two to three years – an expansionary monetary policy may still be having an impact, perhaps its major impact, on the economy at a time when

the underlying situation has changed completely and restriction is what is required; and vice versa. The second problem is that if the lag is unstable and unpredictable, timing becomes much more difficult and calculation of the effects little better than guesswork.

These problems among others led Friedman to propose that we should abandon any 'fine tuning' type of monetary policy and adopt instead a monetary rule, instructing the monetary authority to increase the money supply by a fixed percentage per annum, roughly equal to the projected growth rate of output capacity. This would avoid the need to forecast, inherent in discretionary policy, and the penalties for fallible judgment. It would itself have an automatic contra-cyclical effect: the money supply would increase faster than transactions demand in a recession, more slowly during an expansion. By enabling aggregate demand to grow at the same rate as aggregate output at full employment, it would maintain full employment at stable prices, or at gently rising or gently falling prices if we so wish, according to the chosen rate of increase of the money supply.

The theoretical basis of this proposal is, of course, that the rate of growth of income is closely related to the rate of growth of the money supply. One criticism is that this strong relationship is by no means firmly established. There are others: first, there is the practical difficulty that the monetary authority does not have firm and precise control of the quantity of money. Further, the monetary quantity which it can control most tightly is not necessarily the one which is the strongest link between the financial sector and the real sector. Second, the rule does not really avoid the problem of variable lags. Presumably the increase in the money supply in, say, a given quarter will have its impact on the real sector some time later; if this lag is variable, a smooth growth in the quantity of money will not have a smooth impact on the economy. Neither does it remove the need to forecast. We need to predict the rate of growth of capacity in order to determine the appropriate rate of growth of the money supply. Capacity and its rate of growth change over time with technical progress and changes in the supply of factors of production; these changes must be predicted and the rate of growth of money supply altered accordingly. Third, it is argued that events beyond the control of the monetary authority would still have destabilising effects. Destabilising changes in the real sector, such as shifts in the investment function, would still occur; and in the money sector, changes in the velocity of circulation would sometimes reinforce, sometimes offset, the change in the supply of money. Monetary equilibrium requires that the demand for money shall equal the supply, and a constant rate of growth of the money supply coupled with a demand for money which did not grow at a uniform rate would be destabilising.

Clearly, a basic difference between the monetarists and critics of the rule is that the former believe that the real sector is, in the main, stable; much of the fluctuation which has occurred has been caused by mistaken monetary action. This belief in turn implies that decision-makers in the private sector base their behaviour on *rational expectations* (see Ch. 11); that is, they have sufficient knowledge of the workings of the economic system, the several macro-economic interactions and reciprocities, to

313

judge correctly the consequences of random shocks and adjust optimally to them. They can, as Budd (1975: 59) has put it, '. . . recognise the equilibrium and the path to it . . . The appropriate role for Government is then to minimise the unpredictability of its actions (as would occur for example by following a monetary rule).'[8]

Some difficulties and defects of monetary policy

Control of the money supply

Control of the money supply is not perfect: it consists mainly of bank deposits, which are a function of the banks' reserves and the behavioural ratios which determine the deposit multiplier. One crucial component of bank reserves, cash ('high-powered money'), is, in turn, a function of flows of funds, some of which (the accumulation and repayment of public sector debt) are not determined by the monetary authority, and others (transactions in non-marketable debt and international flows of funds) which are, additionally, likely to respond to interest rate changes in the opposite way to that required. In principle, the authorities can neutralise any undesired flow of funds or creation of high-powered money from any of these sources. In practice, neutralising action is subject to inhibitions or constraints, to be discussed in later paragraphs. The control of bank reserves is weakened by the fact that the banks can acquire reserve assets from the discount houses or the public. The deposit multiplier is a function of leakages of reserves out of the banking system: none of these can be accurately predicted, and at least one of them – the drain of currency into non-bank holdings – has been responsible for significant variations in the ratio of deposits to high-powered money (see Ch. 13).

Money and credit

Control of the supply of money is not synonymous with control of the supply of finance or of credit:

1 Firms have access to supplies of finance from sources other than the banks and other intermediaries. They regularly finance a significant proportion of their investment from internal reserves. The situation appears, however, to be changing. The percentage of total funds, from all sources, generated internally fell from 77.6% in 1967 to 63.3% in 1974; the share coming from bank loans rose from 5% in 1966 to 34.8% in 1974; it fell back to *c*. 6% in 1975, but recovered sharply to 32% in 1976. In the subsequent period it has fallen from this figure to a level of 12.5% in 1979 and around 6% in 1983. Many of them also hold securities which they can sell to finance expenditure. They can raise external finance by new issues of shares and loan stock, or by the mortgage or sale-and-lease-back of property. All these alternative ways of raising funds become more expensive, of course, in times of monetary restraint; that is one

way in which rising interest rates exert whatever restraining influence they have. Furthermore, we must ask the question: what would have happened to these funds if firms had not acquired them? Only by activating idle balances, their own or other people's, and so increasing the velocity of circulation, do they offset the credit squeeze. If the money they obtain would otherwise have been spent, or loaned-and-spent, or invested-and-spent elsewhere, these alternative ways of raising funds do not increase aggregate expenditure; they only change its distribution.

2 The financial system is potentially flexible; it can increase the supply of credit on the basis of a given money supply. Banks can borrow from each other on the inter-bank market, firms can borrow from each other on the inter-company market, and thus put to use any spare balances. The banks can, and do, sell or run off investments to meet demands for overdrafts, within a given total of deposits. In 35 out of the 52 quarters 1959/II to 1972/II, for example, advances and investments changed inversely (Wadsworth 1971: 462–3).

The non-bank financial intermediaries can make the same kind of switch, but most of them hold only small quantities of marketable securities in excess of their minimum reserve requirements. They can also sell other assets to provide loans. The building societies are the exception: they held in 1983 some 13.8% of their assets in government securities, their interest rates are sticky, and they can also attract more deposits from the public by the offer of higher interest rates or by advertising. One would suppose, however, that what matters here is a rise in rates relative to those paid on deposit accounts at the banks, and most non-bank intermediaries seem to have changed their rates more or less in line with penal rates. It has been suggested that it is only as rates in general rise that deposit-holders become 'rate-conscious' and switch funds (Clayton 1962; Gaskin 1960). Advertising will contribute to this awareness of differentials. Again, whether or not these sources of funds offset the effect of monetary restraint on aggregate expenditure depends, of course, on the source of the money used to buy the bonds or lent to the intermediaries. If the money would otherwise have been spent, or lent direct to or invested with deficit spenders, there is no offset; if it is current saving, the borrowing or sale and on-lending of the funds acquired simply ensures that the savings are not hoarded; only if it would otherwise have been held idle is the operation expansionary, by activating idle money.

The ability of the intermediaries to thwart a restrictive monetary policy is, however, limited, for three reasons. First, as the intermediaries expand their operations they must attract ever more reluctant lenders, those whose elasticities of supply of deposits with respect to interest rates and/or persuasive advertising are comparatively low. There is, presumably, a limit to the funds which the public will wish to place with the intermediaries, a limit to the amount of idle money they can attract, and before that limit is reached the rates they have to pay on deposits may rise so high that they cannot find credit-worthy borrowers willing to pay the rates they must, in turn, charge on loans. Second, the credit restriction may well cause a reverse movement of funds, out of the intermediaries. People denied bank credit, or who find any credit too expensive, might withdraw deposits held with the intermediaries to finance their own spending. Third, as the lending-and-spending of intermediary funds raises incomes, bigger transactions balances will be needed and, in the circumstance of a constrained total supply of money, these can only come from idle balances.

The ease with which the financial intermediaries can attract funds depends first on whether bank deposits are complementary with, or substitutes for, the liabilities of other intermediaries. If they are complementary, the public will tend to hold the two kinds of asset in fairly constant proportions, and a reduction of bank deposits will induce the withdrawal of funds from the non-bank intermediaries. If they are substitutes, the ability of the intermediaries to attract bank deposits will, of course, be a function of the degree of substitutability.[9] The evidence both from the USA and the UK is that bank deposits are substitutes for intermediaries' liabilities rather than complements, but there is a conflict of evidence on the degree of substitutability. Lee (1966, 1967), Hamburger (1968), and Chetty (1969) find them closer substitutes than does Feige (1964, 1967, 1974).[10]

Barrett *et al.* (1975) estimate the demand for money by the personal sector with respect to the rates on a variety of non-money assets – special investment deposits at the TSBs, tax reserve certificates, deposits with building societies and HP finance houses, and three categories of National Savings assets – over the period 1957/IV to 1966/IV. With the possible exception of building society deposits, where the results were uncertain, the elasticities ranged from 0.01 to 0.4. Sheppard (1968) does not examine substitutability between money and other assets, but regressions between holdings of National Savings Bank, building society and Trustee Savings Bank liabilities show that households' relative preference 'are quite sensitive to the difference in the net of tax returns paid on such assets' (p. 104). Gibson (1967) found no simple relation between changes in interest-rate differentials and switching of funds between banks and intermediaries; choices within the non-bank sector appeared to be more sensitive to differentials. Townend's report (1972) of his study of personal holdings of current and deposit accounts with deposit banks, building society deposits, National Savings, and deposits with local authorities and finance companies says depositors were 'relatively sensitive to interest rates ...' (although 'investors may ... take up to two years to adjust fully to a new pattern of interest rates'). The elasticity of demand for current accounts with respect to the average rate on other assets was, however, only about 0.1, while that for deposit accounts with respect to bank rate was 1.0.

The evidence is that the intermediaries have not seriously thwarted monetary policy by lending more in periods of tight money. Timberlake (1964) found no evidence that money substitutes had grown faster than the quantity of money, or were better correlated with income, in the period 1897–1960. Melitz and Martin (1971) found that in the period February 1951 to June 1966, changes in high-powered money controlled M_3 (which included all savings deposits) as effectively as M_1 or M_2. Entine (1964) looked at monthly changes in the twelve-month moving averages of holdings of government debt by mutual savings banks, life insurance companies, and savings and loans associations over the years 1954–62. By varying their rates of sale/purchase of bonds they provided relatively more funds for borrowers in periods of tight money but 'the dollar magnitudes of change are small'.

It appears that the faster growth of the financial intermediaries, relative to that of the deposit banks, was a secular change, a change in asset-holding behaviour which has been variously ascribed to the growth of savings seeking a profitable use, an increasing respectability of borrowing on hire purchase, a greater willingness to enter into hire-purchase contracts as people became accustomed to continuous full employment, and an increasing awareness of these institutions both as borrowers and as lenders. If the intermediaries do persistently thwart monetary policy, one obvious answer is to bring them within the net of controls. The trouble is that such controls must be comprehensive. Specific controls on particular intermediaries would, as the Radcliffe Committee saw, encourage the growth of new institutions. And there is a danger that controls will dampen the initiative of the most enterprising institutions, who have done much to maintain London's position as a financial centre and earner of foreign exchange (around £4.6 billion in 1983).

Conclusion

This long discussion of the difficulties and weaknesses of monetary policy must not be taken to imply that monetary policy is useless. Unless one is prepared to follow one of the more extreme protagonists of one or other view, for or against monetary action, one must conclude that monetary policy can help to achieve the ultimate objectives of macro-economic policy, but it should not be expected to carry the whole burden; and we cannot be sure how big a burden it can carry. That is in the nature of things. The success of economic policy depends on the reaction to it of large numbers of people exercising free choice. The nature or direction of the overall response to any given act of policy frequently cannot be taken for granted, and the size of the response is never precisely predictable. Moreover, economic behaviour is influenced by many events other than government action. One could make the same comment on fiscal policy, or any other attempts to control the economy. There are analogous areas of doubt, ignorance and uncertainty in the appraisal of every branch of economic policy; every single one.

Notes

1 Obviously the deposit multiplier outlined in this chapter does not take account of either the non-bank financial intermediaries nor such sources of credit as the Eurocurrency market. For a full discussion of these, see Chick (1979: 21).

2 Of course, as we noted on page 192, the evidence does not fully support these 'regressive expectations'.

3 This diagram shows the difficulty of measuring the degree of credit rationing. Rationing is essentially a 'disequilibrium phenomenon'; if credit is cut off at L_2, the remainder of the S'L curve never becomes operational and we cannot, therefore, know that the equilibrium situation would have been a supply of OL_1 credit at a 'price' RL_1.

4 The Radcliffe Committee seemed to lay some emphasis on this aspect: see, for example, paragraphs 317 to 460.

5 Yields on the kinds of securities bought by the banks, however, will have fallen because the supply to the non-bank private sector has declined.

6 Keynes, incidentally, makes the same point on page 151 of the *General theory*.

7 Laidler (1973) has shown that the lagged response of the demand for money to a change in interest rates, prices and income speeds up the response of these latter variables to a change in the supply of money; their variation from their pre-action values is greater in the short run than in the longer run. Changes in these eventually, but not immediately, increase the demand for money to match a bigger supply, and as the demand for money increases, the effect of money supply changes on interest rates, money income and/or price gradually weakens.

8 It should be noted that some empirical tests have supported the Friedman rule. For example, Mayer (1971) demolishes Modigliani's claim (1964) to have established the superiority of discretionary policy. (See also the reference to Starleaf and Floyd in Chapter 10, page 230.)

9 See also the survey by Feige and Pearce (1974). There are two well-known metaphors used to typify the two situations. *Complementarity* means that the credit system is like a concertina; pressure on one part is transmitted to the whole. *Subsitutability* means that the system is like a balloon; squeeze one end and the other end expands.

10 Hamburger's study related to time deposits, while Feige was concerned with demand deposits.

CHAPTER THIRTEEN

Monetary policy in practice

Introduction

For twenty years up to 1951, there was virtually no direct control of the money supply; indeed, no active monetary policy at all. The Bank never had a set particular quantity of money as its target; the object of policy had rather been to maintain an 'appropriate' level of interest rates, and the occasion of a change in rates was usually an imbalance on the external account. Bank rate had always been the primary instrument of control, operating on the price of bank credit. Open market operations – that is, outright purchases and sales of securities – were really a post-1918 phenomenon. In June 1932, bank rate was reduced to 2%, where it remained until November 1951, except for a period of two months following the outbreak of war in 1939. Any constraint on bank deposits in the 1930s came not from a shortage of cash reserves but from a shortage of bills and a decline in the demand for advances. During the war, the orthodox relationship between bank cash and deposits was reversed: deposits determined cash. The 'backdoor' was never closed. Private expenditure was restrained by physical controls, allocations of essential raw materials and rationing, and the limit to deposits was set indirectly by these controls on spending and by appeals to the public to buy the government securities, marketable and non-marketable, issued to pay for the war. The banks were asked to curb advances, and commercial bill finance declined. Their place was taken by loans to the Government as the banks made obligatory purchases of Treasury deposit receipts and took up new issues of bonds.

During the 1950s and 1960s, fiscal policy assumed greater importance than monetary policy. Probably the main reason for this was the belief that changes in interest rates had little effect on investment or aggregate demand generally. Nevertheless, the authorities did try to excercise some control over liquidity, with the emphasis on direct controls on bank lending and hire purchase (Dow 1970; Croome and Johnson 1970; Cohen 1971; Chalmers 1974).

Liquidity and the Radcliffe approach

The 'locking-in effect' (see Ch. 12) was a particular manifestation of the concept of liquidity on which the Radcliffe Report laid great emphasis. They were highly sceptical of the current 'orthodox' theory of monetary policy, that it operates by reducing the supply of money created by the banks and by engineering changes in interest rates, thus deterring borrowers by making bank credit scarce and expensive. Firms denied bank credit can use internal finance or turn to other borrowers, and 'changes in interest rates only very exceptionally have direct effects on the level of demand' (paragraph 437). The essence of their theory is to be found in paragraphs 387–97.

They are at some pains to play down the importance of the quantity of money. 'Though we do not regard the quantity of money as an unimportant quantity, we view it as only part of the wider structure of liquidity in the economy.' 'The decision to spend . . . depends on liquidity in the broad sense, not upon immediate access to the money' (paragraphs 389, 390). It is on this 'whole liquidity position' that policy must operate. The banks are important 'not because they are "creators of money"' but because they are 'the biggest lenders at the shortest (most liquid) end of the range of credit markets' (paragraph 504).

Though 'liquidity' and 'the liquidity position' were never actually defined in the Report, except as the amount of money people think they can get hold of (paragraph 390), the analysis appears to proceed thus: Decisions to spend are 'the decisions that determine the level of total demand' (paragraph 389). The old Keynesian liquidity preference orthodoxy would say that the accompanying rise in the velocity of circulation (equals activation of idle balances) would be accompanied by a rise in interest rates which would gradually choke off the demand for loans. Not so, according to the Radcliffe Report, for two reasons. Firstly, because borrowing, and spending, is interest inelastic. Secondly, because interest rates 'will not, unaided, rise by much, because in a highly developed financial system . . . there are many highly liquid assets which are close substitutes for money, as good to hold and only inferior when the actual moment for a payment arrives' (paragraph 392). It can be assumed that the close substitutes they had in mind were the liabilities of lending institutions. Because they attract funds from a large number of primary lenders, they can offer quick and easy withdrawal facilities – i.e. liquidity – to any one lender. Their liabilities are therefore almost as liquid as, or close substitutes for, money itself. With such alternatives to money available, the demand for money as an asset becomes highly interest elastic; that is, only a small rise in interest rates is required to attract large flows of idle money to the intermediaries, who then activate it as they lend.

The authorities can operate on liquidity in three ways:

1 First, by variations in the quantity of money. These will affect maturity, since money is the most 'mature' of all assets. Second, they will have both a direct effect on financial strength, of which holdings of money are a part, and a valuation effect: the market values of securities change directly with the supply of money. Third, they determine 'easiness' (Newlyn 1971).
2 By manipulating interest. There are three methods, other than variations in the money supply, by which the authorities can influence interest rates:
(a) By their influence on interest-rate expectations. If the authorities let it be known that they wish to see interest rates rise, or fall, the very fact that they have power to influence the rate by other means will persuade the market to change its views about the appropriate current rate, and market rates will move in the desired direction.

(b)   By the manipulation of administered rates; namely, the old bank rate and minimum lending rate (MLR) and the rates closely associated with it.

(c)   Debt management. Net sales and purchases of debt affect the supply of money and the level of rates; 'funding' and 'disfunding' influence the structure of rates.

3   Credit restrictions have an 'announcement effect'. They create uncertainty about the future among borrowers, spenders and lenders. They affect 'the mood of the market'. And the Report said, 'it is perhaps the emergence of this uncertainty that is the main direct link between a tightening of credit and decisions to limit industrial investment' (paragraph 317; see also paragraph 470).

During these years, the operation of monetary policy, or more accurately debt management policy, was circumscribed by two main elements. The first was the Government's attitude to the bond market. It was during this period that the phrase 'leaning into the wind' was increasingly used to describe government involvement in the bond market. The second was the device of special deposits, which until quite recently has played a significant part in monetary policy, in a day-to-day sense.

The authorities' view of the bond market: 'Leaning into the wind'

The authorities' view of the bond market was dictated by the nature of the market itself. The bulk of the transactions are by the major holders, in particular institutions such as banks, insurance companies, pension funds, discount houses, and big firms putting reserves into gilt-edged temporarily. They want to be able to deal freely in large amounts without moving the market against them. Demand is strongly influenced by expectations. The institutions' overall investment policy includes matching the maturity structures of their assets to that of their liabilities; but in the short run, policy is decided largely by expectations of capital gain or loss. They tend to have 'short horizons'; that is, they look to prices in the near and medium-term future rather than the prospects of long-term capital gains; expectations are extrapolative, inducing perverse reactions to changes in prices.

There is also frequently a 'consensus of opinion' in the market, giving a preponderance either of buyers, or of sellers, so that a fall in prices can quickly develop into a demoralising landslide, particularly since, in an active market with single deals often running into millions of pounds, the jobbers' resources cannot cope with large-scale fluctuations. A rise in prices may equally go too far and end in an abrupt and damaging reaction.

Tactics in the gilt-edged market

1   New stocks were issued in maturities tailored to meet the current demands of large investors. Some buyers would want to pay for the new issue by selling

holdings of existing stock to the jobbers, and thus switch from shorter to longer maturities. The Bank would help by taking up the shorter stocks from the jobbers. If, on the other hand, holders of debt wanted to shorten their holdings by switching from longs to shorts, the authorities would not help unless the jobbers could not take all the stock being offered, and then only at prices which reflected the disadvantage for the authorities of switches of this type.

2 The practice, begun in the 1930s, of buying in maturing issues in the months before maturity also helped holders to switch out of short maturities into the new tap stock.

3 If the authorities wanted stability of rates, they could not force stock onto an unwilling market. Standing ready to buy or sell at any time, they supplied stocks wanted by the jobbers and relieved them of surplus stocks: they acted as 'the jobbers' jobber'. They could influence prices in the market by the prices at which the Government broker was instructed to deal when asked; his prices indicated whether or not the authorities wanted a change in current market prices. They believed that the alternative method of active intervention to move rates up or down 'would strike investors as being more arbitrary and capricious and would therefore make them reluctant to commit themselves to the same extent in the gilt edged market' (*BEQB*, June 1966: 143).

In setting the prices to be charged/offered by their broker they followed, generally speaking, a policy of 'leaning into the wind', buying when the market in general was selling and vice versa, and in this way they restrained any tendency for prices to move sharply up or down. The objective of 'leaning into the wind' was not to impede a general trend in rates, *unless* that trend was thought to be inappropriate to general economic conditions at the time, but rather to retard any sharp day-to-day movements or to moderate 'the more exaggerated day to day fluctuations that occur when markets are thin or nervous' (Ibid: 148). The authorities did on occasion intervene more positively in the market as, for example, in 1957–59.

The generally passive attitude on purchases and sales of stocks meant that funding tended to coincide with falling yields: for example, 1952–54, late 1956 to early 1957, 1961–62, 1966–67 and 1970. In most of these years funding allowed the Treasury to borrow less at short term and reduced the supply of Treasury bills; commentators at the time spoke of shortages of Treasury bills and tightening of bank liquidity. The authorities' view was that sales were more likely on a rising market, when buyers expected a fall in yields and so hoped for capital gains. It also meant that funding usually occurred when general monetary and fiscal policy was either expansionary or neutral.

There were some exceptions to the practice of selling only on a rising market. The departments were buying in stock in late 1954, when prices were rising; they sold stock on a falling market in the two middle quarters of 1955 (£216 million), in the first half of 1956 (£83 million) and in the last quarter of 1967 (£297 million), and bought in the last quarter of 1958 and the first quarter of 1959, when prices were rising slightly. However, Goodhart (1972: 465–6) tested the operation of the 'leaning to the wind' policy over the years 1953–66 and found a small $R^2(=0.27)$ but significant inverse correlation between quarterly sales of stock and changes in the yield on $2\frac{1}{2}\%$ consols.

Operations in the short-term market

The authorities again wanted an orderly market for two reasons:

1 The Treasury depends on the money market for its day-to-day finance by the sale of Treasury bills at weekly tender; the discount houses cover the tender and their purchases are financed by call money from the banks. The discount houses also sell Treasury bills to the banks on most days, and rates which fluctuate widely from day to day would impose on them unpredictable and unwarranted capital gains and losses on their short-term holdings of bills. Relative stability of rates is one way of ensuring that the discount houses remain willing to cover the tender.
2 As the Radcliffe Report (paragraph 583) put it: 'The authorities have feared that irregularities in bill rates would spread through to the short end and then to the long end of the bond market with undesirable repercussions in confidence in the bond market, impeding the authorities' funding programme.'

Loss of control of the money supply

This concern for short-term stability in the two markets meant that the authorities had little or no control over the supply of money by orthodox means. The traditional instruments of control were bank rate and open market operations, operating in conjunction on the cash ratio and liquidity ratio of the banks. To enforce a reduction in bank cash, the Bank must sell bills or bonds to the non-bank public. Other things being equal, they can only be persuaded to hold more non-money assets by the offer of higher yields. The authorities can only control the distribution of public debt between bank and non-bank holders (except by decree) by setting interest rates free: they cannot determine both interest rates and the quantity of money. Moreover, the banks were so well supplied with liquid assets – particularly with 'reserve liquid assets' in the shape of bonds held in *echelon* – that it would have required a large rise in interest rates to shift enough of these assets into the hands of the non-bank public to put pressure on the banks. This freedom, or manipulation, of interest rates was, as we have seen, a policy the authorities were not prepared to accept. And, in view of the supposed nature of the gilt-edged market, such a policy would probably not have succeeded. They believed, rightly or wrongly, that short-term stability of rates was necessary both to maintain an assured market for Treasury bills to achieve their longer-term aim of funding the debt and attracting firm holders of debt other than the banks, and these aims were given priority over control of the banks' cash reserves. Therefore no attempt was made to use the cash ratio for this purpose of controlling the cost and availability of bank credit.

It was in these circumstances that the liquidity ratio, rather than the cash ratio, became the supposed fulcrum of control. Day-to-day operations in the money market were used to determine short-term interest rates, not the supply of cash; that was supplied as necessary to meet the 8% cash/deposit ratio. 'Cash and Treasury bills have come to be practically interchangeable and . . . the supply of Treasury bills and not the supply of cash has come to be the effective regulatory base of the domestic banking system' (Radcliffe Report, paragraph 583).

The authorities themselves appear to have had little faith, in the 1950s at any rate, in the prospects of squeezing the banks' liquidity: they were afraid of the consequences, that is 'irregularities in bill rates', and 'considered the market in Treasury bills as narrowly limited' (Ibid.). In any case, the conventional liquidity ratio was not a true measure of the banks' liquidity to starve them of conventional liquid assets. As noted earlier, their investments are a reserve of liquidity; it is their total holdings of government debt, of all kinds, which largely determined their liquidity and the evidence of liquidity pressure was a 'sign of unwillingness . . . to reduce further their holdings of gilt-edged . . . ' (Ibid.). They have at times used their investment to maintain the liquidity ratio. In the financial year 1968–69, for example, they reduced their bond holdings by £141 million to maintain their liquidity ratio.

By March 1971, the Bank was admitting that neither the liquid assets ratio nor the bank rate were reliable for regulating the expansion of the clearing banks' lending. Bank rate gave them control over many short-term rates. But not only did rates in the increasingly important parallel market break loose from the bank rate in the 1960s, in the long-term market they had only the control achieved by 'leaning into the wind', and that, in the Bank's view, was tenuous.

Moreover, 'leaning into the wind' also meant some loss of control over the effects on the money supply of the balance on external account. A rise in interest rates, undertaken as part of a restrictive policy, will, other things being equal, attract funds from abroad which are converted into sterling and lent or spent, thus increasing the domestic money supply, contrary to the restrictive measures. The EEA mechanism can neutralise this effect, but it involves the sale of bonds or bills to the non-bank public (see pages 294–300). Since large sales will raise interest rates, a policy of day-to-day stabilisation of rates inhibits action to counteract the inflow of funds. Press comment in the later 1960s spoke of 'the controls being overwhelmed' by the inflow of borrowed funds. Conversely, an outflow of funds reduces the domestic money supply and this should, after a lag, raise the interest rates which attract funds to London. But this would 'disturb' the gilt-edged market, which is likely to be weak anyway as foreign investors withdrew funds from it. A policy of 'leaning into the wind' means that the authorities must step in to support the market by buying gilt-edged, which both stops the rise in yields and pumps cash into the banks. An example of this occurred in the currency crisis in the second half of November 1968; there was heavy selling of gilt-edged and the authorities stepped in to 'steady the market until the outlook was a little clearer' (*BEQB*, March 1969: 15).

Special deposits

A special deposit is 'a compulsory deposit by a bank with the Bank of England additional to any bankers' deposit which it might normally hold there as part of its reserves'. In 1958 when, for the first time since the war, all monetary restraints were relaxed, it was announced that the Bank of England would from time to time, and with the approval of the Chancellor of the Exchequer, call for such special deposits from the London clearing banks and Scottish banks, the call being expressed as a percentage of each bank's gross deposits. The calls would be announced on Thursdays, at the same time as bank rate. Special deposits would not count as part of the bank's cash or liquidity ratio, but they would carry interest at the Treasury bill rate. They are created by transfer from bankers' deposits to a special account. The first impact of a call is therefore on the bank's cash reserve. Special deposits could, therefore, be a method of depriving the banks of cash alternative to open market operations. Their advantage over such operations could be that the consequent squeeze on deposits would be effected without the rise in interest rates associated with a large open market sale. A reduction in the money supply (deposits) would also, of course, be expected to raise the interest rates; but the effect would be more gradual, and the immediate effect would not be concentrated on the Treasury bills and/or gilt-edged market. However, the Bank of England said in its evidence to the Radcliffe Committee that special deposits would not be used to deprive the banks of cash, 'the cash required by the banks to make the deposits will be provided by the Bank . . . normally by the purchase of Treasury bills', or very short bonds, from the banks (*Memorandum of Evidence* Vol 1: 41).

The reason for thus planning to use special deposits as a means of squeezing the liquidity ratio rather than the cash ratio was, apparently, that the authorities accepted the mistaken thesis that it was the liquidity ratio, not the cash ratio, which was the basis of monetary control.

The Bank of England could take up Treasury bills in one or both of two ways:

1 A reduction in the cash ratio was also a reduction in the liquidity ratio. A bank's normal first reaction to a shortage of cash is to run off liquid assets by calling in loans to the discount market and perhaps running off Treasury bills. The Bank could take up bills being unloaded by the banks or by the discount houses in order to meet calls from the bank.
2 It could take up tap bills, thus allowing a reduction in the number of bills offered at the weekly tender. There would then be an excess of maturing bills over new bills. Both methods replace the cash lost in special deposits. Since special deposits were not liquid assets, the net effect of a call for special

deposits and the provision of cash by the bank to meet the call was to change the pressure on the cash ratio into pressure on the liquidity ratio.

The banks could react to a call for special deposits in one or two ways. One response would be to reduce their non-liquid assets, and deposits, to conform to their new holdings of liquid assets. This would be a co-operative or obedient reaction to the call: but it would not be a profit-maximising reaction. Alternatively, the banks could avoid a reduction in their deposits by switching from advances and investments to liquid assets. They could call in or run off loans, which would be repaid with cheques on bank deposit, and buy bills with deposits newly created for the purpose. They could sell investments, which would be paid for with cheques on deposits, and buy bills. They could run off investments (for cash) and so finance more Treasury bill purchases via the discount market.

Clearly, the authorities would prefer them to react in the first way. But a large sale of gilt-edged by the banks would have the same effect on gilt-edged prices as a funding operation, an effect which the special deposit scheme was presumably intended to avoid. The authorities' intention was that the banks should react by reducing advances; the Chancellor said, when the first call was made in April 1960, that special deposits were an alternative to requests to the banks to limit their lending. A tighter rationing of overdrafts would not affect gilt-edged prices in the same direct way. However, some deficit spenders, denied a bank loan, would get the funds they wanted by selling gilt-edged out of their own portfolios. Limiting overdrafts tends to raise interest rates generally by putting pressure on other sources of funds.

Special deposits came into operation in April 1960, with a call on the London clearing banks equal to 1% of their gross deposits and a call on the Scottish banks equal to $\frac{1}{2}$% of their gross deposits. Further calls of 1% were made in June 1960 and July 1961. The next calls, again at 1 and $\frac{1}{2}$% of gross deposits, came in April 1965 and July 1966. In May 1970, the totals of special deposits were raised to $2\frac{1}{2}$ and $1\frac{1}{4}$% and in November to $3\frac{1}{2}$ and $1\frac{3}{4}$%, at which level they remained until the new measures of monetary control were brought into operation in September 1971.

The 1960 call achieved very little. The growth of advances slowed down a little, but was £347 million over the year to March 1961, from 44.3% of deposits to 48.2%; investments fell £294 million. The authorities were not prepared to see interest rates rise, hence there was no penalty on sales of bonds. The later calls, except that of 1970, were followed by falls in the level of advances to the private sector, £118 million in the second half of 1965, £320 million in the second half of 1966, and £121 million in the last quarter of 1970; but we do not know, of course, how far, if at all, these were due to this particular one or all the determinants of the volume of bank credit. What we do know is that the authorities never relied on special deposits alone. Every call was combined with one or more other elements of a package deal, for example: rises in bank rate in 1960, 1961 and 1966; a tightening of hire purchase controls in 1960, 1965 and 1966. Further, throughout this period, except for a few months in 1967, requests to restrict lending to the private sector, or ceilings on advances, were in operation. And on at least two occasions, in 1961 and 1965, the banks were specifically asked that the call should be reflected in their advances. The fact that such requests were necessary reveals the weakness of special deposits or, rather, the flaw in the particular technique employed. If calls for special deposits were used to deprive the banks of irreplaceable cash instead of replaceable liquid assets, they could be used to enforce a multiple contraction of deposits. If at the same time interest rates were allowed to rise, or if the authorities intervened to push interest rates up, capital losses might possibly deter the banks from selling investment and the major part of the contraction might fall or advance.

Neither was the new weapon used flexibly enough to be comparable with open market operations. The first calls remained in operation for two years and the Bank held special deposits continuously from April 1965 to September 1971. The percentages held remained unchanged for three years after the Chancellor's announcement in April 1967 that, in future, special deposits would be used more flexibly.

As so often happens, studies of the data give different results. Crouch's thesis (1970) is that the banks will buy Treasury bills from the public (either directly or through the discount houses putting in higher bids at the tender, leaving fewer bills for the public) in exchange for deposits. Deposits and liquid assets both increase and the banks can, if the 'back door' is open, get more cash by surrendering some of their newly acquired Treasury bills. If the back door is closed, they exchange non-liquid assets. Looking at the data for 1960–62, he noted 'a positive ... relationship between special deposits and liquid assets' and 'when special deposits were being increased, bank deposits increased uninterruptedly too'. The figures for 1965–66 and 1970 apear to tell a similar story. Norton (1969) found no correlation whatever between advances and special deposits up to 1966, and concluded that special deposits had no effect on the quantity of money or expenditure. He also found that when the banks were selling investments in response to calls, the non-bank private sector was also selling; hence the public sector must have been buying. Gibson (1964) comes to the same conclusion as Norton as to the ineffectiveness of special deposits. Nobay's (1974) study of monetary policy, 1959–69, on the other hand, gave results which indicated that the authorities reinforced calls for special deposits by undertaking net open market sales, and it was the non-bank private sector which absorbed bonds sold by the banks, thus reducing deposits. Parkin, Gray and Barratt's study (1970: 245) concludes that a '£1 million increase in special deposits leads to a decrease in the banks' holdings of government loans of £1.3 million and an increase in call loans of 0.3 million'. Incidentally, they also concluded that variable reserve ratios would have a similar effect; a £1 million increase in required reserves would be met simply by a reduction of £1 million in their holdings of government securities.

Official views on the money supply

The authorities' own attitude to the money supply, and to monetary policy, over this period is not clear. In evidence to the Radcliffe Committee, the Bank wrote: 'The basic need remains the ability to regulate the total quantity of currency and bank deposits. Monetary measurements will, in the long run, only be effective if government policy as a whole is directed to keeping the money supply under control' (*Memorandum of Evidence*, Vol 1: 36). But a Treasury witness implied that the size of advances (credit) is more important than the size of deposits (money): (Q:1591): 'And your view was that the sales of investments must be thought of as primarily extinguishing idle deposits whereas the advances they substituted were actively used? (Ans): 'That was the diagnosis.' Even at the end of this period, when they were already changing their policies on gilt-edged prices and the money supply, the Governor of the Bank said 'The liabilities of the banks have always been significant for policy, of course, since deposits are a key factor in the determination of advances'; and on monetary policy, 'while we are keeping a close watch on developments in the monetary aggregate, we are looking at them as guidelines rather than as targets . . .' (*BEQB*, March 1971: 42, 43 and 44).[1]

Whatever the official view may have been, with the exception of the years 1956 and 1957, it was never the declared objective to operate directly on the supply of money. In his 1956 Budget, the Chancellor raised interest rates on National Savings, with a 'new objective': 'The financial critics tell me that I must reduce bank deposits and the floating debt if I am to reduce the money supply. Very well. Let us see bank deposits turned into National Savings . . .' In September 1957, when bank rate was raised to 7%, the highest rate since 1921, the Chancellor said that this and other increases would strike at 'the root of any inflation – namely the supply of money' and 'there can be no remedy for inflation . . . which does not include, and indeed is not founded upon, the control of the money supply . . .' Yet the money supply rose £250 million in the year to September 1958, much the same as in the previous two years. Thereafter, there appears to have been no official public mention of the money supply for a decade.

They did, however, pursue an active monetary policy throughout the period. There were occasions when all or most of the burden of adjustment was carried by monetary measures. In general, however, monetary policy was, for internal purposes, employed as an adjunct to fiscal policy.

But it was not an 'orthodox' monetary policy. Throughout these two decades, the banks were subject to minimum ratios of cash and liquid assets to deposits, the Bank was active in both the money market and the gilt-edged market, and bank rate was changed forty times. But the object was not to change the money supply – the authorities 'broadly accommodated the rising demand for money balances as incomes rose' (*BEQB*, March 1971: 43) – but to change interest rates and to use bank rate as a psychological weapon. More often than not, changes in bank rate and other monetary measures were used not for domestic reasons alone, the maintenance of full employment without inflation, but for external reasons alone, or for a mixture of domestic and external reasons. On several occasions – February 1955, February 1957, March and May 1958, October/December 1960, October 1961, September 1968, March 1970 – bank rate was reduced to bring it into line with rates overseas, or because of the continued strength of sterling, or (as in March 1970) to stop the inflow of 'hot' money (that is, money which could just as easily flow out again), but the reduction was accompanied by a warning from the Chancellor that this did not imply that there would be any easing of monetary restraints.

The target of monetary policy in this period was not, then, the supply of money, but the cost and availability of credit, especially bank and hire purchase credit, and its indicator was the level of bank advances. The authorities' concern was with bank lending rather than bank deposits. Bank rate determined the cost of bank credit; to control availability, as opposed to cost, the authorities brought into play a number of direct controls. Changes in bank rate were almost invariably accompanied by, or shortly preceded or followed by, the application of these direct controls, and usually some fiscal measure also, in what became known as 'a package deal'. Halfway through this period, in 1959, came the Radcliffe Report. Its analysis and conclusions were for the most part, it appears, in accord with official thinking at the time: it stressed the importance of the flow of credit, as opposed to the supply of money. However, it argued that in the long run the flow of credit could be controlled by variations in interest rates; it regarded the battery of direct controls, which were used continuously, especially in the 1960s, as instruments more suited to an emergency.

Was policy successful?

It is really impossible to say how effective monetary policy was in this period, because it never operated in isolation; monetary changes were nearly always combined with fiscal policy. Economic policy as a whole was not particularly successful in these twenty years. Fiscal policy tended to be destabilising rather than stabilising and only one of the objectives of economic policy, full employment, was achieved with any consistency. The same point applies even more forcibly, of course, to an attempt to assess the effect of any one instrument of control. Even the effect on one category of expenditure or other target is not 'pure': expenditure on consumer durables, for example, will be affected by changes in indirect tax and other determinants of relative price, by competition from imports, and so on. The demand for bank loans might have been curbed by higher interest rates or by administrative controls, or by the non-quantifiable effect of changes in expectations about future costs, prices, market opportunities, etc. Nevertheless, there is some evidence, of a *post hoc propter hoc* nature, that some changes in the target variables were at least partly a consequence of particular acts of policy, although we cannot say how far policy was responsible for these changes.

However, on one thing there can be little doubt, namely that debt management policy failed, probably because it tried to pursue incompatible ends. Sustained funding was incompatible with sustained support of the bond market. It was therefore not surprising that the authorities found themselves buying bonds at times when they were following a restrictive policy and, as part of that policy, wished to sell bonds. They succeeded neither in controlling bank lending by funding nor, in the long run, in funding. With 27% of the non-floating debt held outside the public sector having a life of 5 years or less, 23% in the 5 to 15 years bracket, and 50% over 15 years, the average maturity of bonds was shorter in 1971 than in 1951.

Competition and Credit Control

From 16 September 1971, the methods of control of the banks and the conduct of monetary policy changed radically. The details of proposed changes were set out in a consultative document, 'Competition and Credit Control', issued on 14 May and discussed with the banks, and published in *BEQB*, June 1971.

The essential changes from the methods of control currently operating were:

1 Greater freedom of competition between monetary institutions, especially in the determination of their interest rates.
2 The extension of controls to all the banks, the discount houses and major finance houses.
3 A change from controls on bank lending to more emphasis on 'the broader monetary aggregates'.
4 A change from direct quantitative controls to reliance on the market mechanism: 'what we have in mind is a system under which the allocation of credit is primarily determined by its cost . . .' (*Munich Address*: 196).

The background

The reasons for the proposed changes were:

1 Dissatisfaction with the results of current methods of monetary control, in particular the direct controls on the clearing banks. The minimum cash and liquidity ratios, and special deposits, applied only to the clearing banks and were therefore a discriminatory control. Until 1970, limits on advances restricted competition between banks; the inefficient were protected against the efficient. They diverted demand for credit to other sources, as the Radcliffe Report said they would. This diversion of borrowers to other sources of credit meant that the authorities did not control the total supply of credit. Finally, money and credit are not synonymous, and control of the supply of credit is not control of supply of money; deposits are created by net payments from the public to the private sector and by the bank purchases of bonds from the non-bank private sector, as well as by lending.
2 A gradual change of opinion away from the Radcliffe concept of money as *only one* of a variety of liquid assets whose totality is the significant quanitity in the determination of expenditure, towards the view that some concept of the supply of money is a proper target of monetary policy. As we saw earlier, official acceptance of the new view was not wholehearted: nevertheless 'the conclusion had been reached that the Bank's operation in the gilt-edged market should pay

more regard to their quantitative effects on the monetary aggregates and less regard to the behaviour of interest rates' (*Sykes Memorial Lecture*: 477).

3 Growing criticism of the state of competition in the financial system. This had two aspects, one relating to competition between the clearing banks and the other to competition between the clearing banks and other financial intermediaries. The first was concerned chiefly with the clearing banks' cartel and their arrangements with the discount market. It was argued that the cartel fixed common prices (that is, rates paid and charged), and this allowed the clearing banks to restrict output (deposits) and raise prices. It restricted competition between the inefficient and the efficient. The practice of not paying interest on current accounts and not charging the true cost of administering them meant that the use of these accounts probably diverged from the social optimum. It encouraged an excessive use of current accounts, and those who used them intensively gained at the expense of those who did not. Instead of price competition there was competition by a proliferation of branches and the provision of ancillary services free or at a below-cost price. Customers might prefer cheaper banking, but they were not given a choice. The limits set on the rates charged for loans necessitated discriminatory non-price rationing of advances. The Treasury bill tender convention – that the banks did not bid – reduced competition for Treasury bills, and probably meant that rates were higher than they would otherwise be; the Treasury loses, the banks lose because call-money earns less than the bills it is used to purchase, and the discount houses benefit.

Cartelisation also inhibited competition between clearing banks and other financial intermediaries. The clearing banks did not offer the same variety of maturities and terms of deposits as their rivals. Ceilings on advances and administered interest rates restricted competition with other lenders. It was also pointed out that controls on the banks put them at a disadvantage in comparison with other lenders. The banks were obliged to keep a minimum proportion of their assets in non-earning cash and low-yielding liquid assets and special deposits. Similarly, ceilings on advances, their most profitable asset, compelled them to hold a higher proportion of their assets than they might wish in lower-yielding bonds.[2] All these restraints, since they were not applied to other institutions, were a discriminatory tax on the clearing banks.

The banks, and others, made several rejoinders to these criticisms. The price and supply of bank credit were fixed not by oligopolist bankers but by the authorities, who set the bank rate which determined the banks' rates and limited the supply of credit from the banks either by open market operations or by direct controls. The clearing banks could not compete freely with other intermediaries until these discriminatory controls were either removed or extended to the rest.

In spite of the minimum cash and liquidity ratios, their prices for credit were lower, not higher, than those in the competitive market. The rates agreement on advances applied only to minimum rates, those charged to 'blue chip' borrowers;

331

charges to other borrowers were negotiable. If the banks were to compete for deposits, at a variety of terms, it would be by offering higher interest rates; they would then have to offer similar rates on the deposits they managed to attract already. Inevitably, they would have to charge more for loans. The banks made proposals for more freedom of rates in 1963, but they were rejected by the Chancellor on the grounds that they would make credit for industry and commerce more expensive. Moreover, rates competitive with 'the market' would not only be higher; they would also be more widely and freely fluctuating rates, both on deposits and advances. To pay higher rates on deposits, they would have to take on more profitable lending. It would also be riskier lending, and the deposit banks' emphasis on safe, self-liquidating loans is a measure of their recognition that their first duty is to depositors; other kinds of lending are best left to other institutions. The banks had shown both their willingness to compete and their adherence to the principles of sound deposit banking by selling up or buying into subsidiary merchant banks, finance houses, and leasing and factoring companies, to provide higher-risk credit. They were all offering medium-term loans of various kinds: for example, personal loans, loans to finance exports and for home improvement, and accepting some large deposits for differing periods at differing interest rates. They operated in some parallel markets through their subsidiaries, and three of them (Barclays, Midland, and Williams and Glyn's) had ventured into the field of long-term industrial finance with equity participation. If the banks did offer higher rates on deposits, what would be the effect on building society deposits and the supply of mortgages to home-buyers? What would be the effect on National Savings?

The new policy

The twin tasks of the new arrangements were to establish a more competitive financial system and to institute a more effective control of money and credit which did not rely on direct and discriminatory restraints. There were, in principle, three possible policies. The first was to set the whole market free by removing the controls on the deposit banks which, of course, the authorities would not accept. The second was to extend the existing controls to the whole market. The third was to try for a compromise solution, a combination of new freedoms and more wide-ranging controls. This was the solution chosen, and there were three major changes:

1 *Reserve ratios.* The old cash and liquidity ratios were replaced by a new reserve asset ratio. All banks would be required to hold 'eligible reserve assets' in a minimum day-to-day ratio, to 'eligible liabilities' of $12\frac{1}{2}\%$. The merchant banks and foreign and overseas banks were, therefore, for the first time subject to the same reserve ratio as the clearing banks.
2 *Eligible liabilities.* These included:
(a) All sterling deposit liabilities with an original maturity of two years or less, from UK residents, other than banks, and from overseas. (The dividing line, set at two years, 'must be arbitrary'.)

(b)   All sterling deposits, whatever their term, from other banks in the United Kingdom, less any sterling claims on other banks, and all sterling certificates of deposit issued by the bank concerned, of whatever term, less any holdings of such certificates. Either of these items could, of course, be negative for an individual bank, and the first would cancel out in the aggregate. The abandonment of the interest-rate cartel (noted later) enabled the clearing banks to deal direct on the inter-bank market instead of through subsidiaries; the netting-out' rule made both inter-bank and certificate of deposit operations more attractive. One of the most noticeable effects of the new system was an enormous expansion in these two markets.

(c)   Any net liability to a wholly owned overseas branch or head office, denominated in sterling.

(d)   Any net liability in currencies other than sterling. They could be switched into sterling and the general criterion of eligibility was availability for use in the UK.

(e)   Sixty per cent of the net value of 'transit items' in the bank's balance sheet. A cheque paid in is credited to the account immediately, but the account on which it was drawn is not debited until the cheque has passed through the clearing. Recorded deposit liabilities therefore exceed true liabilities by the value of these cheques in course of collection, these 'transit items'. Conversely in the case of credit transfers, the paying account will have been debited and the receiving account not yet credited. And some cheques in course of collection will increase overdrafts rather than reduce deposits. An adjustment formula was therefore agreed that each bank should deduct 60% of the net value of all debit transit items less credit transit items shown in its books. These transit items are the difference between 'gross deposits' and the 'net deposits' (which are part of the money stock). The other 40% of total transit items was added to advances.

3   Reserve assets comprising:

(a)   Balances at the Bank of England. Notes and coin held in banks' tills did not count as reserve assets.

(b)   British and Northern Ireland Government Treasury bills.

(c)   Company tax reserve certificates. A company could pre-pay taxes by buying these government securities, issued ad hoc; they carried interest and were negotiable.

(d)   Call money lent to discount houses, to discount brokers and the money trading departments of six banks, to the money brokers and to Stock Exchange brokers if secured on British government or nationalised industry stocks.[3] This had to be money actually callable; 'fixtures' – that is, money lent for a fixed period – did not count as a reserve asset.

(e)   Government and nationalised industry stocks with a life of one year or less to final maturity.

(f)   Local authority bills eligible for rediscount at the Bank: that is, with an original term of less than six months.

(g) Commercial bills eligible for rediscount at the Bank: that is, drawn in sterling and bearing a 'good' British name; but, only up to a maximum of 2% of eligible liabilities. Without this limit, the banks would have been able to substitute claims on the private sector for claims on the public sector in their reserves.

Reserve assets were not, it will be realised, identical with pre-1971 liquid assets. The following items were excluded:

1 Cash in tills.
2 Holdings of foreign currency and any claims expressed in foreign currencies in excess of similar liabilities.
3 Short-term deposits with local authorities.
4 Call loans to other banks and to borrowers outside the money market: for example, stockbrokers.
5 Commercial bills in excess of 2% of deposits.
6 Bills not rediscountable at the Bank: for example, the acceptance of foreign banks.
7 Treasury bills issued by overseas governments.
8 Credits arising from special medium-term loans for shipbuilding and exports, refinanceable at the Bank. On the other hand, government stocks with a life of one year or less were not part of the old definition of liquid assets.

Eligible liabilities were not synonymous with deposits. Taking all banks in the UK, there was a big difference; eligible liabilities in late 1971 were less than 40% of deposits. The difference was due to the netting out of certain assets and deposit liabilities. In the case of the deposit banks, most of whose business relations were with non-bank residents in the UK, eligible liabilities were more than 90% of deposits. But the acceptance houses and other banks, especially the American and other foreign banks, did a much bigger proportion of their business, both borrowing and lending, with other banks and customers overseas, and there was thus a large netting out of assets against liabilities, and therefore a much bigger difference between deposits and eligible liabilities.

Precise control of currency and eligible liabilities would not give precise control of the money supply: sterling deposits of overseas residents were part of eligible liabilities but not part of the money supply; vice versa with foreign currency deposits of UK residents. Inverse changes in the two can open up a gap between the two monetary aggregates; for example, in the six months to December 1972, changes in the two kinds of deposit were −£322 million and +£150 million respectively, and in the six months to December 1973, they were −£211 million and +£286 million.

Another differential aspect of the new scheme was that the London clearing banks agreed to keep balances with the head office of the Bank of England to the value of $1\frac{1}{2}$% of eligible liabilities. Balances held with branches of the Bank counted as reserve assets but not as part of this $1\frac{1}{2}$% ratio.

Reserve assets were so defined as to include cash at the Bank 'and certain assets which the Bank will normally be prepared to convert into cash'[4] (*CCC*: 190). The minimum reserve assets ratio was 'intended to provide the authorities with a known firm base for the operation of monetary policy' (Ibid.). A uniform ratio applied to all banks would make control of the banks 'more efficient and less imprecise'. The monetary aggregate which it was intended to control was eligible liabilities, which comprised 'sterling deposits obtained outside the banking system, including sterling resources acquired by switching foreign currencies into sterling' (*CCC*: 190).

The discount market – the discount houses, discount brokers, money brokers, and the money trading departments of six banks – were not subject to the reserve ratio, but agreed to keep not less than 50% of their borrowed funds in certain categories of public debt: Treasury and other public sector bills, tax reserve certificates, and government, nationalised industry and local authority bonds with not more than five years to final maturity. This was rather less than the proportion of such assets they held in September 1971. This rule was changed in July 1973.

Hire purchase finance houses with liabilities of £5 million or more were to maintain a reserve ratio of 10%. This group comprised fourteen houses, responsible for 80–85% of all instalment credit. Reserve assets were the same as those of the banks; eligible liabilities were defined as 'all deposits with an original maturity of two years or less received from UK residents other than banks, or from overseas'. Loans from banks were excluded since the banks concerned would be obliged to hold reserve assets against them. On 20 October 1971, their reserve ratio was only 1.7% and they were allowed up to a year 'to build up the required proportion of reserve assets in four equal stages'. It was fixed at 10% partly because their existing ratio was so low, partly because 'the return obtainable on reserve assets has recently been less than their cost of borrowing' (*BEQB*, 1971: 489). They brought their reserve ratio up to the minimum by September 1972.

A finance house could apply to be recognised as a bank. This would bring certain advantages:

1 They could issue certificates of deposit, giving them cheaper access to longer-term funds (up to five years) than their usual sources. They would get easy access to the inter-bank market, since loans to 'finance house banks' could be set off against a bank's own loans from other banks in calculating its eligible liabilities.

2 They might get permission to operate in the foreign exchange market.

3 Their acceptances would be treated as bank bills without a second acceptance signature.

4 They might gain access to the bankers' clearing house, which would be of great assistance in establishing a solid current account and cheque-issuing business.

5 They could obtain exemption from the Protection of Depositors Act.

As a result, five houses – First National Finance, Julian S Hodge, Lombard

North Central, Mercantile Credit, and United Dominions Trust – applied successfully for recognition and Forward Trust, a subsidiary of the Midland Bank, acquired banking status in April 1973.

The new methods of control

1 The clearing banks abandoned their agreed rates on deposits, call money and overdrafts. These rates were not now linked to bank rate, but were to be fixed in relation to a base rate decided by each bank individually. The banks were therefore free to pay and charge what rates they wished, but subject to one qualification: if they competed too strongly for savings deposits with the building societies and National Savings, the Bank might set an upper limit on the rates offered.

2 Quantitative ceilings on bank lending were abandoned, but 'the authorities would continue to provide the banks with such qualitative guidance as may be appropriate' (*CCC*: 192). Subject to this exception, the allocation of credit would be determined primarily by its cost, not by discriminatory ceilings and rationing of loans.

3 The monetary controls would be open market operations and calls for special deposits. The latter would be extended uniformly to cover all banks, and normally expressed as a percentage of eligible liabilities. Competition and Credit Control did suggest that it might sometimes be calculated by reference to only some of the banks' liabilities' – for example, domestic deposits – or applied differentially to different liabilities – for example, domestic and overseas deposits. In the extreme case, the effect of an inflow of funds on the domestic money supply, for example, could be completely neutralised by a 100% call against increases in non-resident deposits. These instruments would operate on 'the known firm base' of $12\frac{1}{2}\%$ reserve ratio 'to neutralise excess liquidity which the banking system may acquire . . .' The object, however, would not be 'to achieve some precise multiple contraction or expansion of bank assets' but rather to 'use our control over liquidity . . . to influence the structure of interest rates. The resultant changes in relative rates of return will then induce shifts in the asset portfolios of both the public and the banks . . .' (Ibid.: 197). For example, if interest rates rise, the public might take up more new government debt. Higher bond rates meant unfavourable terms for sales of assets not eligible for the reserve ratio. If the authorities do not support the market, pressure on the banks to sell would itself change the level and structure of interest rates, and both portfolio adjustments would affect the money supply.

4 Operations in the gilt-edged market would be founded on a view of the market very different from that of 1966. It was here that 'regard to the quantitative effects on the monetary aggregates' (Ibid.: 477) would be exercised. The Bank would continue to support the financing and refinancing of government debt; it would continue to sell new stocks on tap and engage in switching operations

336

which would maintain or increase the length of the debt, and would continue to smooth redemptions by buying any stock offered to it with one year or less to run to maturity. But that was the only stock it would guarantee to buy outright. The proposals presaged an end to the policy of continuously leaning into the wind. The Bank would not undertake switches 'which unduly shorten the life of the debt . . .' Open market operations and calls for special deposits could be used to reduce the banks reserve assets. If they tried to protect their reserve ratios and their advances by unloading bonds, they may only be able to do so at a high cost in terms of capital losses.

Further, there would be 'lesser intervention by the authorities in the gilt-edged market so as to leave more freedom for prices to be affected by market conditions and for others to operate if they so wish . . .' (Ibid.: 192). In April 1972 it was announced that the Government broker would no longer name the price at which he would deal. Instead, the market must make a bid and the broker accept or refuse it. The Bank was now prepared to see wider fluctuations in prices.

5 Operations in the short-term money market would continue much as before. Two changes, already in operation, would be continued. First, instead of dealing in Treasury bills day-to-day at the ruling market prices and influencing those prices only by its conduct of the tender, the Bank was now fixing its own prices at which it would deal day-to-day. The price at which it dealt was to be used as a signal to the market that the authorities desired a rise (or no fall) in interest rates. Second, the market had limited borrowing facilities at the Bank, at non-penal rates, in order to give the discount houses sufficient time to adjust to fluctuations in short-term interest rates.

The new system of control was, then, intended to be more *laissez-faire* and market oriented than the pre-1971 system, giving the banks more freedom to compete on equal terms and relying on flexible interest rates rather than direct controls to regulate the volume and allocation of credit. The only relics of the pre-1971 system were the reserve powers to give qualitative directions on lending and to limit competition by the banks for 'individuals' savings at present invested in public sector debt or in the finance of housing' (*CCC*: 192). In these respects, and in the new attitude to the gilt-edged market, the new policy ostensibly discarded that followed in the 1960s.

In the stated intention to control the liquidity of the banks, and in its reliance on interest rates as the means of control, Competition and Credit Control followed the Radcliffe prescription. Radcliffe, however, was concerned with the liquidity of the whole economy, and doubted the efficacy of extending controls to a wide range of financial institutions, except in an emergency.

The proposed controls were also in part – open market operations and a more flexible bank rate – a reversion to 'traditional' methods. But there were significant differences between the new position and textbook orthodoxy. First, the banks were more free in some ways, less free in others. They were subject to possible restraints on competition with savings institutions, free to charge what rates they wish. No rates would be tied to bank rate; that fulcrum of control would now operate in a broader sphere but more loosely. And there was no longer a fixed cash ratio. On the other hand, the categories of reserve assets were closely specified, the discount houses were obliged to keep 50% of their assets in specified categories of public sector debt, and the authorities reserved the right to issue qualitative guidance on lending. Second, the new controls applied not just to the clearing banks, but to all other banks, to discount houses, and to the larger finance houses. Third, special deposits were not a traditional weapon.

Minimum lending rate

On 13 October 1972, bank rate, which had been in existence for 270 years, was replaced by Minimum Lending Rate (MLR). It was announced weekly on Fridays at the same time as the result of the Treasury bill tender, and was determined by the formula: MLR = the average rate at which bills have been allotted $+\frac{1}{2}\%$ rounded up to the nearest $\frac{1}{4}\%$; MLR was always a multiple of $\frac{1}{4}\%$. The fact that MLR followed the Treasury bill rate did not mean that the authorities had no control over it. Bids at the tender depend on the cost of call money and the Bank can influence this, and force the market into the Bank, by open market operations and calls for special deposits. Its connection with CCC was that it was in line with the new philosophy of freeing interest rates from direct administrative controls.

The immediate occasion of the change was a rise in the Treasury bill rate above bank rate in September 1972. This tended to nullify the penal element attached to the Bank's last resort lending, and emphasised the need to have a rate for enforced borrowing which nevertheless would respond flexibly to market conditions. The usefulness of bank rate had been questioned for some time. Moreover, with the abandonment of the clearing banks' interest rate cartel, there was not the same link between bank rate and other market rates as there had been before September 1971. In any case, the rates not linked to it – those in the parallel markets – had become more important than the clearing banks' rates over the previous decade. In another sense, bank rate was too important. It had an important announcement effect on business sentiment, and especially on overseas holders and potential holders of sterling; a change in bank rate was taken as a sign of a change in economic policy. A change in MLR would, it was hoped, be regarded simply as an indication of a change in market trends. Finally, because of the psychological impact of changes – which was a major part of its efficacy – bank rate could not be changed frequently; the new rate would change automatically with changes in the Treasury bill rate and would thus be more flexible.

On the other hand, there are times when we need an instrument with announcement effects, one which signals a change of direction and which markets expect to be effective. Further, doubts were expressed about the operation of MLR as a penal rate. Treasury bills are only a small part, usually about 15% of discount house assets;

most of their funds yield more than Treasury bills. It was the official buying rate for Treasury bills which the authorities charged in the following week which may be the penal rate.

Competition and credit control in practice

Competition

The immediate effect of CCC was that the banks, released from the strait-jackets of ceilings, quickly expanded their lending. Total liabilities increased to 36% within a year, total advances rose nearly 50% and sterling advances 70% from 43 to 52% of sterling deposits (Kern 1971).

The clearing banks began to compete more strongly with each other and with other banks. Much of the competition was by advertising, reduced charges on current account services, and a broader range of loans, but they also competed in price to some extent. Originally, all base rates were set equal to bank rate. Barclays first broke ranks with a cut in its base rate in October 1971. The others did not follow for six weeks, in which time Barclays reserve ratio fell. In January 1973, all except National Westminster raised their rates; National Westminster waited a month, then came into line in two stages. In May 1974, Lloyds was the first to move; Barclays and National Westminster followed within a fortnight, and Midland and Williams and Glyn's a little later. This has been the usual pattern: one or more banks taking the lead and the others following shortly. In a competitive market, with little to choose between the services offered (except when one bank produces an innovation, which cannot be copied quickly) and the geographical coverage of their branch network, a bank which pays and charges less than the others will lose deposits and be pressed for loans, and its reserve ratio will slip. The base rates were also flexible, not tied to bank rate but fixed ad hoc in the light of other market rates. They tended to vary with MLR but sluggishly, being closely related to the inter-bank three-month rate. A substantial part of their term lending was at rates linked to inter-bank rates.

The clearing banks also began immediately to move more strongly into what were for them comparatively new types of loan – for example, mortgage loans and fixed-term loans up to five or seven years, and more recently up to ten years – and began to operate for the first time in the inter-bank market and to issue certificates of deposit. They also begain to operate in their own names, as well as through subsidiaries, in some parallel markets: for example, the Eurodollar market. The other banks quickly replied with innovations in their own activities. Some merchant banks began to take a bigger interest in the small depositor, some moved into leasing and hire purchase finance. Some of the smaller banks began to compete for business with new services. The Co-operative Bank, for example, offered $6\frac{1}{2}\%$ on small fixed-term deposits, and Williams and Glyn's introduced an insurance-linked savings scheme. Some overseas banks and some finance houses opened 'money shops'. Situated in the

High Street, they offered unconventional banking services: attractive rates on current as well as deposit accounts, a wide range of personal and business loans and other financial services, low charges and long opening hours. By mid-1973 there were about seventy of these shops. However, this innovation appears to have been not particularly successful; several of the money shops have closed.

Departures from competition and credit control

The authorities did not adhere strictly to the principles of CCC. Their interference in mortgage rates and bank deposit rates in 1973–74 and the qualitative guidance on bank lending which began in August 1972 were examples. The Bank could claim, quite properly, that such interventions were foreshadowed in the consultative document, but some saw them as contrary to the spirit, if not the letter, of CCC. As part of a package of deflationary measures in December 1973, controls were re-imposed on hire purchase, credit sales and hiring agreements. There was to be a minimum deposit of 20% on some goods and $33\frac{1}{3}$% on others, and a maximum repayment period of 24 months; initial payments on hiring agreements to be 42 weeks' rental in advance; the minimum monthly repayment on credit cards to be the greater of £6.00 or 15%.

Support for gilt-edged

On 23 June 1972, the fixed exchange rates for sterling established by the Smithsonian Agreement in December 1971[5] were abandoned; the pound was allowed to float. Sterling had been under pressure for some weeks since the UK joined (on 1 May) the 'snake in the tunnel' agreement under which the EEC countries kept the rates between their own currencies within $2\frac{1}{4}$% of the Smithsonian cross-rates with the dollar. The banks had been losing reserves, particularly heavily in the week before the float, through sales of sterling assets and withdrawals of deposits by non-residents; with advances rising, some banks' reserve ratios fell below the $12\frac{1}{2}$% minimum. The banks could have bid for deposits in the money markets, or could have sold gilt-edged, to maintain their ratios. Either course would, however, have raised interest rates; indeed, most rates had been rising for a month or more, perhaps in anticipation of these difficulties: but the current inflation and industrial trouble on the railways and the docks also played a part. This was the period of Mr Barber's 'dash for growth' and rising rates would, it was thought, hamper growth by their effect on investment. On 28 June, therefore, the Bank announced a purchase from and resale to the banks of £358 million of government stock; the purchase was made on 30 June and the resale on 14 July. It was a loan to the banks with gilt-edged as collateral, to avoid sales of gilt-edged by them. In this, the first real test of the new system, the authorities back-tracked and, in effect, supported the market. The Governor could claim that this was 'emergency help' which arose from 'our proper concern to avoid an exceptional event having too disruptive an effect', but it leaves two questions: what, in the Bank's view, constituted an emergency? And in what circumstances, and how often, would a similar support operation be thought necessary?

Supplementary deposits (IBELS)

On 17 December 1973, the Bank announced a new arrangement for improving control over the money supply and bank lending, to come into operation immediately. The money supply had been growing rapidly, especially the broader concept M_3, and this growth had been partly the result of arbitraging. Individual banks had been bidding actively for deposits and reserve assets, and the competition for the pool of deposits had pushed up rates in the wholesale markets to levels at which arbitraging was profitable for anyone who could get bank loans at the lowest rates. Thus both advances and deposits increased; it was 'a merry-go-round process which inflated both sides of the banks' balance sheets' (*BEQB*, June 1973: 139). The authorities were following a generally restrictive policy at the time, and wished to restrain the growth of the money supply, but interest rates were already high; MLR was at 13% and the Treasury bill rate, local authority loan rates, and inter-bank and Eurodollar deposit rates had all risen by a half through the year, and they did not want a further rise. They therefore turned to a direct attack on a particular category of deposits, interest-bearing eligible liabilities (IBELS). The Bank coupled with the new arrangements a revocation of $2\frac{1}{2}\%$ calls for special deposits due to be lodged in December and January. But the new scheme was not intended to replace operations in special deposits. Indeed, by deterring banks from bidding for deposits (which would be interest-bearing, of course), they would make a call for special deposits more effective. The arrangement, the details of which were published in *BEQB*, March 1974, was with all banks whose IBELS totalled £5 million or more, and the finance houses subject to CCC. They had agreed that each institution would place supplementary non-interest-bearing deposits at the Bank if its IBELS grew faster than a specified rate. Initially, that rate was fixed at 8% over six months: any institution whose average of IBELS in the quarter April/June 1974 exceeded their average in the quarter October/December 1973 by more than 8% would place supplementary deposits at the Bank on a graduated scale related to the excess. If the excess were 1%, the institution would lodge deposits to the value of 5% of the excess; on an excess of 1–3% the penalty would be 25%, and on an excess higher than 3% it would be 50%; the penalty was steeply progressive. The deposits would be repayable if and as IBELS fell back towards the specified level. The financial penalty was, of course, the interest lost when assets were converted into zero-yielding supplementary deposits. The object was to curb bank lending by restraining the banks from increasing their reserves by bidding competitively for deposits and reserve assets, for example by the issue of certificates of deposit. Bank deposits, we remember, can only be transferred, but an individual bank may be able to get a bigger share of the total and with it cash through the clearing. 'Hidden' reserve assets – for example, Treasury bills and short bonds held outside the banking sector – could be bought by the banks as a whole in exchange for interest-bearing deposits.

The banks could have responded to the new arrangement by reducing the rates on deposit accounts and term deposits and offering more cheap or free services to holders of current accounts, with the object of transferring some of their liabilities from interest-bearing to non-interest-bearing accounts. However, the cross-elasticity of demand between the two types of account with respect to relative interest rates is probably low, and the response would in any case have probably been too slow to help the banks much in adjusting their IBELS. They could also have tried to recoup the penalty by charging more on overdrafts; but the purpose of the scheme was to 'restrain the pace of monetary expansion, including . . . bank lending, without requiring rises in short term interest rates and bank lending rates to unacceptable levels . . .' (*BEQB*, March 1974: 37), and 'Banks and deposit-taking finance houses are not expected to respond to the introduction of these arrangements with a general rise in their lending rates' (*BEQB*, March 1974: 39). The Bank did, however, approve of the steps the clearing banks were taking, at about the same time, to stop arbitraging: they proposed to adjust base rates more flexibly, in line with rates in the inter-bank market and/or on certificates of deposit, and to link their lending rates to local authorities, finance houses and non-clearing banks and some other customers to market rates rather than to their own base rates.

Clearly, the supplementary deposits scheme was, like ceilings on lending, a direct quantitative control. The Bank admitted that it restricted competition between the banks insofar as they would all be restrained to growth at the same maximum pace. It was also suggested at the time that the arrangement discriminated against the clearing banks, who would find it more difficult to control their IBELS than the non-clearers. The former always have unused overdraft limits outstanding which borrowers can draw on at their own initiative; faced with such an increase in its advances, the bank must either reduce other assets or bid for deposits (interest-bearing, of course) from other banks. The arrangement turned away from controlling credit by its cost; its declared purpose was to restrain the growth of credit and the money supply by other means. The rate of growth of IBELS depended partly on the rates offered on deposits, and the new scheme was intended to make competitive bidding for deposits unprofitable. In all this, the new arrangement was a step back from the ideals of CCC. It was, however, as the Bank claimed, more flexible than absolute ceilings on advances or maximum interest rates on deposits. It was also likely to be more effective than a control on one asset, such as advances, whose effect on total assets and liabilities could be avoided by buying another asset – for example, bonds – with deposits. At the same time, it left the banks free to arrange their portfolios of assets as they thought best.[6]

One authority argued that the likely effect of the new arrangements would be a fall in interest rates (*MBR*, August 1974). This could stem from three sources:

1 Deposits taken from other banks are IBELS against which can be offset deposits with other banks. If bank A makes a net payment of such deposits to B, bank B's 'deductibles' fall, increasing its net IBELS by the same sum. Bank B would then probably repay some of the deposits it held, and there would be a chain reaction, with each bank trying to repel deposits, and to place deposits with other banks, by reducing the rates offered and accepted. Total IBELS would not, however, be affected, since inter-bank IBELS are equal to inter-bank deductibles.

2 Loans to local authorities are not deductibles, and the banks would try to reduce these loans. The local authorities would borrow elsewhere and use the deposits so acquired to repay the banks, thus cancelling the deposits. IBELS in total would fall and so would interest rates, since the banks would have less need to bid for deposits.[7]

3 Holdings of certificates of deposit are deductibles, and the banks would try to buy more of them, outside the banking system (only thus can aggregate IBELS be reduced), probably from the discount houses, who are the major non-bank holders. 'The discount houses would no doubt exact a price for the CDs' (Ibid. 14), that is, rates on CDs would fall.

In April and November 1974, the arrangement was prolonged, on each occasion, for a further six months, with a permitted 'free' increase on IBELS of $1\frac{1}{2}$% per month. The November Notice also changed the rates of supplementary deposit to 5% 'in respect of an excess of 3% or less', 25% in respect of an excess of 3–5% and 50% thereafter.

In the event, the new arrangement never came into significant use. Demand for advances slackened, and in the first two years of operation only fourteen small banks ever had to place supplementary deposits, which at their maximum were £6 million. The scheme was suspended on 28 February 1975, but re-imposed in November 1976 to August 1977. It was reintroduced again in June 1978, but abolished finally in June 1980.

The problem with the Supplementary Special Deposits Scheme, or 'the Corset' as it became known as, was that control of IBELS was not synonymous with control of money supply. Eligible liabilities are not identical with any concept of the money supply, nor even with bank deposits. Moreover, constraints on IBELS will curb the growth of bank lending to the private sector, but do nothing to restrict money growth arising from public sector borrowing.

Monetary policy under competition and credit control

The monetary history of this period is shown in Table 13.1. Since there is still disagreement as to which is the more relevant and significant version of the money supply, we include both M_1 and M_3. From the fourth quarter of 1971 to the third quarter of 1976, M_1 increased by 74% and M_3 by 115%. In the second quarter of 1972 and the third quarter of 1973, M_3 was growing at a rate of 35% p.a., and in the fourth quarter of 1974, M_1 rose at an annual rate of 33%.

Where does the responsibility for this enormous monetary expansion lie? The layout of Table 13.2 provides a convenient framework for the analysis. We begin with the public sector borrowing requirement (PSBR), which increased alarmingly 1973–76. It arises because central government and other public bodies put more money into the system than they recoup by taxation, leaving a private sector surplus

Table 13.1 Money stock variations (seasonally adjusted) 1971–77

		Percentage change between period*			Velocity of circulation**		
		M_1	Sterling M_3	M_3	M_1	Sterling M_3	M_3
1971	1st quarter	+4.1	+3.1	+2.9	5.648	3.094	3.009
	2nd quarter	+0.7	+2.3	+2.3	5.747	3.139	3.055
	3rd quarter	+3.4	+2.4	+2.4	5.864	3.196	3.111
	4th quarter	+1.0	+4.9	+4.3	5.742	3.148	3.073
1972	1st quarter	+3.8	+5.1	+5.5	5.560	3.029	2.958
	2nd quarter	+4.1	+7.0	+7.2	5.523	2.921	2.846
	3rd quarter	+1.1	+4.2	+4.2	5.459	2.790	2.716
	4th quarter	+4.3	+6.4	+6.9	5.557	2.776	2.695
1973	1st quarter	−0.1	+5.5	+6.1	5.914	2.837	2.738
	2nd quarter	+6.3	+5.1	+4.8	5.671	2.662	2.562
	3rd quarter	−4.3	+7.0	+7.6	5.772	2.586	2.482
	4th quarter	+4.9	+7.5	+7.5	5.924	2.488	2.381
1974	1st quarter	−2.7	+2.5	+3.4	5.855	2.365	2.252
	2nd quarter	+2.7	+0.6	+1.7	6.266	2.486	2.343
	3rd quarter	+3.0	+2.5	+3.3	6.606	2.652	2.477
	4th quarter	+7.9	+4.3	+3.8	6.422	2.626	2.450
1975	1st quarter	+2.0	+0.6	+0.9	6.524	2.733	2.553
	2nd quarter	+2.4	+2.0	+1.4	6.709	2.874	2.689
	3rd quarter	+5.0	+3.3	+4.3	6.617	2.930	2.737
	4th quarter	+3.4	+0.6	+1.0	6.618	3.027	2.810
1976	1st quarter	+3.5	+1.2	+1.6	6.743	3.169	2.929
	2nd quarter	+2.4	+3.1	+3.9	6.626	3.144	2.890
	3rd quarter	+4.5	+4.1	+4.9	6.654	3.150	2.874
	4th quarter	−0.4	+0.4	+0.2	6.815	3.218	2.928
1977	1st quarter	+3.2	+0.2	+0.9	6.847	3.273	2.971
	2nd quarter	+3.7	+3.2	+3.5	6.886	3.349	3.027
	3rd quarter	+6.7	+2.3	+1.6			

* The seasonally adjusted change shown is expressed as a percentage of the previously adjusted level.
** Ratio of GNP at current market prices seasonally adjusted expressed at an annual rate to the centred quarterly average of money stock seasonally adjusted.

Source: *Financial Statistics*, Apr., Dec., 1977: 75

equal to the public sector deficit less any net deficit on the public sector's foreign payments and receipts: that creates a surplus for foreigners, 'the overseas sector'. The non-bank private sector may also have a foreign deficit, which will reduce its own net surplus. These surpluses – of the overseas sector, if any, and of the private sector – are obvious sources of finance to meet the public sector deficit. If the overseas sector accepts its surplus in sterling, that sterling can be, and much of it usually is, used to buy government debt of one kind or another. If they take it in foreign currency, domestic holders of sterling deposits surrender them to the EEA for foreign exchange and the EEA lend them to the Government. Part of any remaining surplus of the non-bank domestic private sector is likely to be used to buy notes

Table 13.2 Money supply and public sector borrowing requirement

| | | | Net acquisition of public sector debt | | | Changes in financial assets and liabilities of the banking sector | | | |
| | | Public sector borrowing require-ment | By overseas sector | By UK residents other than the Banks | | Lending to | | Deposits by (less lending to) non-residents | Non-deposit liabilities* |
	Change in money stock M3			Currency	Other	Public sector	Private sector		
1969	503	−466	−593	146	354	−373	597	−141	8
1970	1,586	−17	−1,353	321	102	913	1,315	753	210
1971	2,366	1,373	−2,670	273	2,104	1,666	1,856	1,061	368
1972	5,299	2,040	1,564	495	1,007	−1,026	6,434	−48	652
1973	7,232	4,182	−108	305	1,990	1,995	6,828	1,411	485
1974	4,221	6,362	1,489	709	3,463	701	4,671	1,178	682
1975	2,884	10,501	754	814	5,569	3,364	139	1,066	747
Financial years									
1970/71	2,031	803	−1,193	288	530	1,178	1,267	618	84
1971/72	2,811	1,014	−1,879	433	1,694	766	3,142	1,091	439
1972/73	5,733	2,498	1,426	421	884	−233	6,288	−59	802
1973/74	6,799	4,432	125	411	2,514	1,382	6,672	1,320	346
1974/75	3,484	7,932	1,514	874	4,311	1,233	3,264	1,261	626
1975/76	3,045	10,612	1,200	463	5,575	3,374	207	689	852
1975									
1st qtr	−276	1,501	216	363	1,476	−554	83	158	10
2nd qtr	774	3,109	568	−81	1,050	1,572	499	1,104	315
3rd qtr	1,428	2,493	−355	111	1,101	1,636	−432	−30	54
4th qtr	958	3,398	325	421	1,942	710	−11	−166	368
1976									
1st qtr	−115	1,612	662	12	1,482	−544	151	−219	115
2nd qtr	1,782	2,968	1,408	273	1,337	−50	1,056	−529	248
3rd qtr	1,990	2,310	452	307	788	763	883	−43	239

*Comprising the banking sectors's total identified financial assets less accruals adjustment and purchase of bank securities plus capital issues.

Source: *Financial Statistics*, Jan. 1977: 72

and coin from the public sector via the banks and/or to take up government debt. Apart from any increase in notes and coin in circulation, these sources of deficit finance do not affect the money supply directly; they simply re-transfer deposits to the public sector. What cannot be borrowed from these two sources must be borrowed from the banks.[8] The other major source of money supply is bank lending to the private sector; loans create deposits. The two questions we may ask, therefore, are:

Table 13.3 Reserve assets of banks, 1971–1981 (£ million)

	Balances with Bank of England	Money at call†	*	UK and Northern Ireland Treasury bills	Local authority bills	Commercial bills	British Government stocks up to 12 months	Other assets	Total	Reserve ratio
17/11/71	230	1,677	52	215	37	174	312	—	2,696	15.7
19/ 7/72	199	2,219	57	126	52	198	273	—	3,122	14.6
15/11/72	215	1,969	53	354	78	358	162	—	3,190	14.3
18/ 7/73	282	2,520	19	67	38	422	412	3	3,764	14.0
21/11/73	270	2,552	13	426	75	516	325	4	4,179	14.3
17/ 7/74	227	2,330	3	239	140	570	619	5	4,132	13.4
16/10/74	231	2,228	—	407	154	573	572	5	4,169	13.4
21/ 5/75	314	2,313	—	735	143	613	356	5	4,479	13.7
15/10/75	244	1,677	—	2,173	125	524	494	—	5,238	15.7
19/ 5/76	292	1,898	—	1,682	77	577	604	—	5,130	15.2
21/ 7/76	305	1,984	—	1,446	144	611	476	—	4,966	14.2
15/ 9/76	272	1,642	—	2,396	208	596	412	—	5,526	15.4
17/11/76	320	2,056	—	1,547	106	639	522	—	5,190	13.9
14/12/77	425	2,781	—	1,549	164	710	432	—	6,061	14.8
15/11/78	413	2,873	—	1,041	183	798	776	—	6,033	13.5
12/12/79	449	3,629	—	1,118	152	947	565	—	6,861	13.3
10/12/80	485	4,896	—	1,168	502	1,251	782	—	9,084	13.5
19/ 8/81‡	564	4,396	—	1,163	339	1,149	745	—	8,356	11.0

* At discount market
† Other
‡ Reserve assets and the reserve ratio were abolished on 20 August 1981.

Source: *BEQB*: various issues.

1 How much of the increase in the money supply arose from lending to the Government and how much by way of lending to the private sector? Table 13.2 shows that although lending to the public sector was important, it was heavily outweighed except in the year 1975/76 by lending to the private sector, especially in the years 1972 and 1973, when the most extraordinary increases in the quantity of money occurred. But the significance of bank lending to the public sector lies not only in the amount but also in the form it takes. The banks could not have created deposits without reserve assets to support them.

2 How far did lending to the public sector supply the banks with the reserve assets they required? Table 13.3 shows the size and composition of reserve assets normally in November or October, and at some intervening dates to show some of the fluctuations which occurred within the year.

Total reserve assets more than doubled over the five years to September 1976, and some three-quarters of this increase was accounted for by the rise in holdings of Treasury bills. But by far the greater part of this increase in holdings of Treasury bills came in the middle quarters of 1975, and again in the third quarter of 1976 when there were large offerings of Treasury bills at the tender. Holdings of call money and commercial bills accounted for most of the increase in reserve assets in 1972, and for three quarters in 1973, the two years which saw the biggest increase in M_3. Nor was there a big increase in call money on-lent to the public sector by discount houses.

The public sector assets ratio fell (undefined assets multiple rose) almost continuously. It was, then, lending to the private sector which accounted for most of the increase in the money supply up to 1975.

Only rarely did reserve ratios come under really severe pressure; the overall average fell below 13.5% in only four months: August 1973, and July, August and October 1974. These reductions in the ratio in the second half of 1974 were not due to a squeeze on reserve assets – they fell £127 million January to June, then rose £169 million to December – but to a £1,500 million increase in eligible liabilities.

Ultimately, of course, responsibility for the money supply rests with the authorities. It is within their power – for example, by a reduction in the public sector borrowing requirement and a vigorous use of open market operations and special deposits – to restrain it; but only if they are prepared to accept the required level of interest rates, or higher taxation and/or reduced public expenditure, and whatever action may be required to restrain or neutralise inflows of funds across the exchanges.

Not until the second half of 1972 did the authorities appear to make a serious attempt to restrain monetary growth (and not until early 1974 did ΔM moderate significantly). Their policy was then first to push up interest rates by open market operations and a rise in bank rate from 5 to 6% in June. The first calls for special deposits came in November and December, each for 1%. More than £1,300 million was mopped up by special deposits in 1973, and the rate of call rose to 5%. Releases in February, April and May 1974 brought the rate down to 3%. Thereafter, apart from a temporary release of 1% for three weeks in January/February 1976, 'designed to avoid an upward twist in short term rates', there were no further calls or releases up to May 1976. Minimum lending rate was used flexibly; it changed thirty-seven times in three and a half years from October 1972 to 31 March 1976. The authorities could determine it by the terms – at, below, or above MLR – on which they lent to the market, and they used this power freely. Interest rate policy continued to be strongly influenced by external considerations, but domestic were usually in harmony with the external requirements. The erratic growth of the money supply may be linked with these frequent changes in MLR.

The course of gilt-edged operations appeared, on the surface, to have been much the same as before. In general, significant sales were made only on rising markets, and the authorities occasionally bought in stock to steady the market.

It appears from comments in Bank of England publications that the authorities continued to believe, from experience, that heavy sales were only possible on rising markets, and the best situation for selling was one when gilts offer a good return and seem likely to move up. The authorities on occasion initiated an upward movement in short-term rates to produce a chain reaction on long-term rates and provide a firm low base for a selling operation. For example, in September 1975,

> the continued weakness of sterling, and further increases in rates in the United States and in the Eurodollar markets, suggested that another increase in UK short term rates would be appropriate. Furthermore, some rise in domestic interest rates also seemed desirable on internal grounds in order to help secure additional finance for the public sector from outside the banking system, and thereby maintain appropriate restraint on the growth of the money supply (*BEQB*, Dec 1975: 334).

In the financial year 1975–76, M_1 rose 16%, M_3 rose 8%. The increase is explained by the huge public sector borrowing requirement; bank lending to the private sector was little changed. In July 1976, the Government set a 'guideline' rate of growth for M_3 of 12% for the whole financial year, but it was only in October, when the rate of growth had accelerated and M_3 had already risen 9% in six months, that a definite target of 12% for the whole year was set. Meanwhile, two other events combined to change the form of target setting. The first was the realisation that some $1\frac{1}{4}\%$ of the 9% increase in the money supply was the result of an up valuation, in sterling terms, of residents' deposits denominated in foreign currency. The second was that, with the application for a loan of $3.9 billion from the International Monetary Fund, DCE became the relevant target (see Ch. 10). The M_3 target was, therefore, within a few weeks revised to an increase of between 9 and 13% in the sterling component of M_3.

The big expansion (5%) of M_3 in the third quarter of 1976 was associated with the drying up of gilt-edged sales and a consequent increase in government borrowing from the banks (they took up £569 million of Treasury bills; the corresponding figure for the second quarter was £159 million). Sales of gilt-edged stocks were £770 million in the March quarter, £860 million in the June quarter, and only £590

348

million in the third quarter. For most of the year the authorities had been trying to find a base for a major funding to meet the huge projected public sector borrowing requirement of £11 billion. But they had not been prepared to fund aggressively; they only made two issues of long-term stock in the first half of the year, one of £600 million in February to give a yield to maturity of just over 13% and one of £800 million in June offering about 1%. Instead, they had pushed up short rates gradually hoping that long-term rates would follow.

Various reasons have been suggested for the depressed market; one is that those who had bought the February and June issues had seen the value of their holdings decline and were now both cautious and resentful. The decline of sterling since March, and the accelerating increase in the money supply, both of which presaged higher interest rates and a large funding operation, were obviously important factors. Failure to sell stock would, of course, lead to a further increase in the money supply and bring further pressure on sterling. In September, alarmed by the money supply data, the authorities raised MLR to 13%, made a 1% call for special deposits, and announced an issue of £600 million of stock, repayable in 1994, with a yield to maturity of a little over 15%. This issue was over-subscribed and never went on tap. But gilt-edged prices fell abruptly as a new sterling crisis developed, and very little of a new short-term tap stock, £600 million of $11\frac{1}{2}$% 1979 at £98.75, was sold.

In October the authorities took another bite at the cherry. MLR was raised to 15% independently of the formula (see page 338 above) and there was a 2% call for special deposits. They also issued a long tap stock offering 16.16% to redemption and a short stock offering $10\frac{1}{2}$%. Both were sold out within a month. Further issues were made over the following three months, and from the beginning of October to the end of January 1977 some £$7\frac{1}{4}$ billion of new gilt-edged was sold. The Government had more than met its funding requirement for 1976–77, but at a high interest cost to the taxpayer. Meanwhile, the public sector borrowing requirement for 1977–78 had been reduced by £3 billion in two 'mini-budgets' in July and December. This was for the future; currently, the Government were relying on monetary policy, placing the major burden of restraint on the private sector. To help sales, MLR was reduced to $12\frac{1}{4}$% in six stages between November and January; both domestic and foreign money was flooding into gilt-edged and Treasury bills, pushing rates down probably faster than the authorities wished. In February, the Bank cut MLR by a further $\frac{1}{4}$% independently of the formula. This was seen as an attempt by the Bank to re-assert its control over short-term rates and avert the larger fall in MLR which, on the formula, would have occurred the following day.

This delayed success in the funding of debt was reflected in a slowing down of the rate of growth of the money supply. M_1 actually fell 1.8% in October and M_3, seasonally adjusted, fell 0.6% in the three weeks to 8 December (sterling M_3 fell 0.3%). The flow of money into gilt-edged, together with tax payments, created such a tightness in the money market that in January the authorities cancelled 1% of the October call for special deposits and made two releases totalling about £1.5 billion.

The October 1976 figures showed that much of the increase in bank deposits over the previous six months was the counterpart of private sector borrowing. On 18

November the Bank announced the re-imposition of the 'corset' control on the growth of IBELS. The conditions were more stringent than on the previous occasion. The base period was August–September 1976, and the banks were asked to limit the growth of IBELS over the next six months to 3% and to ½% in each of the following two months (considerably lower than the current rate of inflation). The scale of 'penalties' (non-interest-bearing supplementary deposits) was as follows: in respect of an excess growth of 3% or less, 5% of the total growth; 25% in respect of an excess growth of 3–5%, and 50% thereafter. Some relief from this restriction would be provided by another regulation introduced at the same time, forbidding the use of sterling to finance trade between third countries. It was estimated that some hundreds of millions of pounds of foreign currency would come in across the exchanges as current loans were wound up, and the banks would have available for domestic use funds previously tied up abroad.

Monetary policy 1979 – to date

In the period since the election of a Conservative Government in 1979 and the adoption of the so-called Medium Term Financial Strategy (MTFS), monetary policy has undergone substantial change both in substance and emphasis. Much discussion has focused on which of the appropriate definitions of the money supply should be controlled by the monetary authorities, and the debate will no doubt continue for some time to come. Also, since 1979 there have been a number of changes to monetary policy at the operational level. Policy documents such as the 1980 Report of the Committee to Review the Functioning of Financial Institutions (Cmnd 7937) (*the Wilson Report*) and the 1980 paper entitled 'Monetary Control' (Cmnd 7858) have heralded a 'radical' re-appraisal of monetary policy in this country (Dennis 1981).

There have also been a number of significant events which have had a bearing on policy. These include the following:

1 Exchange controls were abolished in October 1979.
2 The supplementary Special Deposits Scheme ('the Corset') was abolished in June 1980.
3 The discontinuation of the reserve assets ratio was announced in November 1980, with an interim reduction in the ratio from 12.5 to 10% from January 1981 onwards.
4 In November 1980, new operational techniques for open market operations (OMO) were announced.
5 In March 1981, the authorities initiated discussions on the feasibility of 'monetary base' control.
6 In September 1981, minimum lending rate (MLR) was scrapped.[9]
7 In October 1983, the Chancellor (Nigel Lawson) introduced a new definition of the money supply, M_0, defined as the monetary liabilities of the monetary authorities. It consists of notes and coin issued by the Bank of England and the

Royal Mint respectively (about 90% of the total) plus the deposits which banks keep voluntarily at the Bank (*MBR*, Winter 1983).

There is some debate in the literature as to whether these 'reforms' can be viewed as a resurrection of the spirit of Competition and Credit Control (Artis and Lewis 1981), with greater emphasis being placed on control of monetary aggregates via interest rate movements. The reserve assets ratio, in particular, had been viewed as redundant for controlling interest rates. Additionally, its existence had altered the relationship between Treasury bill yields and other market rates in a manner which made control of the money supply more difficult. In the event, with its phasing out, it was to be replaced by new prudential liquidity norms.

The adoption of monetary targets

Money supply targets were first adopted in the UK in 1976. Initally, emphasis was placed on board measures of the money supply, specifically sterling M_3. Between 1976 and 1982 this was the single money supply variable targeted by the authorities. In the 1982 Budget, however, the targets were extended to include M_1, a narrower definition, and PSL_2, a broader definition (see Appendix).

The reason for this change of emphasis was clear. Apart from the doubt that any

Table 13.4 Monetary targets in the UK: targets (percentage annual growth rate) and outcome

Period	Monetary variable	
	Target	Outcome
April 1976–April 1977	9–13 (£M3)	7.8
April 1977–April 1978	9–13 (£M3)	16.1
April 1978–April 1979	8–12 (£M3)	10.6
October 1978–October 1979	8–12 (£M3)	13.3
June 1979–October 1980	7–12 (£M3)	16.5
February 1980–April 1981	7–11 (£M3)	19.7
February 1981–April 1982	6–10 (£M3)	13.1
February 1982–April 1983	8–12 (£M1)	12.0
	8–12 (£M3)	10.8
	8–12 (PSL2)	11.1
February 1983–April 1984	7–11 (M1)	13.5
	(£M3)	9.5
	(PSL2)	13.2
October 1983–October 1984*	6–10 (£M3)	8.3
	6–10 (PSL2)	11.5
	4–8 (MO)	4.8

*The figures shown in the final column for £M3, PSL2 and MO cover the 12 months from May 1983 to May 1984.

Source: Adapted from Table 1 *Barclays Review*, Feb. 1984: 2; and *Barclays UK Financial Survey*, May 1984.

single measure of money fully described monetary conditions, the evidence showed that sterling M_3 had repeatedly outstripped the targets set between 1979 and 1982 (see Table 13.4).

Some believed that sterling M_3 was insufficiently broad, particularly as it excludes building society deposits. Others felt that the target variable should be narrow money growth, M_1. Another factor, already alluded to, was that the existence of a large interest-bearing component in broad measures of money rendered interpretation of their movement difficult, particularly during a period of high interest rates. In his Mansion House speech of 20 October 1983, the Chancellor opted for the narrow measure, mainly because the evidence had indicated a closer correspondence between narrow aggregates and inflation, at least from the mid-70s onwards (see Fig. 13.1).

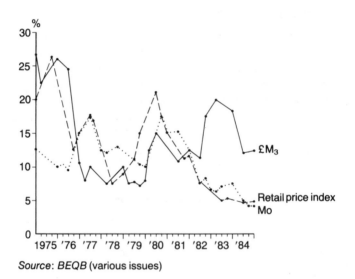

Source: BEQB (various issues)

Fig 13.1   Money supply and inflation (% change on same quarter in previous year)

An additional reason, however, was the belief that narrow measures responded more predictably to changes in the short-term interest rates, with the broader aggregates being influenced more by the structure of interest rates.

However, like sterling M_3, M_1 has in recent years accrued a significant interest-bearing component (around 25% of the total). M_2 was, at one time, considered as an alternative. This incorporates notes and coin, plus the retail deposits of banks and building societies. In the event, the Chancellor elected for M_0 (the wider monetary base). Given the higher proportion of notes and coin in this aggretate, the view was that it was potentially more stable than M_1 or even M_2. M_0, therefore, is likely to remain the target variable, thereby replacing sterling M_3. In recent times the Government, of course, has been somewhat more cock-shy about announcing monetary targets at all, preferring instead to control the public sector borrowing requirement (PSBR).

The evidence does lend some weight to the belief that narrow monetary aggregates should be the focus of policy. Figure 13.2 shows trends for velocity (the ratio of GDP to money supply) for various aggregates, and the narrow monetary aggregates M_0 and M_1 have clearly been more stable over the period 1963–84. By contrast, the velocity of broad money supply, sterling M_3, has displayed wider fluctuations.

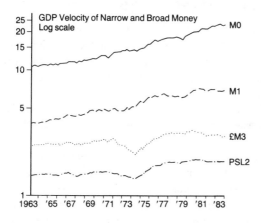

Source: Davies AE 'Monetary aggregates in the United Kingdom',
Barclays Review February 1984: 3.

Fig 13.2   GDP velocity of narrow and broad money

Though M_0 and M_1 velocity have been characterised by rising trends over the period, this is mainly explained by the increasingly 'cashless' nature of the UK economy. Certainly, control of sterling M_3 has some merits in that it can be linked more closely with other policy instruments such as the PSBR, bank lending, government debt sales and even DCE.[10] Nevertheless, it does remain surprising that an avowedly 'monetarist' administration such as the Conservative one of post-1979 should continue to adhere to a broad aggregate. This is perhaps explained by the growing importance of the PSBR at a time of large budget deficits, as well as the imposition of DCE targets on the instruction of the IMF in 1976.

Yet, in recent years the real paradox has been that even with high rates of increase of sterling M_3 and to some extent PSL_2, there has been no corresponding acceleration of inflation. In fact, as we saw in Chapter 11, quite the reverse has happened. Between 1979 and 1984 the velocity of sterling M_3 fell; in other words, money growth exceeded the growth in incomes. One explanation for this may be that the high interest rates that characterised this period (including high real interest rates) may have increased the willingness to hold money. If interest rates were to fall, this may therefore have the perverse effect of increasing inflation as the excess of broad money is converted into transactions demand. However, interest rate policy is no longer (if it ever was) exclusively determined by money supply growth, broad or narrow, but is the outcome of a complex interaction of money supply figures, UK–US interest rate differentials, and exchange rates; as events during 1984–85 clearly indicate (Davies 1984).

Interest rates and monetary aggregates

In the final analysis, the real test is the relationship between interest rates and the various monetary aggregates. It is reasonable to believe that demand for M_1 is interest-sensitive because of the response of non-interest-bearing current accounts to interest rate changes. Holders of non-interest-bearing deposits will normally economise on such deposits whenever interest rates are high, and vice versa. Yet, this need not necessarily imply effective monetary control if all that is happening is a transfer between narrowly defined transactions balances and a broader measure of money liquidity.

What has to be ascertained is whether there is any substitutability between narrow money aggregates and the whole spectrum of assets, financial and non-financial. If this cannot be adequately demonstrated, the movement in non-interest-bearing accounts may be swamped totally by the direct repercussions of interest rate changes in the economy as a whole, of which there is much evidence in the period subsequent to 1979.

Notes

1   *BEQB* began publication in 1961, but not until 1970 did it publish serial statistics of the monetary stock.
2   Their ratio of investments to deposits did, however, fall through the 1960s, and by 1971 was down to their supposed minimum of 10%. The advances ratio rose almost continuously from 30% in the mid 1950s to 51.6% in September 1971.
3   This was extended in 1973 to include stocks of local authorities and public boards, local and national governments of Commonwealth countries, and South African government stock.
4   Some assets of this kind were excluded; for example, commercial bills in excess of 2% of eligible liabilities and refinanceable medium-term credits.
5   Rates were not rigidly fixed; spot market rates against the dollar were allowed to vary by up to 2¼% on either side of the agreed ratio.
6   In curtailing the growth of liabilities the device also, of course, curtailed the growth of assets, for example advances. Also, in late 1973 the Bank announced

that it would no longer pay interest on special deposits to current accounts. The occasion was a big increase in bank profits arising from high interest rates.

7 In both these cases the banks are withdrawing from their intermediary activities, a process of *disintermediation*.

8 Special Deposits at the Bank are lent to the Government. This borrowing from the banks, of course, has a restrictive effect on the money supply.

9 MLR, of course, was temporarily re-introduced on 15 January 1985 in order to put a halt to the dramatic run on the pound which had occurred during most of 1984. This had caused the value of the pound to reach an all-time low against the dollar on the foreign exchange markets, at $1.11, as well as in terms of its trade-weighted index.

10 *The public sector borrowing requirement* (PSBR) is the excess of public expenditure over taxation, which can be financed in four ways: by issuing additional cash (notes and coin) to the public; by selling debt in the form of government bonds, National Savings etc. to the non-bank private sector; by borrowing from overseas or in foreign currency; and by borrowing from the banking system. *Domestic credit expansion* (DCE) is a measure of the increase in the money stock (sterling M_3) created by domestically generated credit. It equals the increase in sterling bank lending to the private sector and overseas residents *plus* the PSBR *minus* sales of public debt to the non-bank private sector. Between 1976 and 1979 targets were also set for DCE. In the first two years the outcome was well within the target. However, in the period April 1978 to April 1979 actual growth rate exceeded the target by a substantial amount (£7.3 billion as opposed to £6 billion).

Monetary definitions in the United Kingdom

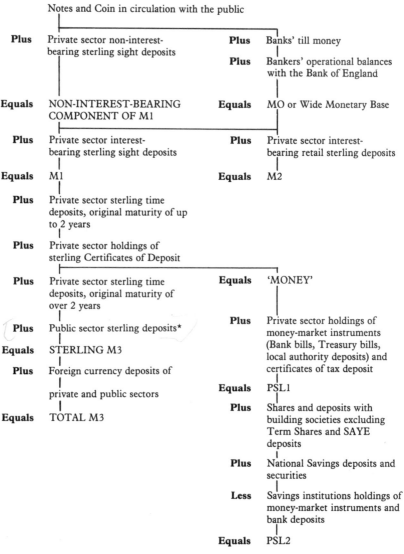

Notes and Coin in circulation with the public

Plus	Private sector non-interest-bearing sterling sight deposits	**Plus**	Banks' till money
		Plus	Bankers' operational balances with the Bank of England
Equals	NON-INTEREST-BEARING COMPONENT OF M1	**Equals**	MO or Wide Monetary Base
Plus	Private sector interest-bearing sterling sight deposits	**Plus**	Private sector interest-bearing retail sterling deposits
Equals	M1	**Equals**	M2

Plus Private sector sterling time deposits, original maturity of up to 2 years

Plus Private sector holdings of sterling Certificates of Deposit

Plus Private sector sterling time deposits, original maturity of over 2 years   **Equals** 'MONEY'

Plus Public sector sterling deposits*

Equals STERLING M3   **Plus** Private sector holdings of money-market instruments (Bank bills, Treasury bills, local authority deposits) and certificates of tax deposit

Plus Foreign currency deposits of private and public sectors   **Equals** PSL1

Equals TOTAL M3   **Plus** Shares and deposits with building societies excluding Term Shares and SAYE deposits

Plus National Savings deposits and securities

Less Savings institutions holdings of money-market instruments and bank deposits

Equals PSL2

* With effect from 1984/85 public sector deposits are to be excluded from the *BEQB* definition of sterling M_3 and M_3. Source: *Bank of England Quarterly Bulletin*, (Mar. 1984: 79).

References

Akerlof G (1980) 'A theory of social custom of which unemployment may be one consequence', *Quarterly Journal of Economics* **94**: 749–75

Alexander S (1952) 'Effects of a devaluation on a trade balance', *International Monetary Fund Staff Papers* **2**: 263–78

Alexander S (1959) 'Effects of a devaluation: a simplified synthesis of elasticities and absorption approaches', *American Economic Review* **49**: 22–42

Allais M (1966) 'A restatement of the quantity theory of money', *American Economic Review* **55**: 1123–57.

Allen RGD (1975) 'The immediate contributions to inflation', *Economic Journal* **85**: 607–11

Almon S (1965) 'The distributed lag between capital appropriations and expenditures' *Econometrica* **33**: 178–96

Anderson LC, Carlson KM (1970) 'A monetarist model for economic stabilisation' Federal Reserve Bank of St Louis Review **52**: April 7–25

Anderson LC, Jordan KM (1968) 'The monetary base: explanation and analytical use', *Federal Reserve Bank of St Louis Review* **50**: No 8, August

Ando A, Modigliani F (1965) 'The relative stability of monetary velocity and the investment multiplier', *American Economic Review* **55**: 693–728

Angell J (1937) 'The components of the circular velocity of money', *Quarterly Journal of Economics* **51**: 224–73

Argy V (1981) *The Post-War International Money Crisis: an analysis.* George Allen and Unwin, London, Ch. 7: 68–87

Arthur T (1978) 'Pensions: the role of the state', *National Westminster Bank Quarterly Review* August: 36–46

Artis M, Lewis M (1981) *Monetary Control in the United Kingdom.* Philip Allan, Oxford

Artis M, Lewis M (1984) 'How unstable is the demand for money in the United Kingdom?' *Economica* **51**: 473–6

Artis M, Nobay AR (1969) 'Two aspects of the monetary debate', *National Institute of Economic and Social Research* **49**: 33–51

Ash DC, Smyth DJ (1973) 'Who forecasts the British economy best?' *The Banker's Magazine* October, **216**: 153–9

Atkin J (1981) 'Does the City let Industry down?' *The Banker*, September: 51–54

Azariadis C (1975) 'Implicit contracts and under-employment equilibria', *Journal of Political Economy* **83**: 118–202

Bacon R, Eltis W (1976) *Britain's Economic Problem: too few producers*. Macmillan, London

Baily M (1974) 'Wages and employment under uncertain demand', *Review of Economic Studies* **41**: 119–55

Bain A (1980) *The Control of the Money Supply* (2nd edn). Penguin, London

Bain A (1981) *The Economics of the Financial System*. Martin Robertson, Oxford

Bain A (1983) 'The Wilson Report – three years on', *Three Banks Review* **138**: 3–19

Ball R (1965) 'Some econometric analysis of the long-term rate of interest in the United Kingdom 1921–61', *The Manchester School of Economic and Social Studies* **33**: 45–96

Baltensberger E (1980) 'Alternative approaches to the theory of the banking firm', *Journal of Monetary Economics* **6**: 1–38

Bank of England Quarterly Bulletin (BEQB): various issues

The Banker (TB): various issues

Bank of England Annual Reports and Accounts: various issues

Bank of England Panel of Academic Consultants: 'Monetary trends in the United Kingdom', papers by RCO Mathews, AJ Brown and DF Hendry and NR Ericsson (Panel paper no. 22)

Barr N (1975) 'Real rates of return to financial assets since the war', *Three Banks Review* **101**: 23–40

Barrett C, Gray E, Parkin M (1975) 'The demand for financial assets by the personal sector' in GA Renton (ed.) *Modelling the economy*. Heinemann, London

Barrett C, Walters D (1966) 'The stability of Keynesian and monetary multipliers in the United Kingdom', *Review of Economics and Statistics* **48**: 395–405

Barro R, Grossman H (1971) 'A general disquilibrium model of income and employment', *American Economic Review* **61**: 82–93

Baumol W (1952) 'The transactions demand for cash: an inventory theoretic approach', *Quarterly Journal of Economics* **66**: 545–56

Baumol W (1965) *Economic theory and operations analysis*. Prentice-Hall, Englewood Cliffs, New Jersey

Becker G, Baumol W (1952) 'The classical monetary theory, the outcome of the discussion', *Economica* **19**: 355–76

Bee RN (1984) 'London consortium banks and the debt crisis', *The Banker*, January: 37–9

Begg D (1982) *The Rational Expectations Revolution in Macroeconomics*. Philip Allan, Oxford

Bell G (1973) *The Euro-dollar Market and the International Financial System*. Macmillan, London

Benson W (1978) 'London clearing banks evidence to the Wilson Committee', *National Westminster Bank Quarterly Review* May: 2–7

BEQB (Bank of England Quarterly Bulletin): various issues

Besen S (1965) 'An empirical analysis of commercial bank lending behaviour', *Yale Economic Essays* **5**, 2: 283–315

Bewley R (1981) 'The portfolio behaviour of the London clearing banks 1963–1971', *The Manchester School of Economic and Social Studies* **49**: 191–210

Blanden M (1981) 'Why banks choose to work together', *The Banker* March: 93–131

Blinder A, Solow R (1973) 'Does fiscal policy matter?' *Journal of Public Economics* **2**: 319–37

Bohi D (1972) 'Tobin v Keynes on liquidity preference', *Review of Economics and Statistics* **44**: 479

Boleat M (1979) 'Banks and building societies – controls are not the answer', *The Banker* July: 55–61

Boleat M (1980) 'Competition between banks and building societies', *National Westminster Bank Quarterly Review* November: 43–57

Boleat M (1982) *The Building Society Industry*. Macmillan, London

Boleat M (1983) 'Banks and building societies in the 1980s', *The Banker* August: 51–5

Brainard W, Cooper I (1975) 'Empirical monetary macroeconomics: what have we learned in the last 25 years?' *American Economic Review* (Papers and Proceedings): 167–76

Brechling F (1973) 'Wage inflation and the structure of regional unemployment', *Journal of Money Credit and.Banking* **5**: 355–79

Brechling F, Clayton G (1965) 'Commercial banks, portfolio behaviour', *Economic Journal* **75**: 290–316

Bronfrenbrenner M (1963) 'A sample survey of the Commission on Money and Credit Research papers', *Review of Economics and Statistics* (supplement) **45**: 111–28

Brown A (1955) *The Great Inflation 1931–1951*. Oxford University Press, Oxford

Brunner K (1965) 'Institutions, policy and monetary analysis', *Journal of Political Economy* **73**: 197–218

Brunner K, Meltzer A (1967) 'Economies of scale in cash balances reconsidered', *Quarterly Journal of Economics* **81**: 422–36

Budd A (1975) 'The debate on fine-tuning: the basic issues', *National Institute of Economic Review* **74**: 56–9

Building Societies: A new framework, (1984) HMSO, Cmnd 9316.

Buiter W (1980) 'The macroeconomics of Dr. Pangloss: a critical survey of the new classical macroeconomics', *Economic Journal* **90**: 34–50

Burton J (1972) *Wage inflation*. Macmillan, London

Burton J (1982) 'The varieties of monetarism and their policy implications', *Three Banks Review* **134**: 14–31

Cagan P (1956) 'The monetary dynamics of hyper-inflation' in M Friedman (ed.) *Studies in the Quantity Theory of Money*. University of Chicago Press, Chicago

Cantillon R (1755) *Essai sur la Nature du Commerce en General.* Royal Economic Society, London

Carlson J, Parkin M (1975) 'Inflation expectations', *Economica* **42**: 123–38

Carter H, Partington I (1981) *Applied Economics in Banking and Finance* (2nd ed). Oxford University Press, Oxford

CCC (1971) 'Competition and Credit Control' *BEQB* 11 June: 189–93

Challen D. *et al.* (1984) *Unemployment and Inflation in the United Kingdom: an introduction to macroeconomics.* Longman, London

Chalmers E (1974) *The money world: a guide to money and banking in the age of inflation.* Macmillan, London

Chant J (1967) 'Depreciation realised on security sales by the London clearing banks', *Bulletin of the Oxford Institute of Economics and Statistics* **29**: 171–84

Chase SB (1967) 'The lock-in effect: bank reactions to securities losses' in LS Ritter (ed.) *Money and Economic Activity.* Houghton Mifflin, Boston: 283–90

Chetty V (1969) 'On measuring the nearness of near-money', *American Economic Review* **59**: 270–81

Chick V (1979) *The Theory of Monetary Policy.* Basil Blackwell, Oxford

Chick V (1983) *Macro-economics after Keynes: a reconsideration of The General Theory* Philip Allan, Oxford

Chow G (1967) 'Multiplier, accelerator and liquidity preference in the determinants of national income in the United States', *Review of Economics and Statistics* **49**: 1–15

Christ C (1968) 'A simple macro-economic model with a government budget constraint', *Journal of Political Economy* **76**: 53–67

Christ C (1973) 'Monetary and fiscal influences on U.S. money income 1891–1970', *Journal of Money Credit and Banking* Part 2 (**1**): 279–300

Clarke W (1979) *Inside the City: a guide to London as a financial centre.* George Allen and Unwin, London

Clay C, Wheble B (1978) *Modern Merchant Banking.* Woodhead and Faulkner, Cambridge

Clayton G (1962) 'British financial institutions in theory and practice', *Economic Journal* **72**: 869–86

Cobham D (1977) 'The debate over the letter of intent', *The Banker* February: 47–54

Cobham D (1982) 'Domestic credit expansion, confidence and the foreign exchange market: sterling in 1976', *Kredit und Kapital* **15**: 434–52

Coghlan R (1981) *Money Credit and the Economy.* George Allan and Unwin, London

Cohen C (1971) *British Economic Policy 1960–69.* Butterworth, London

Congdon T (1978) *Monetarism: an essay in definition.* Centre for Policy Studies, London

Congdon T (1979) 'Building societies are already within the framework of monetary control', *The Building Societies Gazette* April: 358–60

Congdon T (1980a) 'Should Britain adopt monetary base control?' *The Banker* February: 31–8

Congdon T (1980b) 'The monetary base debate: another instalment in the currency school and banking school controversy', *National Westminster Bank Quarterly Review* August: 2–13

Congdon T (1982a) 'A new approach to the balance of payments', *Lloyds Bank Review* **146**: 1–14

Congdon T (1982b) *Monetary Control in Britain*. Macmillan, London

Coppock D (1978) 'Some thoughts on the monetary approach to the balance of payments theory', *Manchester School of Economic and Social Studies* September: 186–208

Crockett A (1970) 'Timing relationships between movements of monetary and national income variables', *Bank of England Quarterly Bulletin* **10**: 459–68

Croome D, Johnson H (1970) *Money in Britain 1959–69*. Oxford University Press, Oxford

Crouch R (1970) 'Special deposits and the British monetary mechanism', *Economic Studies* **5**: 3–16

Crouch R (1971) 'Tobin v Keynes on liquidity preference', *Review of Economics and Statistics* **53**: 368–71

Cubbin J, Foley K (1977) 'The extent of benefit-induced unemployment in Great Britain, some new evidence', *Oxford Economic Papers* **29**: 128–40

Currie D (1976) 'Some criticisms of the monetary theory of the balance of payments', *Economic Journal* **86**: 508–22

Davies AE (1984) 'Monetary aggregates in the United Kingdom: narrowing the choice', *Barclays Review* February: 1–6

Davis R (1968) 'The role of the money supply in business cycles' *Federal Reserve Bank of New York Monthly Review* **50** (April): 63–73

Davis R (1969) 'Monetary theory: discussion', *American Economic Review* (Papers and Proceedings) **59**: 315–24

De Leeuw F, Gramlich E (1969) 'The channels of monetary policy: a further report on the Federal Reserve – MIT Model', *Journal of Finance* **24**: 265–90

De Leeuw F, Kalchenbrenner J (1969) 'Monetary and fiscal actions: a test of their relative importance in economic stabilisation', *Federal Reserve Bank of St Louis Review* **51**: 6–11

Dennis G (1981) *Monetary Economics*. Longman, London

De Prano M, Mayer T (1965) 'Tests of the relative importance of autonomous expenditure and money', *American Economic Review* **55**: 729–52

Desai M (1975) 'The Phillips Curve: a revisionist interpretation', *Economica* **42**: 1–19

Desai M (1982) *Testing Monetarism*. Francis Pinter, London

Dicks–Mireaux L (1961) 'The inter-relationship between cost and price changes 1948–59: a study of inflation in post-war Britain', *Oxford Economic Papers* **13**: 267–92

Dicks–Mireaux L, Dow J (1959) 'The determinants of wage inflation: United Kingdom 1946–1956', *Journal of the Royal Statistical Society* **22** (2), Series A: 145–74

Dow J (1970) *The Management of the British Economy 1945–60*. Oxford University Press, Oxford

Dow S, Earl S (1982) *Money Matters: a Keynesian approach to monetary economics.* Martin Robertson, Oxford

Drury A (1982) *Finance houses: their development and role in the modern financial sector.* Waterlow Publishers, London

Dufey G, Giddy I (1978) *The International Money Market.* Prentice-Hall, Englewood Cliffs, New Jersey (chapter 3: 107–54)

Eckstein O, Wilson T (1962) 'The determinants of money wages in American industry', *Quarterly Journal of Economics* **76**: 379–414

Edge S (1967) 'The relative stability of monetary velocity and the investment multiplier', *Australian Economic Papers* **4**: 192–207

Einzig P (1966) *Primitive Money.* Pergamon, London

Einzig P (1971) *The Parallel Money Markets vol. 1.* Macmillan, London

Einzig P (1973) *The Eurodollar System.* Macmillan, London

Ellis H (1938) 'Some fundamentals in the theory of velocity', *Quarterly Journal of Economics* **52**: 431–72. Reprinted in E Lutz and L Murk (ed.) *Readings in Monetary Theory.* Blackiston for the American Economic Association 1951

El-Mokadem M (1973) *Econometric Models of Personal Savings in the United Kingdom 1948–66.* Butterworth, London

Eltis W, Sinclair J (eds) (1981) 'The money supply and the exchange rate', *Oxford Economic Papers* Summer Supplement: 33

Entine AD (1964) 'Government securities holdings of selected financial institutions' 1945–62 *Journal of Finance* **19**: 644–51

Fama E (1970) 'Efficient capital markets: a review of theory and empirical work', *Journal of Finance* **25**: 383–417

Feige E (1964) *The Demand for Liquid Assets: a temporal cross-section analysis.* Prentice-Hall, Englewood Cliffs, New Jersey

Feige E (1967) 'Expectations and adjustments in the monetary sector', *American Economic Review* **57** (Papers and Proceedings): 462–73

Feige E (1974) 'Alternative temporal cross-section specifications of the demand for demand deposits', in HG Johnson, AR Nobay (eds) *Issues in Monetary Economics.* Oxford University Press, Oxford

Feige E, Pearce D (1977) 'The substitutability of money and near-monies: a survey of the times-series evidence', *Journal of Economic Literature* **15**: 439–69

Feldstein M (1978) 'The effect of unemployment insurance on temporary lay-off unemployment', *American Economic Review* **68**: 834–46

Fieleke N (1984) 'Barter trade: an American viewpoint', *Commercial Courier* **11**, Aug 13: 393

Financial Times (1984) 'World Banking Surveys' 21 May, 28 May (see also 'UK Banking Survey' 24 September)

Fisher, G, Sheppard D (1974) 'Interrelationships between real and monetary variables: some evidence from recent US empirical studies' in HG Johnson, AR Nobay *op. cit.*

Fisher I (1911) *The Purchasing Power of Money*. Macmillan, London

Fleming M (1964) 'The timing of payments and the demand for money', *Economica* **31**: 132–57

Ford J, Stark T (1965) 'Some statistical analysis of the long-term rate of interest in the United Kingdom', *Bulletin of the Oxford Institute of Economics and Statistics* **27**: 287–97

Foster J, Gregory M (1977) 'Inflation expectations: the use of qualitative survey data', *Applied Economics* **9**: 319–29

Fraser D, Rose P (1973) 'Short-run bank portfolio behaviour: an examination of selected liquid assets', *Journal of Finance* **28**: 531–7

Frenkel J, Johnson H (1976) *The Monetary Approach to the Balance of Payments*. George Allen and Unwin, London

Friedman BM (1972) 'Optimal economic stabilisation policy: an extended framework', *Journal of Political Economy* **83**: 1002–22

Friedman BM (1977) 'Even the St Louis model now believes in fiscal policy', *Journal of Money Credit and Banking* **9**: 365–7

Friedman BM (1978) 'Crowding out or crowding in? Economic consequences of financing government deficits', *Brookings Papers on Economic Activity* **3**: 593–641

Friedman M (1956) 'The quantity theory of money – a re-statement' in M Friedman (ed.) *Studies in the Quantity Theory of Money*. Chicago University Press, Chicago

Friedman M (1959) 'The demand for money: some theoretical and empirical results', *Journal of Policial Economy* **67**: 327–51

Friedman M (1966) 'Interest rates and the demand for money', *Journal of Law and Economics* **9**: 71–85

Friedman M (1968) 'The role of monetary policy', *American Economic Review* **58**: 1–17

Friedman M (1969) *The Optimum Quantity of Money and Other Essays*. Macmillan, London

Friedman M (1970) 'A theoretical framework for monetary analysis', *Journal of Political Economy* **78**: 193–238

Friedman M (1971) 'A monetary theory of nominal income', *Journal of Political Economy* **79**: 323–37

Friedman M (1972) 'Comments on the critics' *Journal of Political Economy* **80**: 905–50

Friedman M (1975a) 'Unemployment versus inflation', *Institute of Economic Affairs* Occasional Paper 44, London

Friedman M (1975b) 'Letter to *The Times*', London, 22 January 1975

Friedman M (1976) 'Comments on Tobin and Buiter' in JL Stein (ed) *Monetarism.* North-Holland, Amsterdam

Friedman M, Meiselman D (1963) 'The relative stability of the investment multiplier and monetary velocity in the United States 1897–1958', *Commission on Money and Credit and Stabilisation Policies.* Prentice-Hall, Englewood Cliffs, New Jersey

Friedman M, Meiselman D (1965) 'Reply to Ando and Modigliani and to De Prano and Mayer', *American Economic Review* **55**: 753–85

Friedman M, Schwartz A (1963) *A Monetary History of the United States 1867–1960.* Princetown University Press, New Jersey

Friedman M, Schwartz A (1963a) 'Money and business cycles', *Review of Economics and Statistics* (Supplement) **45**: 32–64

Friedman M, Schwartz A (1970) *Monetary Statistics of the United States.* Columbia University Press, New York

Friedman M, Schwartz A (1982) *Monetary Trends in the United States and the United Kingdom.* National Bureau of Economic Research, University of Chicago Press, Chicago

Frost P (1977) 'Short-run fluctuations in the money multiplier and monetary control', *Journal of Money Credit and Banking* **9**: 165–81

Frydman R *et al.* (1982) 'Rational expectations of government policy: an application of Newcomb's problem', *Southern Economic Journal* **49**: 311–19

Fullarton J (1844) *On the Regulation of Currencies.* John Murray, London

Gaskin M (1960) 'Liquidity and the monetary mechanism', *Oxford Economic Papers* **12**: 274–93

Ghosh D (1974) *The Economics of Building Societies.* Saxon House, Farnborough

Gibson N (1964) 'Special deposits as an instrument of monetary policy', *The Manchester School of Economic and Social Studies* **32**: 239–59

Gibson N (1967) 'Financial intermediaries and monetary policy', *Institute of Economic Affairs* Occasional Paper 39, London

Gibson W (1972) 'Interest rates and inflationary expectations: new evidence', *American Economic Review* **62**: 854–65

Glendinning C (1970) *The Eurodollar Market.* Oxford University Press, Oxford

Godfrey L (1971) 'The Phillips curve: incomes policy and trade union effects' in HG Johnson, AR Nobay (eds) *The Current Inflation.* Macmillan, London

Goldfeld S (1973) 'The demand for money revisited' *Brookings Papers on Economic Activity* **3**: 577–638

Goldfeld S (1976) 'The case of the missing money', *Brookings Papers on Economic Activity* **7**: 683–739

Goldsmith D (1976) 'Transactions costs and the theory of portfolio selection', *Journal of Finance* **31**: 1127–39

Goodhart C, Crockett A (1970) 'The importance of money', *Bank of England Quarterly Bulletin* June 10: 159–98

Goodhart C (1972) 'The gilt-edged market' in HG Johnson (ed.) *Readings in British Monetary Economics.* Oxford University Press, Oxford

Goodhart C (1973) 'Analysis of the determinants of the stock of money' in AR Nobay (ed.) *Essays in Modern Economics.* Longman, London

Goodhart C (1978) *Money Information and Uncertainty.* Macmillan, London

Goodhart C (1984) *Monetary Theory and Policy.* Macmillan, London

Gould J, Nelson C (1974) 'The stochastic structure of the velocity of money', *American Economic Review* **64**: 405–18

Gowland D (1979) *Monetary Policy and Credit Control.* Croom Helm, London

Gowland D (1982) *Controlling the Money Supply.* Croom Helm, London

Gramm W, Timberlake R (1969) 'The stock of money and investment in the United States 1897–1960', *American Economic Review* **59**: 991–6

Grossman H (1980) 'Rational expectations, business cycles and government behaviour' in S Fisher (ed.) *Rational Expectations and Economic Policy.* University of Chicago Press, Chicago

Hacche G (1974) 'The demand for money in the United Kingdom experience since 1971', *Bank of England Quarterly Bulletin* **14**: 284–30

Hagen E (1971) 'The classical theory of the level of output and employment' in MG Mueller (ed.) *Readings in Macroeconomics.* Holt Rinehart and Winston, London

Hahn F (1973) *On the Notion of Equilibrium in Economics.* Cambridge University Press, Cambridge

Hahn F (1977) 'The monetary approach to the balance of payments', *Journal of International Economics* August

Hahn F (1980) 'Monetarism and economic theory', *Economica* **47**: 1–17

Hall M (1984) *Monetary Policy since 1971 – conduct and performance.* Macmillan, London

Hamburger M (1968) 'Household demand for financial assets', *Econometrica* **38**: 97–118

Hamburger M (1977) 'Behaviour of the money stock: is there a puzzle?' *Journal of Monetary Economics* **3**: 265–88

Hamburger M, Silber WL (1971) 'Debt management and interest rates: a re-examination of the evidence', *The Manchester School of Economic and Social Studies* **39**: 261–7

Hansen A (1949) *Monetary Theory and Fiscal Policy.* McGraw-Hill, New York

Hansen A (1953) *A Guide to Keynes.* McGraw-Hill, New York

Heathfield D (1979) *Perspectives on Inflation.* Longman, London

Hegeland H (1951) *The Quantity of Money.* Goteburg

Henry S *et al.* (1976) 'Models of inflation in the United Kingdom: an evaluation', *National Institute of Economic and Social Research* **77**: 60–71

Hester D (1964) 'Keynes and the quantity theory: comment on the Friedman–Meiselman CMC paper', *Review of Economics and Statistics* **46**: 364–8

Hewson J (1974) 'The eurodollar deposit multiplier: a portfolio approach', *International Monetary Fund Staff Papers* **21**: 307–28

Hewson J (1975) *Liquidity Creation and Distribution in the Eurocurrency Markets.* Lexington Books, Lexington

Hewson J, Sakakibara E (1974) *The Eurocurrency Markets and their Implications.* Lexington Books, Lexington

Hicks J (1946) *Value and Capital.* Clarendon Press, Oxford

Hicks J (1937) 'Mr Keynes and the Classics: a suggested interpretation', *Econometrica* **5**: 147–59

Hicks J (1974) *The Crisis in Keynesian Economics.* Basil Blackwell, Oxford

Hilton K, Heathfield D (1970) *The Econometric Study of the UK.* Macmillan, London

Hindle T (1978) 'Britain's banking bill – umbrella or safety net?' *The Banker* August: 23–27

Hines A (1964) 'Trade unions and wage inflation in the United Kingdom 1893–1961', *Review of Economic Studies* **31**: 221–52

Hines A (1969) 'Wage inflation in the United Kingdom 1948–62: a disaggregated study', *Economic Journal* **79**: 66–89

Hines A (1971) *On the Reappraisal of Keynesian Economics.* Martin Robertson, London

Hogan W, Pearce I (1982) *The Incredible Eurodollar.* George Allen and Unwin, London

Holt C (1970) 'Job search, Phillips wage relation and union influence: theory and evidence' in ES Phelps (ed.) *The Microfoundations of Unemployment and Inflation Theory.* WW Norton, New York

Hudson J (1982) *Inflation: a theoretical survey and synthesis,* George Allen and Unwin, London

Hudson M (1976) 'What was the quantity theory of money?' *University of Leeds Discussion Paper* 44

Hume D (1825) 'Of money' reprinted in Eugene Rotwein (ed.) *Writings on economics* (consisting of nine essays from Hume's *Political Discourses*). Nelson, Edinburgh 1955

Jackson H *et al.* (1972) *Do Trade Unions Cause Inflation?* Cambridge University Press, Cambridge

Johnson C (1979) 'Banks and building societies – when is competition unfair?' *The Banker* July: 49–55

Johnson G, Ball A (1980) 'The euromarkets and monetary expansion: do they distort the monetary aggregates?' *Barclays Bank Review* February: 9–12

Johnson HG (1958) 'Towards a general theory of the balance of payments' in *International Trade and Economic Growth.* George Allen and Unwin, London

Johnson HG (1971) *Macroeconomics and Monetary Theory.* Gray-Mills, London

Johnson HG (1972) 'The monetary approach to balance of payments theory', *Journal of Financial and Quantitative analysis* 7 March: 1155–71

Johnson HG (1977a) 'The monetary approach to balance of payments: theory and policy implications', *Economica 44*: 217–29

Johnson HG (1977b) 'The monetary approach to the balance of payments', *Journal of International Economics* 7 August: 251–68

Johnson HG, Nobay A (eds) (1971) *The current inflation.* Macmillan, London

Johnson HG, Nobay A (eds) (1974) *Issues in monetary economics.* Oxford University Press, Oxford

Jones C (1984) 'The future of building societies', *National Westminster Bank Quarterly Review* May: 33–45

Jones S (1984) *North–South countertrade: Barter and reciprocal trade with developing countries.* Economic Intelligence Unit, London

Kaldor N (1970) 'The new monetarism, *Lloyds Bank Review* **97**: 1–18

Kaldor N, Trevithick J (1981) 'A Keynesian perspective on money', *Lloyds Bank Review* **139**: 1–20

Kane D (1983) *The Eurodollar Market and the Years of Crisis.* Croom Helm, London

Karakitsos E (1977) 'Expectations and the term structure of interest rates', *Bulletin of the Oxford Institute of Economics and Statistics* **39**: 139–51

Kareken J, Solow R (1963) 'Monetary policy: lags versus simultaneity' in *CMC Stabilisation Policies.* Prentice-Hall, Englewood Cliffs, New Jersey

Kavanagh N, Walters A (1966) 'The demand for money in the United Kingdom 1877–1961: preliminary findings', *Bulletin of the Oxford Institute of Economics and Statistics* **28**: 93–116

Kern D (1971) 'Monetary policy and CCC', *National Westminster Bank Quarterly Review* November: 29–44

Kern D (1979) 'Neither alarm nor complacency', *Euromoney* April: 110–16

Keynes JM (1930) *A Treatise on Money.* Macmillan, London

Keynes JM (1936) *The General Theory of Employment, Interest and Money.* Macmillan, London

Keynes JM (1937) 'The general theory of employment interest and money', *Quarterly Journal of Economics* **51**: 209–23

Klein L, Ball R (1959) 'Some econometrics of the determinants of the absolute level of wages', *Economic Journal* **69**: 465–82

Klopstock F (1968) 'The eurodollar market: some unresolved issues', *Princetown Essays in International Finance* **65**

Knight G (1972) 'Strikes and wage inflation in British manufacturing industry 1950–1968', *Bulletin of the Oxford Institute of Economics and Statistics* **35**: 281–94

Laffer A, Ransom R (1971) 'A formal model of the economy', *Journal of Business* **44**: 247–70

Laidler D (1969) 'The definition of money: theoretical and empirical problems', *Journal of Money Credit and Banking* **1**: 508–25

Laidler D (1973) 'The influence of money on real income and inflation: a simple model with empirical tests for the United States 1953–72', *The Manchester School of Economic and Social Studies* **41**: 367–95

Laidler D (1975) 'The end of demand management: how to reduce unemployment in the 1970s' in Friedman 1975a *op. cit.*

Laidler D (1977) *The Demand for Money: theories and evidence*. Harper and Row, New York

Laidler D, Parkin M (1975) 'Inflation – a survey', *Economic Journal* **85**: 741–809

Lee B (1973) 'The eurodollar multiplier', *Journal of Finance* **28**: 867–74

Lee TH (1966) 'Substitutability of non-bank intermediary liabilities for money: the empirical evidence', *Journal of Finance* **21**: 441–57

Lee TH (1967) 'Alternative interest rates and the demand for money: the empirical issues', *American Economic Review* **57**: 1168–81

Leigh-Pemberton R (1979) 'Banks, building societies and personal savings', *National Westminster Bank Quarterly Review* May: 2–20

Leijonhufvud A (1968) *On Keynesian Economics and the Economics of Keynes*. Oxford University Press, Oxford

Leijonhufvud A (1981) *Information and Coordination: essays in macroeconomic theory*. Oxford University Press, New York

Levi M (1983) *International Finance*. McGraw-Hill, Tokyo

Lipsey R (1960) 'The relation between unemployment and the rate of change of money wage rates in the United Kingdom 1862–1952', *Economica* **27**: 1–31

Little J (1979) 'Liquidity creation by eurobanks: 1973–78', *Federal Reserve Bank of Boston* Jan–Feb: 62–72

Llewellyn D (1979) 'Do building societies take deposits away from banks?' *Lloyds Bank Review* **131**: 21–34

Llewellyn D *et al.* (1982) *The Framework of UK Monetary Policy*. Heinemann, London

Lucas R (1973) 'Some international evidence on output-inflation trade-offs', *American Economic Review* **63**: 326–34

Maddock R, Carter M (1982) 'A child's guide to rational expectations', *Journal of Economic Literature* **20**: 39–51

Makin J (1972) 'Demand and supply functions for stocks of eurodollars: an empirical study', *Review of Economics and Statistics* **54**: 381–91

Marget A (1938) *The Theory of Prices*, King and Sons, London

Marshall A (1923) *Principles of Economics* (8th edn). Macmillan, London

Mason J (1974) 'Friedman's estimate of the income elasticity of the demand for money', *Southern Economic Journal* **40**: 497–9

Mayer (1971) 'Our financial institutions; what needs changing?' *Journal of Money Credit and Banking* **3**: 13–20

McKenna J (1969) *Aggregate Economic Analysis*. Holt Rinehart and Winston, New York

McKinnon R (1977) 'The eurocurrency market', *Essays in International Finance* **135**, Princeton University Press, New Jersey

McLachan S (1981) 'Building societies in transition', *The Banker* October: 49–53

McMahon G (1976) 'Controlling the euromarkets', *Bank of England Quarterly Bulletin* March: 74–7

McRae H, Cairncross F (1974) *Capital City*. Eyre Methuen, London

Meade J (1982) *Wage-fixing*. George Allen and Unwin, London

Meiselman D (1962) *The Term Structure of Interest Rates*. Prentice-Hall, Englewood Cliffs, New Jersey

Melitz J, Martin G (1971) 'Financial intermediaries, money definition and monetary control; comment', *Journal of Money Credit and Banking* **3**: 693–701

Meltzer A (1963) 'The demand for money: the evidence from the time-series', *Journal of Political Economy* **71**: 219–46

Memorandum of Evidence (1959) Vol 1:41 to the Radcliffe Committee on the working of the monetary system. HMSO, Cmnd 827, August

Michaelson J (1973) *The Term Structure of Interest Rates*. Intext, New York

Midland Bank Review (MBR): various issues

Mill James (1826) *Elements of Political Economy*. Baldwin & Co., London

Mill JS (1852) *Essays on Some Unsettled Questions of Political Economy*. John W Parker, London

Miller E (1981) 'Barter trade in East–West commerce: Extending the "Parallel Market"', *Association for Comparative Economic Studies Bulletin* Fall–Winter **23**: 91–91

Minsky H (1961) 'Employment, growth and price levels: a review article', *Review of Economics and Statistics* **43**: 1–12

Modigliani F (1964) 'Some empirical tests of monetary management and of rules versus discretion', *Journal of Political Economy* **72**: 211–45

Modigliani F (1977) 'The monetarist controversy or should we forsake stabilisation', *American Economic Review* **67**: 1–19

Modigliani F, Sutch R (1969) 'The term structure of interest rates: a re-examination of the evidence', *Journal of Money Credit and Banking* February **1**: 112–20

Monetary Control (1980) HMSO. Cmnd 7858, November

Moore B (1968) *An Introduction to the Theory of Finance*. The Free Press, London

Moore BJ, Threadgold AR (1980) 'Bank lending and the money supply', *Bank of England Discussion Paper* **10**

Morgan B (1979) *Monetarists and Keynesians – their contribution to monetary theory*. Macmillan, London

Moroney J, Mason J (1971) 'The dynamic impacts of autonomous expenditure and the monetary base on aggregate income' *Journal of Money Credit and Banking* **3**: 793–814

Mortenson D (1970) 'Job search, the duration of unemployment and the Phillips Curve', *American Economic Review* **60**: 847–62

Mulvey C, Trevithick J (1974) 'Some evidence on the wage leadership model', *Scottish Journal of Political Economy* **21**: 1–11

Munich Address (1971) Address by the Governor of the Bank of England to the International Banking Conference, Munich, May

Muth J (1961) 'Rational expectations and the theory of price movements', *Econometrica* **29**: 315–35

Nerlove M (1958) 'Adaptive expectations and cobweb phenomenon', *Quarterly Journal of Economics* **72**: 227–40

Nevin E, Davis E (1970) *The London Clearing Banks*. Elek Books, London

Newlyn W (1971) *Theory of Money*. Clarendon Press, Oxford

Nickell S (1979) 'The effects of unemployment and related benefits on the duration of unemployment', *Economic Journal* **89**: 34–9

Niehans J, Hewson J (1976) 'The eurodollar market and monetary theory', *Journal of Money Credit and Banking* **8**: 1–27

Nobay AR (1974) 'A model of the UK monetary authorities behaviour 1959–69' in HG Johnson, AR Nobay (eds) *Issues in Monetary Economics*. Oxford University Press, Oxford

Norton WE (1969) 'Debt management and monetary policy in the UK', *Economic Journal* **79**: 475–94

Okun A (1975) 'Inflation: Its mechanisms and welfare costs', *Brookings Papers on Economic Activity* **2**: 351–90

Oliver F (1977) 'The volume of instalment credit 1968–76', *Credit* – the quarterly review of the Finance Houses Association, September

Park Y (1974) *The Eurobond Market: Function and Structure*. Praeger, New York

Parker C (1977) 'Old and new in London', *The Banker* July: 59–64

Parkin JM (1971) 'The Phillips Curve: a historical perspective, lessons from recent empirical studies and alternative policy choices' in HG Johnson, AR Nobay *op. cit.*

Parkin JM (1975) 'Where is Britain's inflation going?' *Lloyds Bank Review* **117**: 1–13

Parkin JM, Gray MR, Barrett RJ (1970) 'The portfolio behaviour of commercial banks' in K Hilton, D Heathfield *op. cit.*

Patinkin D (1965) *Money Interest and Prices*. Harper and Row, New York

Peterson R (1974) 'A cross-section study of the demand for money: the United States 1960–62', *Journal of Finance* **29**: 73–88

Phelps ES (1968) 'Money-wage dynamics and labour-market equilibrium', *Journal of Political Economy* **76**: 678–711

Phelps Brown EH (1971) 'The analysis of wage movements under full employment', *Scottish Journal of Political Economy* **18**: 233–43

Phillips A (1958) 'The relationship between unemployment and the rate of change of money wage rates in the UK 1861–1957', *Economica* **25**: 283–99

Phillips K (1969) 'The short-run stability of velocity and the autonomous expenditure multiplier', *Journal of Political Economy* **77**: 418–29

Pierson G (1968) 'The effect of union strength on the US Phillips Curve', *American Economic Review* **58**: 456–67

Pigou A (1917) 'The value of money', *Quarterly Journal of Economics* **32**: 38–65

Poole W (1970) 'Optimal choice of monetary policy instruments in a simple stochastic macromodel', *Quarterly Journal of Economics* **84**: 197–216

Poole W, Kornblith E (1973) 'The Friedman–Meiselman CMC Paper: new evidence on an old controversy', *American Economic Review* **63**: 903–17

Pratten C (1979) 'Building societies versus equities', *Lloyds Bank Review* **132**: 38–48

Price L (1972) 'The demand for money in the UK: a further investigation', *Bank of England Quarterly Bulletin* **12**: 43–55

Purdy D, Zis G (1973) 'Trade unions and wage inflation in the UK: a reappraisal' in JM Parkin, AR Nobay (eds) *Essays in Modern Economics*. Longman, London

Purvis D (1980) 'Monetarism: a review', *Canadian Journal of Economics* **13**: 96–122

Pyle D (1972) 'Observed price expectations and interest rates', *Review of Economics and Statistics* **54**: 275–80

Quinn B (1975) *The New Euromarkets*. Macmillan, London

Radcliffe Report (1959) Committee on the working of the monetary system. HMSO Cmnd 827, August

Revell J (1973) *The British Financial System*. Macmillan, London

Robertson D (1965) *Lectures on Economic Principles* vol 111. Fontana Library, London

Roosa R (1951) 'Interest rates and the Central Bank' in *Money, Trade and Economic Growth*. Macmillan, London

Rowan D, O'Brien R (1970) 'Expectations, the interest rate structure and debt policy' in K Hilton, DF Heathfield *op. cit.*

Sargan J (1964) 'Wages and prices in the United Kingdom' in PE Hart *et al. Econometric Analysis for National Economic Planning*. Butterworth, London

Sargan J (1971) 'A study of wages and prices in the UK 1949–68' in HG Johnson, AR Nobay *op. cit.*

Sayers R (1967) *Modern Banking* (7th edn). Oxford University Press, Oxford

Sayers R (1977) *The Bank of England 1891–1944* vols 1–3. Cambridge University Press, Cambridge

Scammell W (1968) *The London Discount Market*. Elek Books, London

Schwartz A (1969) 'Why money matters', *Lloyds Bank Review* **94**: 1–16

Shackle G (1967) *The Years of High Theory: invention and tradition in economic thought 1926–39*. Cambridge University Press, Cambridge

Shackle G (1972) *Epistemics and Economics*. Cambridge University Press, Cambridge

Shackle G (1974) *Keynesian Kaleidics*. Edinburgh University Press, Edinburgh

Shackle G, Phelps Brown E (1938) 'Statistics of monetary circulation in England and Wales 1917–37', Royal Economic Society special memorandum 74

Shaw E (1975) *The London Money Market*. Heinemann, London

Sheppard D (1968) 'Changes in the money supply in the UK 1954–65: comment on Bell and Berman', *Economica* **35**: 297–302

Sheppard D (1971) *The Growth and Role of Financial Institutions*. Methuen, London

Silber W (1970) 'Fiscal policy in IS–LM analysis: a correction', *Journal of Money Credit and Banking* **2**: 461–72

Silbertson A (1970) 'Surveys of applied economics: price behaviour of firms', *Economic Journal* **80**: 565–7

Sims C (1972) 'Money, income and causality', *American Economic Review* **62**: 540–52

Skinner A (1967) 'Say's Law: origin and content', *Economica* **34**: 153–66

Smith A (1976) *The wealth of nations* eds RH Cambell and AS Skinner. Oxford University Press, Oxford

Smith W, Teigen R (1965) *Readings in Money, National Income and Stabilisation Policy*. RD Irwin, Homewood, Illinois

Snodgrass D (1963) 'Wage changes in 24 manufacturing industries 1948–59: a comparative analysis', *Yale Economic Essays* **3**: 171–221

Spencer R, Yohe W (1972) 'The "crowding out" of private expenditures by fiscal policy actions' in JT Boorman, TM Havrilesky *Money supply money demand and macroeconomics*. Allyn and Bacon, Boston

Spiegelberg R (1973) *The City*. Quartet Books, London

Sprenkle C (1969) 'The usefulness of transactions demand models', *Journal of Finance* **24**: 835–47

Sprenkle C (1972) 'On the observed transactions demand for money', *The Manchester School of Economic and Social Studies* **40**: 261–7

Stapleton R (1970) *The Theory of Corporate Finance*. Harrap, London

Starleaf D, Floyd R (1972) 'Some evidence with respect to the efficiency of Friedman's monetary policy', *Journal of Money Credit and Banking* **4**: 713–22

Starleaf D, Reimer R (1967) 'The Keynesian demand function for money: some statistical tests', *Journal of Finance* **22**: 71–6

Stein J (ed.) (1976) *Monetarism*. North-Holland, Amsterdam

Stigler G (1962) 'Administered prices and oligopolistic inflation', *Journal of Business* **35**: 1–13

Struthers J (1981) 'Inflation in Ghana (1966–78): a perspective on the monetarists versus structuralists debate', *Development and Change* **12**: 177–213

Struthers J (1984a) 'The UK economy in 1984', *Yearbook 84: A Review of UK and International Affairs*. Modern Studies Association, Glasgow (see also Yearbook 83)

Struthers J (1984b) 'Rational expectations: a promising research programme or a case of monetarist fundamentalism?' *Journal of Economic Issues* December

Sumner M, Ward R (1983) 'The reappearing Phillips Curve', *Oxford Economic Papers* **35** (Supplement): 306–20

Sutcliffe C (1982) 'Inflation and prisoners dilemmas', *Journal of Post-Keynesian Economics* **4**: 574–85

Sykes Memorial Lecture (1971) Lecture by the Chief Cashier of the Bank of England published in the *Bank of England Quarterly Bulletin* December: 477–81

Tanner J (1969) 'Lags in the effects of monetary policy: a statistical investigation', *American Economic Review* **59**: 794–805

Taylor J (1972) 'Incomes policy, the structure of unemployment and the Phillips Curve: the United Kingdom experience 1953–70' in JM Parkin, MT Sumner (eds) *Incomes Policy and Inflation*. Manchester University Press, Manchester

Taylor J (1974) *Unemployment and Wage Inflation*. Longman, London

TB (The Banker): various issues

Teigen RL (1965) 'The demand for the supply of money' in WL Smith, RL Teigen (eds) *Readings in Money, National Income and Stabilisation*. Irwin, Homewood, Illinois

Thirwall AP (1978) 'The UK's economic problem: a balance of payments constraint', *National Westminster Bank Quarterly Review* February: 24–32

Thirwall AP (1980) *Balance of Payments Theory and the United Kingdom Experience*. Macmillan, London

Thornton H (1802) *An Enquiry into the Nature and Effects of the Paper Credit of Great Briain* (ed. with an introduction by FA Hayek), Holt Rinehart and Winston, New York

Thorpe R (ed.) (1979) *Inflation and Stabilisation in Latin America*. Macmillan, London

Timberlake R (1964) 'The stock of money and money substitutes', *Southern Economic Journal* **30**: 253–60

Tobin J (1956) 'The interest elasticity of transactions demands for cash', *Review of Economics and Statistics* **38**: 241–7

Tobin J (1958) 'Liquidity preference as behaviour towards risk', *Review of Economics Studies* **25**: 65–86

Tobin J (1961) 'Money, capital and other stores of value', *American Economic Review* **51**: 26–37

Tobin J (1965) 'The monetary interpretation of history', *American Economic Review* **55**: 464–85

Tobin J (1965) 'The theory of portfolio selection' in FH Hahn, FP Brechling (eds) *The Theory of Interest Rates*. Macmillan, London

Tobin J (1969) 'A general equilibrium approach to monetary theory', *Journal of Money Credit and Banking* **1**: 15–29

Tobin J, Buiter W (1976) 'Long-run effects of fiscal and monetary policy on aggregate demand' in JL Stein *op. cit.*

Tooke T (1838) *History of Prices and the State of Circulation*. John Murray, London

Townend JC (1972) 'Summary of a research paper on substitution among capital-certain assets in the personal sector of the UK economy 1963–71', *Bank of England Quarterly Bulletin* **12**: 509–51

Trevithick J, Mulvey C (1974) 'Some evidence on the wage leadership hypothesis', *Scottish Journal of Political Economy* **21**: 1–12

Trevithick J, Mulvey C (1975) *The Economics of Inflation*. Martin Robertson, London

Tucker D (1966) 'Dynamic income adjustment to money supply changes', *American Economic Review* **56**: 433–49

Turnbull P (1979) 'Building societies and monetary policies – equality in misery', *The Building Societies Gazette* September: 1056–60

Turner AJ (1972) 'The evolution of reserve ratios in English banking', *National Westminster Bank Quarterly Review* February: 52–62

Turner HA, Jackson DAS (1970) 'On the determination of the general wage level – a world analysis: or unlimited labour?' *Economic Journal* 80: 827–49

Turner HA, Jackson DA (1972) 'The determination of the general wage level', *Economic Journal* 82: 686–93

Tussing AD (1966) 'Can monetary policy influence the availability of credit?' *Journal of Finance* 21: 1–13

Vanderkamp J (1960) 'Wage and price level determination: an empirical model for Canada', *Economica* 33: 194–218

Vogel R, Maddala A (1967) 'Cross-section estimates of liquid assets demand by manufacturing corporations', *Journal of Finance* 22: 557–75

Wachter S (1976) *Latin American Inflation*. Lexington Books, Lexington

Wadsworth J (1971) *The Banks and the Monetary System in the UK 1959–71*. Methuen, London

Walden H (1984) 'How building societies see their role in the financial services revolution', *The Banker* March: 33–8

Walters A (1967) 'Lags and the demand for money', *Journal of Economic Studies* 2: 3–22

Walters A (1970) 'The Radcliffe Report – ten years after: a survey of the empirical evidence' in DR Croome, HG Johnson *op. cit.*

Ward R (1973) 'Proximate targets and monetary policy', *Economic Journal* 83: 1–20

Ward R, Zis G (1974) 'Trade union militancy as an explanation of inflation: an international comparison', *The Manchester School of Economic and Social Studies* 42: 46–65

Welham P (1969) *Monetary Circulation in the United Kingdom*. Basil Blackwell, Oxford

Wilson K (1983) *British Financial Institutions*. Pitman, London

Wilson JSG *et al* (1976) *The Development of Financial Institutions in Europe 1956–76*. Societé Universitairé Européene de Recherches (SUERF), Stijthoff, Leyden

Wilson T (1979) 'Crowding out: the real issues', *Banco Nazionale del Lavoro Quarterly Review* 130: 227142

Wilson Report (1980) Committee to review the functioning of financial institutions. HMSO Cmnd 7937 (and Appendices), June

Wood G (1979) 'Cash base control of the money supply – its institutional implications', *The Banker* July: 37–43

Yassukovich SM (1976) 'Consortium banks on course', *The Banker* February: 909–21

Yohe W, Karnasky D (1969) 'Interest rates and price level changes 1952–69', *Federal Reserve Bank of St Louis Review* 51: 18–38

Index

and 'lifeboat committee', 24
balance sheet of, 25
Bank of Ireland, 32
Bank of London, 73
Bank of Scotland, 32, 59, 83
bank overdrafts, 120
bank rate, 27, 324, 329
  and minimum lending rate (MLR), 338–9
  see also minimum lending rate
Banque Arabe et Internationale
  d'Investissement, 83n
Banque de Paris, 72
banks
  classification of, 61–2
  secondary, 17, 69–82
  merchant, 17, 69–73
  British overseas and foreign, 73–6
  overseas and foreign, 17, 31, 78–82
  commonwealth, 74
  consortium, 76–8
  savings banks, 115–17
  deposit, 32–4, 61
  retail, 32–4
  primary, 32–4
  joint stock, 32–4
  London clearing (LCBs), 32–3
  and creation of money, 36–43
  and corporate finance, 56–9
  as multi-product firms, 50
  and leasing, 57
  nationalisation of, 57
  and Wilson Committee, 57
  and OFIs, 59
  and monetary policy, 59
  and Free Banking Services, 59
  and 'near banks', 61
  and reserve assets, 347
bank supervision, 65–8
Barclays Bank, 32, 71, 78, 85, 332, 339
  International, 33
Barr, N., 256
barter, 3, 14n
  disadvantages of, 3–5
Barrett, C., 229, 300, 312, 316, 327
Barro, R., 280
'base money', 285
Baumol, W., 159, 195, 196, 198
'bears', 179
Bee, R., 77, 82
Becker, G., 165
Begg, D., 172, 280, 281, 283n
Bell, G., 123
Benson, W., 93
Besen, S., 60n
Bewley, R., 60n
bilateral monopoly, 261
  and cost inflation, 261

bills of exchange, 26, 70
  Act, 65
  'accmmodation bills', 87
  bill finance, 120
Birmingham Trustee Savings Bank, 116
Blanden, M., 81
Blinder, A., 239
'block discounting', 86
Bodin, J., 148
Bohi, D., 202
Boleat, M., 96, 97, 99
BOLSA, 73
bonds, 16, 119–20
  'short', 16–17
  local authority, 16–17, 27, 30
  gilt-edged, 16–17
  government, 23
  redemption value of, 47
  in echelon, 49, 289, 299, 323
  and quantity theory, 157–8, 163
  and Keynesian analysis, 177–90
  and speculative motive, 178–9
  and liquidity preference curve, 181–4
  and Post-Keynesian monetary theory, 192–5
  and risk, 199–207
  and new quantity theory, 214
  and crowing out effect, 238–44
  and Keynesian transmission mechanism,
    295–6
  and credit-rationing effect, 296–8
  and 'locking-in effect', 298–9
  and portfolio balance, 300–302
  and monetarist transmission mechanism,
    302–3
  and term structure of interest rates,
    303–4
  and 'leaning into the wind', 322–5
Bowmaker, 85
Brazil
  euroloan to, 124
Brechling, F., 54, 270, 300
Britannia's Japan Fund, 118n
British Electricity Council, euroloan to, 124
British Linen Bank, 83
British Telecom, flotation of, 70
Broad Money, GDP velocity of, 353
Bronfrenbrenner, M., 229
Brown, A., 235, 257
Brown Shipley & Co., 71
Brunner, K., 210n, 234
Budd, A., 314
building societies, 61, 63, 89–104
  growth of, 89–90
  liabilities of, 90–1
  assets of, 91–2
  effects of CCC on, 91
  and interest rates, 92

Wachter, S., 270
Wadsworth, J., 48, 315
'wage drift', 261
Walden, H., 97, 98
Walras' Law, 159–60
Walters, A., 210n, 229, 312
Ward, R., 267, 309
Wardley, 74
ways and means advances, 21
wealth coefficient ratio, 243
wealth effect, 201
Welham, P., 148
Western Credit, 86
Wheble, B., 73
Whole-life insurance, 105
wholesale intermediation, 69
William Brandt, 72, 74
Williams and Glyn's Bank, 32, 78, 83, 332, 339
Wilson, J., 34n

Wilson, T., 239, 270
'window dressing', 31
Wilson Committee, 35n, 56, 57, 350
  and instalment credit, 86
  and building societies, 93–4, 103
  and insurance companies, 105, 106, 108
  and pension funds, 109
  and investment funds, 111
  and savings banks, 116
'withdrawable on demand', 11
World Bank, 21

Yassukovich, S., 77
'yearling bonds', 102
'yearlings', 120
'yield' of security, 14, 54
Yohe, W., 247n, 248n

Zis, G., 267